CHICKEN SOUP
FOR THE
TEENAGE SOUL III

Chicken Soup for the Teenage Soul III
More Stories of Life, Love and Learning
Jack Canfield, Mark Victor Hansen, Kimberly Kirberger

Published by Backlist, LLC,
a unit of Chicken Soup for the Soul Publishing, LLC. www.chickensoup.com

Front cover design by Andrea Perrine Brower
Originally published in 2000 by Health Communications, Inc.

Back cover and spine redesign by Pneuma Books, LLC

Distributed to the booktrade by Simon & Schuster. SAN: 200-2442

Publisher's Cataloging-in-Publication Data
(Prepared by The Donohue Group)

Chicken soup for the teenage soul III : more stories of life, love and learning
/ [compiled by] Jack Canfield, Mark Victor Hansen, [and] Kimberly Kirberger.

   p. : ill. ; cm.

   Originally published: Deerfield Beach, FL : Health Communications, c2000.
   ISBN: 978-1-62361-091-3

   1. Teenagers--Conduct of life--Anecdotes. 2. Anecdotes. I. Canfield, Jack,
1944- II. Hansen, Mark Victor. III. Kirberger, Kimberly, 1953-

BJ1661 .C173 2012
158.1/28/0835   2012944879

PRINTED IN THE UNITED STATES OF AMERICA
on acid free paper

24 23   08 09 10

CHICKEN SOUP
FOR THE
TEENAGE SOUL III

More Stories of Life,
Love and Learning

Jack Canfield
Mark Victor Hansen
Kimberly Kirberger

Backlist, LLC, a unit of
Chicken Soup for the Soul Publishing, LLC
Cos Cob, CT
www.chickensoup.com

CHICKEN SOUP
FOR THE
TEENAGE SOUL III

More Stories of Life,
Love and Learning

Jack Canfield
Mark Victor Hansen
Kimberly Kirberger

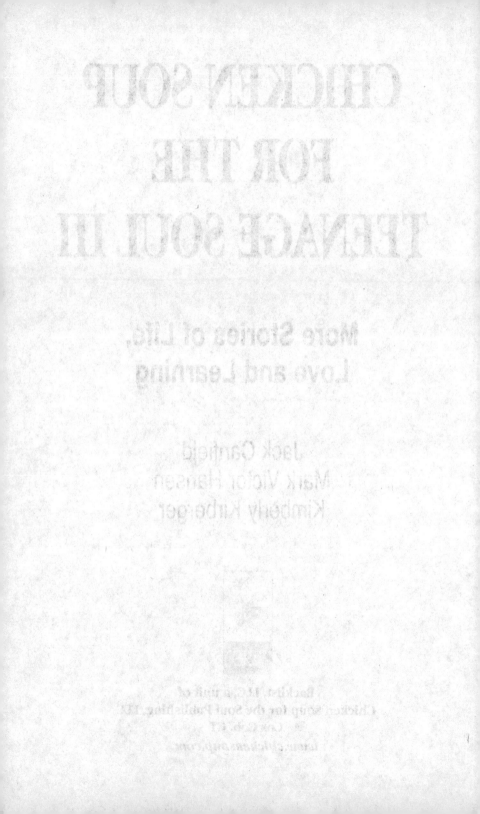

Backlist, LLC, a unit of
Chicken Soup for the Soul Publishing, LLC
www.chickensoup.com

Contents

2. FRIENDSHIP

3. THE POWER OF LOVE

4. FAMILY

5. LESSONS

6. TOUGH STUFF

7. OVERCOMING OBSTACLES

8. SELF-DISCOVERY

9. GROWING UP

Introduction

The Faces of Our Youth

Many older people seem to take an unmerited pride in
the mere fact they are adults.

When youth comes crashing in on them with
enthusiasm and ideals, they put on their
most patronizing smiles and send them out with
what they call their blessings.

But you and I know that they have not given their
blessings but a cold shower.

They pat the young man or young woman on the back
and say:

"You're young. Enjoy your enthusiasm and your
ideals while you can.

For when you grow up and grow out into the world
you'll see how foolish your ideas actually were."

And, the trouble is, young people do grow up and
grow away from their ideals.

And that is one reason why the world into which they
go gets better so slowly.

Franklin Delano Roosevelt

Dear Teen,

We are so excited. After two years of reading thousands upon thousands of stories and poems we have compiled what we believe to be the best *Chicken Soup for the Teenage Soul* book yet. It hasn't been easy. In fact, for some reason this book took more hard work than its two predecessors put together.

We received over fifty thousand submissions for this book, and letters and stories are still pouring in by the hundreds. (We will use them in *Teen IV*.) There were twenty teenagers who read each story that came in and picked their favorites. (Their favorites consisted of over five thousand stories!) We then read each one and picked our favorites based on subject matter, writing style, and, most important, shared wisdom. What we ended up with is a book so packed with experience, emotion, happiness and heartache that whoever reads it will certainly be changed for life.

It is hard to express the gratitude we feel to all the teenagers who so courageously shared their stories and poetry with us. Every single submission touched us deeply and affected the final results of this book.

We are also very grateful to all the teenagers who have written to thank us for compiling these books. We do work hard to make these books what they are, but please know that it is you, the teenager, who is the main force that drives these books and their success, and for that you should be very proud.

Please feel free to read this book in whatever manner works best for you. Skip around, go from front to back, read it all at once or over time. This is your book. We hope it serves you well.

With love,

Jack, Mark and Kimberly

1

RELATIONSHIPS

Love means each person is free to follow his or her own heart.

Melody Beattie

Never Been Dissed—Until Now

What can I say? Sometimes I'm a little dumb. I consider Cheetos a major food group. I play air guitar. I think burping is funny. And, worst of all, I screwed up my chance with Darcy by listening to a bunch of other jerks who were just as clueless as me.

Darcy was kinda like the Jewel CD I loved. I played that thing over and over on the way to school, but the second I pulled into the parking lot, it got stuffed under my seat for, uh, safekeeping and replaced with the Beastie Boys.

Imagine me confessing to my friends that I, captain of the basketball team, was dating Darcy, captain of the debate team. Believe me, I didn't plan on falling for the school brain. But I was blown away by the first words she ever spoke to me.

"Uh, are you lost? This is the li-brar-y. The gym is on the other side of the school, remember?" she said, enunciating the words like she was talking to a toddler. Ouch.

Even though we went to the same school, Darcy and I lived in completely different worlds. She spent her time with the Net nerds, and I roamed the halls like Moses parting the Red Sea of fans who worshipped the guys on my team. I was totally knocked for a loop when she broke the silence.

"Books. I need a book," I stammered, suddenly unable to remember my assignment. She pointed to a row of books on Thomas Edison—just the man I was looking for—and before I could turn to thank her, she was gone.

When I did catch up with her again, she was on her tippy toes reaching for an encyclopedia in the next aisle. "Need a ladder? Or how 'bout some platforms?" I asked giving her a taste of her own sarcasm.

"How about giving me a hand?" she replied. "Oh, that's right. Books are *square*, not round like a basketball. Think you can hold one?" *Cha-ching!* This girl has guts, I thought. When I started laughing, Darcy totally cracked up and started snort-laughing. The number-two pencils holding up her hair were shaking.

"I can't believe I said that to you. I can't believe you're laughing. This is so surreal," she laughed. "Oh, sorry, that's a big word. Do you need a dictionary?" More laughing, more snorting. We went on like that for a while, ripping on each other until I thought my sides would split.

For the rest of the day—okay, the rest of the *week*—every time I thought about her, I felt the same gut-socking, dizzy feeling I get before a big game. Then I found myself taking different routes to get to class just to see if I'd bump into her, and when I did . . . doh! We didn't say a word to each other, but the joke was still going. I'd innocently make gorilla noises, and she'd die laughing. Or she'd take off her glasses and bump into walls, sending her books, pen and protractor flying everywhere. She taped Brain Gum to my locker. I glued a pair of sweaty gym socks to hers. Two weeks into our secret game, Darcy asked me out. Correction: she blackmailed me into a date. I found a ransom note in my locker saying that if I ever wanted to see my lucky jockstrap again, I'd better meet her at a nearby coffee shop. What guy wouldn't love a girl with that sense of humor?

After that first date, we spent nearly every day together talking about everything—cheesy Kung Fu movies (our shared obsession), how I hated being judged as a jock despite my 3.5 GPA, why I hadn't lost my virginity—all of the things I could *never* talk about with the guys or would even think about mentioning to any of the other girls I had dated. Then again, Darcy wasn't like anyone I had ever been with before. She was a lot of firsts for me. She was the first girl who had the guts to ask me out. She was the first girl I didn't judge by her bra size or reputation. She was the first person who made me feel I had more to offer the world than a killer turnaround jumper. She was the first girl I dated who didn't obsess about her hair, her weight or what she was wearing. And she was the first girl I didn't blab about in the locker room when the guys started bragging about their weekend conquests.

It didn't take long for everyone to start wondering why I was flaking on basketball practice or missing the weekly Duke Nukem marathons at Kyle's. I had been making up *the* lamest excuses to cover for hanging out with Darcy and was feeling pretty skanky about it when the guys confronted me about it. So I told them about her.

"Who?" Steve asked.

"Not the girl in overalls and hightops?" Eric asked.

"Why are you wasting time on *that?*" Kyle asked.

I sat there as they teased me about slumming with a "geeky chick," assuming that once they exhausted all of their lame jokes about Darcy, they'd move onto their next target. Wrong. After that day, whenever I told them I was doing stuff with Darcy, they unloaded on her again. At first, I didn't let it bother me. Then one morning, Dave asked, "Have you figured out how to get her to wear a bag over her head to the prom yet?" That really pissed me off and eventually the little things turned into big things, like "accidentally" forgetting to tell me about practice or suddenly not having enough room at the lunch table for me.

After a few weeks of getting the cold shoulder from my friends, I started to doubt my own judgment. Darcy *wasn't* one of the prettiest girls in the school. Was I actually planning to take her to my senior prom? She'd probably wear number-two pencils in her hair *and* those hideous hightops. Once I finished picking her apart, I was convinced she was totally wrong for me. Darcy didn't like basketball or my friends. She refused to go to any of the team parties. I'd been blowing off practices to be with her, and my game was totally suffering. In my mind, the relationship was doomed.

I tried to be subtle at first by taking different routes to my classes to avoid her. I'd promise to call her but never did. She finally cornered me in the hall one day and demanded an explanation, so I swore I'd meet her after school. Then I blew her off. I was hoping she'd get the hint and go away if I flaked, but she didn't let me off that easily. The next day, in front of the entire school, Darcy let me have it. She yelled at me, called me a coward, a jerk and an idiot, and, worst of all, tossed my friends a box of notes I'd written to her. I stood there speechless as they read each one aloud and laughed like hyenas. The funny thing was that for the first time (*another* first with Darcy) I didn't really care what the guys were saying or who saw me standing there like an idiot, because I knew she was right. When I looked at my friends howling and high-fiving each other, I finally realized that I was going to be the first guy in our pathetic circle to grow up.

I wish I could say there was a happy ending to the story, that I begged Darcy to take me back and she did, but it didn't happen. Well, at least not the part about her taking me back. I begged. I pleaded. I stuffed notes in her locker. I followed her around school. I was practically stalking her by the time I realized it was too late. She had already gotten over slumming with a dummy.

Last I heard, Darcy graduated early and got accepted to an out-of-state college. I still feel a little sad when I think about her and what could have been, but I'm also grateful that I learned what I did, when I did. I know a little bit more about who I am—the *whole* me, not just the big man on campus part—and who I can be, regardless of what my friends think or say. So, Darcy, if you're reading this . . . thanks.

Shad Powers

Loving Yourself First

In high school, the student council had a fund-raiser where we could buy a flower for someone special and have it delivered to them on Valentine's Day morning in their first-period class.

That year, I sent out three carnations to three unsuspecting girls. I figured there might be a chance to attract at least one of them. Besides, if any one of them had sent me a flower and I didn't send them one in return, it would be over before it began.

A carnation went out to Melanie, Susie and Jenny (Jenny was the long shot).

The whole week, I anticipated who might send me some carnations. My friend Brian sent one to his girlfriend. Stephanie sent one to Jason, a guy she had a crush on all semester. My friend Lisa sent one to her good friend Tracy just for fun.

That entire week a list of girls ran through my mind. I wondered who would be the one to try to win me over. I had two potentials in mind, but I was more than ready to be completely surprised by any random girl out there for me.

Finally, the morning of February 14 arrived.

After thirty minutes of math class, I spotted the student council flower delivery person outside the classroom in the hallway. She entered the room carrying a massive bouquet of flowers for distribution in Mr. Aaron's math class.

Mr. Aaron reluctantly stopped his class and organized the flowers. As he shuffled through the thick stack of cards, the room filled with anticipation. At long last, Mr. Aaron finally had our undivided attention.

He asked for a helper and started handing out the flowers. He announced the names on the cards as he delivered the goods. "Neil, Brian, Jennifer, Scott, Chad, Anne, Amy . . ." The list went on for a good ten minutes. Flowers began sprouting up on desktops all around me.

Some guys were already on their second and third flowers. One guy even scored a good half-dozen. Even though it was public knowledge that he had a girlfriend, the reality was that he already had six times as many flowers as me.

The list was now coming to an end and there was still a good six or seven of us in the room left holding nothing but a pencil. We had no flowers, no cards, only a small bit of hope that one of the remaining flowers would be for us.

Mr. Aaron read out the last couple names, "Two more for Neil and, oh good, one for Harlan." Yes! There was one for me! Total relief. I had a pretty good idea who had sent it to me.

I looked down at the card and it confirmed exactly what I expected. It wasn't from Melanie, it wasn't from Susie, and it definitely wasn't from Jenny. The card simply read, "Happy Valentine's Day—Love, Harlan."

My friends asked me who sent it. I told them it was someone very special, and left it at that. They never knew. They didn't need to know.

Harlan Cohen

Dear Girl

Dear Girl,

I feel that the time has come for me to have a girlfriend. I know you're out there somewhere. Don't worry, I'll find you.

And when I do, I hope that you will love me because I'm Derek, not because I'm Mike's younger brother. I hope you won't be embarrassed when my clothes don't match, or be annoyed when I want to watch the Lakers on ESPN, instead of *Party of Five*.

I hope that you will remember I play soccer, not football, and that I play midfield, not defense, and that every weekend I live with my dad.

I pray that you'll love me despite my tendency to forget birthdays, and if your parents invite me to dinner, please write their names really small on my hand so I can use it as reference.

Please know that I will constantly act strong and in control, but inside I am actually lost and confused. (Just don't tell my friends.) Please don't worry if I hurt myself skateboarding. Instead, be there to mend my wounds with kisses.

Understand that loving each other means being together, but not all of the time. We should never bail on our friends. Also understand that I may at times act jealous and overly protective, but only because *I* have insecurities not because *you* are doing anything wrong.

And if we fall out of love with one another, please don't hate me. And if I cry in front of you, please don't laugh at me. Please know that I am sensitive . . . in a manly, tough kind of way.

Please be honest with me without being hurtful. After all, I am a *boy*. And I promise to always be honest with you, because you deserve honesty. And I promise to open doors for you and buy your ticket when we go to the movies.

And no, you aren't fat, so please don't constantly ask. And you don't need makeup either. Oh, and don't be upset if you cut your hair and I don't notice. I will love you even in Levi's and a T-shirt.

I hope you don't think I'm asking too much of you. I just want to be happy making you happy. I'm coming to find you, so don't go anywhere. Stay where you are, whoever you are. And by the way, my name's Derek.

Yours Always,
Derek

Derek Whittier

Experience Is a Teacher

The true test of character is not how much we know how to do, but how we behave when we don't know what to do.

John Holt

I was shaking when I heard the car pull into the driveway. I blamed it on the chill in my house, although most likely it was because of my uncontrollable nerves. When I opened the door, Becca was standing on my porch with a smile plastered on her face.

"Hey," she said. As she stepped inside the doorway, the guys behind her became visible. "Oh, ya," she added. "This is Dan, Josh and Kevin."

"Hi," I said, and they replied the same in unison. They looked kind of like deer in headlights, standing outside the door, hands jammed in pockets, mouths half-open. As Becca made her way into the house, the guys followed her, and I felt awkwardly lost, unsure of what to say. To avoid forced conversation, I took the opportunity to jot a note to my mom, explaining where I was going.

Eventually, we made it out of the house, and I found

myself in the back seat of a navy-blue truck, wedged between Josh and Kevin, two older guys from a different school. Becca was chattering away in the passenger seat, changing the radio station and singing along. My legs began to shake, a sure indicator of my nervousness, and I had to put my hands on my thighs to steady them. We soon reached the restaurant, and I was thankful for the chance to get out of the truck.

Dan was toying with the miniature coffee creamers at the end of the table. "I don't trust these," he announced. "They've probably been sitting here since 1982."

At the opposite end of the table, next to Kevin, I giggled, probably for the eighth time since we'd sat down. I wanted to smack myself. Between my legs shaking and my ridiculous giggling, my immature nervous habits were driving me crazy, and I prayed that nobody else noticed.

Suddenly, Becca stood up. "I have to call my mom. Dan, come with me."

"Um, I'll come, too," I said. Feeling the need to elaborate, I continued, "I have to call my mom, too." I felt stupid following Becca and Dan out to the lobby, like a girl in elementary school who can't go anywhere without her best friend.

As we waited while Becca called her mom, Dan nudged me and said, "So, what do you think of Josh and Kevin?"

"Josh is pretty cute," I said, figuring that honesty was the best way to go.

"Not Kevin?" Dan's eyes sparkled, and I knew what Becca had been talking about when she said how wonderful he was.

"No . . ." I looked out the window. "But don't tell him that I said that."

"I won't." Of course he wouldn't. What did I think this was, elementary school? I felt like a child in a world of adults, unsure how to act or what to say.

"Josh thinks you're really hot," Dan continued.

His statement immediately grabbed my attention. "Oh, really?" I was flattered.

Becca hung up the phone and caught the end of our conversation, saying excitedly, "You have to sit by him when we go back to the table!"

"No," I protested. "That'll look dumb."

"No it won't," she insisted, and Dan agreed.

"Yeah, we'll just move stuff around or whatever." It was obvious that this was an argument I was not going to win.

When we returned to the table and assumed our new seats, Josh didn't say anything. I wondered if he had figured out our juvenile plan, and then I wondered if he even cared. But I quickly tried to brush the thoughts out of my head and proceeded to giggle at everything Dan said.

Next we went to the movies. Without Becca next to me in the theater, I felt completely defenseless. I gripped my knees for support, angry at myself for being nervous. Why couldn't I have more self-confidence and be as charming as other girls are? I leaned my head back against the headrest, watching Dan and Becca out of the corner of my eye. No contact yet, I noted. I didn't know what to do with my hands, and it seemed like they took on a life of their own as they repetitiously roamed from my knees to my thighs and eventually gripped the edge of my purse.

I felt a nudge on my right arm. I looked over at Dan and watched as he mouthed the words, "Make a move." He then grinned at me and raised his eyebrows in Josh's direction.

"No!" I whispered emphatically.

"Why not?" he replied with a kind of urgency.

I half-shrugged my shoulders. "I don't know." How could I explain to him the way my mind works? I could never "make a move" on anyone; I didn't have the nerve.

My fear of rejection was too intense. Out of the corner of my eye, I saw that Becca was leaning on Dan's shoulder, and his hand was resting on her knee. I sank farther into my seat.

On the way home from the movies, Becca asked Dan if he had a piece of paper. I knew immediately what she was doing and wanted to object, but couldn't. When she handed me Josh's number on a torn piece of paper, I didn't even look at it. I just played with it between my fingers, bending the edges and running it along the folds of my jeans. Josh's reaction to the piece of paper in his hand was similar.

We pulled into my driveway, and I thought that I was finally safe at home as I said good-bye to everyone and sauntered up to my porch. But as I turned around to give a final wave good-bye, I found Josh standing on the lawn.

"Hey," he said, in a way only older guys can. "When are you going to be home tomorrow?"

"Probably all day," I managed and immediately thought of how dumb I sounded.

"Okay, then. I'll, um, call you around one."

I flashed a slight smile. "Okay. Bye!" I stepped inside my house, allowing myself to breathe only when I had closed the door and was safe inside.

I washed my face, wondering if he would think that I was "really hot" without makeup. As I curled up in bed, the phrase "If only I had . . ." crossed my mind so many times that I became exhausted. But then I remembered that experience, even if awkward and uncomfortable, or in the form of a guy named Josh, is always a teacher. With that, I gradually fell asleep, knowing tomorrow was a new day, and I could rest assured there would be more lessons to learn.

Julia Travis

Dear Boy

Dear Boy,

I do not know who you are, or where or when we will meet, but I do hope it is soon.

I pray that when we meet and fall in love, you will love me, for me, and not hope for someone who is thinner or prettier. I hope you won't compare me to girls who may have brighter smiles. I hope that you will make me laugh, take care of me if I get sick, and be trustworthy.

I hope you will remember that I prefer daisies to roses, and that my favorite color changes with my mood. Please know that my eyes aren't blue, they're gray, with flecks of navy.

Please know that I might be too shy to kiss you first, but please don't be afraid to kiss me. I won't slap you or push you away. I'm sure your kisses will be perfect. When we go on a date, please don't stress about where to take me; what's important is that I'll be with you.

If I cry, please know it isn't because of you, just hold me close, and I'll heal quickly. And, if it is because of you, I'll heal just the same.

And if we decide to break up, please understand that I

may be bitter, but I'd like to be your friend if you'll let me. I promise to remember that you have feelings too, even though you'll never admit it, and when you are ready we'll have a friendship.

Please tell me if anything I do bothers you, or if something just doesn't sit right. I would like you to always be honest with me. If I have a bad day, I hope you will shower me with confidence and smiles.

I hope you don't think that I'm asking too much of you. I hope you understand that I'm a little bit nervous and very scared. I wish I could tell you how or when we will meet, and if we will be in love forever. Every relationship is a new game of cards, and . . . (sigh) . . . I've never been good at cards. But I will try my best to be kind and love you dearly for all that you are, without expecting too much from you. Thank you for listening; this is all that I ask.

Yours always,
Sarah

Sarah Bercot

It took a lot of self-resistance for Luann to keep from picking up the phone, but she knew it was for the best.

A Crush

I'm not afraid of storms, for I am learning how to sail my ship.

Helen Keller

"Aaarghhhmmmmm . . . Hello?"

It was about 10:00 on a beautiful July morning, and I had just been woken up from a deep slumber by the untimely ring of the telephone. Little did I know my destiny was on the other end of the line.

"Is Leigh there?" the rich tenor voice asked.

"Yeah. This is." I sat bolt upright, smacking my head on the headboard in the process. I rubbed my forehead and stared in disbelief at the receiver in my hand.

I met Josh while we worked together at the same pizza parlor. It was love at first sight for me, and the whole restaurant knew about it. Never mind that Josh was five years older than I was or that he didn't know my name (or so I thought, until this fateful phone call proved otherwise). I was 100 percent head over heels for the guy, the guy who was at this very moment on the other end of my telephone wire, calling my name. . . .

"Leigh? Hello? Leigh?"

I regained my senses enough to answer. "Yes. I'm here. Um, hi."

"Leigh, I need to talk with you. Can I pick you up in a half hour?"

Could he? "Yeah. Sure." I responded, trying to sound casual. We hung up, and I stared at the telephone for another moment, until I realized that I had twenty-eight minutes left before the love of my life would arrive at my front door to confess his undying passion for me.

Thirty-two minutes later, I stood gazing up at Josh's figure in my doorway. This was simply too good to be true. He looked slightly uncomfortable as he stood, his tall, slim frame moving restlessly.

"Let's go," he said.

Josh led the way to his car, and we both got in. As we pulled out of my driveway, I again gazed at his beautiful face. His lips were full but firm, his nose straight and perfect, his hair sun-streaked blond (from a side job landscaping, as a little investigative research had revealed to me), and his eyes, his gorgeous, wide-set, polished mahogany eyes were ... staring right back at me! I flushed in embarrassment, as I began to say something, but Josh interrupted me. He didn't bother with small talk, but got right down to business.

"I've been hearing some rumors at work," he began.

This was *not* the opening I had anticipated.

"What kind of rumors?" I ventured.

Josh presented me with an accusatory glance. "Oh, just that you and I are dating. That we're practically engaged. All sorts of great stuff." He gave me a pointed look. "Since I have never even *talked* to you until this morning, I don't know how anybody could have gotten that impression. Unless *somebody*," he paused dramatically, "told them."

I stared at him, shocked. I was speechless for a long

minute, my mouth attempting to form denials that wouldn't make it past my throat. A vice took hold of my heart, squeezing painfully. Finally, I managed to collect myself enough to say, "I swear, I never said anything like that. I might have had a"—my throat began to close up, but I was able to continue in a humiliated whisper—"a little crush on you, and some people knew about it, but I promise, I swear to you, I never insinuated anything else. I'm sorry."

Josh looked at me. My shock at his accusation and every ounce of my humiliation were evident on my face. After a moment, he accepted my admission for the truth that it was, and he tried to change the topic to more light-hearted chit-chat, but I was too occupied trying to keep the tears from streaming down my face, to be a good conversationalist.

After about five minutes, I requested that he take me to my friend Annette's house. As he pulled away, the tears overflowed down my cheeks. I turned to see Annette rushing outside. I ran toward her, sobs making my body shake, and she hugged me until I finally began to calm down. When my crying had diminished to random hic-cuping sighs, my best friend took my face between her hands and said softly, with wisdom beyond her years, "If it were supposed to feel good, they wouldn't call it a crush."

J. Leigh Turner

Sea Glass

We're sitting on the cold shore combing the sand around us looking for sea glass. It's windy, and the cool mist coming off the waves feels cold and charming. We're bundled up in all our layers, and he gently touches my face and kisses my lips. His blue-green eyes stare deep into mine, and I feel him looking straight into my heart.

The brilliant rays of purple, gold and turquoise start to fade as the sun finishes setting. We stand up, wipe the sand off our pants and start walking to the parking lot. I take a deep breath and smell the salt and seaweed crawling in with the tide.

On our walk home, he holds my hand, and we laugh and talk about nothing of real significance. We walk slowly to savor the moment, to savor the time we have together. The trees seem to make a tunnel, surrounding us and isolating us in our own little world.

When we get back to my house, we take the sea glass and put it in my jar. "It's almost halfway filled," he remarks, as I look at the tiny pieces filling the jar. There must be at least a hundred pieces in there, all of them different shapes and different colors. I suppose that if I counted them, there would be just as many as the days we have spent together, and the nights we have comforted each other on the phone.

Each piece of glass is a different color. I decide that they represent the ordinary days filled with insight and love. They are the most frequent ones, the everyday ones. I notice that I put in a green one today. It is a day like today that we shared together that the green ones represent. The green ones frosted with white specks represent the days in which one of us was upset and confided in the other. Although there are only a few, there are some and they're big. I think those are the ones that help the relationship grow the most. The white pieces are the biggest and the shiniest. They reflect the time one of us accomplished something or was really happy about something. One might represent him winning his car, another might be when I made the team, and yet there are so many I can't remember what each one represents. There are so few dark-brown ones. Those have the sharpest edges and cut your fingertips when you touch them. They cause tears and hurt. They're the ex-girlfriends, the not-too-long-ago crushes, the jealousy, the fights. They are the painful parts of our relationship that will never go away, but have become smoother over time.

There is one brilliant bluish-purple piece of glass. It is very small, and I know exactly what it represents. It is the first time he said those three words that before that night were just tossed around and used carelessly by other guys. It represents the time when he looked deep into my eyes, brushed back my hair and told me he loved me.

All of the pieces of sea glass are strong. No matter how hard you try (and people have tried), they won't break. They may get smoother, maybe a little smaller, but so do all memories. They are strong and will always be there and will never be lost.

Then there's a big rock, a big pink rock in the shape of a heart, down at the bottom. Its shape represents exactly what it is. It's our hearts, with all the sea glass and memories and good times to come piled on top. Our small, pink hearts, learning about each other and ourselves, piling little green days on top of big white ones, avoiding the sharp brown ones and trying to find another blue one. It's our hearts, the ones that have grown to love each other. The ones that have spent over two years piling memories on top, good and bad, to make two different, wonderful people. The glass jar will never break. The jar is our bodies that protect our hearts and memories. Like the sea glass, it is strong and even if one of us goes away, it will still be there with all the memories left behind.

Stacey Doerner

Kiss

Point your lashes down
　and you can picture my face—
　　I'm smiling . . .

Open your mouth, speak with your heart
　and you can see my soul—
　　I'm waiting . . .

Place your arms around my waist
　and you can embrace my uncertainty—
　　I'm shaking . . .

Press your lips against mine
　and try to catch me—
　　I'm falling . . .

Emily Crane

He Finally Said, "I Love You"

As I looked into his eyes
And found his longing stare
I stopped myself from saying words
That would show how much I care
I put my hand up to his face
To hold my feelings in
I wouldn't say the words again
To show my love for him
The last time I had told him
How much he meant to me
He put my hands away from his
And said to leave him be
I never spoke the words again
For fear of his deep fright
I thought it was the last time
Until that blissful night
His fingers traced around my face
Pushing hair away
And I was quite unprepared
For what he was to say
My heart beat quickly, my head raced on

I thought that I might cry
He looked as if he might faint—
Imagine this strong guy
But never would I be more impressed
With anything he'd do
Than when he took that heartfelt leap
And told me, "I love you."

Jennifer Orendach

Why Girls Like Guys

In *Chicken Soup for the Teenage Soul II*, we included "A Few Reasons Why Guys Like Girls." We thought it would be fun to keep the momentum going for this book, so we asked you write to us with more reasons "Why Guys Like Girls" or even "Why Girls Like Guys." And write you did! We had such a good time reading all the imaginative and entertaining responses you came up with.

Since we heard from the guys for *Teen II*, we thought we'd let the girls have their say for this book. The following is a compilation of the sweetest lists we received from the girls:

1. They always wear your favorite cologne (which happens to be the one that you bought them for their birthday).
2. The way they run their fingers through your hair.
3. That look they give you that makes you just want to die right then and there.
4. The way they kiss away your tears.

5. The way they get mad when they can't make your problem go away.

6. The way they show off around their friends, even though you know you would love him if he missed a basket or two.

7. The way they make it their personal mission to ensure that you are never cold.

8. That confused look they get on their faces when you are mad at them—guaranteed to make your heart melt and the anger fade away.

9. The way they always let you win any game you play together.

10. . . . And when you point this out to them they pretend not to know what you are talking about.

11. That smile they flash that can make your stomach drop to your feet.

12. The way they call to apologize after you had a big fight.

13. The way they touch and hold you so gently, as if they are afraid they will break you.

14. The way they say, "I love you."

15. The way they would die before saying "I love you" in front of their friends.

16. The way they kiss you.

17. The way they kiss you after making up from a fight.

18. The way they hold you when you are crying.

19. The way they think they are your big protector.

20. The way they say, "I miss you," even though they hate to admit it.

21. The way you miss everything about them when they are gone.

22. The way they comfort you when you have had a bad day.

23. The way they write you love letters even if they think it's uncool.

24. Regardless of whether you love them, hate them, wish they would die or know that you would die without them ... it matters not. Because once they enter your life, whatever you were to the world, they become everything to you. When you look them in the eyes, traveling to the depths of their souls and you say a million things without even speaking, you know that your own life is consumed by their love. We love them for a million reasons; it is a thing, an indescribable feeling.

Compiled by Kimberly Kirberger

The Funeral of My Rose

*You will find as you look back upon your life,
that the moments when you have truly lived, are
the moments when you have done things in the
spirit of love.*

Henry Drummond

I turn on my high beams as I drive home from play rehearsal one night. The outside air is calm as it brushes my cheek through an open window. Hearing a good song, I turn the radio up a little louder. The song takes me to a different place. I begin daydreaming about my crush again. I notice a grocery store on my right, and, spontaneously, I swerve into the parking lot. Tonight is the night. I walk in through the automatic doors and head straight for my destination: the floral department. My choice is a single beautiful red rose. I wrap it in green tissue paper and head back to my car. My heart begins beating rapidly as I strategize. Tonight seems different, though. I've had enough planning, and I am now acting on impulse. It must be a sign.

After a fairly long drive, I turn into one of North

Augusta's more classy subdivisions. I glance at my watch: 9:00 P.M. It seems like a good, solid time. My palms have begun to sweat, but I press on. I find myself parked in a driveway of an amazing house. I take a breath and pull myself out of the car. I leave the rose on the back seat, promising myself that I will return for it later. My footsteps are determined, and I swiftly walk to the front door. *Ding*, the doorbell rings as I nervously press it. The door opens.

"Hello, Derek," a familiar face greets me.

"Hi, Mrs. Johnson, is Lauren home?" I sheepishly ask.

My cheeks burn as she turns and shouts for her daughter. It seems like an eternity, but soon enough I hear a door open. Lauren comes clumping down the stairs, and my heart jumps to my throat. One look into her big brown eyes, and I forget my own name. I have never had a problem communicating until I met this mythological siren disguised in Gap clothing. Her lips part to reveal white teeth, and her brilliant smile lights the dim room. She greets me with a look of confusion.

"Hey, Derek, what's up?" she asks, tilting her head to the side, perplexed. Her eyes examine me as if she is putting a puzzle together. I attempt to speak, but words don't seem to come.

"Can I speak to you out on the porch?" I finally spit out.

I open the door and let her pass. We take seats on the front stoop, and I turn to her. I try choosing my words carefully.

"So, are you going out with Kevin?" I blurt out abruptly and regrettably.

Taken by surprise, she waits a moment to let the question sink in.

"Umm . . . I think so," she slowly replies as she twirls a piece of her hair.

I had taken the time to investigate their relationship. I

knew Kevin would eventually hurt her, and I knew what I had to do.

"He doesn't deserve you, Lauren," I tell her assertively. "Why do you say that?" she asks, again looking confused.

"Because ... look ... umm ..." I struggle and finally get back on track. "Because I like you, Lauren. I like you a lot." I turn away. *What have I done? Why did I say that?* I look back in her eyes. They are more confused than ever now. They look hurt, and I so badly want to go over to her, take her in my arms and live happily ever after with her.

"Well ... Kevin is funny, and sweet. He's not that bad." My mind reels. *What just happened?* I proclaimed my love to her. I had just told the girl of my dreams that I liked her. Did she hear me? I look back in her eyes, the eyes of the girl I fell for as a little boy. The eyes of the girl my heart skips a beat for each time she passes me in the hall. Crushed, I know I have to leave. I have to get out of there. I have to escape. I have revealed something that has tormented me for days, and now my entire body feels like it is shriveling up in embarrassment. After saying good-bye, I get in my car and drive away from her house.

The next day I am in my car after a particularly wretched day at school. I sit there for a few moments letting my mind drift back to last night's activity. Suddenly I notice the rose I had left in the car. This beautiful, red rose has now transformed into a black, stiff, thorny twig. I hold it in my hands for a few moments, and a tear rolls down my cheek. It is time to move on. I realize I have done the right thing. Although I did not get the response I had hoped for, I have learned an invaluable lesson: You cannot make someone love you, you can only make yourself someone who can be loved.

Derek Gamba

My Childhood Sweetheart

Love can sometimes be magic. But magic can sometimes . . . just be an illusion.

Javan

I met Jake when I was eleven. To me, he wasn't just "my older brother's friend." He was a thirteen-year-old—an older man. Jake and my brother would sit in my brother's room, door closed, and shake their heads to the music of Guns 'n Roses. I would desperately try to think of excuses to knock on my brother's door, just to get a peek or a quick smile at Jake. I found something attractive in this geeky computer whiz. But I was just "Phil's baby sister," so the lines were drawn: He was the friend, and I was the annoying little sister, two seemingly incompatible titles.

Jake went away to private school, and I missed his presence in the house, even if it had just been behind my brother's locked door. A few months after he left, Jake wrote a letter to Phil, and at the end of the letter, in barely legible script, he scribbled, "Say hello to your sister for me. Is she still cute?" I lived on that line for months; it was enough to give me a constant flutter in my stomach.

In the summer of 1993, Jake came home. One evening, the phone rang. When I answered it, the voice on the other line responded, "Hi, Leesa, is Phil around?" I searched my memory, trying to remember the familiar voice on the other line. After a few seconds, I realized it was Jake. JAKE!

"Actually, he's not here. Where are you?" My voice shook. I couldn't believe it when he replied, "Cranbrook." He was home.

Our friendship began the instant he spoke again and said, "Well, if Phil isn't around, I guess *you* are going to have to talk to me." That night, we got together and sat in the park for hours.

I brought a friend along, with the intention of setting her up with the friend who accompanied Jake. I watched as Jake talked and laughed with my friend, Mel. I realized I wasn't going to be the one setting anyone up. Jake was obviously interested in Mel.

When Jake and Mel became a couple, my heart sank. To my selfish pleasure, I felt smug later that month when they broke up, and Jake called me to complain. We ended up talking again, and my anger toward his dating Mel wore off rather quickly. It was hard to stay mad at him.

Although he left for school again soon after that, his letters were now addressed to me, with side notes that read, "Say hi to Phil for me." Our friendship was growing stronger and stronger.

He left his school two years later, only to move farther away. I thought we would both move on, since we were so far apart, but we only grew closer. It wasn't long before I realized that I was officially in love with him. Whenever he came to visit, it was like a whole new adventure. We felt free to act like kids, but at the same time, we had endless conversations. We laughed and shared our secrets, and I always dreaded the day he had to go back home.

Every time he visited, I told myself, *This is it. I am going to tell him how I feel.* I promised myself that I would before he left, but I never got the guts to confess my true feelings.

Jake came home again a few days ago. I swore to myself that there was no more next time, that it was now or never, and that I couldn't hold it in anymore. While we had hinted at our feelings, we had never talked about them. I worked up the nerve to tell him how I felt, that I loved him and had for some time. The words just flowed out of me. He cut me off, leaned over and kissed me. I expected to feel complete bliss, but, surprisingly, I didn't. *This is Jake,* I reminded myself. *Remember? You love him!* Still, I felt nothing. When he looked at me, I could tell he felt the same. I believed that kissing Jake would be the last piece of the puzzle to complete my perfect fantasy. Yet somehow, the puzzle pieces just didn't match up.

Jake left again today, and for once, his leaving doesn't feel like a tragedy. We are best friends, nothing more, and always will be.

So maybe this isn't a storybook ending. Perhaps my childhood sweetheart will not become my fairy-tale prince, but we can still live happily ever after.

Leesa Dean

I Had to Let Him Go

"I'm sorry, I just don't really remember . . ."

His words tore through me, piercing every inch of my body and cutting jaggedly through to my heart. Just one week earlier, we had watched the sun set and held each other. He comforted me while I asked him why my best friend and I just couldn't get along anymore. But tonight, his mind was somewhere else; he couldn't remember that special night.

Why was he so distant? Was he so lost in the pain that had been haunting him for so long?

There were nights he cried himself to sleep, remembering the harsh words of his mother. He told me how much he dreaded the weekends spent with her, because it meant another seventy-two hours of being blamed for everything that went wrong. The nagging didn't stop—she harassed him because his grades were lower than his brother's and he wasn't the perfect son she wanted him to be. She said he was dumb; that he wouldn't get into college, wouldn't succeed in life. She called him a loser, a disappointment to her. His gift at art was undeniable, yet her criticism caused him to believe he had no talent, when actually, he was winning prizes for his work.

What kept him alive, he told me, was our love. Friends for years, and now dating, he needed me. He counted on me. In one letter I received from him, he said, "You're like my family. Just you. We can be a family. Do you need anyone else? I don't. Just keep loving me," he wrote, "and I'll be okay."

For a while, I believed him. I promised I would never hurt him like she had, never leave him, never stop loving him. I would be his family; the one he needed in good times and in bad, the one who held him when he was sick and cheered for him at track meets. I thought that if I held him tightly enough, his pain would disappear.

It was like a roller coaster, though, our relationship. Sometimes, he was the happiest kid I knew—laughing, joking, smiling and kissing. I always knew if he was happy by his eyes. Crystal clear and blue, they told me no lies. If he was happy, they sparkled. But if he was sad, they seemed more gray than blue. On those sad days, he didn't joke. When I tried to cheer him with a kiss, he would refuse. He wouldn't let me touch him. I couldn't show him how much I loved him. When he was hurt, all he knew was to return the hurt to those undeserving. He said things he knew were cruel, apologizing the next day. The cycle never ended—the cruelties, the apologies. Yet I knew why.

Though I loved him, I couldn't take away his pain. It stemmed from events that occurred long before I knew him. Soon I realized my love couldn't compete with his inner pain. Though it hurt, I realized that I couldn't help him; rather, he had to seek professional help. I had to let him go.

The night I told him this couldn't continue, the tears stung my eyes more painfully than ever before. He now would have to face his worst fear—to be alone to confront the real demons within him. He thought I had deceived him, that I had lied to him when I whispered the word *forever*. But I hadn't lied to anyone but myself because I believed that all he needed was my love. Right now, my love was only causing pain.

He had built a separate world, in which only he and I existed. For a while, it had been nice to dream of such a happy place, a mystical Eden for just the two of us. Before long, however, I knew the walls would crumble if he kept relying only on me. Deep down I knew it wasn't healthy for either of us. I simply couldn't hold on to us and this fantasy any longer.

Yesterday, I saw him for the first time in a year. His eyes sparkled, and the light came from within. The darkness is lifting, because he allowed other people into his life, people who helped him in more ways than I ever could have done on my own. Now, he sees the special gifts that he has, and although the painful memories will always remain, he is now beginning to believe in himself. Yesterday, I realized that even perfect love can't protect someone from himself. And, sometimes, the most loving thing you can do for someone is to let him go.

Andrea Barkoukis

I Never Thought It Would End This Way

A twig snaps under my foot, and we both jump. Anticipation tingles my skin, and his hand is cold as it rests in mine. The shadows of the forest dance on his troubled face. Moonlight eerily bounces off the pond. The moonlight reflects the cold beads of sweat that have built up on his neck.

We come to a clearing in the woods, our clearing. It's the place where he first told me that he loved me. It's the first place we ever kissed. It's where "we" started, and it's where "we" will end.

The winter darkness has turned his blue eyes into pools of black. A cold shiver runs through my body. The cold's not from the outside, but the inside.

We both involuntarily sit on a rock, hand in hand, shoulder to shoulder, leg to leg. Unconsciously, he brushes a stray strand of blond hair off my face. Silence has become normal between us. Not the nice kind of silence or the comfortable kind of silence, but the awkward silence of strangers. Our silence is an avoidance of the truth.

For two years, this guy has been my world. He's been

my best friend, my boyfriend, my comfort, my strength. Now I've come to break this pact, this bond. And I know that once I've said what I need to say nothing will ever be the same again. I want to sit here and hold him. I want to know that everything will be okay.

If we talk about the truth, everything will be over. So we choose silence. In this place of beginnings, it is so ironic that now it is the place for endings. Everything in my world is changing, and there is nothing I can do about it. Suddenly, my shivering stops as his jacket surrounds my shaking body.

How can I live without him? The owl's hooting above reflects the lonely song in my heart. My heart is slowly being torn to pieces. I look up into his eyes. He turns away at my tears.

"Don't. I can't handle that," he says. His voice is quiet and filled with pain. He wipes my tears away with his thumbs. His mouth is so close to mine that my lips reach for his, but he turns away. The sting of rejection is more pain than I can handle. I wish that I could fall asleep and wake up when this nightmare is over and all the pain is gone.

"I love you." My words are a peace offering, sent out cautiously and carefully. They are meant to stop further missiles from coming my way.

"Don't. You're just making it worse."

"How could it be worse?" My voice is pleading and desperate. My whole world is crumbling around me, and he's worried that it could be worse.

All around me the stars are shining their heavenly light. How can they stay so brilliant and bright while all the lights in my world are cut off?

Instinctively, I reach for my ring and twirl it around my finger. I've been wearing this ring for two years now. He gave it to me for our first Valentine's Day together. Out here in the cold, the gold of the moonlight looks pale and its luminosity has lost its sparkle. Out here the world looks bleak and dismal.

If the sun were shining and sending its happy rays everywhere, would we be happy, too? Or would our hearts still be dark and cold like the atmosphere now?

"Do you feel like this is unreal? Do you feel like this should never have happened to us?" I ask. "This was not supposed to happen to us!" He puts his head in his hands, as if he is trying to avoid my questions. Slowly, he rubs his hands back and forth like he's trying to wipe away a bad dream.

"We can work this out. I know we can. This is us we are talking about," he says, laughing.

What about this could be funny? I wonder. "Are you laughing at me?" I ask. The look in his eyes tells me no. It tells me that his laughter is to prevent sobbing. I can't resist the urge to touch his face. He grabs my hand, and for a moment we freeze. We are stopped in a moment of time that in our minds will last forever.

He leans in to kiss me. His lips seek reconciliation. The moonlight bathes us in a luminous light, but it's just dark enough to see only silhouettes. The frogs on the pond sing a lovely melody. And for one brief shining moment I know that life will go on, with or without him. So, I disentangle myself from his arms and start the long lonely walk to the car, and somehow I know I will find myself again.

Jennifer Gearhart

"This time it's *really* over, Jared. I threw out all your pictures *and* deleted all your e-mails."

Reprinted with permission of David Cooney.

Please Sign My Yearbook

The hardest of all is learning to be a well of affection, and not a fountain; to show them we love them not when we feel like it, but when they do.

Nan Fairbother

Sitting in class, I concentrated on the back of Brian's neck. Evil thoughts filled my mind; I was secretly waiting for his head to explode. It didn't, and I was forced to watch my ex-boyfriend laugh and chat with every person in the room while he blatantly ignored me.

After Brian and I broke up, third period became pure torture. While I was still nursing what I considered to be the world's worst broken heart, I was bombarded with the sight of my ex's excessive flirting, as if he were proving to me that he was so obviously over his heartache. During class, Brian would gossip loudly about his weekend, his latest party and his new car.

Maybe Brian was trying to get back at me for breaking off our six-month relationship. Maybe he thought that if he looked happy, it would hurt me more than I had hurt him.

At the end of the relationship, I let him cry on my shoulder but held a strong heart as he begged me not to go. Of course, he covered his pain very well at school, as if our tearful good-bye had never occurred.

Immediately after the breakup, Brian started dating another girl. She was graduating that spring, as if that were a big feat for a junior-year boy. She took him to the prom and announced it right beside me in math class. I, too, had a date for the prom, but it still hurt. My hurt curdled and turned to anger. It felt like he was trying to upset me, trying to rub his happiness in my face. Every time I saw them together, I wanted to scream. It felt like the pain was going to tear me in half, or at least force me to consider tearing her in half.

School was coming to an end, and I eagerly waited for summer vacation, my savior. No more Algebra Two and that gnawing feeling in my stomach each day.

One day in dreaded third period, Brian leaned over to me, and to my surprise, he asked me to sign his yearbook. I must have sat there for a full minute before I got over the shock and said yes.

I thought to myself, *This is my chance.* I could really let him have it! I could tell him that I knew what he was doing, that he was trying to hurt me, and that it wasn't fair. I could tell him that I saw through his act, that he and I both knew it was exactly that, an act. But then it hit me, what good would come of that? Would belittling him make me feel better, or would it just perpetuate the pain that we both needed to recover from?

Instead of writing of the pain I had endured, I listed all of the fun times we had shared. I wrote about the first place we had ever kissed, the gifts he had given me, the lessons I had learned—the ones he had taught me—and the first "I love you" that was whispered between us. It took up one page, and that quickly became two, until my hand was tired of writing. There were still a million more great memories crowding the corners of my mind, and I remembered many more throughout the day. It made me realize the things I learned from him and what great experiences we had shared. I finished by telling him I held no hard feelings, and I hoped he felt the same.

Maybe what I wrote in his yearbook made me look weak, maybe he thought I was pathetic for still holding onto the memories of our relationship. But writing all those things helped me; it helped me heal the wounds that still hurt in my heart. It felt liberating to let go of the grudge; I finally felt free from my anger.

I realized that Brian had taught me one final lesson: forgiveness. Someday, when he is fifty and has his own children, he may stumble upon his high school yearbook, and they will ask who Stacy was. I hope he can look back and say I was someone who really cared about him, loved him, and most importantly, that I was someone who taught him about forgiveness.

Stacy Brakebush

Wayne was deeply touched
by the personal inscriptions in his yearbook.

My Knight on His White Horse

I expected to meet my first love in a magical way. Not necessarily "Knight on White Horse" magical, but I had a definite picture in my head—tall, blond, chiseled body, deep voice, designer clothes. He would be romantic, smart and very witty. He would be perfect. One day he did come along, my perfect love, although his perfection wasn't quite there—at first.

He was five years older than I and about five inches shorter. He had a high squeaky voice, considering he was nineteen at the time, and a scrawny little body. He wasn't what you would call "good-looking."

We met at the beach. A mutual friend introduced us. He was annoying and kept cracking jokes and flirting with me. Somehow, he ended up giving my friends and me a ride home that night.

I rolled my eyes as the car pulled up to us. The brakes were shot, the door was broken, and he had to sit on a phone book to actually see over the dashboard. I could not help but laugh at the situation. *How embarrassing*, I thought. But he was far from embarrassed. He kept cracking jokes about his "trusty steed" and had us all laughing to tears. We stopped off at his house on the way home, and I asked him if I could use his bathroom. He stopped, turned and said, "Yes, but . . . those who use my bathroom must give me their phone numbers." He was grinning.

"Whatever. Here." I jotted down my number and then sought out the bathroom.

I guess you could say that was where it all started. We became friends instantly. He would take me out to dinner and to the movies. He even brought me as his date to a Halloween party and stayed by my side the whole night. That Halloween was the night I realized that Chris was more to me than just a friend. We came to the party as "hitch hikers that escaped from prison" and won the prize for most creative costume.

His creativity and silliness was what did it. That's how he won my heart. I was in love with this beautiful friend.

Did I tell him? Oh, no way! I was very proud . . . and very stubborn. I had been hurt many times before meeting Chris, and needless to say, had learned that love confessions are dangerous. But this was different; it felt real. We had been friends for almost a year and knew each other inside out. I knew that he liked me. He told me so all the time. I was confused. I didn't want to ruin the amazing friendship we had.

I hid my feelings for him for another year. It drove me crazy. He gave up on me and got a girlfriend, and I dated off and on; thus, we grew apart. I was never happy with any other guy. I compared every date and hug and voice to his. It hurt inside, and I denied my own true feelings and hid them very well until one day. . . .

He had just broken up with his girlfriend, and I called out of the blue. He asked if I wanted to come over and watch a movie, and I agreed.

"We have some catching up to do," he whispered, his voice giving me chills.

"Yeah, you're right. I've missed ya. . . . You haven't grown have you?" I joked.

"Just come over," he laughed. So I did.

It felt good to be back. I threw my arms around him immediately as I walked through the door. Our eyes met awkwardly, and I pulled away.

We talked about our lives, each other and ourselves. We talked for hours, about everything and anything, until silence interrupted our conversation.

I had always wondered how it would feel to kiss him— soft, sloppy, passionate?

And in that moment I decided that I needed to know. Our eyes met, and I leaned in and kissed him. His lips were soft, the kiss perfect. I was floating in his touch, his arms, his affection. It had been two years of flirting and friendship, and finally we were trapped in the moment, between our own true feelings.

I spilled to him the truth about my feelings. I told him how scared I was that I would lose him as a friend, but that he had become much more than that to me. I told him that I had never cared about someone this way. I told him that he was beautiful and that I was falling in love with him. I even began to cry.

He smiled and kissed me lightly on the cheek. " I love you, too," he whispered. "And I know how you feel. We go perfectly together, Becca."

"I know, Chris." At that moment he was the most beautiful person I had ever seen, every inch, up to his perfect ears. His voice was music, his touch tender. That was when our friendship became more. We were in love.

Months passed and our stability floundered. Love is a roller coaster, and I must admit sometimes all the turns and twists made me sick. But through everything we had an amazing and beautiful relationship. He taught me how to love and admired my passion for life. He instilled confidence in me and supported my individuality.

Love has a tendency to fade. Ours did. We had given each other a lot, including the confidence to grow into our own people, and, ultimately, to grow apart. One day, I just didn't see the love in his eyes any more. His kiss was different. We both felt the slow drift apart, yet neither of us really wanted to admit that our fire was blowing out. We had been together for a year-and-a-half and, secretly, I knew, no longer.

Although our relationship ended, our connection stayed strong. My friends had always warned me never to date your best friend; that you will ruin your friendship and it can never be the same again.

Three years later, he remains one of my best friends. We have changed and grown. I am involved with someone new and wonderful, and so is he. And yet we still remain major priorities in one another's lives.

The fantasy of my magical man has faded, and I no longer search for perfection. I know that it doesn't exist. What I do know is that love is mysterious, beautiful, and, oftentimes, very unexpected.

Rebecca Woolf

Fading Fast

Looking down at the interior side of my Strawberry Shortcake running shoes, I realize that his name, Forrest David, is fading. I trace my finger over his signature, remembering the day he autographed my shoe with his dad's pen as I sat in the Austin airport, tears blurring my vision.

That's what he's doing, I think, *slowly fading out of my life.* And yet, I remember everything and every moment I was with him, savoring his every move, smile and kiss. I never thought a person could be so precious to me. He was so beautiful, it hurt to look at him. But now it hurts to think of him. I memorized his face: dark eyebrows, greenish-blue eyes, tousled hair. His hands, tan and strong, could swallow my own. I had never loved anyone else the way I loved Forrest.

The first time I saw him, I stood there quietly, drinking him in. And when I finally had him, I was almost in tears because I had never felt so alive. I don't know how long I stood there holding him, breathing in his scent with my face pressed against his shirt. I knew I didn't want to let go.

I cried bitterly the day we parted, feeling utterly alone

as I watched him vanish down the airplane terminal. I tasted the salt as I wept, feeling so angry at the world and at life. I had found my love, the one I wanted to be with forever, and life had chosen to be cruel and unfair, keeping us over six hundred miles away from each other. It might as well have been 10 million. I thought my heart would break.

I sigh as I remember these painful memories, but I don't cry. I have no tears left for him.

They say real love is forever. I don't know the exact definition of it, but Forrest is as close as I've ever come to it. He's gone now, and my dreams have been shattered by the harsh reality of the situation. I thought we were meant to be together, and I dearly loved him. Two teenagers living so far away from each other usually can't make it. I thought we would be different, that we were strong enough to make it. I was wrong. When he left, he took a piece of my heart with him. It's now floating somewhere in Austin.

For a while, I couldn't eat or sleep. I felt so sick and empty. I didn't think I'd be able to go on without him. As I look back now, I see that it was a time of mourning—I was mourning the loss of a two-year relationship. I didn't think the hurt would ever end.

Then, one morning I woke up, and the sick feeling in my stomach was gone. I knew then that I was going to be okay, that I no longer needed him. I began to live again. As I look back, the only thing he ever gave me that I'll be able to carry with me forever is the discovery of my inner strength. It will carry me through all the pain, all the hurt, and I will survive. I had it in me the entire time; I just couldn't quite find it. Thank you, Forrest.

I smile as I remember him, and then I gently slip my running shoes off and let go.

Kendal Kelly

2

FRIENDSHIP

Live your life from your heart. Share from your heart. And your story will touch and heal people's souls.

Melody Beattie

Why Rion Should Live

Believe that life is worth living and your belief will help create the fact.

William James

High school didn't frighten me. Oh sure, the endless halls and hundreds of classrooms were overwhelming, but I took it in with all the pleasure of starting a new adventure. My freshman year was full of possibilities and new people. With a class of nearly two thousand new-comers, you just couldn't go wrong. So I, still possessing the innocence of a child concealed in a touch of mascara and lipstick, set out to meet them all.

Spanish One introduced me to Rion. By the student definition, he was a "freak": the black jeans, the well-worn Metallica shirts, the wallet chains, the works. But his unique personality and family troubles drew me to him. Not a crush, more of a curiosity. He was fun to talk to, and where interrupted whispering sessions left off, hours of phone conversations picked up.

During one of these evening conversations, "it," as we like to address the incident, unfolded. We were discussing the spectacular height of Ms. Canaple's over-styled bangs when I heard Rion's dad yelling in the back-ground. "Hold on," Rion muttered before a question could be asked. I could tell that he was trying to muffle the receiver, but you could still hear the horror as if his room were a dungeon, maximizing the bellows. Then the line went dead.

Shaking, I listened to the flatline of the phone for a minute before gently placing it in its cradle, too scared to call back for fear of what I might hear. I had grown up in an ideal family setting: a mom and a dad and an older sis-ter as a role model. This kind of situation took me by sur-prise, and I felt confused and helpless at the same time. A couple of tense hours later, after his father had gone to bed, Rion called me to apologize. He told me his dad had received a letter from his ex-wife, Rion's mom, saying she refused to pay child support. Having no other scapegoat, he stumbled into Rion's room in rage.

"I can't take this anymore. All the fighting . . . it's always there. . . ." His voice had trailed off, lost in painful thought. "All I have to do is pull the trigger, and it will be over."

"No!" I screamed. "Don't talk like that! You know you have so much to live for." It was becoming clearer every second how threatening the situation was. A cold, forced chuckle came from the other end of the line. "Yeah, right," was his response. We got off the phone, but only after promising to go right to sleep.

Sleep, however, was light years away from me. I was so worried and had a feeling I was Rion's only hope. He had told me repeatedly that it was hard to open up to anyone but me. How could someone not want to live? I could lit-erally list the reasons why I loved waking up every morn-ing. Frantically, I racked my brain for ways to convince Rion of this. Then the lightbulb clicked on. I took a piece of notebook paper and entitled it, "Why Rion Should

Live." Below, I began listing every reason I could think of that a person had to exist. What started as a few sentences turned into twenty, then thirty-two, then forty-seven. By midnight, I had penned fifty-seven reasons for Rion to live. The last ten were as follows:

48) Six feet of earth is pretty heavy.
49) They don't play Metallica in cemeteries.
50) Braces aren't biodegradable.
51) God loves you.
52) Believe it or not, your father loves you, too.
53) Spanish One would be so boring.
54) Two words: driver's license.
55) Satan isn't exactly the type of guy you want to hang out with for eternity.
56) How could you live without Twinkies?
57) You should never regret who you are, only what you have become.

Believing that I had done my best, I crawled into bed to await tomorrow's chore: saving Rion.

I waited for him at the door to Spanish the next day and handed him the paper as he walked in. I watched him from the opposite side of the room while he read the creased sheet in his lap. I waited, but he didn't look up for the entire period. After class, I approached him, concerned, but before I could say a word, his arms were around me in a tight embrace. I hugged him for a while, tears almost blinding me. He let go, and with a soft look into my eyes, he walked out of the room. No thank you was needed, his face said it all.

A week later, Rion was transferred to another school district so that he could live with his grandmother. For weeks I heard nothing, until one night the phone rang. "Sarah, is it you?" I heard the familiar voice say. Well, it was like we had never missed a day. I updated him on Ms.

Canaple's new haircut, and he told me his grades were much better, and he was on the soccer team. He is even going to counseling with his dad to help them build a stronger relationship. "But do you know what the best part is?" I sensed true happiness in his voice. "I don't regret who I am, nor what I've become."

Sarah Barnett

[EDITORS' NOTE: *Rion was lucky. Everyone isn't as fortunate. If you are depressed or thinking about hurting yourself, (or if you think any of your friends are in this situation),* please call for help, toll-free: **1-800-SUICIDE**. *Remember, you are not alone. People care and can help you.* **WE LOVE YOU!!**]

My Fairy Tale

The road to a friend's house is never long.

Danish Proverb

He was the stuff fairy tales are made of—not unrealistically suave, but definitely charming. Tall and handsome, he was a prince by all conventional definitions and had the ability to steal unsuspecting young girls' hearts.

Our first kiss was perfect, and from that moment on, our relationship soared. Some days, he picked me up early for school so that we could eat breakfast together, and other days we sneaked away for snowball fights during study hall. On weekends, I watched him play soccer, and he came to all of my softball games. And then we'd end our week with the ritual of a Saturday night movie at his house. Without fail, we talked on the phone every night until we fell asleep. A few months into our relationship, I had no time for anyone but him. But at the time, I liked it that way. I was perfectly content to be with him every second, because I was, without a doubt, in love.

But sometime during our nine-month walk in the

clouds, the honeymoon stage ended, and our relationship lost its spontaneity and sparkle. Saturday nights spent together became routine, and phone calls and kisses became as natural and expected as breathing.

On one particularly cold June day, Chris broke up with me. He said that he woke up that morning and realized he didn't love me. He said our relationship consisted of nothing but the memories of our past. It was two days before our nine-month anniversary. I felt empty inside, and the thought of being alone was uncomfortable and scary. Moreover, the person on whom I depended to pull me through hard times was the cause of my pain. My heart literally hurt.

Not knowing what else to do, I ran to a familiar place, Ashley's house. It was a place I hadn't visited often in the nine months before this afternoon. I stood at the door, and Ashley, seeing my tears, immediately understood what had happened. Within an hour, my three closest friends, the girls I had once spent so much time with, all arrived at Ashley's house. For the next two days, we camped out at Ashley's and analyzed every aspect of Chris's and my relationship, attempting to pinpoint where it went wrong.

Unable to form any meaningful conclusions, we agreed that we would never understand the male population, and so we moved on to bashing Prince Charming until he was reduced to a creature with the appeal of a toad. It felt good, and I even caught myself laughing for brief moments. Slowly, I began to reclaim my pre-boys, pre-broken-heart days with a little more wisdom and experience than I had before. I realized that life would go on, and I loved and appreciated my girlfriends for that invaluable realization.

Toward the end of our healing party, while we were laughing over ice cream sundaes, Erica looked at me and said, "We've missed you." The truth was, I had really missed them, too. I had unfairly neglected them in the midst of love's wake, and the past two days had shown me just how precious my friends were.

When love had removed its blindfold and all was said and done, I realized that maybe I hadn't had such a fairy-tale boyfriend after all. What I had were fairy-tale friendships. It took a heartbreak to realize the special gift I possessed all along: my girlfriends.

Kathryn Vacca

Colorful Shades of Gray

Moths are very ugly creatures. At least that is what I always thought until a reliable source told me otherwise. When I was about five or six years old, my brother Joseph and I stayed overnight at our Aunt Linda's house, our favorite relative. She spoke to us like adults, and she always had the best stories.

Joseph was only four years old and still afraid of the dark, so Aunt Linda left the door open and the hall light on when she tucked us into bed. Joe couldn't sleep, so he just lay there staring at the ceiling. Just as I dozed off to sleep, he woke me up and asked, "Jennie, what are those ugly things near the light?" (I had always liked that he asked me questions because I was older and supposed to know the answers. I didn't always know the answers, of course, but I could always pretend I did.) He was pointing to the moths fluttering around the hall light. "They're just moths. Go to sleep," I told him.

He wasn't content with that answer or the moths near his night light, so the next time my Aunt walked by the door he asked her to make the ugly moths go away. When she asked why, he said simply, "Because they're ugly and scary, and I don't like them!" She just laughed, rubbed his head, and said, "Joe, just because something is ugly outside doesn't mean it's not beautiful inside. Do you know why moths are brown?" Joe just shook his head.

"Moths were the most beautiful insects in the animal kingdom. At one time they were more colorful than the butterflies. They have always been helpful, kind and generous creatures. One day the angels up in heaven were crying. They were sad because it was cloudy and they couldn't look down upon the people on earth. Their tears fell down to the earth as rain. The sweet little moths hated to see everyone so sad; they decided to make a rainbow. The moths figured that if they asked their cousins, the butterflies, to help, they could all give up just a little bit of their colors, and they could make a beautiful rainbow.

"One of the littlest moths flew to ask the queen of the butterflies for help. The butterflies were too vain and selfish to give up any of their colors for either the people or the angels. So, the moths decided to try to make the rainbow themselves. They beat their wings very hard and the powder on them formed little clouds that the winds smoothed over like glass. Unfortunately, the rainbow wasn't big enough so the moths kept giving a little more and a little more until the rainbow stretched all the way across the sky. They had given away all their color except brown, which didn't fit into their beautiful rainbow.

"Now, the once-colorful moths were plain and brown. The angels up in heaven saw the rainbow and became joyous. They smiled, and the warmth of their smiles shone down on the earth as sunshine. The warm sunshine made the people on earth happy, and they smiled, too. Now every time it rains the baby moths, who still have their colors, spread them across the sky to make more rainbows."

My brother sank off to sleep with that story and hasn't

feared moths since. The story my aunt told us had been gathering dust in the back corners of my brain for years, but recently came back to me.

I have a friend named Abigail who always wears gray clothes. She is also one of the most kind and generous people I've ever met. When people ask her why she doesn't wear more colors, she just smiles that smile and says, "Gray is my color." She knows herself, and she doesn't compromise that to appease other people. Some may see her as plain like a moth, but I know that underneath the gray, Abigail is every color of the rainbow.

Jennie Gratton

My Best Friend Mike

A friend is one who knows you and loves you just the same.

Elbert Hubbard

"Hi. It's Mike . . ."

"Hi, Mike, what's the matter?" Mike had been going through a lot lately, and it was not unusual for him to sound upset.

"I need to tell you something, but I'm not sure if I should," he said. Curiosity got the best of me, and I convinced him to let me in on his big secret. "I can't tell you on the phone. Come over." I walked for five minutes around the block, rang his doorbell and followed his mother's instructions to go up to his room.

Mike had been my best friend for the past two years. At first I thought he was weird. We met during our freshman year of high school and soon became inseparable. The summer after that year was the highlight of our friendship. I never had more fun with any other person. We spent every night and every day together. Time flies when you are having fun, however, and we soon found ourselves back in school. I began to notice a change in Mike. The fun ceased, and I felt a strain in our friendship. Mike was suffering from depression, and I could not understand why. He seemed to have everything going for him. He was doing well in school, there were no problems at home, and he had many friends who loved him. I soon found myself spending every weekend in his bedroom, trying to convince him to cheer up. Nothing seemed to work. His parents became worried and decided to seek professional help.

Mike began to take medication to counteract his depression, and things seemed a little better, but they were not what they used to be. I was still clueless as to what had been causing this change in his behavior. I did not want to give up on my true best friend, so I continued spending painful hours trying to drag him out of his house.

It was one of those weekends, and there I was, sitting on his bed, waiting to hear what he had to say. I had a sense that he was about to tell me something serious. There was a strange look in his eyes, and he would not focus them on me. The silence was overbearing. He finally looked up at me.

"I'm gay." It hit me like a bolt of lightning. I was shocked. "Okay" was all I managed to utter. Silence followed for minutes afterward.

It took some getting used to, but I decided right then and there that I was not going to lose my best friend over it. Mike seems to be back to his normal self these days. We're seniors now, and I still spend a large portion of my time with him and his friends.

A smile comes to my face every time I think back to the first day we met, and the first thought that came to my mind as I approached the bus stop that day: *Who is that weird kid?* That weird kid is my true best friend, Mike, and there is nothing weird about him.

Brian Leykum

Kim

Friends are treasures.

Horace Bruns

We both lie sideways on her bed, the screen door slapping open and shut with the California breeze. We thumb through fashion magazines, laughing at the hairstyles and smelling the perfume samples. It seems like any other Sunday between girlfriends; laughter filling the room, a half-eaten carton of cookies between the two of us. This was my Sunday afternoon ritual, the two of us and our magazines, and from the time I was twelve, I lived for these afternoons. She was my friend, but more than that, she was a safe place, an unconditional love, and she was an adult.

I had known Kim most of my life. For the first ten years of my life, Kim wasn't one of the closest adults in my life, but her husband John doted on me and was one of the only "grown-ups" to understand my fearless and abundant energy.

When I was twelve, I moved to Los Angeles to live with

my father. Kim and John also lived nearby, and soon after my move, I began spending time at their home. Kim was fun; she liked to laugh and talk about boys. She listened to me while I talked about my crushes and fights with my family. She spoke to me as an equal, as a friend, not a child.

As I grew older, these visits became more important. I would cry over heartbreaks and whine about the latest rejection. The gap in age between us stayed the same, but the space between us grew closer. I called her with secrets, which she kept, and went to her when I couldn't handle my world for a while.

I think my parents went through periods of jealousy and hurt regarding Kim and our friendship, because they wished they could be the ones to whom I came with my stories. I had reached an age where it was harder to relate to my parents, but I still needed guidance. Kim offered that guidance; she didn't force-feed it.

Soon I was sixteen, and things began to change. I sunk into sadness, and I was slipping away from everyone, including Kim. I was taken to the hospital after swallowing a bottle of pain medication, and there, without question, was Kim. She was two hours away when the call came, and she showed up at the hospital with hair things and, of course, magazines. We didn't talk about the incident, but when she pulled my hair up for me, I saw in her eyes true fear and heartache. She used to say to me, "You wouldn't want to spend so much time with me if I really was your mom." I didn't understand those words until that day when she offered me the feeling of love without obligation. She wasn't my mom; she wasn't obligated to love me, she just did.

After my suicide attempt, things between us, though unspoken, began to change. I stopped spending Sunday afternoons at her house. I called, but not as often. I didn't feel good about myself, so I couldn't feel good about our friendship. I figured I had grown up and that we had just grown apart. Like any normal friendship, it had transformed, and I believed that I no longer needed Kim or the friendship.

The summer before I left for college, I went to say goodbye to Kim. Though we hadn't been as close for the last two years, we both cried when I left. I walked down the walkway from her house, and she called out from the kitchen window, "Call me if you need anything." I knew she meant that.

My first semester was hard. I was far from home, a little lonely, and things began to swing back down for me. With pure instinct, I picked up the phone. It was late. Kim picked up the phone, and I asked, "Were you sleeping?" She replied, "Yes, but it's okay. What's wrong? What do you need?" What I needed was Kim. I needed to hear her voice, and feel that California breeze in her back bedroom. I needed to tell her that our friendship had finally surpassed the age gap.

We talked about once a week after that, every Sunday afternoon. I called with the stress of my finals and with my newest boy problem. When I returned home for the summer, I went to Kim's, and we read magazines and ate cookies. I had become an adult, what she had always been. When I was younger, she had related to me on a level that I needed at that time, and now she relates to me as an equal. She was right; things would have been different if she were my mom. I didn't need another mom. I had one. I needed exactly what she gave: love, unconditional. And because she wanted me in her life, not because she had to have me.

Lia Gay

When Forever Ends

An insincere and evil friend is more to be feared than a wild beast; a wild beast may wound your body, but an evil friend will wound your mind.

Buddha

I look back on it now with only sorrow; the passing of time has worn down the sharp edges of bitterness that plagued me for so long. I switch the bracelet from hand to hand, first yanking at it, then soothingly stroking the well-formed stitches, and admiring the skill and precision of the intricately woven strands. Each tightly pulled knot lends the bracelet a nice shape, but does not destroy its delicate softness. I finger the cheap plastic beads, but I don't think scornfully of the inferior material anymore; I can only cherish the way the beads catch the light, reflecting a deep aquamarine, like the shimmering sea before me. In the imitation crystal surface of each little bead I see myself, I see a precious friendship lost, and I wonder for the thousandth time how it could possibly be that I didn't see it coming.

The sunlight streamed in the French windows of the colonial cottage, an odd location to house ninety middle-schoolers during the daytime hours. I knelt on the rough, maroon carpeting and spun the dial of my combination lock. Clockwise to sixteen, opposite to twenty-four, around and back again to eight. I tossed my American history test into my neat and tidy locker, smiling again in satisfaction at the scarlet "A" scrawled on top. I hastily removed the books that I would need over the weekend and stuffed them into my backpack. As I slammed my locker door shut, I caught a glimpse of the pictures and magazine clippings adorning the inside, and, for a split-second, thought of nothing but the happy times shared with friends and captured for posterity in those photographs. Just then, I noticed a small, white envelope flutter to the ground. Stooping, I picked it up. My name was printed on the front in plain block letters, but the generic envelope and handwriting gave no indication of its author. Consumed with curiosity, I tore it open.

"Dear Molly," it began, "I'm sorry, but we can't be friends anymore."

It went on, but my eyes cut quickly to the bottom, searching for a signature. Katie. Katie wrote it? My best friend wrote me a hate letter? Why in the world . . . ? I took a deep breath and started again from the beginning.

"Look, it's nothing you did, I just don't want to be friends anymore, okay?"

Nothing I did?! Why couldn't we be friends if it's nothing I did?!

The letter continued nebulously, a lot of wishy-washy garbage that skirted around any real issues that should have been addressed (not that I could think of any). Nowhere did she state any reason for writing such a thing to me. We hadn't fought in a long time, not really fought, anyway, just the kind of teasing and bantering that are part of healthy friendship. Out of the blue, my best friend hated me? How could she have put up such a casual veneer if all the while her mind was filled with hatred toward me?

A honk from outside jarred me out of my trance. My ride had arrived. Still contemplating the bizarre and unsettling occurrence, I picked up my bag (which suddenly felt like it was filled with bricks) and, with an even heavier heart, headed outside.

Someone was entering as I was leaving, and I started to brush past until I lifted my eyes from the floor and saw who it was. The crumpled note fell from my dangling palm and tumbled down the gray staircase. The tall, gangly blond started to apologize for running into me, but stopped short when she saw the open confusion and horror that creased my dramatic features. Her mouth opened and closed a few times, but she was lost for words, much like I was at the moment. She knew that I had read it. The anxiety was apparent on her ghostly pale face.

She broke the stare first as her eyes looked to the bottom of the staircase, where her note lay in a wrinkled ball. I heard a cough, and at once realized that we were not alone to do battle. Two piercing orbs behind wire-rim glasses and boy-cut bangs approached when Bev stepped forward, as if to shield Katie from the tongue-lashing she mistakenly thought I was prepared to give.

"Look, Molly, Katie doesn't want to be friends with you anymore, okay? She's my friend now."

If I were good at giving retorts on the spur of the moment, I would have unleashed every bit of antipathy within my petite body towards the controlling witch standing before me. If I had, maybe it would have given my former friend the courage she needed to stand up against her new "leader." However, my mind was unable to process what was happening that quickly, and the hundreds of verbally abusive comments that would flash before me in neon lights five minutes later did me no good. I stood, empty inside, as Bev grabbed Katie's sleeve and pulled her up the stairs. My ex-friend shot me one last helpless look, then straightened her mouth into a grim line and marched up the stairs behind her new friend, leaving her old one lost and powerless at the bottom, left to toy with a simple bracelet of beads and string. I had worn her handiwork from the emergence of our friendship through to its demise at that very moment.

Years later, I fiddle with the very same bracelet as I did on that very afternoon. I ask myself the same questions that tormented me then, and I wonder if fighting back would have saved a friendship that was worth fighting for. Katie was weak; she followed Bev as a sheep follows a herder, without question, without fail. I knew that the two of them had grown dependent on each other over the previous couple of years, widening the swiftly growing chasm between Katie and me, but I never dreamt of such a sudden end to our friendship. It shook me to learn that Bev's jealousy of my relationship with "her" friend would surface so spontaneously and drive her to such cruel and desperate measures. I later learned that she had given Katie an ultimatum: Break off her friendship with me or Bev would stop being friends with her. Bev was clever and conniving; she knew whom Katie would choose. I ask myself for the last time why I didn't see it coming. Then I lift the unwieldy and troublesome burden off my shoulders, and heave it into the ocean in the form of a small, string bracelet. Friendships rise and fall like the tide. I cannot stop the tide; I cannot stop what is beyond my control. We swore to be friends forever, but was it right for us to make that promise?

As the beaded trinket sails through the air, another question for the first time enters my thoughts: *Does she still have the bracelet that I made for her?*

Molly Karlin

Falling Out

Dear Travis,

What's happened to us? I used to feel so close to you, but now it's as if there are miles between us. I have always believed that friends come before everything else—girlfriends and boyfriends—everything. I guess I was wrong. Thanks for the push back to reality. I am sorry that we have had a falling out, but I want you to know that I will still be here when (and if) you need me. I will miss you.

Melissa

No "love you," no "yours sincerely" . . . as I noticed how plain my name looked on the paper all by itself, Travis walked into the hallway where I stood waiting by his locker. I glanced around quickly, looking for a way to escape, but before I could leave without being seen, I heard his all-too-familiar "Hey," as he spotted me.

I put my head down as he approached, hoping that he wouldn't see the pain in my eyes. I handed over the letter, which he took with a small smile. "Thanks, Melissa."

"Can you call me tonight?" I replied, "After you read the

letter?" My voice was shaking, and my words were unsure, but if he noticed, he didn't let on. I gave him a quick hug and left the hall, though turning from him was one of the hardest things I've ever done.

An hour later, as I talked with my friend Caitlan on the phone, I explained that I couldn't believe what I had actually given to him. What was he going to think?

"He's your *friend*, Melissa. It's going to be okay," Caitlan reassured me. As I listened to her words, I thought of just how important a friend he was. I had always found it easier to confide in guys, because somehow they seem to judge you a little less, while understanding you a little more. That was definitely what I had with Travis. He could understand me when the rest of the world couldn't. He trusted me, let me grow and listened to what I had to say without judgment—whether it was something he wanted to hear or not.

When I had realized that Travis had a thing for my other best friend Janette, I never thought that his asking her out would affect as many things as it did. Suddenly, it was as if he and I had no chance to talk on the phone or write letters, no freedom to hug or be ourselves. Suddenly Janette, whom I had known since the second grade, didn't trust me enough to be with her new boyfriend. She felt jealous . . . but she didn't realize that I, too, had my own feelings of jealousy. I was jealous of the time she got to spend with Travis, and resentful of the time I could not.

The click of call waiting brought my thoughts back to the present, and I answered the other line knowing that it was Travis.

"Hey, so um . . . yeah, that was the saddest letter I have ever read," he began. "I never knew you felt that way."

"Yeah, well, you weren't exactly around to ask, either," I replied harshly.

"Yeah Missa, I know, I know . . . I am sorry that we

haven't had much time together, but all I can say is that it will get better. I mean, it can't get any worse. But we can beat this—you and I will always be friends."

"Trav, everybody says that, but you and I both know that it is not going to happen." My voice trembled, and tears welled up in my eyes, threatening to spill over.

"It's different with us, remember? Nothing can tear us apart. We will be friends forever." I hung up the phone that night feeling a little bit better, yet at the same time, wondering if the promise would last.

Time went on, and nothing seemed to change. We seemed to grow farther and farther apart, and the thought that we would ever be friends again slowly faded. We talked once in a while, usually a polite "hi" in the hallway, but our "friendship," as it was, was making me crazy. The night before winter break, I made the decision to bring closure to the situation. I put everything that reminded me of Travis into a box, and put the box in my closet. There was one thing I could not put away: a stuffed lobster named Allen that I had won on a trip to Las Vegas. It was a trip I had spent with Travis. I knew what I had to do.

I saw him at school the next day, and handed him the stuffed animal.

"What's this?" he asked.

"Allen—you do remember him, don't you?"

"Yeah, but ... " he started to say.

"It's so he can be with you ... while I can't." My last few words trickled out, and big tears started rolling down my face as I realized this was the last time I could call him a friend. Travis looked at me, motionless and silent, as if only realizing then that we had grown apart, too far beyond repair.

"Are you sure you want to do this?" he asked me. I nodded my head as more tears streamed down my face. He pulled me into his arms, Allen and all. It was one of those hugs that reassures you that someday everything will be all right. And now, I do not regret what happened between us. It was an experience that will make me stronger and help me grow. I had never paid attention to the saying about how boyfriends and girlfriends will come and go, while your friends will last forever. But now, I see it as the most important advice I had ever been given. One day, I know it will be better. Sometimes I see him with Janette, and before he passes, he always gives me that famous smile. . . .

Melissa Lew

My Best Friend

Mmm. Look at those eyes, crystal-blue with just a touch of green. Those long eyelashes are just reaching for me. I can feel it. Oh, my God! Is he looking over here? No, that's silly. I'm looking at him; therefore, there is no way that he'd be looking at me. I mean, that doesn't happen in my life. Or maybe he actually is! No, no, that's just my imagination playing tricks on me. Well, you never know, crazy things do . . .

"What's up, Katie?"

"Oh, hey," I replied as my best friend, Michelle, abruptly interrupted my ongoing battle of mind versus heart.

"So who have you got your eye on tonight? I see those thoughts circling around in that mind of yours. Maybe tonight you'll actually act upon them!"

"What are you talking about? I don't have any of *those* thoughts in my head, as you like to put it. I'm perfectly content to be by myself right now."

I could feel the obviousness of the lie throughout my entire body as I tried to look Michelle straight in the eyes. I'd never lied to her before, and I'm not exactly sure why I did right then. I couldn't believe that I pulled it off. I mean, that's what best friends are for, to obsess over our crushes with. But something inside me prevented me from telling her about this one. I really liked this guy and, as horrible as this sounds, I didn't want any of my friends to mess it up. Every time I even mention that I think a guy is cute, Michelle goes into full matchmaker mode and won't snap out of it until she feels she has accomplished something. Needless to say, that never happens. She makes my crush into such a big deal that I become completely nervous around the guy, and then he thinks I am a complete idiot. I wasn't about to let that happen this time.

"Well, whatever you say. Let's go talk to Tommy, he's hot!"

What did she say? Tommy?!! How did she know? I didn't even tell her this time. No! Now she's going to become little miss matchmaker again and screw things up. Maybe I'm overreacting. Maybe she just thinks Tommy is cute. No, that's terrible! We can't go after the same guy. Michelle would never be interested in Tommy. He's too short for her. Okay, nothing to worry about.

"Come on, Katie! He's walking away!" Michelle screamed as she forcefully tugged on my cute new suede jacket.

"Okay, okay, I'm comin'."

All right, so now we are approaching him. My right foot just got closer. Now my left, right, left, right. STOP THIS! I'm not in the army! It's okay. I can do this. What is the big deal about talking to a guy anyway? He's just a human like me. Oh, but he's such a beautiful human! Look at that body! I can't do this. I can't do . . .

"Hi, Tommy. How's it goin'?" *Oh, my God, I must have sounded like the biggest nerd!*

"What's up, Katie? Hey, Michelle. You girls are looking good tonight. Having fun?"

His voice is so sexy. And he said I looked good!! But he said girlssss. He can't flirt with both of us. That's not allowed.

"Oh, Tommy, stop it. You're so silly. Ha ha. You're tickling me."

Michelle's giggling was loud enough to interrupt all of the conversations at that party. I couldn't believe how much she was flirting with him. Even worse, he was flirting back! Here is my best friend with the guy of my dreams—even though she doesn't know that—and the guy of my dreams was rejecting me more and more by the second. I couldn't exactly pull Michelle aside and ask her to stop. That would only make things worse. She would either be mad at me for not telling her before or she wouldn't even believe me. The only thing I could do was sit there and be quiet.

The whole drive home from the party I had to listen to Michelle go on and on about how amazing Tommy is. She was completely "in love" with him.

"Did you see the way he was flirting with me? I think he likes me. We were talking for an hour and he didn't seem to be paying attention to anyone else! Aren't you happy for me?"

I had always admired Michelle for the amount of confidence she had when it came to guys. If she wanted one, she went for him. Now she just sounded arrogant, as if any guy would be stupid not to like her. I just clenched my teeth, nodded my head and kept on driving.

After what seemed like the longest car ride in human history, we finally reached Michelle's house. I dropped her off, and the second I heard the door shut I started bawling.

Why was this making me so mad? She is my best friend. I should be happy for her. But I thought this was going to be my turn. I was really going to go for Tommy and make something happen with him. Michelle doesn't like him the way I do. But it's too late to say anything. We always promised each other never to let a guy come between us. I guess this is the tester.

I was awakened the next morning with a phone call, which I thought would be Michelle calling to obsess more about Tommy.

"Hello," I said in that groggy, don't-want-to-answer-it-but-feel-I have-to kind of tone.

"Hi, Katie?" A thick male voice replied through the phone, and I knew in an instant it was Tommy!

Why is he calling me? If this is to ask for Michelle's number, then I'm gonna hang up right now. No, I have to be mature about this. I should be nice. Yeah, right, man, I don't have to be nice to anybody.

"Katie, are you there?"

"Yeah, yeah, I'm here."

"Well, how are you?"

He wants to know how I am! I'll tell him how I am! I'm a depressed teenage girl who thought she had a chance with a guy who she thought had some class. But now she finds out that this guy is in love with her best friend when he has no clue what he'd be missing by going out with her. I've been bawling and tossing all night as if I was trying to quit an addiction, and hearing his voice right now drives me even crazier because it reminds me how much I still like him.

"Oh, I'm fine, just catching up on some sleep." It's amazing how the lie seemed to shoot right out of my mouth.

"I'm sorry if I woke you. I was just calling . . . well . . . I feel kind of weird doing this . . ."

Just get it out already! I'll give you her number!

"Okay, here goes. Do you want to see a movie or something tonight? You probably think I'm really weird since we haven't even spoken that much. But you seemed really cool, and I thought I would take a chance. If you really don't want to it's okay, I'll understand. I just thought . . ."

Oh, my God! Oh, my God! What's happening here? He's asking me out! What happened to Michelle? This can't be right.

But it is. It is! It is! It is! I have to say something now. Breathe. Calm. Act like a sane person.

"That sounds great, Tommy. Which movie were you thinking?"

Which movie?! Why did I say that? It doesn't matter which movie we see!

"I don't know. Why don't I pick you up at seven and we'll go and see which ones are playing?"

He sounds so calm. I wonder if I sound that calm.

"Okay, great, I'll see you at seven. Bye."

"Bye."

I am going on a date with TOMMY!!! I can't believe this. This is amazing, it's incredible, it's . . . terrible! What about Michelle? She's going to kill me. I have to call her.

"Michelle, I really need to talk to you." My voice was as shaky as my body, she had to know something was up.

"What's wrong? Are you okay?" She was worried about me. Great, I'm about to hurt my best friend.

"Yeah, I'm fine. I just wanted to tell you that Tommy called me. He wanted . . ."

"He wanted my phone number, huh? I knew it!"

"Well, not exactly. He seemed kind of, well, I don't know . . . he asked me to go see a movie tonight." The words came out slower than imaginable. I thought I was about to be attacked by Michelle's raging hormones any second now. "Before you get mad, I want to explain myself, and you have to believe me."

I was completely honest with Michelle. I explained how I liked Tommy for a long time and apologized profusely for not telling her sooner. I told her about her matchmaker disease and how I had cried the whole night before. I recited my conversation with Tommy word for word and poured out a million more apologies. The weight had been lifted off my shoulders, but I felt I had just passed it on to her. The long period of silence that followed assured me that Michelle was not going to accept my apology that quickly.

After not being able to take the silence any more, I broke in and asked, "Are you all right? What are you thinking? Do you hate me? Do you want me to break my date? What? At least give me an idea of how you feel."

The heavy breathing on the other side of the phone was about to become a whimper when I heard the *click*. She didn't even say a word, just hung up. I called her back fifty times that day only to hear an answering machine that demanded that I never call her again. I have never felt so torn before in my life. The first time that something exciting actually happens to me, it has to break up the only solid relationship that I have in my life. Michelle and I always thought we were above this type of situation. Our friendship was too strong to let a boy break it up. We refused to be like those other cliques of girls that back-stabbed each other all the time.

I called Tommy and explained the whole situation. He felt terrible and agreed that we could cancel our date for the night. He was disappointed but he understood. Every day for the following three weeks, I felt like I was in some never-ending chase. I would track Michelle down whenever I could and try to convince her to talk to me. I would fail each time. She would either snicker some rude comment or just shoot me down or she wouldn't say anything at all. I never realized she had the ability to be so cruel. After the countless number of rejections, I slowly began to give up. I couldn't keep chasing after something that she seemed to have given up on a long time ago. It was too frustrating and disappointing.

Tommy was great throughout the whole ordeal. We continued to see each other and became extremely close. I could safely say he was my best friend. As for Michelle, her hostility toward me slowly began to wear down but we still weren't friends. We had one of those say-hi-to-each-other-in-the-hallway relationships. The pain of losing her friendship never diminished either. I would find myself suddenly crying sometimes when I would think of what happened to our relationship. I wondered if she ever even missed me.

About a week ago, eight months after everything had happened, I built up the courage to ask Michelle if she wanted to go out to lunch with me. To my ultimate surprise, she agreed. We spent most of the lunch having little chit-chat conversations about the things happening in our lives. The whole time I wanted to scream at her about how much I missed her. I wanted to go back to my house, change into our pajamas, and gossip about every little detail about every little thing that could possibly be gossiped about! I wanted to laugh with her and feel comfortable around her. I wanted to curl up and eat five scoops of Häagen-Dazs coffee chip ice cream while we watched our favorite movies that we've both seen 50 million times. Most of all, I wanted the security of knowing that I had my best friend back.

The meaningless chit-chat continued until I reached Michelle's house to drop her off. The last time I had dropped Michelle off I had wanted to strangle her for obsessing over Tommy so much. Now all I wanted to do was hug her so tight so that she could never leave me again. Fortunately, I didn't have to. As I pulled the car over to the curb, Michelle looked at me with her welcoming warm eyes and said the four words that brought my whole eight months of misery to an end, "I've really missed you!"

Tears began to fall down my face but no words would come out. I looked into her eyes, leaned forward and gave my best friend a big hug.

Lisa Rothbard

My Perfect Friend

Sometimes people look at me like I'm strange. I catch them staring out of the corner of my eye and shudder. Their sideways glances pass through me, and I feel judged, unaccepted. My best friend, Mariah, never looks at me that way, though. Even though we are opposites— I spend my time in the world of books, escaping into other stories, while she spends hers in the world of boys and crushes—we have always gotten along perfectly. Somehow, our differences just seem to work well to create a relationship of comfort and acceptance.

On our first day of high school, Mariah and I walked into school together. It was intimidating, so I was glad that I had Mariah at my side. As we turned the corner toward our first class, we both saw him. He was beautiful. We giggled like little girls and followed him. When we lost sight of him, we both sighed with regret, wishing he had passed our way.

After school, Mariah and I waited at the bus stop together, discussing the day's events, eating whatever snack was left over from our lunch that day, and laughing. In mid-sentence, I looked over, and there he was, standing right next to us! I threw my half-eaten banana to the side and fiddled nervously.

Although I'm painfully shy, Mariah doesn't have that problem. As I stood petrified by his looks, she walked boldly up to him and asked him his name. "Jonathan," he said, while he ran a hand through his hair, brushing it out of his pale blue eyes. That is when my infatuation began, even though I knew nothing about him. And for the first time in our whole lives, Mariah and I had the same crush.

"So, where are you from . . . Jonathan?" Mariah asked, emphasizing his name. As the bus pulled up and we boarded, I caught Mariah's eye. She winked, and I giggled. Jonathan sat across from me on the bus, and as he sat, he smiled. I awkwardly attempted to smile back.

That began the routine that I followed for about a week: seeing him in the hall, nervously sitting near him on the bus, and calling Mariah each night to reconstruct every detail. Our school had a dance planned, and the date was approaching. Mariah was determined to go with Jonathan, but she had a list of guys, just in case he didn't work out. I laughed, the chances of Jonathan asking me were slim to none, but it was fun to fantasize.

Then, one afternoon, we boarded the bus in the same fashion, hoping to sit as close to Jonathan as possible. But this afternoon was different. I didn't have to try to sit near him, for he sat right down beside me. I caught Mariah's eye and shot her a quizzical look. I thought to myself, *No one has liked me before, what is this guy doing?*

Then, my question was answered. He leaned over to me and whispered, "Hey, how about you let me take you to the dance on Friday?" It was more a statement than a question. I nearly choked on my gum.

I barely squeaked out my reply, "Yeah, sure, I guess . . . I mean, if you want to."

He smiled and said, "Cool."

Without words, Mariah motioned for me to get off at her stop. I quickly took inventory of the situation: the same guy who had been plaguing my thoughts just asked me out. I was on cloud nine. We remained calm until the bus was out of sight, and then, as the coast became clear, we grabbed onto each other and started jumping up and down. For once, I didn't feel so different. Mariah screeched, "Danielle, this is s-o-o-o-o-o cool!"

"I know. Was I shaking?" I replied.

She gave me a hug. "No. You were so calm, you did great." We split at the road and left it at that. I had done great.

The night of the dance, I was frantic. Desperately trying to apply my makeup in a hurry while talking to Mariah on the phone at the same time, I heard my mother yell that I was going to be late. Soon Mariah's parents dropped her off.

On our way to the dance, we met up with Mariah's date, Ben. When we reached the school, Jonathan wasn't there yet, so I waited outside and motioned for Mariah and Ben to go on ahead while I waited. I looked up and saw him. There he stood, with those pale blue eyes, that soft hair, that smooth skin and that sweet smile. There he stood, but . . . with another girl! He wasn't alone, and he definitely wasn't waiting for me.

I hid myself behind a tree. *How could I have been so stupid?* I should have known it was too good to be true. He was popular, and I wasn't. I let myself feel ugly and undesirable. But worst of all, worse than the embarrassment and the shame, I felt heartbroken.

I made my way out from behind the tree, just in time to see their backs as they entered the dance together. I walked home and into my room, ignoring my mother's questions of why I had returned so early. Sitting alone on my bed, I was plagued by a voice in my head, the voice that told me I was ugly and unloved.

Later, my phone rang. It was Mariah. I knew she wasn't calling to torture me with the dance details, but, rather, to comfort me. This was my first time playing in her world, and I had been hurt. She knew that, and her soothing words helped mend my aching heart and silence that voice in my head that told me I wasn't good enough. Maybe Jonathan didn't think I was good enough, but who cared? Mariah reminded me that there would always be other guys. She told me I was beautiful, and most of all, that I was loved. The self-deprecating voice quickly faded. Mariah and I may be different, even worlds apart, but she accepts me for who I am, and she is my perfect friend.

Danielle Eberschlag

Sometimes Things Are Never the Same

I wish they would only take me as I am.

Vincent van Gogh

Michelle and I had been best friends since the fourth grade. She was a beautiful person inside and out, one of the kindest I'd ever met. We were like paper and glue—completely inseparable.

When we began junior high, the new social life was a tough adjustment. But our friendship endured, and we were there for each other. I took comfort in the fact that I could tell her anything and always trust her.

Sixth grade passed, as did seventh, and soon eighth grade was upon us. It was that year that things slowly started to change between Michelle and me. I became a social butterfly, fluttering around to different cliques of friends, discussing the hottest gossip and relishing my new categorization as "popular." Although I made many new friends that year, I still loved Michelle and wanted her to hang out with my new, fairly large social group. I attempted to drag her along to my social gatherings, but I soon noticed the disapproving looks and whispers about Michelle—a clear message that she was not "cool enough" to hang out with us.

My new, so-called friends made up lies and rumors about Michelle in order to ruin our friendship. And somewhere along the way, I fell into their trap. I started to believe that I shouldn't be friends with Michelle just because my other friends didn't like her.

One night, one of my new friends, Jamie, came over after school. I was thrilled that she wanted to come over to my house and spend time with me. After a couple of hours of laughing and having a great time, Michelle's name came up in our conversation. Slowly, a mischievous grin formed on Jamie's face. Remembering that Michelle was madly in love with a boy named Zach, Jamie ordered that I tell Michelle that Jamie was going out with Zach, and then rub it in her face. Afraid that my new friends would dislike me if I refused, just like they did Michelle, I picked up the phone, dialed Michelle's number and blurted it out to her. She was more sad, heartbroken and furious than I'd expected, and as I listened to her hysterically cry over the phone, I remembered how close we used to be. At that moment, I realized how much I treasured her friendship, and the cruelty of my actions sunk in. Needing to think about what I had just done, I got off the phone.

I soon called Michelle back and told her the truth. Zach was not going out with Jamie, and I was deeply sorry that I decided to betray her. I was sorry for not being there for her in the last few months, and I was sorry for letting my friends pressure me into situations like these. I wanted to be her best friend again. But she was not as forgiving as I had hoped. "It's not that easy," she said solemnly.

For the next couple of weeks, I did everything I could to win back Michelle's friendship. I sent her a thousand apology notes, I gave her pictures of the two of us, and I called her every night. I even stopped hanging out with my new group of friends who had been so cruel to Michelle. They weren't true friends anyway.

One night, I was sitting on my bed doing homework when I heard the doorbell ring. Unsure of who was at the door, I opened it tentatively, and there stood Michelle. I was shocked. "I forgive you," she said. "I wanted to let you know."

"Really?" I responded excitedly. "So, do you want to come in? Maybe you could sleep over, and we can talk."

"No, I can't. I don't want to," she said.

"Well, maybe we can catch a movie this weekend," I said with a hint of desperation.

"No," she answered.

"I thought you forgave me, Michelle," I said, unable to hide the disappointment in my voice.

"I do forgive you, but what you did changed what we used to be and what we are now. There is still a hole in my heart from what you did; it will never be the same."

She turned away. "I'll see ya around," she said, without looking back.

Every once in a while, Michelle and I run into each other at school, and she waves without saying a word. I always held out hope that our friendship would rekindle. But it hasn't, and things between us will never be the same. I lost my best friend, and it changed my heart forever. I wish I could undo the damage and take back what I have done. Never again will I let the influences of others get in the way of genuine friendships. I owe that to Michelle.

Celine Geday

I Don't Talk to My Closest Friend

I remember when they introduced us. "This is one of the girls from Sweden," my counselor told me, in Spanish. "Her name is Ellen."

I looked up at the girl and smiled. I attempted to introduce myself in my broken English, but her counselor had to tell her for me, in Swedish. Ellen smiled apologetically, and I smiled back. She shyly outstretched her pale hand, and I took it eagerly. We walked into the adjacent woods together, as our counselors stared after us in surprise.

They had introduced us two girls as a formality, but they had not really expected us to get along, I think. After all, neither one of us could speak English very well, and we couldn't possibly be any more different.

But I had never seen anyone like Ellen before, and her beauty mesmerized me. Her eyes were a dim, graying blue, and her hair was the color of sunlight. I looked at the deep chocolate of my skin against her fragile hand and could imagine no greater contrast.

I desperately wished my English were better, that I could ask her of the world that produced such living porcelain dolls. But she was much more interested in learning about me than talking about herself. She delighted in taking my dark curls in her hands and stared at them with a profound wonder.

I soon found out that it would have done me no good to speak better English, because she understood as little of it as I did. We could find no similarities between her lyrical Swedish tongue and my Spanish and were therefore removed from any possibility of real verbal communication.

If we had been able to speak, I would have told her of the idyllic beaches of Honduras, where the warm ocean hugs the soft sand and brings strange treasures in for the children almost every day. And she would have told me of the white blankets that cover her mountains and of the tiny flakes of dissipating beauty that fall from her sky every year. I would have told her of the charming adobe houses that line the hot, tropical streets of our towns, and she would have spoken of the buildings that seem to touch the sky in her gigantic cities.

But we could not speak, so instead we smiled and held hands, put flowers in each other's hair, and laughed and laughed. We traced the paths of the quiet woods of the camp over and over again, finding companionship in each other's virtually mute presence.

We were inseparable, and that fact amazed everybody. We would crawl into bed at night when it was time for the lights to go out, and listen to the voices of the other children and the wondrous counselors. We could not understand that they were trying to explain to themselves the bond that existed between Ellen and me.

If we had understood them, we would have told them that two teenage girls away at an international summer camp share the same closeness as any other pair of teenage girls.

I'm not so young anymore, and I'm back in Honduras.

My English is better, and so is Ellen's, and we write each other frequently. She remains one of my closest friends, and we are no more different now than we were then. Although now we communicate verbally, we include a lot of pictures in our letters (though neither one of us is skilled at drawing). We know, better than anyone, that beauty transcends words and culture. We know that to share something all you need are two open hearts.

Melissa Cantor

Have a Seat upon a Cloud

Have a seat upon a cloud and make yourself at home
You are now inside my dreams, inside a book, inside a
  poem.

Where anything can happen if you only make it real
Plunge into my waters if you're not afraid to feel.

Take off your shoes and close your eyes, relax upon my
  sand
Join me in my land of dreams, reach out and take my
  hand.

Let me share my dreams with you until you find your
  own
I'll take you there if you believe, take mine out on loan.

Where birds are words so gracefully they glide across
  the sky
Leave behind your worries, here the rules do not apply.

Pick my flowers if you like and plant a seed or two
Paint the sky in polka dots if you do not like it blue.

Climb my trees, face your fears; erase them one by one
See the world from up above and don't stop at the sun.

When the world starts raining down and the sun is out
of sight
Let your dreams control your mind and help you
through the night.

There's a place inside my dreams for all who care to
roam
So have a seat upon a cloud and make yourself at home.

Danielle Rosenblatt

3
THE POWER OF LOVE

You can give without loving, but you cannot love without giving.

Amy Carmichael

Coffee-Shop Kindness

If you can't return a favor, pass it on.

Louise Brown

My senior year of high school was an extremely hectic one, to say the least. If I wasn't studying and worrying about my grades, I was juggling multiple extracurricular activities or attempting to make sense of my plans for college. It seemed as if my life had turned into one crazy cloud of confusion, and I was stumbling around blindly, hoping to find some sort of direction.

Finally, as senior year began to wind down, I got a part-time job working at the local coffee shop. I had figured that the job would be easy and, for the most part, stress-free. I pictured myself pouring the best gourmet coffees, making delicious doughnuts and becoming close friends with the regular customers.

What I hadn't counted on were the people with enormous orders who chose to use the drive-thru window, or the women who felt that the coffee was much too creamy, or the men who wanted their iced coffees remade again and again until they reached a certain level of perfection. There were moments when I was exasperated with the human race as a whole, simply because I couldn't seem to please anyone. There was always too much sugar, too little ice and not enough skim milk. Nevertheless, I kept at it.

One miserable rainy day, one of my regular customers came in looking depressed and defeated. My coworker and I asked what the problem was and if we could help, but the customer wouldn't reveal any details. He just said he felt like crawling into bed, pulling the sheets up over his head and staying there for a few years. I knew exactly how he felt.

Before he left, I handed him a bag along with his iced coffee. He looked at me questioningly because he hadn't ordered anything but the coffee. He opened the bag and saw that I had given him his favorite type of doughnut.

"It's on me," I told him. "Have a nice day."

He smiled and thanked me before turning around and heading back out into the rain.

The next day was miserable as well, rain spilling from the sky. Everyone in town seemed to be using the drive-thru window because no one wanted to brave the black skies or the thunder and lightning.

I spent my afternoon hanging out the window, handing people their orders and waiting as they slowly counted their pennies. I tried to smile as the customers complained about the weather, but it was difficult to smile as they sat in their temperature-controlled cars with the windows rolled up, while I dealt with huge droplets of water hanging from my visor, a shirt that was thoroughly soaked around the collar and an air conditioner that blasted out cold air despite sixty-seven-degree weather. On top of that, no one was tipping. Every time I looked into our nearly empty tip jar, I grew more depressed.

Around seven o'clock that evening, I was in the middle of making another pot of vanilla hazelnut decaf when the customer from the day before drove up to the window. But instead of ordering anything, he handed me a single pink rose and a little note. He said that not too many people take the time to care about others, and he was glad there were still people like me in the world. I was speechless and very touched; I nearly forgot yesterday's deed. After a moment, I happily thanked him. He told me I was welcome and, with a friendly wave, drove away.

I waited until I saw his Jeep exit the parking lot, then I ran to the back of the shop and read the note. It read:

Christine,

Thanks for being so sweet, kind and thoughtful yesterday. I was sincerely touched by you. It is so nice to meet someone who's genuinely nice, warm, and sensitive and unselfish. Please don't change your ways because I truly believe that you will excel. Have a great day!

Hank

As the day passed, I had plenty of complaining customers, but anytime I felt depressed or frustrated, I thought of Hank and his kindness. I would smile, hold my head up high, clear my throat and politely ask, "How can I help you?"

Christine Walsh

Mary Lou

It was my first day as newcomer to Miss Hargrove's seventh-grade class. Past "newcomer" experiences had been difficult, so I was very anxious to fit in. After being introduced to the class, I bravely put on a smile and took my seat, expecting to be shunned.

Lunchtime was a pleasant surprise when the girls all crowded around my table. Their chatter was friendly, so I began to relax. My new classmates filled me in on the school, the teachers and the other kids. It wasn't long before the class nerd was pointed out to me: Mary Lou English. Actually she called herself Mary Louise. A prim, prissy young girl with a stern visage and old-fashioned clothes. She wasn't ugly—not even funny looking. I thought she was quite pretty, but I had sense enough not to say so. Dark-eyed and olive-skinned, she had long, silky black hair, but—she had pipe curls! Practical shoes, long wool skirt and a starched, frilly blouse completed the image of a total dork. The girls' whispers and giggles got louder and louder. Mary Lou made eye contact with no one as she strode past our table, chin held high with iron determination. She ate alone.

After school, the girls invited me to join them in front of the school. I was thrilled to be a member of the club, however tentative. We waited. For what, I didn't yet know. Oh, how I wish I had gone home, but I had a lesson to learn.

Arms wrapped around her backpack, Mary Lou came down the school steps. The taunting began—rude, biting comments and jeering from the girls. I paused, then joined right in. My momentum began to pick up as I approached her. Nasty, mean remarks fell unabated from my lips. No one could tell I'd never done this before. The other girls stepped back and became my cheerleaders. Emboldened, I yanked the strap of her backpack and then pushed her. The strap broke, Mary Lou fell, and I backed off. Everyone was laughing and patting me. I fit in. I was a leader.

I was not proud. Something inside me hurt. If you've ever picked a wing off a butterfly, you know how I felt.

Mary Lou got up, gathered her books and—without a tear shed or retort given—off she went. She held her head high as a small trickle of blood ran down from her bruised knee. I watched her limp away down the street.

I turned to leave with my laughing friends and noticed a man standing beside his car. His olive skin, dark hair and handsome features told me this was her father. Respectful of Mary Lou's proud spirit, he remained still and watched the lonely girl walk toward him. Only his eyes—shining with both grief and pride—followed. As I passed, he looked at me in silence with burning tears that spoke to my shame and scalded my heart. He didn't speak a word.

No scolding from a teacher or preaching from a parent could linger as much as that hurt in my heart from the day a father's eyes taught me kindness and strength and dignity. I never again joined the cruel herds. I never again hurt someone for my own gain.

Lynne Zielinski

Lessons of Life

*The supreme happiness in life is the conviction
that we are all loved.*

Victor Hugo

If the lesson of life is happiness, then I have met the
most dramatic of teachers. By the world's standards, my
"teacher's" words are far from eloquent, his style far from
graceful, his works far from wondrous. Yet, in his determination and courage I see a hero, a hero unlike those we
normally choose. He is Patrick, and, by the way, he has
Down's syndrome.

Working as the dance and movement specialist during
the summer of 1994 at Carousel Farm, a summer camp for
mentally challenged and neurologically impaired children, has shown me what true goodness really is. Pure
souls do exist, and Patrick is one of them. Patrick did not
see the differences of skin color among his camp friends or
notice that Jimmy came to camp every day wearing the
same unwashed clothes. He kissed and hugged everyone
just the same and flirtatiously called everyone "boo-tiful."
Patrick had the talent of savoring the flavor of each and

every moment. No time was wasted with the words "I can't," but rather, "We're done already?" He didn't simply come to camp. He *lived* camp. I marveled at his unending energy and his zest for fun.

The "Incredible Hulk" (as he liked to call himself) and I shared a special friendship during those unforgettable eight weeks. I taught him the "Electric Slide," and he proudly presented me with hand-picked dandelions each morning. He treasured the shiny star stickers I gave him for being a super dancer. We shared potato chips under the trees at lunchtime. Through the sweaty days and the not-so-fun rainy days, we learned from each other. I gave Patrick the feeling that he was wonderful and loved, while he taught me to laugh at the happy and colorful moments that would otherwise have flashed by without a thought—a kickball game with good friends, the tickle of a horse's whiskers on your cheek or a piggyback ride in the pool. Patrick had a jack-o-lantern smile for every occasion.

Contrary to the world's standards, I say that Patrick's words really are eloquent. After all, who else could respond to my statement, "I love you very much" with "How many 'verys'?" Every female at camp can surely attest to his unmatched style and charm. His works—the home run in softball, the pencil can in arts and crafts, the "Chicken Dance" lead in our dance finale—were wondrous too, because they were challenges that Patrick met with just a little extra effort. Just a little extra effort, that's all.

I won't see Patrick until Open House during next year's camp season. We are separated by many miles and find ourselves in two different worlds during the school year. Yet Patrick is with me, inside my head and heart. Sensitive and able to see the decency in everyone, he has touched me and changed me. If the lesson of life is happiness, then I surely have met the most inspiring of teachers.

Shari LaGrotte
From The Best College Admission Essays

Healing with Love

On a bitterly cold and cloudy winter's day in upstate New York, I saw my brother again for the first time in a year. As my father and I pulled up to the reform school after four hours of driving, his attempts at cheerful commentary did nothing to ameliorate the dismal apprehension that I felt. I had little hope that my brother would be changed and, furthermore, I had convinced myself that any appearance of change would not necessarily be genuine.

Being with my brother after so long was like getting to know him all over again. Over the next couple of days, I felt a kind of peace developing between us, and, for the first time, I wasn't tense around him, nor was I scared of what he would do or say next. It seemed as though I would finally find a friend in my brother, and, more than that, I would find a true brother in my brother. While part of me rejoiced in his transformation, another part of me thought it was too good to be true, and so I remained skeptical of his seeming progress. Two days was surely not enough time to erase the hostility that had built up between us over the years. I showed this cynical front to my father and brother, while the hopeful voice remained hidden deep inside of my heart, afraid to appear, lest it should be trampled upon. My brother himself commented several times on my depressed disposition, but I knew he would never understand the complexity of my feelings, so I remained elusive.

I wrapped myself in this same protective silence during, what was for me, the most emotionally trying part of the visit. Meals at the school were more than just meals. They were chaperoned with two teachers at each table, and provided a forum for judging the students' progress and/or continued delinquency. My father had told me that these meals often lasted for an hour or two, as each student was treated separately and with the full attention of the table. As we sat down for lunch, I knew I wouldn't be able to make it through the meal without crying.

Several boys and girls were "brought up" in front of the table for transgressions they had committed, but a boy named Brian touched me the most. A fairly new arrival at the school, he hadn't yet lost the initial anger and bitterness at having been brought there against his will. He was an attractive boy, about sixteen years old and was, my father whispered to me, an exceptional soccer player with a promising future in the sport. As the head teacher at our table conducted a heavy interrogation of him, Brian shifted his weight nervously every two seconds, and I saw in his eyes what I had become so good at reading in my brother's. They darted anxiously about the room, resting upon everything except the man addressing him, and I knew that he was searching for someone or something to blame. He wasn't yet aware that only when he stopped looking for excuses could he truly hear and learn from those trying to help him.

Suddenly, out of the corner of my eye, I became aware of a bearded man standing at the closed door and peering

in apprehensively at our solemn gathering, which must
have looked more like an AA meeting than a meal. The
realization that it was Brian's father trying to catch a
glimpse of his son precipitated the first tear I had shed all
weekend.

"Why is Brian here?" I whispered softly to my father.

"Oh, you know, the usual, drugs, violence . . . I think the
last straw was when he hit his father in the head with one
of his soccer trophies. . . . He was chosen for the National
All-Star team, you know. . . . Must be quite a player."

As the tears flowed more freely down my face, Brian
looked straight ahead at the wall and told us that he had
refused to see his father who had driven for many hours
to see him.

Then the teacher spoke, "Brian, I talked to your dad,
and he says he brought you your puppy because he
knows how much you must miss him. He's willing to
accept the fact that you don't want to see him, but he
wants you to know that you can see your puppy."

I was screaming inside. I wanted to stand up and tell
Brian how lucky he was to have a father who obviously
loved him so much, and who loved him enough to do the
hardest thing a parent ever has to do: send his child away.
I was bursting to enlighten him, but I knew it was something he would have to learn on his own, so I remained
still and just let the overwhelming sadness spread over
me like a dark cloud.

That afternoon, I saw my brother waving good-bye as
we pulled up the dirt drive and out of the gates of the
school. I couldn't look back, as I was too busy trying to
suppress the emotion that I felt creeping up on me with
the force of a tidal wave. I was filled with hopelessness
and empathy for these kids who had somehow gotten lost
along the way. I knew there was a fine line between them
and me, a line I had walked like a tightrope at several

times in my life. Indeed, part of my sadness lay in the guilt I felt for not having such a heavy load to bear and for never being able to fully comprehend the nature and sheer weight of this load my brother carried.

Several months later I returned to the school, this time in early spring and accompanied by my whole family, including my mother and two sisters. Everything looked brighter and more colorful in the sun. Wildflowers bloomed on the hillside looking out over the valley, and the water in the pond sparkled like jewels. I closed my eyes, held my face up to the sun and smiled. It was my family's first reunion in over a year. As it was family weekend, everywhere I looked I saw proud, attentive parents and beaming kids. This is when the full force of what I was experiencing hit me. For the first time in a while, I didn't feel the despair and hopelessness of these kids' lives, but the tremendous amount of love and support that surrounded each one of them. After a whole year spent doubting that my brother would ever be able to function normally in society, I allowed the seeds of hope to germinate in my mind, as well as in my heart.

Moments later, my new outlook was strengthened and forever cemented by the most beautiful sight I think I have ever seen. At first I couldn't believe my eyes. Brian and his father were walking arm in arm across the grass towards the pond and seemed to be in quiet discussion about one of those everyday, mundane things that is the business of fathers and their sons. A golden retriever, now fully grown, wagged its tail in delight as he trotted after them.

Cecile Wood

Forgive

Forgive the sun who didn't shine
The sky had asked her in to dine

Forgive the stars that heard your wish
The moon prepared their favorite dish

Forgive the rain for its attack
The clouds have tears they can't hold back

Don't hate the birds 'cause they are free
Don't envy all the things they see

Don't block the wind, but hear its cry
Or else that wind may pass you by

Forgive the storm it means no harm
Could not resist to show its charm

Forgive the earth that never turns
Don't hate the sun, because too much burns

Life intends to not cause pain
The flowers bloom from all the rain

The storm will come and it will pass
The sun that shines, it grows the grass

The wind it cannot help but cry
The stars at night light up the sky

Forgive the world in which we live
We'll all find peace if we forgive

Danielle Rosenblatt

The Gift of Time

What we do for ourselves dies with us. What we do for others and the world remains and is immortal.

Albert Pine

His name was Bryce. I inherited him when I was nine years old. Actually, he became part of our family when my mother married his uncle.

It was a second marriage for my mother, and while it might have been less than desirable for my two older brothers, for me it was a slice of heaven. We moved to a beautiful neighborhood, into a house three times the size of the one in which I had been born and raised. Not only did this marriage come with a big house, a pool and huge yard, it also came with Bryce. He lived in Northern California with his brother and parents, but he visited frequently, sometimes spending entire summers with us.

Bryce became my good friend. He was six years older than I, but we had an instant rapport that belied the gap in our ages. He taught me how to dive and do flips off the diving board, he helped my stepfather build a tree house for me, and he helped me learn how to expertly negotiate my new bicycle built for two that I had won in a contest. By the time I was thirteen, we had become best friends.

Bryce and I spent many summers together, and as the years passed we still remained close. The activities changed—tennis, hiking, beach trips and computers—but our bond didn't. He was handsome, smart and funny, and even though I was only fourteen years old, I fantasized about marrying him someday. I couldn't conceive of my life without him.

Bryce was the eldest of two boys, and he was his parents' pride and joy. He lived nearly a picture-perfect life. Achieving in school, becoming an award-winning athlete, and having this incredibly huge, compassionate heart, he was a parent's dream. When his mother's brother decided to marry my widowed mother, Bryce helped create a bridge that served to unite the two families. He was charismatic, funny and a great mitigating influence for two teenage boys who didn't want their mother to marry this man. But, his family came with Bryce, and at the very least, Bryce was cool.

One summer, Bryce and I went swimming at a friend's house. They had a pool to envy. Complete with diving boards, a slide, waterfalls and a small island in the center, it was by far the coolest pool in the San Fernando Valley. I was fifteen, Bryce was twenty-one. It was one of those perfect days, and we were having so much fun. At one point, I decided to slide down the slide on my belly. Apparently, given the location of the slide, this was not a good idea. I smacked down hard on the bottom of the pool and was knocked out. By the time anyone figured out that I wasn't just playing around (the blood that began to tint the water was probably a good clue) I was starting to drown. Bryce saved my life. He jumped into the pool, pulled me to safety and helped to clear the water out of my lungs so that I could breathe. When I finally regained consciousness, Bryce was kneeling beside me, with tears in his eyes.

He was now my friend and my savior. I grew up with him; he became the first boy that I really loved. He treated me like I was the only person in his life who really mattered, even though I'm sure he had girlfriends.

By the time I turned sixteen, I was already fairly proficient behind the wheel of a car, thanks to Bryce. He made it very clear to me that it was my turn to drive the seven hours it required for us to visit each other. I was more than happy to oblige.

I would drive up to Redding, and we would go to the river and live in the water. We would jet ski, swim, snorkel and sun on the dock until those long summer days finally claimed the sun. Then we'd go back to his parents' house and barbecue, laugh and hang out.

By the end of my senior year in high school, there was only one person I wanted to take me to my prom, so I was thrilled when he finally asked me. I accepted without reservation. Even though there were other boys who had asked, it was Bryce I wanted to share the occasion with. Besides, grad night at Disneyland required someone with the guts to ride all the coasters several times, and I knew he was up for the task.

During that next year, our lives became busy, and we didn't see each other that often. I was starting college, and he was working. We wrote and talked to each other on the phone, but it seemed that our lives were taking us in two different directions. I missed him dearly, so I was overjoyed when I found out he would be coming down for his birthday. My stepfather had a special gift that he wanted to give him.

We had a little party for Bryce, and my stepfather gave him his gift. It was a gold Hamilton tank-style watch that

was given to my stepfather by his mother, Bryce's grandmother, when he was younger. Engraved on the back
were my stepfather's initials and the date, 11/30/48. It was
a special memento that my stepfather held very dear, so
the gesture of giving it to his nephew meant a great deal
to Bryce. He cherished it. He wore it all the time. And
when the band broke, he just put it in his pocket and carried it around that way. He was never without it.

One winter night, Bryce and I were on the phone on
one of those two-hour-long telephone conversations. It
was around eleven o'clock at night, he was at his parents'
house having dinner with them and some guests who
were visiting from out of town. Bryce said that he had to
go. His mother had asked him to take these friends back
to the hotel where they were staying. It was at least an
hour out of town and he was already tired. We made some
vague plans to meet on the dock in the summer.
Sometimes it was the only thing that would get me
through a tough school year. Then before he hung up he
said something that made me smile. He said, "Just remember, no matter what you do in this life, I will always be
there for you if you bump your head." I told him that he
would always be my hero, and then we hung up.

Bryce's car was found the next day. He had driven off
the road when he fell asleep at the wheel. My sweet Bryce
was killed instantly. He was twenty-five years old. The
pain and upset that spread through our family was profound. I was left with a huge hole in my heart, a hole I was
afraid would never mend.

That summer, as agreed, I went to the dock. I sat on the
dock, knowing that Bryce would never come. I sat down
and started to weep, my tears falling into the river. I found
myself getting angry. How could he have done this to
me? Why did he have to die? I was questioning God,
Bryce and whomever else was listening.

Then, remembering our conversation the night before he died, I started to hit my head.

"I'm hitting my head . . . I'm bumping it, where are you? You lied to me! Do I really need to hurt myself?"

In a moment of emotional frenzy, I picked up an oar that was lying on the pier. Suddenly, underneath where the oar had just been, something shiny caught my eye. There was something wedged between the boards. I set the oar down and bent down to retrieve the shiny object. When I finally pried it free, I immediately recognized it. It was the watch my stepfather had given Bryce on his birthday. I sat down and cried. With the object still cradled in my hand, I held it up close to my heart. I soon realized that this little 1948 old-fashioned watch that needed to be wound every twenty-four hours was still ticking. Goose bumps covered my skin, and the warmest, most loving feeling came over me. I felt as if I were being hugged from the inside out. There he was, still with me.

I'll never know exactly how that little watch happened upon that pier. But I think that Bryce left it behind for me. I bought a new band for the watch, and to this very day I still wear it. It will always be a symbol of unconditional love, something time could never stop.

Zan Gaudioso

Someday When I'm Older

I am only seven and a lot of things are confusing to me. Grown-ups tell me that someday I'll understand, but I wish that "someday" were now. Life is really complicated. I always have to say "please," be nice, clean up—and sometimes I just don't want to. Then there is something grown-ups call death. I know it's not a good thing, but I don't know quite what it is. I think I am supposed to understand, but no one wants to help me; maybe someday when I'm older.

* * * *

I don't usually wait with Grace for her bus before school in the morning, but today we are sitting on the steps together. Christmas is just two weeks away, and there is fresh snow outside from last night. I can't wait until recess so I can go out and play in it. The bus has just stopped outside our house. Grace is eleven and she doesn't like to hug me too often, but this morning, she hugs me good-bye. I don't know why.

In art class today, I drew a picture for Grace's teacher: baby Jesus in the manger with an angel above him. But

now school is over, and I don't know where my picture is.
I never gave it to her. One of the teachers tells me that she
has to drive me home. She says that Grace was in an accident. I wonder if she'll have to wear a cast in the
Christmas pictures.

Now I'm walking into my house. Mommy's crying. She
never cries, even when I'm really, really bad. Two police-
men are in our living room. No one is telling me why they
are there. All the grown-ups are talking, but I can't understand what they are saying; maybe someday I will. Daddy
is the only one who says anything to me.

"You have to go to Mrs. Riffs's house for awhile." I like
Mrs. Riffs, but I really want to stay with Mommy and
Daddy. No one is listening to me, so I will just keep that
inside. Mommy is really sad. I think Grace has more than
a broken arm. All I can do is pat Mommy on the shoulder
and whisper like she does when I'm sad.

"Grace is going to be okay," I say. I'm not quite sure
though. No one will tell me how bad things are, and seeing
Mommy crying scares me most of all. But Grace *has* to be
okay. I already made her Christmas present, and we are
supposed to make snow angels together on the front lawn.

Mommy and Daddy are always telling people that I
have a short "tensions pan." I think that means I don't like
to watch movies that are too long. Tonight seems to be
taking a lot longer than the longest movie I have ever
seen. It is past my bedtime, and I just want to go home. I
think I hear a car in the driveway. Mommy and Daddy are
coming inside now. Daddy wants to talk to me, but I don't
want to hear what he is going to say.

"Grace has gone up to heaven."

I'm crying now. I don't really want to, but Mommy is,
and I think it's the right thing to do. I am so confused.
Mommy and Daddy told me that heaven is where we
go when we die, but Grace can't be dead. I want to ask

questions, but I know I'm supposed to just be sad now. This is really complicated. I want someone to explain, but as usual, I'm too young to understand anyway. I feel bad for not feeling like crying, so I am trying my best.

It is past Christmas now, but I still have a lot of questions. I try to keep them inside because I don't want Mommy to cry again. Sometimes they tell me more about "the accident": Grace was waiting for the bus after school with some other kids. A car was driving too fast on the icy road, went out of control and hit her. They tell me she didn't feel any pain. That's good, because I don't want Grace to be hurting.

I am trying very hard to understand death. I read the books that people give me about Joe and what happened when his dog died. I still feel too young to get it. I feel sad and angry and frustrated. I love Grace, and I miss playing with her. Mommy is crying less now. I think it's okay to ask her a question.

"Mommy, why did it have to be Grace that was hit? Why couldn't it have been someone else who was standing there?" Mommy has started crying again and I wish I didn't ask her the question, but now she is smiling and hugging me. She says, "Because then another family would have to go through all the pain and sadness that we feel." I am not sure why she said that, but it's not the time for any more questions.

Now it is a few weeks later. Mommy and Daddy tell me that the man who hit Grace found out that he killed her, so he killed himself. I think I am old enough to understand what this means.

"That's good, right, Mom? Now he has paid for what he did." Mommy speaks very quietly when she answers. She tells me, "No, it's not good. Now his family has to go through everything that we felt. They shouldn't have to do that."

* * * *

I am sixteen now and I know a lot more than I did then. I know that seven years is a short time to learn about forgiveness. Back then, I didn't quite understand why Mom didn't want the man to be punished, but I trusted that she was right. Now Mom's words echo in my heart as clearly as they did when I first heard them nine years ago. Since that time, there have been so many instances when I have found it difficult, almost impossible to forgive someone. Then I hear Mom again. I realize that if Mom could forgive the man who killed her daughter, surely I can forgive my best friend for forgetting our Saturday afternoon plans.

It took me a long time to understand exactly what that horrific day and my sister's death meant. I have gradually accepted that I will not see Grace for a long time, but I know I will see her again in heaven. I also know that Grace is happy and that she is still with me. With time, my wounds have healed. I have learned that it's okay to be sad, and it's also okay not to be sad. As I have learned more about life, I have also come to understand death better. More important than all this, though, I will never forget Mom's lesson of the ultimate forgiveness.

Andrea Gonsalves

Dear Child—A Sister's Message

Today I look into your tender young face, you're all of eleven years old, and I shudder at that thought. Perhaps I am trying to relive my adolescence through you and I recall how tough that age was for me. It was about the time Mom and Dad divorced, the year I had my first real crush and the beginning of junior high—three hard-hitting blows to a confused, awkward kid. That is possibly why I want to write a letter that could somehow condense all my experiences and all my sufferings in one neat page, for you to look at and say, "my mistakes—never!" You see, my experiences weren't unusual or extraordinary, but at the time they took place I felt as if the world would sooner swallow me whole, than allow me to overcome it with some sense of self intact.

So, somehow, I want to call upon that girl I once was and ask her to help me find the words that will give you the armor, that will make all the cruel insults you will surely encounter simply roll off your back. I want to find the potion that will make you see how extraordinary you are so that when that first heartbreak comes along, although you may doubt the love of others, you will never once doubt the love you hold for yourself. I want to make you aware of the beauty that is woman, so that you will always be proud and bold, never flinching in the eye of a man, or most likely a boy, who will try with all his might to convince you that you have a lesser place in the world. I want to show you how to adore this temple in which you house your mind and soul, always respect it and treat it as the jewel that is you. Remember, dear child, that whomever you allow near this temple, this possession that is solely yours, is completely your choice. No amount of convincing or begging could ever change that. Your heart—the treasure box that holds dreams and secret wishes—don't allow it to become a house for fear. Fear will consume you; it will beckon you to keep from shining, to step down for the light on the horizon. Don't hesitate, not even for a moment, because in that moment you may be draining the life of your spirit. Instead, walk with firm, steady steps into the glare of failure and humiliation, two of your greatest foes—believe me, they are no match.

Friends will test your best judgment. You will ask yourself if you chose wisely, or perhaps you will not choose carefully enough and in desperation of walking alone, you will allow yourself to be surrounded by meaningless acquaintances, who have little interest in your true self. These friendships could at times prove to be soul-killing and exhausting, and, although this may seem out of touch right now, I want you to know that at times there is more dignity in marching alone. Loneliness is what you will feel if you build your friendships on longings of being mirrored by visions of your self.

There will always be those that are different from you, in aspects ranging from ethnic background to physical challenges. I wonder, "will she be gracious and kind, an angel cloaked in a child's disguise, or will she be cruel and sharp with a tongue solely shaped to stab at the heart?"

Who will you be, sister? Will those around you regard you as boring and snotty for not wanting to partake in the spirit-bashing of those unaccepted souls? Or will you be leader of such tragic slander? Although you may be cast out for any goodness you exhibit, will you have the commanding strength to remain true to what you've been taught? True to yourself?

Dear child, I know this is huge and unsettling, and perhaps too much to digest at this place and time, but will you tuck this away in a safe, unrelenting place so that its presence will always peer into your conscience? Perhaps you will have a question someday and you will remember these words, my words, which today seem unfitting, uncompromising. I don't think I've covered every possible adolescent terror that you will be struck with, but I can't possibly anticipate all the life that will come your way. What I can say is that you will survive, but not without scars in the most unimaginable place—your heart. Wear them like a badge of courage once you have survived this battle referred to as "growing up." You will be all the wiser, dear child—I know I am.

Danette Julene Gomez

A Message for Ben

Coming of age in this dangerous world is a dauntingly,
    difficult thing.
How will you live up to the promise of what the future
    will bring?
You've shown by example that God has a plan
for helping this old boy become a young man.

We encourage you, Ben, to accept every challenge
with strength and conviction, with patience and balance.
Be truthful, be gentle and always forgive.
Through compassion you learn how to live and let live.

Take to adventure with your eyes open wide.
To steady the journey, travel often inside.
Seek poetry, passion, beauty and art.
Keep magic and wonder tucked close to your heart.

Celebrate failure with just one more try.
Be mindful of the riches that money can't buy.
Be grateful for wealth, but know what's at stake.
And give back to the earth, always, more than you take.

Plant gardens, feed pigeons, walk softly through snow.
When you nurture all life, you help yourself grow.
Be childlike, laugh often, and share every joy.
Honor the man, remember the boy.

Cry at sad movies and when you feel grief.
Tears are the heart's way of bringing relief.
Learn from your pain, it will help make you wise.
Above all, remember that love never dies.

Then, at the end, as you walk your last mile,
Looking back on your life with a well-deserved smile,
Recall all the faces that helped light the way.
Give thanks for their love and remember this day.

Tom Witte

[EDITORS' NOTE: *Ben's uncle, Tom Witte, wrote this poem for Ben for his thirteenth birthday. Tom passed away from complications from AIDS, shortly after he gave him the poem.*]

Finger Paints and Crayons

With chalk in hand she wrote her name across a board
  once bare
And then she sat behind her desk without a single care
And for fifteen minutes, she did not make a sound
Until the final student, had finally settled down
Then she stood before them, and told them all her name
And then politely asked, each student to do the same
Then without hesitation, she took papers from a sack
And placed them in two piles, one white, the other
  black
And deliberately quite slowly, with a slight, mischie-
  vous smile
She began handing out the papers, up and down each
  aisle
And once each student had a piece; she continued
  within their sights
To gather two piles of crayons, one black, the other
  white
And then she took a painting, from behind her walnut
  desk
Then placed a painter's smock, overtop her navy dress

And to no one in particular, she spoke in peaceful tones
"I've been working on this painting, for years in my
   own home."
She stood staring at the painting, its brilliant colors
   mixed as one
Upon a vast horizon, the presence of a sun
It indeed was not a Rembrandt, a Picasso, or Michelangelo
   to say the least
But it nonetheless was beautiful; its presence spoke of
   peace
And no doubt that lovely painting, had taken so much
   time
For every color known to man, seemed to intertwine
And so it came with wonder, what they witnessed with
   surprise
The act that took them all off guard, done right before
   their eyes
With finger paints now gathered, and opened on her
   desk
She smeared the colors upon her hands, in an en-
   tangled awful mess
And then as though she'd lost her mind, she smeared
   her hands across
The painting once so beautiful . . . now a total loss
It did not make a bit of sense, they did not understand
As they sat and watched their teacher, wipe the paints
   from off her hands
And then she took the crayons, and went up and down
   the rows
And handed to each student, the colors that she chose
"Now," she told her students, "I want you to create
A picture filled with beauty, devoid of any hate."
Mouths dropped open widely; mumbles filled the room
And students looked to one another, as unasked ques-
   tions seemed to loom

For the students with white paper, were given crayons
  the same shade
And the students with black crayons, had been given a
  raven-colored page
And how could one create splendor, with no colors to
  mix and match
The students were quite certain, their teacher had left
  out most the facts
"Teacher," a student's voice was heard, "I'm not so sure
  I can"
Staring at the white crayon, and white paper in her hand
Silence overtook the room; it eerily crept about
Causing the teacher's gentle voice, to erupt into a shout
"You each share the same problem, you each possess
  the power to resolve
But only the students with open minds, will have the
  ability to solve."
Minutes ticked away, class was nearing to an end
And not one single student, knew quite how to begin
And when the bell rang out, and they hurried to their feet
Their teacher told them commandingly, to return back
  to their seat
"Before you leave this classroom, I think you each
  should know
For this assignment you receive a failing grade, for you
  have no work to show
And tomorrow and the next day, your assignment shall
  be the same
And those who fail my class, will have only themselves
  to blame."
The next day and the following, students weren't quite
  sure what to do
Until at last, a solution, began to surface through
When one student with his crayon, and paper both in
  black

Turned to the student behind him and asked, "May I
    borrow that?"
The student hesitated, but then gave up his crayon
    made of white
And ultimately the assignment, no longer seemed a
    plight
For students all throughout the class, switched crayons
    up and down the aisles
And certain that they'd found the solution, their faces
    lit with smiles
And just as every student began to draw, across an
    empty page
The teacher whom they'd all began, to see as certainly
    quite strange
Collected all the pages and crayons, without a single
    mark
And then spoke aloud, "Thank you, for bringing hope
    into my heart
You see, I wanted you to realize, that in order to create
A picture filled with beauty, devoid of any hate
You needed first to recognize, that a problem did exist
And that a practical solution, could be found within
    your midst
And that racism is a problem, each of us must face
Working all as one, before it's much too late
And with open eyes and open hearts, we must see the
    person, not the color of their skin
And come to the understanding, that racism has to end
For together we are family, we cry tears, we all feel pain
And though we may not look the part, that's exactly
    what we do
For crayons are just colors, that's all our skin is, too."

Students looked about the room, a variety of colors on
their skin
As the point she was trying to make, began to settle in
The looks upon their faces, readily explained
That they each were trying to contemplate: that indeed
they were the same
A nervous shuffling of papers, and coughs throughout
the room
Portraying the vital image, that fighting over crayons
was a stupid thing to do
It was then each student realized, the purpose of
crayons and papers the same shade
Was to prove they each needed the other color, to help
fill their empty page

Silence seized the moment, as one student raised his
open hand
And then spoke in hesitation, "I just don't understand...
Why you took your painting, the one you seemed to
enjoy so very much
Gathered up your finger paints, to destroy it in a
touch."

Sadness filled her face, as a tear trailed upon her cheek
And in slow and heartfelt words, she began to speak
"To show you each that colors can be beautiful, but they
also can destroy
Everything we love and work for, everything we each
enjoy
And the destruction of something that I loved, was to
make a point to you
That racism destroys the beauty in us all,
And that fighting over colors, is a destructive thing to
do."

Cheryl Costello-Forshey

4

FAMILY

*Other things may change us, but we start and
end with family.*

Anthony Brandt

The Best of Brothers

He was the best of brothers; he was the worst of brothers. Unfortunately, he was the worst—for a long time before I thought otherwise. In short, Mike did not fit my image of the ideal older brother. He was not a friend. Instead, he was my enemy, my nightmare, a bully from whom I could not escape. Just the thought of our horrible childhood encounters makes me cringe.

I can recall the nightly "pounding sessions" that left me screaming for my parents, and my parents screaming at Mike. In fact, it seemed as though they were always focused on my brother, usually for something he had done wrong. My friends' older brothers were their mentors, their protectors, their idols. Not mine. The only interaction we had consisted of physical and verbal abuse. Needless to say, there was not much affection between us.

I can't remember exactly when I discovered I was smarter than my brother, but it was early on and it afforded me the chance to gain at least the intellectual edge. I took great delight in bringing home better grades, beating him at family games, and winning our verbal encounters. I usually paid the price, but at least my pride stayed somewhat intact.

Two winters ago, my family took a ski vacation to Colorado. Many of our school friends were there, as well. We skied, we ate, we partied. I tried to avoid Mike as best I could, but when we were together, he never missed an opportunity to torment me, especially in front of the others.

One particularly frigid morning found my brother, a mutual friend, and me perched tentatively (at least I was) atop a narrow, plunging slope. Trees lined both sides, and the sun had yet to make any impact on the ice-encrusted snow. Mike went first. He made two turns, lost his balance, and began to career downhill, clearly out of control. Our eyes widened as we saw him veer left and disappear into the forest. "Mike!" we screamed several times. There was no sound.

I could feel a churning sensation in my stomach as we quickly made our way down to the spot where we had last seen my brother. The forest was dense and dark, and it swallowed our frantic cries without reply. I had already kicked off my skis and begun to tread through deep snow in the direction of Mike's tracks when I saw him. He lay motionless between two trees, and I was sure he was dead.

"Get a doctor!" I pleaded with our friend. As he skied away, I approached my brother, terrified. "Mike," I repeated several times as I stared at the bloody scrape above his left eye. He did not respond, but I was almost sure he was breathing. I knew not to move him, and the only thing I could think to do was keep him warm until help arrived. I lay at his side and tried to cover as much of him with my body as possible without any weight.

That's when my mind began to race. I had wished him dead so many times and now that it seemed a distinct possibility, somehow I felt responsible. I was actually afraid that it might happen, and feelings began to surface that had been lost or repressed for as long as I could remember. My whole body heaved and shook. As I found myself praying for Mike's life, I began to question my role in our relationship. In my mind I had always been the "victim," the innocent object of his wrath. I had never accepted any responsibility for our lack of closeness, but suddenly I realized that I had played a major part as well. I was a master at infuriating Mike; I knew the right "buttons to push" and enjoyed seeing him and my parents fight. I delighted in the frustration Mike felt when I brought home scholastic awards and straight As. My brother was the perfect foil; and in some twisted way I actually owed him a great deal, for he was the inspiration for much of my motivation and success, a reverse role model.

Suddenly I didn't seem so innocent, I had used Mike as he had used me, and our relationship was the real victim. I truly felt compassion for him and wondered if this new and strange sensation was "brotherly love." As it turned out, Mike had a concussion, no broken bones, and had to sit out the rest of our vacation in bed. I finished the week a slightly better skier and a brother who had found a new level of understanding about accepting responsibility, and one who had rediscovered some long-forgotten emotions.

A year and a half later I am happy to report that our relationship is much improved. We still don't have a great deal in common, but we do have a newfound respect for one another; and although we still bicker and fight, I sense a growing connection between us. Mike called home from college last week and asked to speak with me. We actually had a meaningful conversation, and it felt wonderful.

From The Best College Admission Essays

Kicki

Throughout my childhood, I constantly dreamed of being an only child—having no one around to fight with, to share with, to grab the remote away from me in the middle of a "big game." I would have the biggest bedroom in the house and be able to talk on the phone as long as I wanted, without being asked a million times, "Are you off yet?" But I was not born an only child; I was born with an older sister. I have always called my sister "Kicki," instead of her real name, Christie, because, when I was younger, I had trouble pronouncing the *r* and *s*. To this day, she is still "Kicki."

I started playing basketball when I was eight years old. My dad was the coach of my team, and my mom kept score. So my sister, not old enough to stay home alone, was forced to come to all of my games. I remember looking into the stands for my mother's approval during games and seeing my sister's face, confused. It was obvious that she wasn't thrilled to be there, but she cheered along with the crowd anyway. Her hair was cut short, almost as short as mine, and her teeth stuck out. I teased her often, calling her "bucky beaver." She wasn't a very attractive little girl, and she looked more like my older brother than my sister.

After the games, on the car rides home, my parents and I relived every move I had made on the court. My sister sat in the backseat with me in silence, not knowing how or when to enter the conversation. Most nights she came into my room and said, "Good night, Brad. Good game." I would smile and thank her. I never really took her compliment seriously. I mean, she hardly understood what was going on in the games; she couldn't possibly know whether I had played well or not.

It wasn't until I reached high school that I realized what a truly beautiful person my sister was. Everybody knew her and thought highly of her, and I was referred to as "Christie's little brother." Kicki was on the Homecoming Court her senior year, and she stood tall and beautiful. I was astonished at the person she had become: smart, sweet and beautiful. To me, she was still the ten-year-old little girl with the boyish looks and buckteeth.

I played basketball in high school, and although Christie wasn't forced to attend my games anymore, she still came every week, cheering me on from the stands. I remember one game in particular, the last game of the season. My sister sat in the bleachers with her boyfriend and a large group of friends. Printed on her shirt, in big bright red letters, were the words "BRAD'S SISTER." Suddenly I was embarrassed. But it wasn't her presence that embarrassed me, rather, it was the fact that I had never appreciated her support before. She was never embarrassed to be my sister, even though I had been embarrassed to call her that so many years ago. She didn't care what anyone thought, and she never had.

I am an only child now; my sister left for college a few months after that last game. I finally have the biggest room in the house and the remote control all to myself.

But now that she's gone, I kind of miss having someone to fight with for the phone, and the big bedroom isn't all that great anyway.

I went to visit her at college for a weekend, and as I stood outside her dorm, waiting for her to come out, a friend of hers walked past me and questioned, "Hey, aren't you Christie's brother?" I beamed and said proudly, "Yeah, I am. I'm Christie's brother."

Brad Dixon

Relief

I'm not quite sure when the turning point came. But I know that it came after a fight I had with my mother. It was a typical fight for that rebellious summer. You know how it is, you lie once, and then they all start to pile up. And nothing happens evenly—it's always all at once. That summer I drifted apart from my mother, and my two best friends, whom I needed to turn to, were angry with me. That's where I learned my second lesson (the first being not to lie)—never keep your feelings hidden. That's what my friends did, and when I found out, it was too late.

Anyway, my house was a battle zone. I'd sleep till I had to go to work and then sleep after work. In between, I'd cry and feel sorry for myself, well, when I wasn't fighting with my mom. That day it all changed.

She was screaming at me about how I wasn't a part of the family anymore—that no one liked being around me because I was always so hostile. I yelled back, as most sixteen-year-olds would. But my mom doesn't ground me (well, I was already grounded) or take away the phone; she assigns essays. My assignment was to apologize for my behavior.

I cried tears of rage in my room, yelling about what I could possibly write. But then I started to write. And the apology turned into an explanation. I poured out every pain and emotion, ones that I had hidden behind my rage, the ones I cried about at night. I didn't know how to get back to being me, and I hated what I had become. I felt so lost. And, most of all, I felt like everyone that I had depended on had left me. Alone.

I left the letter on her bed and went to sleep, exhausted from sobbing. I wrapped myself up in my warm, flannel blankets to ease the cold. Although it was a warm and humid summer night, I shivered. The next morning I woke up early enough to go to work so that no one was awake yet. I crept into the bathroom and noticed a card with my name written on it in my mother's handwriting taped to the mirror. I opened it. It said that she understood. She understood that I was lost and scared. And she promised that she would help me.

I got into the hot shower, silently sobbing. My salty tears mixed with the water on my face. Except that this time, the tears were of relief, not of despair.

Kathryn Litzenberger

Don't Cry, Dad

During my years in junior high, I developed an after-school routine. Every day I walked in the back door of my home and proceeded up the three flights of stairs to my bedroom. I closed the door, turned my music up loud and lay on my bed for two hours until someone came to get me for dinner. I ate dinner in silence; I tried desperately to avoid talking to my family and even harder not to make eye contact with them. I hurriedly finished my dinner and rushed back to my room for more music. I locked myself in my room until it was time for school the next day.

Once in a while, my parents would ask me if there was anything wrong. I would snap at them, saying that I was just fine and to stop asking so many questions. The truth was, I couldn't answer them because *I* didn't know what was wrong. Looking back, I was very unhappy. I cried for no reason, and little things made me explode. I didn't eat well, either. It wasn't "cool" at that time to be seen actually eating lunch during school. I wasn't much of a breakfast eater, and if I weren't required to eat dinner with my family every night, I probably wouldn't have eaten at all.

The summer before my freshman year, my dad told me

that he wanted to talk. I was *not* thrilled. In fact, I resented him. I did not want to talk to anyone, especially my dad.

We sat down, and he started the conversation by asking the usual questions: "Are you okay? Is everything all right?" I didn't answer; I refused to make eye contact.

"Every day I come home from work, and you're locked in your room, cut off from the rest of us." He paused a moment, his voice was a little shaky as he began again. "I feel like you're shutting me out of your life." Having said that, my father, a man who I thought was stronger than steel, began to cry. And I don't mean just a few tears rolling down his cheeks. Months of hidden pain flooded from his eyes. I felt like I had been slapped. Never in my fourteen years had I seen my dad cry. Through his tears he went on to tell me that he wanted to be a part of my life and how he ached to be my friend. I loved my dad more than anything in the world, and it killed me to think I had hurt him so deeply. His eyes shifted towards me. They looked tired and full of pain—pain that I had never seen, or maybe that I had ignored. I felt a lump forming in my throat as he continued to cry. Slowly, that lump turned to tears, and they started pouring from my eyes.

"Don't cry, Dad," I said, putting my hand on his shoulder.

"I hope I didn't embarrass you with my tears," he replied.

"Of course not."

We cried together a little more before he left. In the days that followed, I had a hard time breaking the pattern I had become so accustomed to over the last two years. I tried sitting in the living room with my parents while they drank their coffee. I felt lost in their world, while I was desperately trying to adjust to new habits. Still, I made an effort. It took almost another full year before I felt completely comfortable around my family again and included them in my personal life.

Now I'm a sophomore in high school, and almost every day when I come home from school, I sit down and tell my dad about my day while we have our coffee. We talk about my life, and he offers advice sometimes, but mostly, he just listens.

Looking back, I am so glad my father and I had that talk. Not only have I gained a better relationship with my father, I've gained a friend.

Laura Loken

Ghost Mother

Six months before my thirteenth birthday, my parents gave my brother and me "the talk." The one about their loving us, but not each other and how much happier everyone would be if they separated. Yet, my parents rewrote the ending: "We think it would be best if you lived with your father." My mother was the one who said this, running her red nails through my hair. That moment has stayed in the center of my stomach since then, like a jagged stone rolling around.

Mothers are supposed to be that one person who represents home, who somehow makes everything okay when your world is shaking. A mother should be there for you no matter how many times you change your Halloween costume, how messy your room gets or what happens to her marriage. But mine saw motherhood as an optional endeavor, something she could easily discard like a sweater that no longer fit.

She quickly settled into her own life and her new apartment. Having married at twenty-one, this was the first time she was on her own. Her decorating business was growing, and she was more interested in catering to her clients than to two kids and a husband of fifteen years.

A few weeks after she moved out, she called on a Friday night. "Tomorrow, let's have lunch and then go shopping. Okay?" she asked. I was so excited that I could hardly answer. That night I dreamed of riding beside my mom in the car. Saturday, I woke early, put on my favorite overalls and finished my homework in case she wanted to spend Sunday together, too. My friend Jennifer called. "Aren't you coming to the movies?" she asked. "Everyone's going."

"My mom and I have stuff to do. Shopping or something," I said, forcing my tone to be matter-of-fact. But morning turned into afternoon, and she didn't call. I spent the day by the phone pretending to read, playing solitaire and braiding my hair. I wouldn't eat anything because I thought at any minute she'd be there and want to take me out for lunch. And I didn't want my mom to have to eat alone. But she didn't call until after six o'clock. "Sorry, honey, I was working all day and not near a phone," she said quickly. "And now I'm so tired, I just need to take a nap. You understand, don't you?" No Mom, I didn't understand.

This same scenario happened many weekends for several years after she left. The rare times I did see her, she'd rent me four-hour movies like *Tess* and leave me alone to watch them. Or I'd go on her errands or to her office, never really with her, more like a balloon trailing after her. I'd sit alone at a desk in her office eating Chinese food out of a paper carton while she worked or talked on the phone. But I never complained or stopped going. How could I when this was all I had of her?

Almost a year after she moved out, the clothes she didn't want remained in her walk-in closet. My father said he was too busy to pack them, but I think that—just as I did—he hoped it meant she wasn't gone for good. I used to sit in that closet, breathing in the lingering smell of her Ralph Lauren perfume. I'd wrap myself in her ivory cashmere cardigan and run my fingers along the beaded surface of a pink bag, remembering when she'd carried it with a chiffon dress. She had looked just like a princess. I'd rock the bag gently, feeling sorry for it that she had left it behind, too.

Living with my father and brother in their masculine world of boxer shorts and hockey games wasn't easy. Just when I should have been stepping out of my tomboy stage of wearing my brother's worn Levi's and buttondowns and starting to become a young woman, I was screaming at the basketball players on TV and munching on Doritos. Each of my friends watched her mother apply eyeliner and blush and practiced with her makeup while she was out. The only makeup I knew about was the black smudges under football players' eyes.

Growing up without my mother, I always had to carry myself to each new stage of life or get left behind. I wore the same clothes that my friends did, bought my first bra by myself and started shaving my legs when they did. But to me I was just following clumsily behind them, selfconscious that my motherlessness was showing. When I got my period, I huddled in my pink bathroom, feeling like a little girl at this sign of being a woman. Having to say, "I got my period, Dad," was mortifying. But the truth was, I felt more comfortable telling him than my mother. When she called the following week, she said, "Dad told me what happened, but he took care of it." This was a statement, not a question.

My mother became like a distant relative whom I saw several times a year, who sent a birthday card if she remembered and to whom I was stiffly polite and didn't curse in front of. The word "mom" was foreign to me. She never asked about my friends or school or seemed to notice that I was struggling to grow up without her. Each time I said good-bye, I knew it would be months before I saw her again.

Why didn't my mother want me? I wondered. Teachers and friends' parents always wore a look of pity when my father picked me up from parties, came alone to plays and parent-conference day and talked to them to arrange car pools. Hating their pity, I'd mix the few minutes my mother did give me with my imagination. Then I'd casually talk about her at lunch or at friends' houses so they wouldn't see that all I had was a ghost mother who touched my life only in memories.

Although it was tough at first, my father tried to do everything he could to fill the gaps my mother left. He put my brother and me first, at times sacrificing his own happiness for ours. Despite losing his wife and marriage, my father wore a smile on his face. After all, he was the person we looked toward to tell us everything was going to be okay, so we couldn't see him sad. He had no spouse to pick up where he left off or to help him with daily issues and unexpected situations. He took us to the doctor, listened to our problems and helped us with homework. He was there with treats when my friends slept over and told the kind of dumb fatherly jokes that made us laugh and roll our eyes. He was always at all my school plays and softball games. He never missed a gymnastics meet or recital. Most fathers never took off work to come to even one of these things; my father was at all of them. Most of all, he was always conscious of my disappointments and tried to make a bad situation better. After a while, all the people who pitied me noticed my father's intense interest in my well-being and realized, as I did, that though my life was different, there was nothing wrong with it or me. In time, I adjusted to this. And though I never stopped wishing my mother were a more central part of my life, I saw the fact that she wasn't; she was just a part of who I am.

In recent years, I have become closer with her. I accept her for who she is, regardless of the fact that she wasn't always the mother I wanted her to be. As I have gotten older, I can look at what she did from a different perspective. And I think I've reached this point because my father taught me to be understanding of and sensitive to others. I've realized it's okay not to have a storybook home with a mom, dad, two kids and a dog. Who said that is the definition of family? My home may have been unique, but it had in it the same love and loyalty as other families.

Michele Bender

Unspoken Years

To an outsider looking in, my life probably looked pretty great. I had what appeared to be a loving family, I lived in a spacious home in a safe neighborhood, and I attended a good school. But what an outsider couldn't see was the cold atmosphere that permeated my house. My parents' and my endless fights included the shouting of hurtful words, bitter stares, and at times, unbearable silence. Misunderstandings inevitably led to fights.

This particular fight started just like the others. I packed my bag, preparing to leave for an overnight retreat for my confirmation class. I carefully selected my clothes, folding and refolding them, doing everything I could to stall, thereby avoiding a potential fight. I crept down the stairs into our kitchen, only to find my parents glaring up at me.

"What time should I pick you up tomorrow?" my mom demanded impatiently with folded arms.

I told her that I wasn't certain, but that I thought she should pick me up at approximately 8:00 P.M. I quickly gathered that my reply was not the answer she wanted to hear.

"So you don't know what time?" Her face wrinkled with disapproval.

I tried my best not to explode and release years of repressed feelings of anger, resentment and sorrow. These feelings were trapped inside my confused body. Whenever my parents and I fought, usually about small, insignificant misunderstandings, we seemed to convey more. The fight was not just about the topic of that particular quarrel, but the unspoken emotions that hovered over the sixteen years of my life. My parents and I had issues, and we did not know how to voice them.

"You always run around and never tell me where you are going or when you will be home!" my mom yelled, continuing the argument and inflicting as much guilt on me as humanly possible.

I pretended I didn't know what she was talking about, and I left my house for the retreat on bitter terms with my parents, casting a shadow on my experience at the retreat. I did not want to participate or involve myself in anything that night. I sat by myself, drowning in self-pity. Whenever someone asked me what was wrong, I refused to answer.

The next morning, my instructor approached me and asked if I had received my letter.

"What letter?" I wondered, puzzled. Another leader at the retreat handed me an envelope with my name written on it in my mom's handwriting. I stared at the letter with perplexed eyes and strode to the conference room to open it in privacy.

"Make rainbows with faith in yourself. Many beautiful things will happen in your life. Your shine brightens our lives." As I read these statements, I tried to choke back the river of tears swelling in my eyes. I failed, and the tears trickled down my cheeks. As I made my way toward the tissue box at the other end of the room, three supportive friends hugged me. But wishing to be alone and to finish reading the letter, I broke free from their embrace and rushed toward the exit. I sat in my room, attempting to gather my thoughts and emotions. My instructor then knocked on my door and explained to me that she had asked everyone's parents to write a letter to their son or daughter before we went on the retreat. She then left me alone to sort out my feelings.

After rereading those initial statements, I continued reading the rest of the letter. My mom and dad wrote that they loved me, although it didn't always seem like it and that they needed me in their lives. Their honesty made me think about our relationship, and I began to realize the role I played in instigating the arguments and our lack of communication. In reality, everyone contributed. And now it was time for all of us to work toward a better relationship.

My family was more calm when I returned home from the retreat, and my parents and I had a newfound respect for each other. We still have the occasional run-ins, but they're not like they used to be. There are no more cold stares or hurtful shouting matches. Even though my parents and I cannot change the past and the sixteen years lost to incessant bickering, each day we slowly learn how to communicate as a family, ensuring that another sixteen years won't be lost as well.

Kristin Sester

Rikki's Hug

I'm walking up the sidewalk to our brown, three-bedroom condo. I've lived here for so many years that I can't even remember the day we moved in. I know that sidewalk, steps and porch so well that I could easily walk them blind. As I pause at the door to search for my key in my purse, I get a whiff of the familiar dryer sheet smell that is flowing from the vent near the porch. It's a comforting smell, one that most people would overlook. But I've always noticed it. I gaze up at the same old gray Connecticut sky. The cool breeze that frequents early spring in the Northeast whips my windbreaker around my shoulders and leaks through the sleeves, causing me to shiver. My day at school was pretty typical, although I didn't do as well in all of my classes as I wanted to. I'm behind in my outlining for history, which is usually the most lacking area of my schoolwork because I dread it so much.

Tonight I am supposed to go out for a mid-week dinner and then to the gym, but play rehearsal ran over. It's getting late, and I have so much work ahead of me this evening. What began as an ordinary day is now anything but ordinary. The breeze feels like a fierce, wintry gust. My head hurts, my liveliness faded to a shade of tired. It's too much. I can't do it anymore. I struggle to turn the key in the door when it swings wide open.

There she stands, her little body clad in Osh-Koshes that have Pooh on them, her long brown curls free and flowing down her back to her waist. She lets me put her hair up very rarely; she prefers it to be let alone to do what it wants. She's wise beyond her years. Her eyes remind me of milk chocolate with a fleck of summer sunshine in them. They retain the gentle radiance of summer long after the leaves have fallen off the trees and have been replaced with frigid snow. But it's her smile that I notice. Her smile never ceases to amaze me. It lights up her face with an innocent and happy luminescence. It's a contagious smile. "Gaga is home!" She's called me that name since she first started talking. She's put behind her all of the other baby names for friends and family, but mine sticks. That's because I'm her favorite sister, her favorite person. Well, that's what she tells me and I choose not to acknowledge that she's only four and doesn't understand yet what the depths of the word "favorite" are. I understand what it means, so I can legitimately say that she's my favorite. Though she may not understand the extremity in this word, she sure understands me.

Her little arms wrap around me as I hug the little girl whom I still call, "Baby." Only when she misbehaves do I use her real name. Though she's at that age when babies no longer are babies and want to be "big girls," she never corrects me. And only when she's upset with me does she ever use my actual name. With that one gesture, everything's okay again. She puts a butterfly kiss on my cheek. Then come the sweetest words you could ever hear, which could easily be mistaken for the sound of an angel: "I missed you." *Isn't it funny how with one simple display of affection, everything turns around?* The world suddenly seems okay and I can no longer find a reason to be tired. And even though when that moment is over, the toils and troubles of life return, it's always waiting for me at my front door. All I have to do is turn the key.

Kathryn Litzenberger

About Mom

I keep remembering odd things: the way she loved daf-
fodils, her delight at the antics of our dog, jokes she told
at the dinner table, her subtle brand of feminism, the look
in her eyes when she talked about my future. I knew
about college before I'd ever heard of high school; I was
Mom's second chance at the degree she never had.

Her parents pushed her too much, too hard, too fast, and
she always wished she hadn't let the pressure overwhelm
her. She dropped out of college after one semester for marriage and a secretarial job. While she never regretted
marrying my father, she always regretted giving up her
dream of becoming an accountant. She was determined her
eldest daughter would never miss an opportunity, and she
missed out on so many herself so I could succeed.

She was the one person I could talk to about anything:
politics, dating, parties, failed tests, or nail polish. She was
right about so much, so often—much more than I gave
her credit for at the time. We never did agree on clothes.
She favored the J. Crew look, I kept trying for (and failing
at) the neo-sixties style. One year we didn't buy any new
clothes at all in a battle of wills: she refused to buy

anything that didn't "fit me properly" and I refused to wear anything with an alligator on it.

She loved the holidays, Christmas most of all. One of the most intensely special times of my life was Christmas my sophomore year, when I played Tiny Tim in a local community theater production of "A Christmas Carol." Mom delighted in my endless rehearsal stories and spent hours helping me work out ways of disguising my long hair. There's a line in the show: "And it was always said of him that he knew how to keep Christmas well, if any man alive possessed the knowledge." Change the pronouns and that quote describes Mom perfectly.

I never imagined she wouldn't be here now, micromanaging, debating the merits of such-and-such college with me, chasing the dog around the living room, ruining spaghetti, explaining "power colors," and relishing exciting changes in IRS forms. I never thought cancer could strike so quickly, could kill someone so strong and determined in only a year.

She's the one person I couldn't imagine living without; now, since last January, I've had to. Suddenly, I have no one to talk to about meaningless little things, no one whose advice I trust implicitly to help me with decisions. When I come home from school, I come home to an empty house, haunted by memories of the year she spent here dying. I remember the disastrous Thanksgiving when she was nauseous and delusional, our wonderful last Christmas Eve together, the tangle of tubes in the family room, the needlepoint picture of Rainbow Row she labored over while stuck in bed, and the bags of M&M's she always kept within reach.

What I feel cheated of is the future we'll never have.

Stacy Cowley
From The Best College Admission Essays

Dear Diary . . .

*The greatest happiness of life is the conviction
that we are loved—loved for ourselves or rather,
loved in spite of ourselves.*

Victor Hugo

Dear Diary,

*Drip. Drip. Drip. For three hours I've waited in this train
station and for three hours I've heard the faint splash of
water fall from an old water fountain onto the cold, hardwood
floor. The wood is old and worn but somehow doesn't allow
any of the water drops to seep through. Funny, how something . . . Suddenly a horn whistles from a departing train,
interrupting my thoughts and allowing them to come crashing back to reality.*

*I glance at my watch and realize I've missed my train, and
the next one isn't going to leave this town for the next four
hours. What am I going to do now? It's a quarter past midnight, and I'm cold and hungry. I have a meeting with the
admissions officer in a college at 8:00 A.M., and by the look of*

things, I'm not going to make it on time. What a way to make a first impression, huh?

I begin to feel the tears burn the back of my eyes, and soon they are dancing upon my cheek. I am here alone. There isn't a familiar face around to comfort me. My mother was supposed to be here with me, to say one final good-bye before I enter adulthood. But with the many fights and unkept promises we've shared I didn't expect her to want to come here with me. Maybe I shouldn't have left the house this evening without saying I'm sorry. Sorry for the many disagreements and disappointments. Sorry for my hurtful words and actions. But we've passed the point where "sorry" heals things and makes them better again. Still, what I wouldn't give to have her here with me. Maybe she's right. Maybe I'm not the know-it-all mature adult I think I am. Maybe I am still just a scared kid who needs the protection of a mother's love.

It's almost 4:00 now, and the morning sun should be rising soon. I am able to grab a cup of coffee and change my clothes during the wait. I figure if I catch a 7:00 bus in Boston I can still make my appointment. . . .

Until next time,
Me

Putting away my journal I reach into my bag to get out my ticket, but instead a plain white envelope emerges in my hand. I don't need to read the name on the front to know who it's from. She wants us to have a better relationship and put the past behind us. Have a fresh start. My mother even admitted she was sorry for all the arguments we've had over the course of the years. The note also said she would be waiting for me at the train station in Boston and we would walk into college together. Enclosed was an upgraded ticket and a "P.S." telling me to look in the bottom of my bag. There I would find money for a bite to eat and a sweater in case I got cold in the station. As I make my way to the train I pass the broken water fountain, which no longer drips, and I realize, for the first time in this life, I'm about to see a woman for who she truly is. My mother.

Liz Correale

The Turning Point

I stomped out of the house, and the screen door slammed shut behind me. My face was wet with tears. As I started out down the street, I heard my mother call after me, "Dani, take your brother with you." I was in the middle of complete emotional distress, and now my brother was trotting down the driveway behind me. This is exactly why my parents had no idea what was going on. They only talked to me to tell me to take my brother with me or to clean up my room. They had no idea the pain I was enduring.

I walked down the block to my best friend Mike's house. I was going to say good-bye. I didn't want to be here anymore, I couldn't stand that no one understood what I was going through.

Mike opened the door and immediately embraced me in the biggest, tightest hug of my life. My younger brother, whom I had been ignoring, wandered off to play with Mike's brothers.

Mike and I went into his living room to sit down. He didn't ask for an explanation or try to console me; he just held me and let me cry on his shoulder. I sobbed until my sides hurt. I cried about how lonely I was. I cried about how my family didn't seem to understand me at all. And when I was all cried out, I realized that part of the hurt was gone.

It dawned on me that I had been crying and talking with Mike for hours. I called home, and my mother screamed at me for being out past curfew. But instead of picking a fight, I grabbed my brother and started the walk home.

There was something strangely calming about that walk home. Because of this new sense of calm and warmth I was feeling, I decided to tell my brother everything. My brother and I rarely talked, and when we did, it had only to do with him tagging along or arguments over the remote. But on that walk home, I spilled my heart to my sixth-grade brother, someone I had never before looked to for advice or comfort.

He didn't yell at me or lecture me. He didn't tell me my feelings were wrong or that I was wrong for feeling them. He just said, "Please don't die. That would make me sad." It was then, walking hand-in-hand with my kid brother, that I decided I wanted to live.

The next day I turned fifteen.

Dani Allred

A Birthday Gift

She lived a life of solitude.
She lived a life in vain.
She lived a life in which there was
A strong, ongoing pain.

She had no friends on which to lean
And cry her problems to.
She had no friends to give her love
And hope and kindness, too.

She thought about it day and night;
She lay upon her bed.
Her mind made up, she grabbed a gun
And put it to her head.

Just then a ring came from the phone.
She pulled the gun away.
Her mom was on the other end
And wanted just to say,

"Happy Birthday, my dear girl.
Today is just for you.
I care for you with all my heart,
I hope you know that's true."

These words ran through her mind so much.
The gun was down for good.
She changed her mind about her life
And then she changed her mood.

She thought about this special day
And what her mom had said.
The gift her mom gave her that day
Was the gift of life, *again*.

Thad Langenberg

The Mother Who Matters

I have eyes that are said to be "cow brown," and my long blond hair is my best feature. My nose is a little too big; my face is oval shaped. I am not overweight, but I'm not skinny either. The only way to describe my height is "vertically challenged."

I'm relatively happy with my appearance, but where did I get it? Do I share the same features as some unknown stranger? Oftentimes, while walking down the street, I try to pick out that stranger, imagining that one of the women I pass could possibly be my biological mother.

I never met my birth mother. I was adopted the moment I was born, and I was taken into a wonderful family. For a long time I wondered what life would be like with my birth mother. Would I still be the same? Where would I live? Would I be happier? Who would my friends be?

I was never dissatisfied with my life; I just never stopped wondering what it would be like to have been raised by my biological mother. And then one day, I was baby-sitting with a friend, and I came across a poem on the nursery wall. It compared adoption to a seed that was planted by one person and then taken care of by another.

The second person had watered the seed and made it grow to be tall and beautiful. I found that it compared perfectly to my situation.

I realized that my mom had made me who I am today, no matter what either of us looks like. And I started to notice that we had the same silly personality, the same outlook on life, and the same way of treating people, along with some other things. She curled my hair for my first dance. She was there for my first heartbreak. She held my hand every time I got a shot at the doctors. She'd been smiling in the crowd for my first school play. She'd been there for everything that ever mattered, and what could compare to that? She's my mom.

Sometimes when we're out somewhere, people comment on how much we look alike, and we turn to each other and laugh, forgetting until that moment that it wasn't she who carried me in her womb for nine months.

Though I may not know why I look the way I do, I know why I am who I am. The mom I have now is the best one I ever could have hoped for, not only because she holds a tremendous amount of unconditional love, but because she has shaped who I am today, my qualities and characteristics. She is the one who made me beautiful!

Kristy White

Never Enough

Sometimes I know the words to say,
Give thanks for all you've done,
But then they fly up and away,
As quickly as they come.

How could I possibly thank you enough,
The one who makes me whole,
The one to whom I owe my life,
The forming of my soul.

The one who tucked me in at night,
The one who stopped my crying,
The one who was the expert,
At picking up when I was lying.

The one who saw me off to school,
And spent sad days alone,
Yet magically produced a smile,
As soon as I came home.

The one who makes such sacrifices,
To always put me first,

Who lets me test my broken wings,
In spite of how it hurts.

Who paints the world a rainbow,
When it's filled with broken dreams,
Who explains it all so clearly,
When nothing's what it seems.

Are there really any words for this?
I find this question tough . . .
Anything I want to say,
Just doesn't seem enough.

What way is there to thank you,
For your heart, your sweat, your tears,
For ten thousand little things you've done,
For oh-so-many years.

For changing with me as I changed,
Accepting all my flaws,
Not loving 'cause you had to,
But loving "just because."

For never giving up on me,
When your wits had reached their end,
For always being proud of me,
For being my best friend.

And so I come to realize,
The only way to say,
The only thank you that's enough,
Is clear in just one way.

Look at me before you,
See what I've become,
Do you see yourself in me?
The job that you have done?

All your hopes and all your dreams,
The strength that no one sees,
A transfer over many years,
Your best was passed to me.

Thank you for the gifts you give,
For everything you do,
But thank you, Mommy, most of all,
For making dreams come true.

Love,
Your Daughter

Laurie Kalb

Angel

I just sit here, watching the funny looking bird through the window. It is washing itself in the driveway, which is full of rain from last night's shower. I think, *What if I were a bird? Where would I go? What would I do?* Of course, I know that is not possible, especially now. I'm just sitting here, watching my life pass by, second by second, minute by minute. I know I should do something productive, like homework, but I just feel like it's my job to watch the funny looking bird. Then the bird flies away, and I turn on the TV and watch a show about buffalo.

School's almost out, but I'm not there. I have to be sick, stuck inside with the flu, stuck inside underneath this blanket.

It's such a beautiful day outside, and I feel so sick. I feel like I am falling up (which just isn't possible, but I still feel like it). My head is spinning, almost as if I am in a daze. My brain starts pounding, like someone is hitting my skull with a hammer. The sun is shining, which doesn't help; it just makes it worse. I hide under the covers. This is the one time I feel like the sun is a bad thing.

Now my stomach starts to ache, so I move from the

couch to my room to lie on my bed. Even though my brain hurts, I start to think. I let my imagination go.

I think about how much easier it is to tap your foot to a country song than to a rock song. I think about how long a day seems when you're bored, but when you do something fun the time flies by. I think about how they make us go to school for seven hours, then expect us to do three hours of homework every night and endure a big test in science or history the next day.

I start to dream, daydream that is, even more. I wander even further into my imagination. Somehow the thought of an angel comes into my head. *What do they look like? Do they have golden wings? Do they live in the moment, rather than the past or the future? Are they light?*

For some reason I can't stop wondering about them. *Can a human being become an angel after life?* My friends tell me no, but I think my grandpa is my grandma's guardian angel. I take out a piece of paper and start drawing what I think an angel looks like. In the finished drawing, the angel has golden hair as rich as the sun and gold wings that stretch from her body so that she can touch everyone's heart. She is wearing a smile and a pure white robe. A golden halo of stars floats atop her head.

The drawing makes me smile, and I feel a little better. *Tomorrow will be a better day,* I think. At that, I fall asleep.

"Anyone home?" greets me as I awaken.

"Hi, Mom," I reply.

"How are you feeling?" she asks.

"Better."

She insists on making me some chicken noodle soup anyway. Moms sure know how to make me feel better when I'm sick. Seems like she would take my sickness away from me in a second and give it to herself if she could. That's what moms are for, always there for you. Mothers hate to see their children suffer, even if it's just a little flu bug.

I don't need to know what an angel looks like, I think, *I already know.* An angel is a mom, my Mom. Her smile is that light that fills the room when it's dark. And her thoughtfulness touches my heart. My mom is an angel, watching over me. Thanks, Mom.

Nathen Cantwell

5

LESSONS

Obstacles are those frightful things you see when you take your eyes off your goal.

Hannah Moore

China's Story

China was fourteen, she gave what she got
She had many friends, who loved her a lot.
She loved them back, too, and would always be
    there,
But at prettier girls, she could not help but stare.

You must understand, that this group was a sight,
With their Cover Girl masks, and their shirts way
    too tight.
The guys hung around them, as though in a trance,
They were always the first ones who were asked to
    dance.

They seemed so secure, knowing just what to say.
And they said what they said in *the* coolest of ways
They never were seen without smiles on their
    faces.
Their clothes were real tight in all the right places.

You can see what I mean, when I say they were
    cool.
They were by far the sexiest girls in the school.

So China dreamed on, by day and by night,
Wishing her shirts would fit her as tight.
She wondered what contest she would have to win.
For, she'd give up the world, and her life to fit in.

She kept it a secret, hoping nobody knew,
But her friends caught on fast, and they found it
    was true.
They tried to warn her of their pretentious way.
But China grew more and more stubborn each day.

As cool as they were, and as hot as their show,
They struggled in school and their grades were
    quite low.
The groups of girls smoked, and were known to
    drink beer,
But this was not stuff China wanted to hear.

So China tried hard to fit in with the clique,
She giggled at jokes that she knew were just sick.
She gave her attention to these cool girls alone,
She dressed just like them, in a style not her own.

China's old friends feared her drifting away,
They were losing her slowly, and didn't know what
    to say.
They told China the truth, that the group was all fake,
But their words of advice, China just wouldn't take.

Why aren't they happy for me? China thought,
I don't act like myself, but now look where I've got.
She thought her old friends were jealous and tart,
She was truthfully happy, deep down in her heart.

China laughed at her old friends, along with her
   new,
They made fun of so many and smiled at so few.
China's new friends were cool, she was in with the
   clan,
She was treated like they were, she was happy
   again.

China's old group of friends sadly melted away,
They left China alone, but watched close every
   day.
They longed for her friendship, the warmth in her
   smile.
And hoped she'd miss them, and come back in a
   while.

But the jokes kept on coming, so the group with a
   sigh,
Turned their backs on harsh China, and walked
   silently by.
The pain was too deep and the torture too hard,
Her old friend's poor hearts had been torn out and
   scarred.

As all this did happen, the cool did their thing,
They giggled and gossiped and made actions sting.
They mutated China, the best that they could,
And taught her to be like a glamour girl should.

China went to parties, she got into fights,
She became really cool, but during the night,
She tried to discover just what was the scoop,
Why she wasn't content in her newly found group.

Then one day it hit her, came into her head,
That the answer was one that she truly did dread.
She had run ahead quickly and back round the bends,
She had left her companions, she had ditched her
true friends.

China realized her error, "This group's not a sight,
With their makeup done perfect and hair fixed just
right.
That's not what they look like, it's a lie what you
see,
It's the Maybelline models they wish they could
be."

Then early one night, around seven o'clock,
A girl opened her door to the sound of a knock.
Out in the cold, standing there in the rain,
Stood teary-eyed China, her old self again.

Neither one spoke, as she ushered her in,
The girl knew from experience, where China had
been.
She had also once felt that those girls were the best,
But those long-ago thoughts, she had put down to
rest.

The girls sat up talking for a good length of time,
China knew in her heart that she would be just fine.
She couldn't believe just how much she'd been
blessed,
That her loving dear friends would forgive her like
this.

This tale ends happy, but not all stories will,
Some friends aren't so forgiving, they go in for the
kill.

China was lucky, but you may not be,
So choose your friends wisely, and help others see.

The moral is not to have one group of friends,
From a particular table, with particular trends.
It's to teach of the truth, that those girls tried to
    hide,
You will always be cool if it comes from inside.

Libby Barnes

Forever Changed

The great use of life is to spend it for something that will outlast it.

William James

Every morning when I wake up, I peel back the blankets that keep my body warmth hostage and look around my room. I see cherished family photos, my favorite mahogany dresser and of course my love beads that hang from the windows. I can't imagine my life without a loving family surrounding me or a roof shielding me from the night.

This past July, I went on a mission trip to Monterrey, Mexico, with my youth group. I sat on a bus for two days, not knowing what to expect. My friends on the bus described all the bugs that had infested the orphanages we were to work at for the next week. They told me how dirty everything would be and how dangerous the streets were. Secretly, I was hoping the bus would turn around somehow. But it did not. The first night we arrived, a man said, "We have come here to change Mexico, but instead, Mexico will change us."

Each morning during the hour-and-a-half bus ride to the orphanage, I would think of how little I had slept the night before, how tired I was, and how there was no air conditioning on the bus. But, as soon as the orphanage came into view, all those feelings melted away. The children would run up to the gates, scream, and jump up and down because we had finally arrived. The first day I walked cautiously inside the metal gates. I saw one girl with a huge smile on her face. When I walked over to her, she gave me a hug. I looked around at all the other children. All were smiling. All were laughing. They were not upset, nor complaining about their lives and living conditions.

I met a little girl at the orphanage named Erica. She had short black hair and a big scar beneath her nose. I picked her up and swung her around. She squealed with laughter. Every day when we arrived, she always ran up to me, gave me a hug and kissed my cheeks. I began looking forward to this.

The whole time, I was thinking, *Who would give such a wonderful child up?* I saw other children in the orphanage. They did not fight over the toys we brought them. Instead, they shared them because they wanted everyone to experience the joy of the new toys.

On the last day, the kids were singing songs to us. Rose, the lady in charge, told us that one of the children wanted to share her story with us. To my amazement, Erica went up to speak. She smiled at me and began her story: "I am so happy to be here in the orphanage." *Happy,* I thought. *Who would be happy to be in an orphanage?* "When I was in my house," she continued, "my parents used to beat me. They threw me against the wall and hurt me."

When she was done, I ran over to tell her how proud I was of her. I looked down and saw the scar near her nose. Now I knew how she got it.

The day we left is a day I'll never forget. Everyone was crying. I held Erica for fifteen minutes, too scared to put her down. I kissed her scar, hoping, once more, to erase her memories. I told her I loved her. She stopped crying and smiled. When our time with the children was done, they waved once again through the gates. This time it was good-bye.

When I came home, I looked in my room while unpacking. I looked at all my clothes hanging in my closet on multicolored hangers. The visions of Erica's closet with two shirts in it flashed before my eyes. She tried to give me one of her stuffed animals in return for my friendship. I told her I did not need one. She said she didn't either because she had two. Erica is only seven. It will take me a long time to learn what she already knows.

JoLynn Shopteese

Kissing the Bully

I looked down at my skinny body and turned to the side. I was awkward; my knobby knees led down to thin, bony legs. I looked around, enviously watching as the other girls pulled on their bras and hooked the back. I pulled on the bra I barely fit into, the one I had forced my mom to take me to buy, just so you could see the outline through the back of my shirt. I was a late-bloomer; there was no questioning that.

I walked home from school with my equally skinny best friend Laura at my side; she had hidden her embarrassment of her not-yet-developed body with a larger-than-life attitude. It was the normal walk home: She and I were taunted by Ben and a few other boys our age who inevitably found a way to make me cry.

I reached my house, knowing that the phone would ring later that night with some crank call and muffled sounds of prepubescent boy's laughter. I knew that the same pattern would be repeated the next day: They would walk behind us on the way to school, laughing about the "wall," Ben's less-than-endearing reference to my chest.

To ease my despair, I was told, "They only do that because they like you." My dad reassured me that once I blossomed, they'd be begging to go out with me. I hadn't had a boyfriend yet, and it seemed like everyone else was well on his or her way to awkward handholding and spin-the-bottle games. I pined for some sort of attention from the opposite sex. I didn't realize at the time that the torture from Ben and his friends was actually attention.

By the ninth grade, Laura and I were no longer walking to school; we caught the number-three bus on our corner to the local high school. Ben, by this point, had moved on to hitting us with spitballs. So every morning, I had to clean the wads of gross spit-covered paper out of my hair, making sure the evidence was gone. I would yell at him to stop, which only provoked more torture. I had known him for four years at this point, and the funny thing was we considered each other friends. He would talk to me, if the other boys weren't around, and I knew, despite his tough exterior, that he actually enjoyed my company.

Throughout middle school, Ben maintained the ritual of Rollerblading to my house after school, but I'm sure he never told his friends that in the seventh grade he had held my hand down the street, teaching me to use the Rollerblades I had just received for my birthday. It seemed that the nicer he was to me in private, the meaner he had to be to me in public.

I vowed that once I "blossomed," he would want to be my boyfriend, that the group of boys who tortured me in middle school would long for me in high school. I had a cruel fantasy of one of them asking me out and my rejecting him coldly, in front of everyone. I wanted to make them feel the embarrassment I had felt during all those walks home, and on all the bus rides with spitwad-filled hair.

High school finally came along and, better late than

never, I did blossom. I grew out of my awkward, bony body. My wavy red hair grew longer and straightened itself out. Although I didn't transform, I grew up, more in mind than in body. I started to accept the freckles and felt blessed to be naturally thin. I even wore a little makeup. And my dad was right, it did happen. I finally had a boyfriend. He was from a different middle school than I had attended, and he was unaware of my uncomfortable beginnings.

I still saw Ben; we attended the same high school parties and shared the same group of friends. He teased me a bit, but it didn't really bother me as much. I went through a few boyfriends in high school, and it seemed that the awkward years were finally over.

This summer I returned home from my first year of college. Ben and I ran into each other. He stood about a foot taller than I did, and I realized how much he had grown up throughout our eight years of friendship. He lives on his own now and invited me over to see his new apartment. The walls were sparse; it looked like a college boy's room, which struck me as odd. I knew so many college boys, but it was hard for me to picture Ben as one. I still saw the skinny blond boy who sat behind me in eighth grade snapping my bra straps.

We started talking about those years, and we both laughed. A few other old friends filled the apartment, and one of Ben's old partners-in-crime leaned over and said, "You have gotten so pretty." I thanked him, smirking at the same time. It seemed like I had waited eight years for this, for my revenge.

I found myself sitting outside with Ben, and then, it happened. He leaned over, and he kissed me, something that had never happened between us before. For a second, I thought, *This is it, I can finally tell him off and embarrass him for all the times he belittled me.* But I didn't. I no longer needed revenge. I continued to look at him, and I asked, "Did you ever have a crush on me?"

And he responded, "I had a crush on you the whole time. I was just too embarrassed to tell you."

Lia Gay

A Difficult Lesson

*Of all the words of tongue or pen, the saddest
are those . . . it might have been.*

John Greenleaf Whittier

It was August 1984, Kalamazoo, Michigan, Western
Michigan University. The temperature was in the mid-
eighties, the sun was shining and it was my first day of
college. And, as if all this weren't enough, it was also the
day I met Cindy.

She was stunningly beautiful. The type of beauty that
turned heads. Casual attire and sparse amounts of
makeup reflected her confident and self-assured persona.
No need to flaunt her beauty.

Cindy and I met under precarious terms on this special
day. While riding up in the elevator, she gave me a smile,
which I returned. We got off on the same floor, which
shocked me into insinuating that she must have been
mistaken. Boys and girls on the same floor? In college? I
shrugged it off, still not believing. As I stood outside my
room, waiting for my brother's arrival with a load of my
stuff, Cindy walked down the hall directly toward me. As

she approached me, the butterflies began to stir in my stomach. Outwardly I tried to be cool, confident and funny. I calmly said with a wide grin, "I am not waiting for you." Cindy shot back with "You're a jerk" and entered her dorm room key into the very next door. I could not believe the most beautiful girl in the whole dorm lived on the other side of my wall. So much for me having a clue.

I was able to overcome my less-than-desirable first impression and we began to date. By mid-November we were an inseparable pair. We were in love. For me, this type of love was a first. We had many things in common. We were both outgoing, fun seeking and shared the same musical tastes. We shared close to a year-and-a-half of wonderful but tumultuous times. Being in love brought forth many different emotions from within me, the ma - jority of which were positive. Some however were nega- tive. Negative emotions I had never dealt with, like jealousy, the most powerful of those emotions.

Cindy and I broke up, for good, in February of 1986. I had allowed jealousy to consume, smother and destroy my first love. When I last saw Cindy, the only emotion I shared with her was anger. My anger compelled me to present to her a full envelope of pictures of good times we shared together. Pictures that, in anger, I had torn into thousands of little pieces. I did not keep one single pic- ture. Cindy opened the envelope and saw the pictures. The last words she spoke to me were the same as the first: "You're a jerk." This time she was right. The last words I spoke to her I will live with forever. I looked her in the eyes, with passion no longer of the loving kind, and said, "I don't care if I ever see you or hear from you again." And I walked away.

Unfortunately for me the story doesn't end with just another jealous young man messing up. Within that year, I began to grow up. I regretted the way I dealt with my jealousy and anger. I regretted the things I said and did that stemmed from those emotions. I wanted desperately to apologize, to make things right and tell her I didn't mean those hurtful things. I wanted to let her know that she was right, that I was a jerk and if she didn't forgive me I would understand. I wanted to tell her she was really special to me and I would always love her.

I finally got the nerve to call her one night in December however there was no answer. I found out two weeks later that my first love had died. She died the very night I had attempted to say I'm sorry, in a car accident involving a drunk driver. She died not knowing that I was sorry for my actions. She died too soon.

Rick Reed

Terri Jackson

On the first day of sixth grade, I sat in my quiet home-room class and observed all the people who I would even-tually befriend and possibly graduate with. I glanced around the room and noticed that the majority of the middle-class kids were dressed in their nicest first-day outfits. My glance stopped on a shy-looking girl in the back of the room. She wore a stained, yellow plaid shirt with a pair of frayed jeans that had obviously had several owners before her. Her hair was unusually short and unwashed. She wore dress shoes that were once white, and frilly pink socks that had lost their frill with too many wearings. I caught myself thinking, "That's disgusting. Doesn't she know what a bathtub is?" As I looked around, I figured others were probably thinking the same thing.

The teacher began checking the attendance, each per-son casually lifting his or her hand as names were called in turn.

"Terri Jackson?" the teacher asked, following the roll with her finger. Silence. "Um, Terri Jackson?"

Finally we heard a meek answer from the back of the room, followed by the sound of ripping cloth. We all shifted in our seats to see what had happened.

"Scary Terri ripped the armpit of her shirt!" one boy joked.

"Eww, I bet it's a hundred years old!" another girl commented. One comment after another brought a roar of laughter.

I was probably laughing the loudest. Sadly, making Terri feel insecure made me feel secure and confident. It was a good break from the awkward silence and uncomfortable first-day jitters.

Terri Jackson was the joke of the whole sixth grade that year. If we had nothing to talk about, Terri's trip through the lunchroom was an entertaining conversation starter. Her grandma-looking dress, missing front tooth and stained gym clothes kept us mocking and imitating her for hours.

At my twelfth birthday party, ten giggly, gossipy girls were playing Truth or Dare, a favorite party game. We had just finished a Terri Jackson discussion. It was my turn at the game.

"Umm . . . Sydney! Truth or Dare?" one of my friends asked.

"How about a dare? Bring it on. I'll do anything." Oh, if only I'd known what she was about to say.

"Okay, I dare you to invite Terri Jackson over to your house next Friday for two whole hours!"

"Two whole hours?! Please ask something else, *please!*" I begged. "How could anybody do that?" But my question was drowned out by a sea of giggly girls slapping their hands over their mouths and rolling on the floor, trying to contain their laughter.

The next day, I cautiously walked up to Terri as if her body odor was going to make me fall over dead. My friends huddled and watched from a corner to see if I would follow through with the brave dare.

I managed to choke out, "Hey Scary—I mean Terri—
you want to come over for two hours Friday?" I didn't see
her face light up because I had turned to my friends and
made a gagging expression. When I was satisfied with
their laughter of approval, I turned back to Terri. Terri's
face was buried in her filthy hands; she was crying. I
couldn't stand it. Half of me felt the strongest compassion
for her, but the other half wanted to slap her for making
me look so cruel and heartless. That was exactly what I
was being.

"What's got you all upset? All I did was invite you
over," I whispered, trying not to show my concern.

She looked up and watched my eyes for what seemed
like forever. "Really?" That was all she could say. Her
seldom-heard voice almost startled me.

"I guess so, if you're up to it." My voice sounded surprisingly sincere. I'd never seen her flash her toothless
smile so brightly. The rest of the day I had a good feeling,
and I was not dreading the two-hour visit as I had before.
I was almost looking forward to it.

Friday rolled around quickly. My time with Terri passed
by in a flash as the two hours slipped into four hours, and
I found myself actually enjoying her company. We chat-
ted about her family and her battles with poverty. We discovered that we both played violin, and my favorite part
of the afternoon occurred when she played the violin for
me. I was amazed by how beautifully she played.

I would love to tell you that Terri and I became best
friends and that from then on I ignored all my other
friends' comments. But that's not how it happened. While
I no longer participated in the Terri bashings and even
tried to defend her at times, I didn't want to lose everyone
else's acceptance just to gain Terri's.

Terri disappeared after the sixth grade. No one is sure
what happened to her. We think that she may have trans-

ferred to a different school because of how cruelly the kids
treated her. I still think about her sometimes and wonder
what she's doing. I guess all I can do is hope that she is
being accepted and loved wherever she is.

I realize now how insecure and weak I was during that
sixth-grade year. I participated in the cruel, heartless
Terri-bashing sessions because they seemed kind of funny
in a distorted way. But they were only funny because
they falsely boosted my own self-confidence; I felt bigger
by making someone else feel smaller. I know now that
true confidence is not proven by destroying another's
self-esteem, but rather, by having the strength to stand
up for the Terri Jacksons of the world.

Sydney Fox

Children's Eyes

What kind of world is it my friend
    that little children see?
I wonder if they see God first
    because they just believe?

Do they see strength in caring eyes
    who watch them as they play—
or maybe love through gentle hands
    that guide them on their way?

Do you think they dream of future times
    when they would be a king—
    or just enjoy their present life
    while with their friends they sing?

Do they see the acts of kindness
    done for people who are poor?
Is the very best in everyone
    what they are looking for?

And when the day is over,
    as they close their eyes to sleep,

do they look forward to tomorrow
with its promises to keep?

If this is what the children see,
then it should be no surprise,
the world would be a better place
if we all had children's eyes.

Tom Krause

Reprinted with permission of Randy Glasbergen.

Courage

Darkness cannot drive out darkness; only light can do that. Hate cannot drive out hate, only love can do that.

Martin Luther King Jr.

The excited sound of seventh-grade laughter and voices tumbled down the hallway as the students filed into the gym. I scanned the room, searching for my friends, and soon spotted them near the door to the restroom. I weaved my way through the mass of people and sat down next to my best friend, Lauren.

"So, what exactly are we doing here?" she questioned.

"Well, according to Mrs. Marks, we're supposed to be listening to a speaker about bullying, peer pressure and put-downs." I said this somewhat sarcastically, because the entire year our grade had been lectured over and over again on these topics. We were earning the reputation as the worst class in the school, which was not a reputation that my friends nor I were particularly proud of. As our science teacher stood in front of the entire grade level, attempting to get our attention, my friends and I sat back, prepared to sit through another monotonous speech full of harsh remarks about "Kids these days . . ." and "Your maturity level when you put someone down is no greater than that of an eight-year-old."

But as soon as she started talking, I snapped to attention. She had this way about her, as if she knew how to reach into our minds and souls and make us think. And for once, I actually began to think about what it was she was preaching about. I thought about all the kids who came to school every day, despite knowing that they would have to face cruel comments and sneering faces all day long.

One boy, in particular, came to mind. Every day, this boy came to first hour late, and I suspected it was because he needed to get medicine from the nurse. But this didn't stop the kids in the class from making fun of him. They punched him in the shoulder and said, "Hey, man! Where have you been?" And then another would add, "How's that girlfriend of yours? Oh sorry, we forgot. You don't *have* a girlfriend. You only have *boyfriends*." This harassment would continue until the teacher cut in, forcing the boys to stop. But it was too late—it always was. The boy would put his head down on his desk in shame. The worst, though, was when he tried to retaliate. His attackers only laughed and continued the cruelty until the entire room was laughing at his expense.

As I sat in the auditorium, absorbing everything the speaker had to say, thoughts of this poor boy crept into my head. I sighed, thinking how sorry I felt for him, not that there was anything I could do. I tuned back into the speaker and listened intently to her words of wisdom.

"Now, before I leave today, I would like to give everyone here an opportunity to say *anything* he or she wants to on the subject of bullying or peer pressure. You may apologize to a friend, thank someone for his or her kindness, *anything*. And this is the one time I can promise that *no one*, but *no one*, will laugh at you."

The stillness in the room made me believe her. Slowly, I saw a few hands raise tentatively in the air behind me. One girl wanted to apologize to a friend she had been ignoring recently. Another thanked a boy for his kindness when she slipped on the steps the other day. It was then that my moment of courage happened. The speaker called on me, and with shaking hands and clammy palms, I began to talk.

"What you said today really made sense. I know that it's true, because I see it every day in class. There is one person who is always made fun of. It doesn't matter why—it could be the way he looks, talks or even takes notes." My voice shook. "I think that everyone here has made fun of him at one time or another. I know I have. And now I really regret it. To us, it may just be a game, but to him, it must hurt. And I think . . . well, I think we need to stop."

Scared of my classmates' reaction, I felt like the silence that followed lasted forever. But then, soft clapping started in the front of the room, quickly spreading through the entire crowd. By the time I looked up, the soft pitter-patter had turned into a thunderous roar of applause. I had voiced something that everyone was feeling.

Later on that day, the boy whom I had been talking about came up to me privately and said thank you.

I noticed that from that day on, people began to treat him a little better. The teasing stopped, and people greeted him in the halls with a friendly, "Hi!" It was those little, everyday things that I noticed, and I'm sure he noticed them, too.

Ruth Ann Supica

Accentuating Difference

Julia and I met in math class—right before lunch. We soon realized that we both hated word problems, both loved egg salad sandwiches and both thought Bobby Bisbee was the only boy we could ever kiss. During recesses, we were inseparable. One Friday, Julia had an idea. "Hey, let's make plans for the weekend," she said. "We could have a sleep-over or something."

We were both so excited we couldn't sit still during math, or any other class. But when the bell sounded the end of school, I suddenly got very nervous.

"Hi, Talia. How was school today?" my mom asked with a smile. Today, her warm and caring hello did not sound comforting. Instead, all I heard in the loving syllables was her thick foreign accent.

I was so embarrassed. Julia and I were no longer the same. The sound of my mom's voice made me feel like an outsider. What would Julia think?

I didn't have to wait long to find out. From across the schoolyard, I saw Julia pulling her mother towards us.

"Hello, I'm Julia's mother. I hear the girls want to get together this weekend."

"Oh, that sounds wonderful," my mom replied.

But all I heard was the *v* replacing the *w* and the roll of the *r*: *vonderrrful*.

I was mortified. Were they staring? Had Julia changed her mind? Did I dare look into her eyes? I did. She answered my unspoken fears with an excited smile while our moms exchanged phone numbers. That Sunday we went to the movies.

Years later, Julia and I sit on my bed talking. Graduation is only days away. Julia has plans of becoming a math and physics major and I no longer like egg salad sandwiches. Neither of us has ever kissed Bobby Bisbee. (There are others who have left much more permanent marks on our hearts and our lips.) My mom comes into my room to see what we're up to. We tell her of our plans to spend the afternoon with friends at the beach, and maybe see a movie after dinner. "That sounds wonderful," she replies.

I no longer hear the *v* replacing a *w* in her speech. But I think it still does. Somewhere in the passing of math classes and lunch recesses, I realized that it is my mom's cheerful, compassionate nature that people hear, and love. She shares my excitements and frustrations with overflowing compassion, tender words and rolling *r*s. Sometimes, she still reminds me that I am different. But I think that differences between people are as valuable as similarities. As my mom closes the door, I look at Julia and smile. Our friendship has been strengthened not only by our shared interests but also by our distinctly differing ones.

Daphna Renan

$\overline{6}$

TOUGH STUFF

The soul would have no rainbow had the eyes no tears.

John Vance Cheney

Your heart is not living until it has experienced pain . . . the pain of love breaks open the heart, even if it is as hard as a rock.

Hazret Inayat Khan

11:21 A.M.

[AUTHOR'S NOTE: *I was a junior at Columbine High School and was in the choir room when the shootings began. I wrote this poem after the tragedy to help me deal with the pain and grief. My classmates and I are still struggling with the emotional trauma, but we continue to heal. We are so grateful to the officers, firefighters and others who saved people's lives that day. I would like to thank everyone throughout the world for their ongoing support and prayers as we begin to rebuild.*]

> I lie on my bed
>   numb,
>   unemotional,
>   non-feeling.
> Fear stains my memories as I reflect
>   on a placid morning in Littleton.
> A usual day in choir.
> We prepare for concerts,
>   blithely indulging in normal routine.
> Carefree . . . Content . . .
>   Unaware. . . .

A sudden blast startles us.
A chemistry explosion?
Deafening eruptions penetrate "Ave Maria."
Sinuous voices now punctuated by gunshots,
    the demonic splintering the angelic.

The choir hushes
    to the rhythm of pounding hearts.
Students scream through halls
    as terror burns itself on innocent faces.

Tick, Tick, Tick—11:21—
    lives are forever changed.
Shock . . . Hysteria. . . .
    Why?
The sound of bombs ignite horror through our veins
    and send chills
    that pinch the skin like needles.

Some run.
Some stand paralyzed in shock,
    numbness engulfing all other emotions.
Billows of powder now blanket the hall,
    creating ghostly images.
I look through the delicate webs of cotton
    and see the fruits of hatred.
Bullets shatter glass
    and invade bodies,
    as malice sears the souls of the perpetrators.

A student prays;
    another hides in stunned confusion;
    a teacher bleeds.

Like children
    we are helpless,
    longing to be in mama's arms.

Screaming . . . Frantic . . .
    Why?

Two faces
    are plastered against the window.
The horror in their eyes strips away
    my consciousness.
My first instinct is to run;
    I duck as bullets spray the halls.

Our school is now the grounds of warfare—
    mortal fighting
    in a field of bombs and bullets.
Weapons that have fallen into the wrong hands
    have only one purpose and they
    are killing us and all I hear is gunfire.
Crackling, Crackling,
Humming, bursting, screaming, ringing, what now,
Too much
Too soon
Too young
So scared
Help us.

I struggle to escape but am slowed
    as if trudging through water.
Through the front doors I see milky clouds
    that absorb the sun;
I see golden light and sunburned pavement.
I cannot get there fast enough.

I am almost to the door.
A bullet ricochets off the pane.
The glass swirls like a droplet on water,
    creating rings that shiver and spread,
    shattering as I dash through the door—

All is silent.
I have escaped hell.

There is a dark room
  where ten broken bodies lie,
  and where others play dead.
In the darkness of the library,
  angels embrace the lifeless,
  and their wings flicker light
  against a wall of helpless shadows.
God now wraps His arms
  around the school
  and gathers the souls of the lost,
  makes strong the souls of the weak,
  cries for the violence on Earth.

Time picks up and I am
  vulnerable, insecure.
A dog's bark screams like bullets.
Who to trust?
Our haven is destroyed,
  and we are scattered.

I sit immobilized,
  while anxiety and guilt wrap themselves around me
  and consume me.
Angry . . . Numb . . .
  Why?
Are there answers in silence . . . ?
Because I am asking you and you don't answer . . .

Or maybe the silence is just you listening.

Joanna Gates

Tears

I did not cry for Michigan.
It seemed before my time.
I did not cry for Jonesboro,
too far away to mind.
I did not cry for Palisades
even though it may be mine.
I did not cry for Conyers, Georgia
By then it all seemed fine.
But I poured my heart right through my eyes
The day they shot up Columbine.

The tears they fell for children lost
And children on the line.
My head fell quick into my hands
for parents who must pine.
My eyes stayed glossy to a screen
Watching kids of my own climb.

But,
What shook my body up the most,
What made it hard to breathe,

What bolted all my stomach down
And wouldn't let me leave.
What made me think about those boys
And try to empathize
Was the fright, the fear, the look of death
In one scared victim's eyes.

She described a scene so horror filled
So wrapped with movie cuts.
I thought about these kids and film,
what put them in their ruts.
I ruled out only media—
we all watch similar things
But combined with loneliness and fear
Who knows what games can bring?

One lesson to be learned from this,
The only one for which I'm sure,
Is that a gun manufacturer, movie title, music
    lyric, parent, anti-depressant, Internet,
    trench-coat, insult, or whatever else,
Is not the thing at fault.
And no gun policy, censorship, parent in jail,
    drug ban, Web-site check, dress code, sus-
    pension, or whatever else,
Would have removed their every thought.
We must take looks inside ourselves, accept-
    ing looks with love.
For what they didn't like in someone else,
Is what they saw in themselves.

Jamie Rowen

Can That Be?

[AUTHOR'S NOTE: *I would like to submit the enclosed poem by my daughter Kelly, who was a sophomore. Kelly was a beautiful, kind and loving teenager with a heart of gold. She loved to write short stories and poetry, and wanted to become a published author. Kelly's life came to a tragic end, however, on April 20, 1999 when she was shot and killed in the library at Columbine High School. Kelly touched many hearts along her life's journey. A former middle-school teacher described her as "a gentle soul who walked among us that would never be forgotten." Kelly will remain forever in the hearts of those who loved her. This is one of Kelly's poems written in December 1998. Thank you for keeping Littleton in your prayers.*

God bless,
Dee Fleming]

> I step outside what did I hear?
> I heard the whispers and
> The cries of people's fear.
> The loneliness of wisdom,
> Can that be?

The sad, sad sorrow that I see,
That is past in the tree.
Is it true? Can it be real?
Can I let them know how I really feel?
The things that I have seen,
The things that I have felt,
The feelings of sorrow that
I hope will soon melt.
I walked through the distances
And thought how it should be,
Of the smiles and the laughter,
That is what I thought it should be.
But can that be?
I walked past the dark houses,
And crossed the open fields.
I walked to the tree to kneel
I took a deep long breath
Then I closed my eyes.
I counted to three,
Then I open my eyes,
I was in my room,
That was a surprise.
But then I had seen that it was just a dream.
I walked to the window and pulled on the string.
What a surprise to see the sunrise.
In the distance were children with laughter and happiness,
That was the thought that I like to see!
But of course can that really be?
Or can this be another dream?

Kelly Ann Fleming

Fire and Rain

Leslie had the most incredible voice. When she sang everyone would get very quiet as if making a sound would stop this beautiful angel from singing. She played the drums, the piano and was strikingly beautiful. Her presence captivated me. Every time I looked at her or heard her voice, I knew that Leslie was going to do wonderful things with her life.

We used to sit by the piano for hours singing James Taylor and Carly Simon songs. She taught me how to harmonize. When we sang together nothing else mattered. It was always a way for me to achieve instant happiness.

I remember when Leslie met Mike. "This one is different," she would tell me. "He is so grown up, very mature." He wasn't like the high-school boys she was used to dating. She was so excited that he had asked her to pick him up at the airport. He had been out of town visiting relatives, and he couldn't wait an extra minute to see her. She borrowed her parents' car.

I was told two days later that Leslie was dead. She had had a couple beers before leaving for the airport. She had a six-pack in the back seat. It was assumed the beers were for their reunion. She drove off the side of the road and hit a boulder. They didn't find her until thirty-six hours later, although the search had started immediately after Mike reported her missing.

Sometimes I sit quietly, scared to make a sound. I only wish I that I could hear her singing. I softly hum the tune of "Fire and Rain." I am alone. My beautiful angel must be singing somewhere else.

Anonymous

Minutes Like Hours

You walk into the store
and stride down the aisle.
You pick me up and
try to look casual while
you carry me down
to the checkout line.
Pull out your wallet,
you soon will be mine.
Your friends are observing
every move that you make.
The clerk asks for ID—
you show him a fake.
You quickly walk down
to the front of the store.
Your friends are waiting for you
as you step out the door.
You hop in the car
and drive away from the shop.
Then you shut off the ignition,
and pop off my top.
You take a few drinks

and pass me around.
That's when you decide
to take a drive around town.
You turn on your car
and put your foot on the clutch.
I'm sober, you think,
I didn't have very much.
You pull onto the road
with me by your side,
Taking occasional sips
as you enjoy the ride.
Then the brakes on the car
in front of you squeal.
You try hard to stop,
but lose control of the wheel.
You skid off the road,
and you know you have crashed.
The dashboard is shattered,
the windshield is smashed.
Minutes like hours,
You're in treacherous pain,
that washes your senses,
envelops your brain.
The screams all around you
are faint to your ears,
as life flashes before you,
your hopes and your fears.
Minutes like hours,
you plead and you pray,
I'll never touch it again,
just let me live one more day.
Your mind starts to go dark,
it falls apart piece by piece.
And then you slip into blackness,
the pain has finally ceased.

Before you entered that store,
you should have thought twice,
for I am the substance
that cost you your life.

Vidhya Chandrasekaran

Life After Mom

Shopping was one of the few activities my mom and I could manage without arguing. We had a policy of not fighting in public, and besides, I trusted her when it came to clothes. She would tell me if an item was too tight, or too baggy, or too short, and I rarely disagreed. When we weren't rifling the sale racks, though, we couldn't seem to agree on *anything*. We fought fiercely and often—about my boyfriend, my curfew, even my hair, which, she insisted, was always hanging in my eyes. Whenever I refused to help her around the house—which was nearly every time she asked—she complained about my "bad attitude." When I talked back, she said I had a "fresh mouth." I remember screaming at her more than once to get out of my life and get one of her own.

So it was pretty amazing that the moment we stepped into the fluorescent hum of the local mall, the fighting automatically stopped. For an hour or two at a time, it even felt like my mother and I were friends.

That's what made it doubly painful when I had to go shopping for a dress without her one steaming July afternoon just after I'd turned seventeen. My aunt guided me into the fitting room of a local department store, where an overly eager salesclerk kept toting bright, flowered dresses back to me, saying things like, "What about this one?" and "Now I *think* this one would look great on you." As I pulled a dark blue dress over my head, I heard my aunt explaining in a polite whisper, "No flowered dresses, please. We're looking for something to wear to a funeral. Her mother just died."

Her mother just died. I mouthed the words to myself in the mirror. I hated the way they looked, so clipped and to the point, so final.

The words made me think of the social worker who had approached me in the hospital hallway three days earlier, as my mother lay hooked up to tubes and monitors in a nearby room. My younger sister, who'd been rushed home from summer camp that morning, was sitting on the floor crying softly, while my father wandered aimlessly through the hospital halls in his baseball cap, as if he'd forgotten the directions to the field. I was frantically pacing back and forth in front of my mother's door when the social worker backed me up against the wall.

"Your mother is very sick," she said to me in a slow, controlled voice. "And . . ."

"I know," I interrupted. "She's had cancer for more than a year."

She shook her head. "Hope," she said, "listen to me. Your mother is going to die."

"I know," I said quickly, trying to act as if I'd known this all along. But, of course, I hadn't. Yes, I'd been aware that my mother had a breast removed after a doctor found a cancerous lump in it when I was fifteen. Yes, I knew she took huge, white pills with her orange juice every morning, and I'd seen her body swell almost an additional forty pounds from the drugs. And yes, I'd watched helplessly from the bathroom door when she sat on the rim of the tub crying as the first clumps of hair came out in her hand.

But no, I'd never seriously thought about the possibility that my mom might actually die. Because I couldn't imagine the rest of us—my father, my fourteen-year-old sister, my nine-year-old brother, and me—surviving without my mother. As I stood mutely outside the bathroom, listening to her vomit quietly after she came home from her chemotherapy shots, I'd tell myself that cancer was, like most other illnesses, something that time and rest and prescription drugs would eventually heal. If one of my friends said "cancer" in my presence and then looked at me guiltily and apologized, I'd say, "What are you sorry for? My mother's going to be fine." Even as she started growing noticeably weaker and could no longer leave her room, I kept running off to movies and outdoor concerts with my friends as if any morning now she'd wake up in perfect health again.

After the social worker left me with a few pamphlets about grieving—"After the death of a loved one, you may feel angry," one of them said, "You may also want to deny the loss"—I sat alone in the hospital waiting room. *This can't be happening,* I kept thinking. *Someone, please tell me this isn't real.*

We never said a true good-bye, my mother and I. The last time I saw her conscious I said, "I love you," but the words felt clumsy and foreign in my mouth; I couldn't remember ever saying them to her. She said, "I love you, too," but her tone was empty, distracted, vague. The cancer had reached her brain by then, and she was already on her way to someplace else.

After the funeral—after my sister returned to camp, my father went back to work, and my brother started spending afternoons at the house of a friend—I spent days searching our house room by room, looking for the good-bye note I was certain my mother had left for me. I checked underneath each piece of clothing in her drawers, between her cookbooks, even inside her jewelry box and medicine chest. But if there was a note, I never found it, and that preoccupied "I love you, too" has echoed in my head ever since.

That fall, I was greeted at school with a symphony of whispers and furtive nods. Over the summer, I'd transformed from The Girl Who Writes for the Yearbook into The Girl Whose Mother Just Died. It gave me a strange sort of celebrity. Sophomore year, when Linda Grassi's mother died, we'd all solemnly whispered the news to each other in the hallways as she walked by. I remember how Linda had hurried past us as if she were doing just fine, but how up close, you could see that something had gone flat in her eyes. I wondered, as my senior year started, if people could see a difference in me, too.

Because I'd changed that summer. My whole family had. When my father, sister, and I returned from the hospital the morning my mother died, we joined my younger brother at the kitchen table and blinked quizzically at each other, as if to ask, "What now?" Only after my mother was gone did I understand that she'd been the adhesive that had held us all together.

We began eating microwaved dinners with a television on the table in the place where she used to sit, pretending to be absorbed in *Wheel of Fortune* reruns. Silence and awkwardness filled the kitchen, which had once been the site of lively conversations about everyone's day. My sister, brother, and I became afraid to even mention our mother, because one of us might start to cry, and if one person started, the others might too, and there is little in this world more terrifying than watching your father start weeping into his macaroni and cheese.

I wish I could say my family pulled closer together to get through the crisis, but the truth is exactly the opposite.

After dinner we each spun off like satellites into our respective bedrooms. My father watched television and smoked cigarettes in his; I read or talked on the telephone in mine. I don't know how my brother and sister passed those long hours before sleep. I couldn't bear the way their eyes pleaded with me, the oldest sister, to make everything all right. They'd both been close to our mother and they missed her terribly, but I didn't know how to reach out to them when I needed so much comfort myself. If either of them knocked on my door for company, I'd quickly shout, "I'm busy!" and pretend I didn't hear their sad sighs and disappointed footsteps retreating down the hall. After our mother was gone, whatever comfort each of us was to find in the house, we had to find alone.

At school, most of my friends treated me with special caution. "How are you?" they would ask with hesitant smiles. "Fine, I'm fine," was always my reply, because what was I supposed to do, tell them the truth? And then they'd exhale with relief and quickly change the subject. I couldn't really blame them: They'd known my mother well, and her death must have been almost as shocking to them as it was to me.

My friend Gillian recently told me about the thought that she couldn't put out of her mind that year: "I kept telling myself, 'Oh my God. If it could happen to Hope's mother, it could happen to *mine.*'" The few times I tried to talk on the phone with my best friend about my mom I started sobbing uncontrollably and had to hang up. Because I didn't know who to turn to for help, I'd try to force myself into calmness. *Stop being a baby*, I scolded myself. *Grow up. Be strong.*

Eventually, I would. But first I became angry and defensive. I grew furious at the doctors who hadn't saved my mother. I got mad at my father when he asked me to take over a household task my mother had once done; I looked at his request symbolically, as though he was trying to get me to replace my mother somehow. If my sister dared to ask me for a favor, I'd yell at her to grow up and do it herself. I'd even snap at people I barely knew. Any time a well-meaning stranger said, "I'm sorry," after hearing that my mother had died, I'd spit back: "What are *you* sorry for? It wasn't *your* fault."

As my senior year drew to an end, I watched as my friends did things with their mothers—shopping for a prom dress, packing items into boxes bound for college—that I had to do alone. Other girls were slowly starting to view their mothers more as friends, which I resented, because I would never get that chance. But most of all, I was angry with myself, for having fought so much with my mother and for failing to make her life a little easier, as I imagined, in retrospect, that I could have.

My mother always told me all people are fundamentally equal, but her death taught me this wasn't true. By the time I started college, the world felt divided into girls who had mothers and girls who didn't. Linda Grassi, my sister, and I were the only ones I knew in the latter category. I felt ashamed of my fractured family, and I didn't want to be pitied.

So for most of my freshman year, I hardly told anyone that my mother had died. Among my new friends, I made vague references to "my family" rather than "my parents." When the other girls in my dorm pulled their telephones into the halls to call their mothers on Sunday afternoons, I pretended to be absorbed in a history textbook. When a group of friends knocked on my door and invited me to join them to buy Mother's Day cards at a local store, I thanked them but said I had other plans.

It didn't take me long to notice other significant differences between girls who had mothers and me. A C-minus on an exam would shake me up, but it didn't make me phone home in tears. When I received a rejection letter for a summer job I'd applied for, I just shrugged my shoulders and said, "Oh well." My roommate asked, "Why aren't you upset?" and the only answer I could think of was, "I know what a *real* crisis feels like, and this doesn't even compare."

In college, I discovered the special bond that mother-less daughters share. My closest friend there had gone to boarding school since she was twelve and saw her mother only once or twice a year. Two of the women I admired most in my dorm had lost their mother during childhood. As these new friends and I slowly built the trust we needed to share our feelings about something so private, we discovered we had much more in common than the absence of a family member we'd loved. Since then, I've met dozens of other motherless daughters who are similar in very specific ways. Most of us say that our family's house no longer felt much like a "home" after our mothers died, and many of us admit that we often expect our boyfriends to "mother" us, and we get angry and upset when they don't. But most of us also agree that we feel more self-sufficient than our friends because we had to learn how to take care of ourselves at a much earlier age, and that early loss helped toughen us to a point where we feel capable of handling just about anything that comes our way.

People sometimes say to me, "If your mother died when you were in high school, you must be over it by now." But I don't think losing your mother is something you ever really "get over"—I think it's something you have to learn to live with. I know that after a while my mom's death stopped feeling like something awful that happened to me and just became something that was a part of me. That's when I started being able to think about my mother without automatically feeling guilty, or getting angry, or collapsing into tears.

But sometimes I feel like crying when I see a mother and daughter together in a dressing room. I wish I could call her for advice when I'm feeling low. I wish she could meet my boyfriend. I'd even like to hear her tell me my bangs are too long, just one more time.

The other day, a new friend learned that I had lost my mother when I was seventeen. "Oh," he said. "I'm sorry." I couldn't help smiling. "Thank you," I told him. "So am I."

Hope Edelman

Defining Myself

Without a struggle, there can be no progress.

Fredrick Douglass

My dad died when I was four. My brother was two and my sister only one. Soon after, our family grew to five children, as I found myself with a half-sister and then a half-brother. We lived in the poorest part of the city; the projects were only a block away.

My mother, a widow in her twenties with five kids, couldn't handle it. She became an alcoholic and a drug user. Her expensive drug habit caused her to use all the money she could get her hands on for drugs. Although we were on welfare, she didn't use the money for the food we needed. Instead, she used the money to help support her drug habit. Her routine became a normal occurrence: she sent each one of us kids to the store with a food stamp. We'd buy something for a quarter or less, then give the change to her. We soon began to rely on the food given out by homeless shelters in order to eat. We would receive a bag and walk through a line as donated food, such as TV dinners or canned green beans, was dropped in our bags.

Not only were we deprived of a proper diet, but our poverty prevented us from experiencing the normal joys that kids look forward to, such as Christmas. Although we swallowed our pride when we had no choice but to seek food donations, it was hardest during the holidays. Each winter, our thin, hand-me-down clothing and holed shoes forced us to accept free clothes and a voucher for new shoes at the local church, which we then exchanged as Christmas gifts. Knowing that our clothes came from this organization made it impossible to believe in Santa, tainting our holiday spirit.

Soon, my mom began disappearing for days at a time. In a way, it was better when she wasn't around because we didn't have to live in fear of her mental and physical abuse, like the beatings and heartless name-callings. One night, after my mom threw a lamp at me, nailing me on the side of the head, and a plastic vase at my sister, hitting her in the eye, I made the toughest decision that I ever had to make. I called Child Protective Services, while my sisters cried beside me, begging me not to. Although my mom had been reported before for abuse and neglect, we had always been prepared, cleaning the house beforehand and lying about our situation. Since I was a good student and none of us were troublemakers, we were convincing. We made everyone believe that we had a great life. But while we could lie to everyone else, we could no longer lie to ourselves.

We were put into foster care. My sister and I were placed with an elderly couple in the country, my brother stayed in the city with another family, and my half-sister and half-brother went to live with their dads. We were permitted to visit with my mom once a week, that is if she showed up. When she did come to see us, which averaged about once every two months, she promised us that she was getting an apartment so that we could live together once again.

It's been four years now since I made that call. No one has heard from my mom in over two and a half years. We don't even know if she's dead or alive. Although my brother walked down the wrong path for a while having stolen a car, he was released from detention center early for good behavior and vows to turn his life around. My sister has been adopted by a family who lives in a nice neighborhood. She's on a swim team and finally getting good grades. My half-sister still lives with her father. Her dad remarried a wonderful woman who treats her like her own daughter. Unfortunately, we lost contact with our little half-brother, and we haven't had any luck finding him. He'll be turning six soon.

And me? I'd like to say that I'm doing pretty well. I just turned sixteen, and I have finally found stability in my life, which has helped me excel and succeed in many areas. I've been on the honor roll for five years, and I'm involved in way too many school activities. I'm even in a volunteer group that promotes the fight against drugs and alcohol. I'm a good advocate of the anti-drug campaign because I know from firsthand experience what happens when drugs run your life: they ruin not only your own life, but the lives of those around you. I tell my story and amaze people with my positive attitude, despite all that I've been through. My adoptive mom says, "You've definitely made some sweet lemonade out of all the sour lemons you've been handed."

What I went through, all my hardships and pain, they're part of who I am. I'll always feel like I'm different, and I'll always have to fight the feelings that I wasn't good enough, not even for my own mom. But I'm not going to let those feelings define me. I will only let them make me stronger. And I know that I'm going to be somebody. Actually, I already am.

Morgan Mullens-Landis

A Name in the Sand

I sit on the rocky edge of a boulder, letting my feet dangle in the stillness of the water, and gaze out at the rippling waves crawling into shore like an ancient sea turtle. A salty mist hangs above the water, and I can feel it gently kissing my face. I lick my lips and can taste the familiar presence of salt from the ocean water. Above my head seagulls circle, searching the shallow, clear water for food and calling out to one another. And in my hand rests. . . .

The sound of a hospital bed being rolled down the hallway outside my mother's hospital room brought me out of my daydreams. The ocean was gone and all that was left was a bare hospital room, its only decorations consisting of flowers, cards and seashells carefully arranged on a table next to my mother's bed.

My mother was diagnosed with cancer about a year ago, a year full of months spent in various hospitals, radia - tion therapy, doses of chemotherapy and other methods to try to kill the cancer eating away at her life. But the tumors keep growing and spreading, and all the treat- ments have done is weaken her already frail body. The disease is now in its final course and, although nobody has told me, I know my mother won't be coming home this time.

I tried to change my thoughts, and they once again returned to my daydreams. Everything seemed so clear and so real, the sound of the waves, the taste of salt, the seagulls, and the . . . what was in my hand? I glanced down at my hands and realized I was holding my mother's favorite shell. I placed it against my ear, and the sound of the ocean sent cherished memories crashing into my mind.

Every year, my mother, my father and I would spend our summer vacations in a little cabin down by the ocean. As a little girl, I would explore this stretch of sand with my parents. Walking hand-in-hand, they would swing me high into the air as we ran to meet the incoming surf. And it was there, in those gentle waves, where my parents first taught me how to swim. I would wear my favorite navy blue-and-white striped swimsuit, and my father's strong arms would support me, while my mother's gentle hands would guide me through the water. After many mouthfuls of swallowed salty ocean water I could swim by myself, while my parents stood close by, proudly and anxiously watching over me. And it was in those grains of sand, not on a piece of paper that could be saved and displayed on a refrigerator, that I first painstakingly wrote my name.

My family's fondest memories weren't captured on film and put in a photo album, but were captured in the sand, wind and water of the ocean. Last summer was the final time my family would ever go to the ocean all together. This summer was nearly over and had been filled with memories of various hospitals, failed treatments, false hopes, despair, sorrow and tears.

I glanced over at my mother lying in her hospital bed,

peacefully asleep after the doctor had given her some medicine for her pain. I wanted to cry out to God, "Why, why my mother? How can I live without her to help me through my life? Don't take her away from my father and me!" My tears and sobs began to fade away, as the dripping of my mother's IV hypnotized me into a restless sleep.

* * * *

"Ashes to ashes, and dust to dust," droned the pastor, while my father and I spread my mother's ashes over the ocean water. Some of them fell into the water and dissolved, while others were caught in the wind and carried away. This was my mother's final wish—to be in the place she loved the most, where all her favorite memories live on.

As the funeral concluded and people began to drift away saying words of comfort to my father and me, I stayed behind to say my final farewell to Mother. I carried her favorite shell that brought her so much comfort while she was in the hospital and unable to hear the sounds of the ocean. I put it to my ear and the sound of the ocean seemed almost muted. I looked into the shell and was surprised to find a piece of paper stuck inside of it. I pulled the paper out and read its words:

> To my daughter, I will always love you and be with you.

> A name in the sand will never last,
> The waves come rolling into shore high and fast.
> And wash the lines away,
> But not the memories we shared that day
> Where we have trod this sandy shore,
> Our traces we left there will be no more.

But, wherever we are,
   The memories will never be far.
   Although I may not be with you,
   Know that my love for you will always be true.
   Those memories will last forever,
   And in them we shall always be together.
   Hold them close to your heart,
   And know that from your side I will never part.

As I crossed the beach, I stooped and wrote my mother's name in the sand. I continued onward, turning only to cast one last lingering look behind, and the waves had already begun to wash my lines away.

Elizabeth Stumbo

Train Tracks

"Alison, come on out and play," my best friend yelled through the screen door. Many summer mornings, I ran through the old house, my long red hair flying after me, to meet Manda on the rickety front steps.

"Watcha wanna do t'day?" she always asked.

"Oh, I dunno. Let's go play at the Ol' Station again."

The Ol' Station was once a train station in 1912, but it was no longer in use. The tracks were rusty, but trains used them all the same. A narrow gravel road cut through the old train tracks and was used to lead to the housing area in which Manda and I lived.

Playing at the Ol' Station was more than fun, it was an eight-year-old's dream. Imaginations ran wild, friendships blossomed, and the day's worries were forgotten at the Ol' Station. Manda and I loved to run down the train tracks searching for granite rocks and old money that might have been left from the station's productive days. When we were younger, we would dress in our mothers' clothes and pretend we were ladies of America's elite, waiting for a train of riches. When one of us became angry with the other, we would run down the tracks, either as far as we were allowed or until we couldn't breathe.

One day, in a fit of rage against Manda, I started sprinting down the tracks, when her foot caught and she tripped.

"Ouch! Oh my gosh, Alison, help me!"

I looked back to find Manda lying on the tracks, bawling like I'd never seen my tough friend bawl before. I ran back to her. "What's wrong? Are you okay?"

"I tripped and hurt my knee."

I looked at the badly skinned knee.

"It's just a little blood. Here, you hop on my back and I'll carry you home." So that's what we did—I gave her a piggyback ride home.

Over the years, Manda and I had gone our separate ways, but we still considered ourselves friends. Beginning our ninth-grade year, we had only one class together, and that was Algebra I. We both hated math with a violent passion and hated our teacher equally as much. Manda sat behind me, so I spent most of the class time passing notes to Manda that made fun of Mrs. Madlock, whom we'd nicknamed "The Green Heifer" due to her large build and green shirts.

"Guess what today is?" Manda asked me during class one day.

"September nineteenth?"

"Yeah, but today is soccer try-out day!" Manda had always wanted to play soccer. "I've practiced so hard, the coach would be an idiot not to put me on the team."

"Alison, turn around and shut up. You have all weekend to talk to Manda." Mrs. Madlock barked at me. Smiling at Manda, I turned around to learn about the exciting world of algebra.

That night, I went out of town to watch my brother's first football game of the season. I couldn't help but wonder if Manda had made the soccer team; after all, it had been her dream. I called Manda's house as soon as I got home from the football game, but no one answered.

Disappointed that Manda hadn't cared enough to call and tell me the results of the soccer try-outs, I went to the local car show alone. Aimlessly wandering through the maze of cars, wondering why Manda and I had grown apart, I heard a voice shout my name. I turned around to see Jenni Stovers, a girl I was friendly with from school.

"Alison, did you hear about Manda?" The look on her face was difficult to read.

"No," I said casually. "Did she make the soccer team?" Jenni's eyes swelled up with tears as she sympathetically looked at me.

"Alison, Manda was killed last night in an accident."

My mouth dropped and my stomach did a flip-flop, making me feel sick. "Wha . . . what happened?" I stammered.

"Her mother was driving her home from soccer try-outs, and the sun made it hard to see. They were crossing the tracks by your house, and a train smashed into them."

I looked at Jenni's sympathetic face and ran. I ran past Ol' Station, over the railroad crossing, and down the gravel road that seemed to stare angrily up at me like an evil monster ready to attack. I ran up the rickety porch step and through my house, my long red hair flying after me. Throwing myself upon my bed, sobbing into my pillow, I thought back to the carefree days of our childhood when Manda had tripped on the tracks.

"It's just a little blood. Here, you hop on my back and I'll carry you home."

Only this time, I couldn't carry her home.

Alison Hamby

Emergency 911

I never thought the day would come. You stop by me as I get on the tennis bus. "Would you like a ride to practice?" you ask.

"No, Stephanie—but thanks, anyway." My parents would freak if they found out I got into a car with a sixteen-year-old driver.

You drive away after promising to come to our tennis match tomorrow. I wave out of the bus window as you head down the hill.

Five minutes later, our bus is slowing down as we pass a crash on our left side. Crashes are really cool, especially if they are really bloody and gory. The car, a red Honda Civic, looks like yours, but there are lots here in Valley Center. The side is all bashed in, and everyone's faces are covered in blood. People are walking around with cell phones, calling 911. The bus moves on to tennis practice.

My mom is working at the hospital tonight. She calls home to say that two girls from my school are dead, and one is in critical condition. The other was released earlier. I blow it off. The next morning, my mom comes home. She says that you are dead, Stephie, and so is Jenn. I don't believe her and go to school. When I get to school, I suddenly believe her. I start crying as my friends look at each other in amazement. I never cry, at least I haven't in about three years. But this is real. They have a room open for people who can't handle classes. But I'm Danni. Of course I can handle them. But I can't. I can't last five minutes through first period before I start bawling.

I spend the day in the memorial room making cards for your families. Reporters come up to me and ask me how I feel. I say words not befitting a girl. Your family comes in, Stephanie. I am surprised by how much your sisters look like you. I almost mistook your older one for you. But you weren't there. I laid roses in the quad for you. I wrote countless poems and cried countless tears. Did you know you had so many friends?

The memorial service was held today. The song they played was "Lately"—a song about death and learning to live again. It was our favorite. As I step off of the bus back at Ramona High School, the last chords of "Lately" can be heard.

I won all of my matches for you today. I met a guy the other day. You sent him from heaven, didn't you? His name is Tyler. He helped me through this. I wanted to be with you, and almost succeeded. But he helped me realize that life is worth living to the fullest. After all, that's what you did.

Each day I forget a little more, but in my heart will always be the memory of your love and kindness. Oh, and Stephanie: I don't think crashes are cool anymore.

Danni Villemez

Long Road Ahead

Live as if you were to die tomorrow. Learn as if you were to live forever.

Mahatma Gandhi

The road home seemed never-ending. In an attempt to forget about the strange and uneasy feeling I had inside of me, I joined my friends and teammates in our ritual road trip sing-along. Soon enough I was laughing, and my worries dispersed. Mid-song, the bus pulled into the parking lot of Laurel High School.

I was beginning my freshmen year at Laurel, returning from a trip to Michigan with the lacrosse team. As we tossed our luggage out of the bus, I observed the pleasant April day through the small back door. I jumped out of the big yellow schoolbus, so relieved to get out of the cramped bus seats. I grabbed my blue and white floral bag, and waited patiently for my ride.

I wasn't there for long when I was gently pulled aside by my friend's mother. She hugged me while informing me that she was going to wait with me until my mother arrived. When my mother finally came, she appeared exhausted. Her expression scared me. My nagging worry on the bus trip had been justified; something was seriously wrong.

My mother began to load my bag into the trunk. I stopped her. "What happened? Tell me what's wrong," I pleaded. She held her tears back firmly. Then softly and slowly the words came out of her mouth. My father had suffered a massive heart attack earlier that morning. All at once I felt a whirlwind of emotions: shock, fear, confusion, anger, hysteria. I was lost in emotions never before conjured.

When I asked if he was okay, my mother shook her head. He had died. I slowly sat down in the back of the car and was handed a beige box of hospital tissue. Reality crept in; tears filled my eyes and streamed down my face.

Up until that moment, my life had been like a strand of bright and colorful Christmas lights. With my father's death, one bulb was ripped out and the entire strand went black. I was fifteen and unable to put my life back together. Life became confusing. I felt robbed of my innocence and identity. I was faced with emotions and obligations that I never had to deal with before. I constantly faced new obstacles and tasks. I forgot who I was, where I was going, and how to move on.

Each member in my family had devised his or her own technique for dealing with our loss. No matter how they chose to grieve, I knew their method was more effective than mine. In my grief, I felt increasingly isolated. Looking back, I realize that strangely, I had become comfortable in my dark, unstable world. I began to feel safe; I was lonely and sheltered in my nest of hurt and discouragement.

I don't remember exactly why or how I began to climb out of my misery. My friends and family were huge contributions. With their help, I broke tasks into smaller steps. I learned to handle my problems differently. It took time and plenty of willpower, but eventually I pushed myself out into the light. I came to realize the importance of every moment and not to take life for granted.

As tragic as the experience of losing my father was, I feel that it has pushed me to become a stronger person. Life is a gift, and even through pain and complexity, I realize that I cannot and will not give up; I will not abandon my identity. Today I feel that I have developed the strength and knowledge to grow and mature. I have learned to respect life and all of its many blessings. I think my dad would be proud.

Maria Maisano

A Father's Ties

In three words I can sum up everything I've learned about life; it goes on.

Robert Frost

That Sunday night over a year ago was like most other Sunday nights had been. Katie's mom collapsed onto the couch around seven o'clock when she got home from visiting the hospital. The twins, Ryan and Andy, were fighting over who got to pick what video to watch. Katie was thinking about what topic to choose for her ten-page term paper due the next morning. Everything was pretty much the same as usual, except one thing. That Sunday night, Katie's father died.

The minister came over as soon as she heard the news. "I know it's very hard, Katie," Reverend Annie said, so calmly it was hard to believe she really knew what had happened. "But it's time to let go now. Your dad was very sick. He needed to go."

Katie did everything Reverend Annie told her to do. She found something "meaningful" to take to the funeral to put in the long, shiny casket with her dad. It was the little rubber frog she had won at the state fair the summer before. She wondered if maybe sometime during the service, the frog would come to life, jump out of the casket and hop away. If the frog could do it, so could her dad. Then she'd follow them both. They could all live together happily ever after on a lily pad or something. "Boy, am I *dumb* when I work at it," Katie said to herself in disgust.

She went to the counselor at school one day a few weeks later. Reverend Annie had told her to do that, too. "How are you doing, Katie?" Mrs. Mooney asked, flashing her wide smile.

"Okay," she lied.

"I know this is a very hard time for you, dear. Are you sure you're going to be all right?"

"Pretty sure," Katie said. She nodded her head yes, to be more convincing. She was staring at the picture behind her on the wall. It showed Mrs. Mooney's husband with his arms around three kids in bathing suits, caught by the camera in mid-giggle.

"Good. Good," Mrs. Mooney said, patting the hand Katie had laid on the desk. "I want you to come visit me anytime you feel the need, okay?" She took a quick peek at her watch.

"Okay," Katie said. "Thank you for your help." They wiggled their fingers at each other in a good-bye wave.

It hadn't helped, of course. If anything, it had made things worse. It just showed Katie how different she was from everyone else now. How she was really hurt. And they weren't.

The praying that Reverend Annie told her to do didn't help either. It was like she was knocking on a door to an empty room.

So that's why, one night, Katie sat for an hour on the floor of her father's closet. She'd pulled down every one of his neckties. "Dad, you had really *awful* taste in ties," Katie groaned, looking at them as they lay all over her lap and on the carpet like a pile of wacky spaghetti.

"Take the tie off, dear," her mom said the next morning as Katie headed out the door.

"Can't, Mom. Too late," she mumbled through a mouthful of blueberry muffin. Katie could see the bus at the end of the street already. She'd selected a lime-green number, with little M&Ms holding hands and dancing across the front. Her dad had gotten this one on the family's vacation to Hershey, Pennsylvania, a couple of years ago. Katie remembered that the twins threw up on the boat swing, just after they'd all gotten their souvenirs. Her dad sat with them in the bathroom for forty-five minutes. They were all pretty much the same shade of green as the tie when they came out. The tie flapped over her shoulder as she ran for the bus.

It was more than a week later when she finally got called to the principal's office.

"It's about the ties, isn't it?" Katie asked meekly. She was wearing the wide Hawaiian with a cluster of little brown pompoms hanging off the bottom corner. They were meant to look like coconuts. Her dad had bought this when he and her mom were supposed to be in Hawaii for their second honeymoon. Instead, they were in the emergency room. Mom had appendicitis. He got her a muumuu and said when she put it on after her surgery that it was almost as good as being in Hawaii. Where he got a muumuu in Minnesota in the dead of winter, no one ever did figure out.

Mr. Winhaven peered over his glasses at her. "Yes, Katie, it's about the ties. You know we have a dress code here."

"I know, Mr. Winhaven, but it doesn't say anything about wearing ties in the handbook," she said politely. Her dad had always said, if you think you're right, say so.

Just don't say it so that it makes the other person mad.

"Tru-u-ue," he said, pursing his lips and drawing out the word slowly. She could tell that he was thinking it over, deciding what to do. "But it *is* a distraction," he went on.

"Well, maybe if I wore the plainer ones. You know, darker colors?"

"Deal," he said. He put out his hand to shake. "But no baseball caps in class!"

She wondered if Mr. Winhaven would think the tie with the yellow happy faces on it would be okay. It had a black background.

When February rolled around, Katie was really troubled over which tie to wear to the Valentine's Day Dance. She wasn't going to go at first, but she could tell that her mom wanted her to. So, she decided on the black bow tie, the one her dad had worn to her first piano recital. She remembered how embarrassed she'd been that her parents had gotten all dressed up to hear her play. It was the only really normal tie her dad had. And, as she looked in the mirror on her way downstairs, it didn't look half bad with her red dress.

"So," Tyler Minskoff yelled, as they danced to the squeal of their local rock band. "Cool tie. Snap on?" he asked.

"Yes," she huffed. The dance tempo was very fast, and she was having trouble keeping up. It was a song the band had written themselves, called "Let's All Get Together, Okay?" She liked the song, but right in the middle, they stopped playing and had an argument about how the rest of it went. At least she got a chance to catch her breath.

She felt a little guilty when she got home from the dance. She had forgotten about her dad for a while. When everyone was standing around the snack table chattering away about who was dancing with whom, she was right there with them, laughing and gossiping.

"Do you think Dad would really have wanted me to go, Mom?" she asked later, climbing into bed.

"Yes," her mom said, quietly. "I think so." Her mom smiled and ran her fingers along the silk back of the bow tie Katie had left on the bedside table. It was good to see her smile, even if it was a sad smile.

Katie met with Reverend Annie from time to time. Sometimes, they'd talk about how sad she still felt. But when she knocked on that door with a prayer, the room didn't seem so empty anymore. As more time went by, she didn't feel the need to wear one of her dad's ties every day. Then, it was just once a week. Finally, she didn't wear them at all. She placed them carefully in a box and put the box under her bed. She knew that it didn't matter where she put them. Her father's ties would be with her forever.

Bonnie Brightman

$\overline{7}$

OVERCOMING OBSTACLES

The way I see it, if you want the rainbow, you gotta put up with the rain.

Dolly Parton

They always say that time changes things, but you actually have to change them yourselves.

Andy Warhol

Owning the World

Character cannot be developed in ease and quiet. Only through experience of trial and suffering can the soul be strengthened, ambition inspired, and success achieved.

Helen Keller

I slowly came to understand what had been said. Instead of the expected dismissal of my illness and being told to choke down a series of medications, I was told I had leukemia. It was June 27, 1997. The weather was pleasant, and I was calm. From the smaller hospital in Kitchener, my mom and I proceeded directly to London to begin my own personal hell.

As my mom, dad and I sat listening in a vague stupor, what we could come to expect was explained to us in the simplest and nicest way possible. That information was repeated a lot during the next little while. It was a great deal to take in while under such shock. However, I decided right away that my case would be different. I would not lose all my hair, I would not puff up from steroids, I would not get mouth sores, and the chemo-therapy would not be so hard on me as it is on other people. I was wrong.

The next couple of days were the most difficult I had faced in my life. To that point, most of my life had been no problem. I could dismiss whatever was wrong within a couple of days and never face very severe or life-changing consequences. But leukemia was a big deal that I would have to live with for an indeterminate length of time. I decided to complete this temporary obstacle with grace, maturity and an understanding of how much people were helping me, and how much I had to be grateful for.

Meanwhile, back at home people were slowly hearing the news. I started getting lots of cards and gifts. I knew they were meant to cheer me up, but they made me sad. I didn't want to be the center of bad attention. I didn't want people to know I was even sick. I wanted to get the chemotherapy, go home and be happy without every-body knowing. But the gifts and cards piled up, each one a painful reminder of what a difficult and daunting task lay before me.

When it was around time for it to fall out, I cut my shoulder-length black curly hair short. I didn't really care that much; I was too weak from the leukemia and the first strong dose of chemotherapy. My hair fell out about a week later. For the first little while I wore a wig or a hat all the time because I was so ashamed. Eventually, I came not to care if the nurses or my parents saw me without hair. It took quite a while longer for me to show a select group of my friends. I kept in contact with two of my best friends. I didn't have the energy or the strength to reassure them all firsthand.

I spent most of July in the hospital, waiting for my blood counts to come back high enough that I could return home. I completed a number of paintings, finding that painting helped to keep my spirits high and my mood cool, calm and collected. It was amazing therapy. I went home for a week in early August. I needed a break. I had to stay out of the sun, didn't have as much stamina as usual and wore a wig, but other than that it was the closest I would feel to normal for quite a while.

The following cycle of chemotherapy was the worst I have ever experienced. I had no idea what was in store for me. Up until then, I had handled all the chemotherapy with flying colors. At the end of August I was back in the hospital, only this time in pain. It was the worst pain I had ever felt. I wasn't allowed to have pain relievers because the doctors had to know if the pain changed in any way. An endless bombardment of seemingly unimportant questions, which in reality were quite significant, drove me insane. They put a tube down my nose to drain the stomach acid, and I suffered severe nausea and stomach pain for the next month. I finally went home feeling better. My bone marrow transplant was scheduled for October, earlier than anticipated. I went shopping, had my friends over, and had a great time. It was a very well-deserved break.

I was very fortunate to have two donors to choose from. Both my brother and my sister were perfect matches. The doctors chose my brother. We went to Toronto's special bone-marrow transplant unit confident and full of hope that this was finally coming to a close. The round of chemotherapy was strong enough to kill me if I hadn't had my brother's marrow to back me up. I did quite well in isolation. Except for the nausea. It just never went away. Everything I ate just came back up again. I went home promising to eat and drink as much as I could or a minimum of one-and-a-half liters a day. That proved to be extremely difficult.

Within a couple of days I was back in the hospital to get

hydrated and for treatment for shingles. The nausea still hadn't gone away. I was angry with myself for letting everybody down. We all had such high expectations for me after the bone-marrow transplant, and I wasn't meeting them. No matter how hard I tried, I could not bring myself to eat. On top of it, I had to take a great number of pills, which just made me more sick.

Even though the nausea continued, I was able to return home. It was torture. I got bronchitis and sinusitis and had no idea how it could possibly get worse. After a CT scan and routine clinic visit, I found out I had relapsed. The chemotherapy and bone-marrow transplant didn't work. The leukemia was back. All I had just been through was for nothing. This bad news came ten times harder than it had the first time. I had already been through all this, suffered the consequences, and lived through the trials and tribulations.

When a patient with AML relapses, the chances of long-term remission, or cure, with conventional treatments is about 20 percent. That news just never left my mind. However, I was able to remain secure in knowing that I was getting the newest and latest treatment. I was the eighth pediatric patient to try this new treatment through Sick Kids' Hospital, and so far it had worked quite well in adults. So I told myself it would be all right and started it along with another program my dad had heard about.

The medication my dad found was an experimental organic medicine that is injected into the lymph nodes. I had to do that every day for three months. It was up to me when to stop. It was as if a great weight had been taken off my shoulders when I finally felt confident enough to stop.

The hospital treatment was quite different. I had to endure a round of chemotherapy, followed by a dose of my brother's white blood cells, hoping that they would identify the leukemia as foreign "bad stuff" and destroy it. The first chemotherapy and batch of my brother's white blood cells proved inadequate. When I got my bone marrow checked there were still signs of leukemia. I went through the chemotherapy once more, knowing that if it didn't work this time I was as good as gone. They gave me the remaining batch of white blood cells, this time many more of them. My brother and I are such a close match that the blood cells hadn't attacked me enough, so, with the second and final round, they gave me the entire batch.

I am proud to say that I no longer show signs of any leukemia.

Slowly, day by day, I approach summer, regain my strength and remind myself of how valuable and fragile *everybody* is. It has been a long, hard fight, but I would not trade the lessons I have learned in those ten months for the world. I have learned to be brave. I have learned to be strong. And, most important, I have learned to persevere.

Liz Alarie

[EDITOR'S NOTE: *We received the following from the author's parents:*

Two months later, Lizzie relapsed for the last time. Shortly after, she died at home. Lizzie lived her fifteen months of illness with radiant grace, maturity and ever-present gratitude. She accomplished her greatness here on Earth as a teacher. "Her world" witnessed her valiant actions, kind deeds and motivating stories such as this one. Lizzie's wish for mankind was simple: Begin now to live your life to the fullest—it is possible!

Ray and Mary Pat Alarie]

Voices

When she looks in the mirror
She doesn't see what you see
You see,
Skin and bones,
The sunken face,
And dark circles under her eyes.
She looks in the mirror
And sees just the opposite.
She sees a girl,
With too much fat here
And there
And her body figure just not perfect.
You tell her to eat,
And that she's way too thin.
The voices in her head
Are saying,
If she eats she will gain,
And be way too fat to be loved.
She has been told countless times over
You are special,
Unique,

And loved by all.
On the other hand
The strong voices shout,
You are worthless,
And plain,
You don't deserve any of their love.
This child
She needs your ever-lasting support,
And love.
Continue to tell her she is a special,
Worthwhile person
Undeserving of this terrible disease.
The road to recovery will be a bumpy one,
With many curves,
Steep hills,
And valleys.
With the love and support from all
She will again realize she is loved
And wanted.
You may feel your words
Of hopeful strength,
Are sounds she isn't listening to,
But your words will soon
Build up in her head
And conquer her evil thoughts.
She will soon blossom,
And live a life of
Love,
And laughter
Once again.

Micah Twaddle

I Just Wanted to Be Skinny

I couldn't believe that I hadn't let myself see how awful Colleen had become. I was so ashamed of myself at that moment, staring at her in her size zero sundress draped loosely over her. She looked like a little girl swimming in her mother's clothes. It was as if I was seeing her for the first time. Her adorable round baby face had become so gaunt, and her once bright eyes had become dull and faded, now just slightly sunken in as if all her desire for life had been sucked out of her. I began to panic as my eyes frantically scanned the rest of her body. But it was no use. With every glance, I saw skin and bone where there should have been the beginnings of womanly curves. Everything about her was so tiny and frail that she reminded me of a twig that could be snapped with the blow of a harsh winter wind. I was overwhelmed with guilt. I was supposed to be her friend. I was supposed to keep her from doing things like this to herself. I had promised I would always be there for her. And right then, I wanted to run crying from the store because I knew I had failed. Instead, I just stood there next to her, unable to say anything, while she critiqued herself about how fat she looked and how tight the dress was. How had this happened?

I later found out it began in the eighth grade, which was the year when attention on being thin became emphasized. Diets became an obsession for many girls. There was a new one to try every week, each promising better results than the last. They were "in style" the same way green nail polish or jelly sandals were. Colleen was always insecure about being fat, which surprised me because she had such a healthy looking body. But seeing those stick-figured girls talk about their diets only perpetuated Colleen's insecurity.

How could I have been so dumb and so blind? How could I not have realized that her reasoning for all the missed school lunches were just excuses, that she hadn't conveniently just eaten before she came over? And all the times my friends and I invited her to eat with us, how could we not have seen the pattern in her continuous declines, saying she would love to come . . . another time?

Colleen's parents took her to see a doctor, and he confirmed everyone's worst fear: He diagnosed her as anorexic. It sounded so weird to hear her called that; even though everyone knew she was, no one had ever actually said it before. Colleen was anorexic. It was almost as if I had to say it to myself a couple of times before I could really comprehend it. She weighed only eighty-six pounds at a height of 5'4" when she was admitted, and the doctors said that had she continued the destructive pattern much longer, there was a good chance she could have died of a heart attack. Imagine that—dying of a heart attack at age fourteen.

The doctors and psychologists asked Colleen repeatedly, "What made you decide to stop eating?" And she always answered sincerely and simply, "I just wanted to be skinny." This reply frustrated them. I guess they expected to hear a huge psychological reasoning behind her anorexia, like pressure from her parents, school or sports. I'm not really sure what they wanted to hear, but they couldn't seem to accept that Colleen starved herself because she just wanted to be thinner.

It's been a little over a year now, and I'm proud to say that Colleen has only been back to the hospital once. She has worked incredibly hard to gain back her normal, stress-free life, and it's been a difficult struggle. But I know she will win this battle in the end.

It bothers me, though, that Colleen's struggle could have been prevented. What is it that makes girls feel like they must look like waifs before they are considered beautiful? Some people might blame the media, others may fault the girl's lack of self-confidence, or the parents for not providing better examples. Maybe it's a little of all three. If only there were a way to tell each young, impressionable girl that women are *supposed* to be different shapes, that it's all those dozens of unique figures that make our world beautiful. If only there were some way to tell them that it's this variety that makes every woman truly beautiful. Then, maybe, cases like Colleen's could be prevented.

Laura Bloor

Inner Sustenance

All I ever wanted was to be popular. Have the coolest friends. Be in a hot rock band and date the best-looking men—simple wishes for a young girl. Some of my dreams even came true. I started a rock band. And the cutest guy at Melbourne High School even asked me out.

I answered yes of course, but within a week, he complained, "Your hips are too big. You need to lose weight to look thin like the other girls in your band."

Immediately, I tried several different diets to lose weight. For one, I ate grapefruit and vegetables only. That didn't work; I felt faint and had to eat. The second week I tried skipping breakfast and dinner. When I did that, I became so hungry by the time dinner came, I splurged and eventually started gaining weight. Ten pounds I added in a month trying to please my boyfriend. Instead of praising my efforts, he cut me down even more. "You look like a whale," he said, making me feel not as pretty as my other friends who wanted to date him. I felt self-conscious and didn't want to lose him as a boyfriend, so I desperately searched for another way to lose the pounds that were keeping him at bay.

I didn't even think that he was the problem: just me, it was just me. Whatever I ate made me fatter. Whatever I wore, I looked hideous. I was now 110 pounds, a complete blimp!

One evening after a date, I got so angry by his "whale" remarks that I ate an enormous piece of cake. The guilt made me want to try something I had seen other girls in my school doing at lunch break: throw up. I went to my bathroom and without even thinking of the consequences, stuck my finger down my throat and threw up in the toilet.

All I ever wanted was to be as pretty as a model. I wanted my boyfriend to look at me the same way as he did those bikini-poster girls.

It was so easy. That cake I just enjoyed didn't cost me any unwanted calories.

Once a day soon turned into three forced vomits. Becoming malnourished, I was constantly hungry, so I ate more, threw up more. It wasn't until I strangely gained another fifteen pounds and tried to quit a month later that I realized I couldn't stop. I fought to, for several weeks. As soon as I got up from the table, my stomach began convulsing. Now my own stomach somehow believed that's what it was supposed to do. I had to run from the table. I was throwing up without even sticking my finger down my throat or even wanting to!

I wasn't in control anymore. I was caught in a whirlwind. I thought bulimia would help me lose pounds but after the months of doing it, not only hadn't it controlled my weight, but the purging had opened up the pits of hell.

I needed help. My boyfriend's comments and my weight were the least of my problems now and I knew it. At age fifteen I didn't know what to do. Desperate for a solution, I broke down into tears and confided in the only person I could trust: my mom. Unsure, of how she would react and wondering if she'd stop loving me if she knew, I mustered up the courage to write the truth on a note and leave it on her dresser:

"Mom, I'm sick. I tried forcing myself to throw up to lose weight, now I am vomiting every day. I can't stop. I'm afraid I'm going to die."

I locked myself in my room the entire night. My mother knocked on my door several times. I could hear her crying. The next morning she pounded harder and told me she had made a doctor's appointment for me. "Get out here before we're late!" she said.

I opened the door. Instead of a hard and loud scolding, I received a hug. Being in her understanding arms, I had the confidence to go to the doctor with her.

The first meeting with the doctor, I'll never forget. He told me that by using bulimia to lose weight I was actually retaining water, losing hair, ruining the enamel on my teeth and was now developing a very serious stomach condition called gastritis. He informed me I was malnourished and in danger of losing my life. He strongly recommended that I check myself into a hospital for treatment.

Knowing that I would be apart from my friends and my mother, I didn't want to agree. Going to the hospital seemed to be a way of walking away from everything I've ever known. I was terrified about leaving home. I'd never been away from my house, my school or my friends be - fore. I was wondering if anyone would even stay my friend or if they all would think I was a freak. I thought about telling the doctor I wouldn't even consider it, but my conscience reminded me, *If I don't go I'll be spending the rest of my days, however many more I have left, throwing my life away, literally down the toilet.* I told the doctor I would go.

The first day and night were the hardest. Nurses gave me a study schedule for both educational and counseling activities. I would attend six different classes each day: math, English, science, group counseling, PE and a personal session with my doctor. All the people were complete strangers. Most of the patients my age weren't there for eating disorders but for severe mental illnesses or violent behaviors. In my first class, math, I sat down and said hello to the girl sitting next to me. She turned her head and ignored me. I shifted in my chair and waved to the girl on my left and asked what her problem was. She didn't answer and mumbled something about needing medicine. I quickly learned that the other patients were hard to relate to or on heavy medication. They didn't seem to have any desire to make friends. That night, I cried myself to sleep, feeling more alone than I ever had.

The next morning, I was told that my blood work reported that I was not only dehydrated but also starving. The doctor said he wouldn't release me until I was strong inside and out. Months passed like this and I continued attending classes with screaming, irrational kids. I felt so isolated. The doctors tried several types of medicines; none of them seemed to be working to keep my food down. They started feeding me intravenously. A needle was stuck in the top of my hand and stayed there, taped, twenty-four hours a day. It was so gross, having a big needle sticking out in my hand. Every morning they would attach a liquid-filled bag that dripped nutrients into my bloodstream. Each night they gave me pills that made me nauseous and want to throw up. I was becoming more and more discouraged. *Will I ever be normal again?* I wondered. Still, I wouldn't give up. I knew what I had to do and I tried yet another medication.

When that didn't seem to do anything, a nurse came into my room, took that morning's medication out of my hand and suggested that I stand in front of the mirror one hour after each meal and repeat to myself these words,

"Yes, I am perfect because God made me."

I thought she was nuts! If modern medicine couldn't work, how could saying a few words do the trick? Still, I knew I had to try it. It couldn't hurt and if it got me off the feeding tube, it was worth it no matter how crazy it sounded. Beside, if it didn't work, I could tell the nurse that it wasn't the cure and that at least I tried.

The next meal, I said the words for several minutes. Religiously. I said them for an entire week extending the time every day. After a while, I realized I began saying them as if I meant them and I had been keeping my food down. My bulimia was becoming under control because my mind stopped focusing on throwing up, and started focusing on saying those words! Within a week I stopped needing to be fed through tubes, my stomach had stopped rejecting food and my compulsion to vomit ceased. My mind had been tricked into more positive thinking!

With the support of my counselors and nurses, I continued searching for ways to bolster my self-esteem, so that I would never again be so vulnerable to the judgments of others. I began to read self-esteem books and the Bible to further my self-image. By then, my boyfriend had dumped me. Most of my friends had stopped coming to see me. Even on the day I celebrated my newfound ability to keep my food down, I called my brother to tell him the good news and he said, "You're making all this up for attention, aren't you?"

I can't tell you how much that hurt. Still, I wouldn't let the outside world's cruelty diminish my victory or my newly found self-esteem of loving myself no matter what my weight was. Finally, I realized with this new strength, I was well.

I began feeding myself and choosing to be full— literally, spiritually, emotionally and physically. My self-esteem strengthened as I ate, repeated those words, and learned to love myself. By gulping down food, I became the vessel God had created me to be. I was special regardless of what others thought. And, I saw that old boyfriend for what he really was: shallow, close-minded, inconsiderate, and not even worthy of my love in the first place.

It had taken months in the hospital with nurses and counseling to learn a lesson I'll never forget. Being popular is just an illusion. If you love yourself you are in the "in" crowd. You are an individual gift from God to the world. It's comforting to know joy comes from being who I am instead of trying to become somebody else's perfect model.

My first day back to school, my ex-boyfriend actually came up to me and asked me out again. "Wow, you look great. You're so thin! You want to go to the football game on Friday?"

"No," I answered, without regret. "I'd rather date someone who loves my heart."

Me! Accepting me suddenly became a daily celebration of life. I love me! Those three words sound so simple, but living them, believing them makes living so tantalizingly delicious!

Michelle Wallace Campanelli

I Am Not Alone

Here I stand, just another voice, lost in a crowd of noise. Though I am surrounded by familiar faces, I do not recognize anyone. I have never felt so alone. . . .

I am eighteen years old, and in love with the most wonderful person! He is cute, sweet and oh so charming. He makes me so happy. I have never felt so content. He is my best friend. When he looks in my eyes and says, "I love you," I just know we are forever. For us, life is a party.

Reality sets in and threatens to reveal the illusions of my fantasy world. *Where is he now?* I wonder desperately. *Where did I go wrong? Did I fall short of his expectations somehow? Or was he unable to meet mine? Was it that he never really loved me, and if so, did he lie? WHY?* The young man I thought I knew so well does not exist, is someone whose face I do not recognize. His voice sounds strange and distant. I see behind his disguise. I look past his smile and his promises. I see him for who he *really* is.

My stomach hurts lately, and I have trouble eating. I feel dizzy and nauseous. I get so tired, I can hardly stay awake. Yet even after a nap, I still feel cranky and irritable. Maybe it's just the flu. No, it is something else.

I sense a truth I want to ignore.

My friend must know, too. I can tell by the way she watches me. I don't want to say anything because I am afraid. She brings me a pregnancy test and tells me, "You should take it just to be sure."

I pretend that I am not worried, that this is silly. "I know I am not pregnant." I keep saying it to reassure myself more than her. Then I go to the bathroom.

I watch two lines appear quickly. I can hardly breathe. I feel nothing really, except shock and denial. Tears will not come. I just stare in disbelief and then quietly call for my friend. I point at the test stick lying face up on the counter, the faint pink lines rapidly changing to a dark shade of maroon. As calmly as I can, I say, "This can't be right." She knows the test is right, and so do I. Tomorrow, I will go to the doctor. Right now, I just want to lie down.

"Positive. You are definitely pregnant." I look up and catch the nurse's eyes. It is real. There is no way to avoid the truth. She hands me a tissue as I cry. Now, my tears are endless. She listens as I lose myself in despair. I can't think. A million thoughts are colliding in my head, causing a mass of confusion. How will I tell him? He has to know.

I go to see him when I leave the clinic. He is sitting in his bedroom, with the light off. A small ray of light comes through the window, and casts shadows across his face. I turn my head away. I can't look him in the eye. I can feel my lips trembling as I try not to cry, but I will not allow him to witness the panic that grips me. I try to appear brave and unemotional as I tell this stranger I am carrying his child. He, too, seems unemotional. I feel his eyes upon me. Getting my words out is a struggle. I look up and try to smile, a weak attempt. This is not how I had imagined it would be. So, I wait for him to do, or say, something, anything to let me know I am not alone. Instead, his silence chills me. I know that things between us are changed forever; I turn and walk away. I want him to call to me, or run after me. I want him to hold me in his arms. As I am leaving, I vaguely hear him say, "I'm sorry."

I am outside now. The sun shines down upon me like a spotlight. I feel naked. The door shuts behind me, and I burst into tears. I cry for the young man on the other side of the door. I cry for the baby that is growing inside me. I cry because my heart is breaking. I suddenly feel my youth is ending.

Weeks go by, and every day I live in fear. I wish I had been more careful with my heart and my body. I wish I had never met him. I am too young to be a mother. I am scared. I feel sick and alone. Will my baby have a father? I sleep all day and cry all night. I wonder how it feels to laugh. I stare at myself in the mirror, looking for my smile, my happiness.

Now I see the beginning of this tiny creature on a screen. I hear a heartbeat separate from my own. I feel a new kind of love. A love that has confidence and guidance—the love of a mother. I lift my head up, and I stand strong for myself, for my unborn child and for the priorities instilled in me by my pregnancy.

Here I am amidst a crowd of noise, swimming against the current I have accepted as my reality, in a sea where familiar faces fade away, and I am not alone.

Sara Strickland

Four Kisses

I am thirteen and going to a baseball game with my father. I bring binoculars, a little Dutch-boy haircut, my glasses, insecurity, a love for the game and a lack of serotonin in my brain. The fog is twisting around Candlestick Park, leaving the feeling of dampness, dirty water on my jacket and wetness on my glasses, making my perspective skewed like a funhouse mirror. My father wants more than anything else to teach me to keep score, but I am desperately trying to never learn anything new again, because the things I have learned in the last year have been all-around destructive: that I am clinically depressed, that a school day is too long, that I have obsessive-compulsive disorder, and that I am losing even more weight, and am down to eighty-five pounds.

My father grabs my hand. "Did you see that pitch? Right on the money, right on the money. Whoever says they're not going to take it all the way . . ." Asleep in the car on the way home, I can only vaguely hear the music he has on softly so as not to wake me. Something about going home, going home, going home. Mom is asleep in their bed with her red-and-gray quilt that smells just like she does.

My father stops in my room on his way to his. "Good night, Kater." He is standing in the one spot in my doorway where everything echoes. "Good night, Daddy. I love you. Can I have four kisses?" I need four of everything, because obsessive-compulsive disorder has me believing in plastic number power, power I can't have in other arenas. So I make my bed sixteen times and wash my hands until I have slammed the door to the cabinet under the sink just so, so that nobody dies or gets in a car wreck.

My father notes that I have been sleeping wildly. I am usually a still sleeper, the biggest moves I make are a shift from one side to the other, so that I go to sleep staring at the green light from my clock, and wake up with my face towards the wall. But starting last year, I have been waking up having kicked my quilt off, with my stuffed animals relegated unconsciously to the coldness of the floor.

The next day my father says, "Maybe you're getting better." He tries.

"I just want it to end."

"I know you do."

"But I really, really need it to end. Dad, I can't deal with it."

"You know how when you're cleaning out your desk or your room, you have to empty everything out, spread it all over the floor?"

"I guess." I wipe the tears from my face. I hate not being able to see.

"Well, you're there right now."

I hadn't noticed until now how foggy it is. We are walking across the street from a mortuary on the way back from my therapist. It is a Tuesday.

"What?" I asked, not understanding his point.

"Katie, you have everything spread out all over the floor. You have to wait, to pick it all up." This only makes me cry harder, because I am frustrated by the reality of the metaphor blown up, enlarged, unreachable.

My father and my mother are constant reminders to me of what I leave when I go to school for abbreviated days. They are what I stand to lose.

Graduation day. My father and my mother sit in the white plastic chairs; I am on an elevated platform. It is wood painted brown, and parts of it have chipped off so that the chairs that my eighth-grade class sits on are tipping and making plastic-to-wood noises through hollow speeches. Somewhere in the middle, I start to cry. For once it's okay, nobody jeers. I am leaving a part of my life on an uneven platform with my above-the-ears-but-growing-out haircut, bangs clipped back with golden barrettes, a white dress and wonderful parents.

My father drives me to my first day at high school. I haven't been to the therapist in three months. I am walking on legs and feet and ankles that I trust. A senior tells my older sister that I am strutting around school. I keep my bangs pulled away from my face. I hate not being able to see.

My father and I have begun to fight. He does not want me staying out too late. He is upset that my grades are lower than he expected. He always wants to know when I'll be home. When I argue with him, and he leaves, I almost don't know what to do with myself. My obsessive-compulsive power is gone. I am empty so that I can start over.

"Fall came today," my dad says, his first words to me that morning. Since the recent death of my friend's brother, I think of first words and last words more carefully than I should. There have been other first words on other mornings, mostly about the weather or the Giants and how they blew it in the seventh with two runners on, one of them in scoring position. I nod. I'm ineffectual with him that way, letting him bounce off me, because if I let him in, I would be admitting to something. I have thoughts now. And they are mine. My insides and my breaths and my friends and my words, they are all mine. I cling to them more and more.

When my father and I fight, it is loud and articulate. There's something cleansing about it, and it makes me shake. He tells me that he's proud of how well I can argue, that I can always get my point across. My father blames me when my mother gets sick, because it's the stress that I cause, manifesting itself in her.

I am finally sixteen. I have a best friend and contact lenses, a father, a mother and a past. I have beaten something. And that is what I have inside me: strength. I realize, midway through the first quarter of my junior year, that I don't know who bats cleanup for the Giants. I realize that the mortuary across from my old therapist was torn down to build a parking lot. I realize that I haven't talked to my father, sat down and talked to him, since I went away this summer by myself and came back with crisp white inspiration.

I finally have enough serotonin in my brain. I know what I need. I have respect for myself and what I went through. It used to be inexplicable. My father, my mother, a dry bedspread, a song about going home and the National League champion Giants went through it with me. I had built a fresh new me, but I had lost my father. And I wasn't willing to give him up.

I hear his sweaty-feet footsteps coming up the stairs in the house. I lie in my bed tonight, a sixteen-year-old at 110 pounds with long hair, a daughter, home by curfew. Warm and whole, stubborn, stronger, older, and I ask my father for one solitary kiss.

Kate Reder

Mark's Choice

The question is not whether we will die, but how we will live.

Joan Borysenko

"What's wrong?" I still remember asking that question to my teammate as he sat in front of his locker more than twenty years ago. We had just finished polishing off another opponent our senior year and there he sat—head in hands—alone—in pain. He was tough, seventeen years old and a great athlete. His name is Mark Overstreet. The rest of our teammates had showered and left for home, but Mark was still fully dressed in his football uniform. When he raised his head to speak, I saw tears in his eyes. Now I knew something was wrong. This was a young man who took pride in making the opponents cry on the football field. "I don't know," he said silently. "It's as if all the injuries I've ever had are coming back. My whole body hurts. My legs feel like they weigh a hundred pounds each."

A week or so before, an outbreak of the swine flu had swept through our community. One by one, students lined up to take the vaccine to prevent the spread of the illness. I remember we all took the shot and thought nothing of it. When Mark received the vaccine, however, his body developed a very rare allergic reaction to the drug—so rare that his sudden illness was never correctly diagnosed until ten years later.

The next morning after our conversation in the locker room, Mark awoke to find his right foot asleep. No matter how much he tried to rub the foot to alleviate the "pins and needles" feeling, the circulation never returned. Concerned, Mark's mother decided to take him to the doctor. Mark's life was about to change forever.

Baffled by what he saw while examining Mark, the doctor somberly exclaimed, "I don't know what's wrong with you, Mark, but you are going to lose that foot." Shocked, his mother backed up against the wall. Stunned, Mark said, "What are you talking about? What's wrong with me?" The doctor did not know the answer and admitted Mark into the hospital for further tests.

While in the hospital, Mark's left foot fell asleep and, just like the right one, never woke up. Now, not only were both feet losing circulation, but things were getting worse. Finally, after many failed tests, the doctor entered his room to tell him the news. "Mark, whatever it is, it is killing you. It's spreading up to your heart. We have one plan. To hopefully stop the spread we want to amputate both your legs just below the knee. If that doesn't work, you have two weeks."

Two weeks. Two weeks for a young man who had never been sick a day in his life. "What is wrong with me?" Mark again asked. "We don't know," responded the doctor. Mark prepared for the operation not knowing his chances.

When the operation was over, Mark awoke to find the doctor by his bed. "I've got some good news and some bad news," he said. "The good news is, whatever it was, it's gone. The operation was successful. You are going to live. The bad news is, you are probably going to be in a wheelchair your whole life and in and out of hospitals, as well. I'm sorry."

It was at that moment that Mark made a decision—a choice that would shape his whole future. "No!" he responded. "I'm not staying in hospitals—I'm not staying in wheelchairs. I'm going to walk and I'm going to live life! This is just the beginning—not the end."

It took a year, but after learning to use wooden legs, Mark walked out of the hospital for the last time. Later, he decided that since he would never play football or baseball again, he would coach and teach others to play. While in college, Mark met Sharon and fell in love. Sharon didn't mind Mark's wooden legs. She loved him for who he was. After graduation they married and Mark began his first job teaching handicapped students and coaching high school football. Today, Mark and Sharon have four beautiful children and a lovely home. He is a high-school principal in southwest Missouri and my boss. Every morning Mark gets up, puts on his legs and goes to school to greet students and teachers alike. You would never know if he has had a bad day because he would never tell you.

The choice was his. He could still be back in that wheelchair, in and out of hospitals, feeling sorry about the bad break he suffered in high school, but, instead, he is changing lives and living a blessed one himself.

Tom Krause

Ability

Ability is to look at a blank page,
And create a poem.
Ability is to stare into the eyes of fear,
And come out stronger because of it.
Ability is to walk into a room of strangers,
And come out with friends.
Ability is to admit you are wrong,
When you are wrong.
Ability is to get back up,
When you fall down.
Ability is to believe,
When everything seems lost.

Ability—a simple word, with a complex meaning.
For many, ability is never found, but for all ability is within.
Ability stares everyone in the face at one time or another.
Whether your ability is how well you shoot hoops,
How well you flip at dancing,
How smart you are at school.
You have ability.
For some, ability is lost by never trying.

Whether never trying to shoot one more time,
Never trying to bend a little more,
Or never trying to score higher in school.

Ability is within.
Ability is yours.

Selina E. Matis

The Final Game

No pessimist ever discovered the secret of the stars or sailed to an uncharted land, or opened a new doorway for the human spirit.

Helen Keller

Before the final game, life was an ordinary, daily routine. Each day, I awakened with a mental list of the tasks I had to complete before the end of the day. My routine wasn't too complicated: class, soccer practice, studying and sleep. Oftentimes, I returned home from endless hours on the soccer field only to have to study until the early hours of the morning.

Having adapted well to my daily routine, I never imagined it would be altered. However, my life changed the day of the final game. It was the last game of the tournament, and the winner would capture the championship. Not only had my team been under vigorous physical training for the past four years in anticipation of this day, but emotionally, we were ready as well. I was ready. I entered the game with the mindset that the title was in our hands. We deserved it because our desire to win was so great, and we were *hot!*

"Captains!" called the referee. I approached the center of the field, and with confidence, looked my opponent in the eyes while giving her a powerful handshake, wishing her luck. As I took my position on the field, I knew it was time for the final game to begin. I took a deep breath and reassured myself that I would give this game my all, displaying the best of my abilities as if it were the last game I ever played.

"Goalie, Goalie," yelled the man dressed in black and white. The two goalies simultaneously raised their right hands in the air, indicating that they were ready. The game could begin. This was it. The whistle sounded, and the ball was soon kicked in my direction. I received the ball and crossed it twenty feet toward the goal, just in time for my teammate to meet it and pound it right into the net. "Goal!" everyone shouted. The game had started out well.

But the momentum of the game soon grew intense as the opposing team came right back at us with a goal to tie the game at one to one. The game continued at an extremely competitive level throughout the first half and into the second. The score was still tied at one to one, until I received the ball with one minute to go. I needed to put the ball in the net, and I did just that, making the final score two to one. But it didn't go exactly as planned.

In an attempt to block my shot, my opponent challenged me in midair. But instead of heading the ball, her body slammed into mine, leaving me unconscious in the middle of the field, while my teammates shouted cries of victory and horror at the same time.

When I regained consciousness, I found myself in a hospital bed, surrounded by family, friends and teammates, with a huge cast on my right leg. Also at my side were doctors, the determiners of my future. In a matter of moments, they would tell me the severity of my injuries.

To my dismay, I had torn every tendon in my ankle and would have to undergo an extremely rare surgery that had only been performed a limited number of times in the United States, with a mere 50 percent success rate. After hours of contemplation, I decided to chance the surgery, knowing that either way, many challenges would await me. Would I be able to finish the semester? What effect would it have on my social life, my grades, my GPA? These questions circled my head, and unfortunately, only time would provide answers.

After the surgery, I was no longer the independent person I had once been, for I had to depend on my boyfriend, Jordan, to assist me in even the simplest tasks. It was going to be a long, tough road to recovery, and I knew I couldn't get through it without a positive attitude. Needless to say, I engaged in many mind exercises, which helped me attain the positive attitude that would aid in my adjustment to the changes in my life. I began to realize that I didn't have to give up my old life completely, and I focused my energy on a favorite pastime: writing.

Even though it was necessary for Jordan to accompany me everywhere I went, I was still able to produce works of art in the silence and solace of my mind and spirit. Although I was not in physical control of half of my body, I still had control of my mind.

Looking back on the situation in its entirety, I am glad that the final game was, in fact, my final game. I have no regrets. I said I would give it 110 percent and play as if it were my final game. I did just that, and ultimately, I came out a winner. Although my accident robbed me of my physical abilities, it left me with the power of mind and forced me to discover my inner self. That final game, in retrospect, couldn't have been more rewarding. Not only did we win, but I was able to discover a new level within. I guess I gained two victories that day.

Kelly Harrington

Winner

*You can complain because roses have thorns,
or you can rejoice because thorns have roses.*

Ziggy

I am a winner.

I have beaten odds to get where I am today.

I have felt some pain every time I have walked another step forward, yet after having taken even one step back, I have known that regression and giving up were not options for me. I have felt the emptiness of separation as I have moved in the wrong direction.

I have learned the arts of persistence, tenacity and dedication. I know how it feels to watch my world and dreams shatter to a million pieces at my feet. I know what it is to run until there is nothing left inside of me, and then run some more.

I know how it feels to be loved, and I know how it feels when that love grows hard and cold.

I know how to be happy. I know how to smile and spread joy into lives of others with that same smile.

I have learned that one conversation can make or break

a fragile mind and heart, and thus I have learned to choose my words carefully.

I know that enthusiasm is the key to everything, and yet I know how it feels to completely lack enthusiasm.

I have learned that winning is not everything, but sometimes it feels like it is the most important thing. I have learned that other color ribbons only prove to make that blue so much sweeter. I know that my chief competitor is always myself.

I know that sometimes my best isn't good enough for others and that people can be cruel. I know that sometimes I get frustrated with myself, especially when others are frustrated with me.

I know how it feels to have something mean so much to me that it *is* me. I have experienced wrath, outrage and fury, but have still made it through the storm a survivor.

I know what it is to love. I know how to spread joy and how to extract it from even the darkest situations.

I know what hope is, and I rely on it as my last refuge. I know that darkness must exist if only to make those tiny bits of light seem that much brighter.

I know that success is self-made, and that luck is a relative term.

I know that I am strong.

I know that miracles do exist, angels do find us in our hour of need, and there is always something behind me, pushing me forward.

I believe in myself at all times, even when I think that I don't and even when I feel like no one else does.

I know how it feels to be lost. I also know how it feels to be picked out of a crowd. What it is like to be the winner, and how it feels when, for one moment, you are the star of the show.

Above all, though, I know that all of this has made me ME.

I know that being a winner is not about winning what-ever race faces me in the moment. I recognize I am win-ning just by pushing myself every day and by waking up each morning feeling blessed by the day that lies ahead of me. Through this I am winning in the most important race ever, the race I entered at birth—this race we call life.

Amy Huffman

8

SELF-
DISCOVERY

*W*ho in the world am I? Ah, that's the great
   puzzle.

Lewis Carroll

*Y*ou have to be yourself. Be very honest about
   who and what you are. And if people still
   like you, that's fine. If they don't, that's
   their problem.

Sting

An Ode to Shoes

Shiny look-a-likes are they,
empty night time, full all day,
travel miles along the street,
though they only move two feet.

When I was thirteen
I stepped
Off my horse
Out of my tall, black leather boots
And into
Running shoes
Into high school
And high-school track
Into high heels and high-school parties
Strutting
Running
Away from the chaos
And back
Strutting
Swinging my legs, my hips
Just enough
Just so, to get the looks

Not the bad ones,
The good
Expensive boots
All the girls have them
Like all the boys have egos
Fake ones
Like fake plastic heels I would never wear
Call me ritzy
I'll call you cheap
In orange, green, and clear
Four-inch heels
little skirts
and I remember
When no one really cared
When our calves hadn't developed into
The sexy, sloping
Line we exploit
When I tied my LA Gears with
One pink shoe lace
And one chartreuse
Like my socks
Like the style
Before the decade turned
Spun into
Steve Maddens and Doc Martins
And Mary Janes
Each with two names
And we all had two faces
Sometimes more for more occasions
Meaning more shoes
Overflowing our closets like muddy water
Like the muddy circle
The track I run in the spring rains
In the new Nikes
Glossy white leather flushing to red-brown

That cracks and dries in the summer sun
The heat
That beats down in a country where
These shoes are manufactured
By small, brown fingers
Crescents of dirt under unkept nails
Working fine threads into my shoes
Working from dawn until dusk
In a place where nobody knows
Steve Madden or Doc Martin
Or any other doctor that the baby's mother cries for
And the children cry here
For a new pair of shoes
Here in
Distorted Reality
In crowded
Walk-in closets
Full of shoes.

Jessica Pinto

Happiness from Within

Finish each day and be done with it. You have done what you could; some blunders and absurdities have crept in; forget them as soon as you can. Tomorrow is a new day; you shall begin it serenely, and with too high a spirit to be encumbered with your own nonsense.

Ralph Waldo Emerson

Having been raised Catholic by parents who worked hard for every penny they earned, I was taught at an early age that money cannot buy happiness. As much as my parents and the church tried to teach me these values, I had to learn through my own experiences that happiness comes from within and cannot be measured by material possessions.

As a child, I would sit in church, trying to concentrate on the words of the priest, but my attention was soon diverted by the sparkle of the gold and diamonds worn by the Sunday churchgoers. As my eyes began to wander, I noticed men dressed in their tailored suits and monogrammed shirts, accompanied by women in their designer dresses with matching handbags and shoes.

My family, on the other hand, was the opposite of glamorous. Our hand-me-down clothes had been washed so many times that the colors had become dull and lifeless and the material frayed around the seams. Although our clothes revealed the money struggles of our large family, our faces were always washed, our hair neatly combed, and we each tossed our twenty-five cents in the basket even when there was a second collection. As my family piled into our big green and white VW bus after the service, I fantasized about the glamorous lives led by those driving their brand new BMWs, wishing I were more like them.

I continued these fantasies when I was an adolescent attending Catholic school. Since it was a private school, most of the children came from wealthy families. As a result, I constantly felt inferior to the rest of my classmates. Although I could hide my lack of wealth at school by wearing our mandated school uniforms, my poverty was embarrassingly apparent on weekends when my classmates wore designer jeans, and I had no choice but to wear my sister's outgrown jeans. Once, because I could not afford a birthday gift, I gave one of my own used CDs to a friend in school. When she opened the gift, her face twisted into a strange look as if she did not know whether to laugh or say thank you. It was times like these, when the other kids laughed at me and talked behind my back, that convinced me that if I only had the new clothes, the nice house and other such material possessions, then maybe I would have a chance to fit in. Then I would be happy.

I began to believe so much in the material world that I started my first job when I was fourteen so that I could afford those "things" that were going to make me happy. Soon I was working two jobs in order to fulfill my needs.

I began to purchase the clothes, the jewelry and the perfume. Each purchase was a sign of hope. Each time I thought, *This is it, this is really going to make me happy.* Within a few days, sometimes as little as a few hours, that feeling of emptiness came over me again. I would dream bigger and set my goals higher to purchase something even better. Each time I thought it was going to be different, but it never was.

Unfortunately, it took many of these disappointing and painful experiences, not to mention the amount of money spent, for me to realize that what I admired in other people was not about their clothes, their hairstyles or the car they drove. It was their self-confidence. I admired the way they carried themselves, their ability to take on new challenges and the way they looked people in the eye during conversations instead of staring down at their toes as I often found myself doing. I began to notice that it was the qualities that they possessed inside themselves that I was lacking. I knew then that I would never be a complete person until I started to do some work on the inside.

There was no lightning bolt or voice from God that brought me to this realization. I had to go all the way down the wrong road in life to realize that I was headed in the wrong direction. As a result, I now possess those qualities that I had always admired in other people. Long gone are the days of remedying my problems with new clothes and makeup. I confess I still get caught up in the excitement of shopping sprees, but there is a difference today: I know each time I put on a new outfit and look in the mirror, the same person will be underneath it all. I now carry myself with an air of confidence, and I can look people in the eye, for I have no reason to look down.

Dianna McGill

"I think it's so cool that you don't care if you're cool."

Reprinted with permission of Dave Carpenter.

Out of Step

The roots of true achievement lie in the will to become the best that you can become.

Harold Taylor

I wanted to find my niche. I wanted to fit in so badly with some group, any group in high school. Sports didn't really work for me. I sucked at just about all of them. In fact, I dreaded those times in PE when the captains picked teams. Fights sometimes ensued between captains about who would have the misfortune of ending up with me on their team. I was the guy who had a full-scale neurotic episode if you threw the ball to him.

I did run track for awhile. This was a pretty good sport for me because it required very little coordination, and I already had some practice running: away from bullies, their girlfriends and any ball thrown in my general direction. But I wanted to run sprints and only the football players got to run sprints. I was relegated to middle distance—the half-mile, which really didn't work for me. It took about two minutes to run, and the extent of my ability to exert myself athletically was about thirty seconds.

But one day, a girl I liked and sometimes stalked (although we didn't call it stalking back then—just a playful crush) happened into the band office to sign up. Because I had a "playful crush" on Jaclyn, I was hiding behind a tree and noticed her sign up for the band. Okay, sure, the uniforms were pretty dorky and being in the band didn't exactly give you the best reputation in school (which in my case couldn't really get much worse), but I could learn to play the drums and there *was* Jaclyn. I would later learn that many of the greatest musicians of our time were motivated to music by some girl whose name they most likely don't remember anymore.

It was not just the band, but the marching band. I picked the drums for two reasons: (1) it seemed pretty easy, and (2) I thought it would make me look cool. I later found out that the drums are actually quite difficult and that little or nothing could make me look cool. I wanted to play snare drum, but because of my lack of experience I was relegated to the tenor drum.

The first thing to learn was how to hold the drum and play it. We all had to learn the cadence which, to this day, I can still perform with two pencils and a paper cup, which really wows them on job interviews. Holding the drum and playing it is not as easy as it might look. I did, after several private lessons, learn the cadence. Next, as if that weren't difficult enough, I had to learn how to play it while not only walking, but marching.

We were required to march the equivalent of five miles per practice day, while carrying our eighty-pound drums (it was then I wished I had picked the flute) and wearing our big, shiny, black military shoes, in the 104-degree summer heat. And then one day, they delivered the Shakos. For those of you who may not be familiar with high school marching band terminology, the Shako is that really tall, furry-looking hat that you wear with a strap around your chin. Now I was marching five miles a day in my shiny shoes, carrying my eighty-pound drum, playing the cadence about six thousand times, in 104-degree heat, and wearing a big tall, white, furry hat.

Finally, at the end of the summer, our uniforms arrived. The band uniform is a sacred attire. It is carefully sized to fit the individual, hand sewn, and acquired through twenty-seven or so fundraising activities such as car washes, bake sales and door-to-door sales of things like half-melted candy bars at inflated prices. It is cleaned after each use and worn with pride. It is also 100 percent wool. Add now to the excruciatingly painful military shoes, the eighty-pound drum, the silly hat and the 104-degree heat, what I estimate to have been about forty pounds of long-sleeved, neck-to-toe, pure wool.

I forgot to mention something. In addition to an inability to play sports, I was also not so good at marching. If you were not in step, the band director would yell in a loud and embarrassingly annoyed voice, "OUT OF STEP!" It was at this point that I began to question my decision to join the band. How do playing music and marching around in silly formations, all "in step," go together?

The day of our first competition finally arrived. It was the Mother Goose Parade, an annual Thanksgiving Day event in my town. High school bands from all over the county marched while all the people in town lined the streets in lawn chairs and watched them march by. Although the parade didn't start until 9:00 A.M., we had to meet at 6:00 A.M. to get our uniforms from the "band boosters"—those selfless, dedicated parents who provided comfort and assistance to the members of the band.

At 6:00 A.M., to this day, I am not really in existence. Oh sure, you can get me out of bed and dress me, and I will walk and talk, but inside my brain is fast asleep, waiting for a more reasonable hour. I was standing around waiting for my Shako to be cleaned when I noticed a big urn of coffee. *Coffee? That wakes you up, doesn't it?* I poured myself a cup—my first-ever cup of coffee. It tasted pretty bitter, but I had to wake up. I dumped in three sugars and three packets of that white, milky powder that is supposed to scientifically simulate cream. It still tasted bitter but drinkable. I just had to wake up so I could be "IN STEP." After about ten minutes, I was awake. I WAS REALLY AWAKE. I went over to the corner and put on my drum. I wanted to see how fast I could play the cadence. Pretty fast. I started marching around in circles until one of the band boosters came over with a look of concern on her face. She suggested I sit down and rest until it was time to line up. That's when I learned to play the cadence with pencils and a paper cup.

Finally, the moment of truth. They lined us all up and we waited for about forty-five minutes. I had my coffee, and I was raring to go. The drum major blew his whistle and off we went. I beat the cadence out with all my heart. I marched with the precision of a brigadier general. For about the first hour. Then, something happened. Suddenly all my energy drained away. I began to feel sleepy and I fell "OUT OF STEP." No one noticed at first and I tried to skip back into step. But nothing worked. Then I saw one of the band boosters talking to another one and pointing at me. They looked very concerned. They enlisted a third booster and suddenly, to my horror, they all three pointed at me and motioned for me to leave formation. I complied; after all, they had rank. I walked over to them as the band marched on. They told me what I already knew, I was "OUT OF STEP," and would have to stay out of the formation until the band passed the judging stand. I could rejoin the band after the judging stand, but only if I followed along on the side of the road.

I couldn't believe it. Now, I not only couldn't march

with the band, but I had to climb over the lawn chairs, popcorn and arms and legs of my fellow townspeople for the next mile to keep up with the band, in my shiny shoes, carrying my drum and wearing my Shako. I would like to say this was the single most humiliating moment of my life, but unfortunately there were more to follow. But this one did rank pretty high up there on the list.

I never did learn to march "IN STEP." But it hasn't really come up that much in my adult life. I also never did find a niche in high school, but I got through it. As an adult, I have found several niches that I fit into quite nicely, and I look for new ones every day. And I always ask if there is any marching competition before signing up.

Tal Vigderson

Terrifying freshmen on the first day of school is a favorite pastime of many seniors.

She Stands Alone

Don't let life discourage you; everyone who got where he is had to begin where he was.

Richard L. Evans

I got dumped. A young man I had been with for four years, a person who knew me better than I knew myself, the only person I could envision spending the rest of my life with, told me that he didn't want to be with me anymore.

It took me days to crawl out of bed, weeks before I stopped crying. My future, which had once looked bright, was now a complete and total void. I thought about quitting school. I couldn't bear the thought of doing anything without him by my side. My family was at their wits' end. They tried being sympathetic. They tried tough love. Nothing seemed to work.

Then I took up biking. Starting off with a few miles each evening and eventually working my way a little bit further each day. Biking took my mind off things temporarily. The more I pushed my body, the less I thought of my broken heart. But still, when I lay in bed at night, the pain came back.

Eventually my biking took me past a tall, majestic elm tree. It is very unusual to see a mature elm in these parts, as they were all but obliterated early in the century by the Dutch elm disease. I began to think, *what made this tree so different? Why did it survive when so many others could not?* Each night I biked past this tree, and each night I paused in wonder.

One night as I passed the tree, verses wrote themselves in my head. By the time I returned to my house, I had a complete poem, ready to type up and put on my wall:

> *She stands alone, both tall and true*
> *The perfect picture of solitude*
> *The soul of a woman encased in bark*
> *With limbs that move in a majestic arc*
> *Alone she's faced the storms of life*
> *The wind and rain, disease and strife*
> *Others gave up, but no, not she*
> *And there she stands for all to see*
> *She's had her share of troubles and woes*
> *But she made it through, and still she grows*
> *Like her I too know grief and pain*
> *I've faced the wind, I've felt the rain*
> *And like her too, I still stand tall*
> *Though life may beat me, I will not fall*
> *It may throw punches, I may take a blow*
> *But in the end I too shall grow*
> *Each storm I weather increases my strength*
> *And beneath this skin, my soul's to thank*
> *The elm and I, we know what to do*
> *We count on ourselves, and make it*
> *through.*

I didn't quit school, but there were still rough times ahead. Each time I found myself beginning to feel like the world was against me, I read my poem. I had it framed and hung it on my wall, along with a picture I had taken of that great tree. I learned an important lesson that night: I must rely on myself in order to grow stronger through strife. I accepted the fact that I was heartbroken, yet knew in my heart that I would get through it, and like the tree, stand stronger and live on.

Kelly Cook

The Essence of Adolescence

I yelled at Mom yesterday
'Cause she told me I'm going through
A difficult age
And I'm not.
So I slammed the door extra hard
When I got up to my room.
And then I yelled at God for a while
Just for good measure
'Cause he made it snow but
Wouldn't close school.
Besides
He parked that damn streetlight
Just where
He knew it would shine in my eyes
Every night when I'm trying to sleep.
And I yelled at the light, too
'Cause it's too bright
And besides
It lights up the snowman
That the kids next door made.
I was too old to make a snowman this year

But that's okay
I've always hated snowmen anyway.
I yelled at the snowman, too
Before I sat down at my desk
Where this old box was sitting . . .
It had a bunch of
Stupid treasures from when I was little.
Inside was a cotton ball
And some acorns, a dead bee
My eraser collection, and a pen
That had my name on it.
I picked up the box and
Threw it away
'Cause it's dumb to keep that sort of stuff
I put my phone and a romance novel
On the desk instead.
I have to keep my priorities straight.

Then I got home from school today
And I sat down at my desk
I looked for my box.
It wasn't on my desk or in the trash
'Cause today was garbage day
And I sat back down and I guess,
I started to cry.
It's too complicated being mad at the world.

Anne Gepford
Submitted by Katie Shaw

The Two Roads

There was a path
Deep in the woods.
Once it forked—
The bad, the good.

I chose to take
The left-hand path,
I did not know
I had no map.

Now this road that I travel
Is dirty and battered.
It's littered with dreams
That are broken and tattered.

Paved with wrongdoings
And dotted with hearts,
That were taken from people
And just torn apart.

Pain and regret
Are common here.

wherever you turn,
They're always near.

I want to cross
To the other path,
And leave behind
This painful wrath.

I thought I was forever
doomed to walk.
And all the gates
were tightly locked.

But as I continued,
A footbridge I could see.
A Bridge of Hope
called out to me.

Slowly I crossed
to the path of good.
Finally I was on the path
Of which I thought I
should.

Now hidden deep
Within the woods.
The one that forked;
Paths bad and good.

I once was wrong,
But now I'm right.
And before me
Glows a guiding light.

Altered by
A little step.
So close to falling
In darkened depths.

But I was finally
Pulled to hope.
I found that footbridge,
And learned to cope.

My simple mistake
Following the crowd.
Ignoring the heart
That speaks so loud.

The choices you make
Can change your life.
One will bring happiness,
The other brings strife.

Following the crowd,
Won't lead you to right.
If you follow your heart,
You'll be guided by light.

There was a path,
Deep in the woods.
Once it forked—
The bad, the good.

Heed my warning,
Because I know.
Follow your heart—
You know where to go.

Whitney Welch

Suspicion

A teenager—
Closely watched by store security
As to avoid any kind of larceny
Through his eyes, this kid is surely a thief.
He surveys her every move
Waiting for the act
So that he can catch her and set her straight.
Straight, unlike her tousled bright-red hair
He shakes his head in disapproval
Does she expect people not to stare?
Impossible

With her graffiti-colored,
Over-sized jeans; too-wide
black clunky boots; too high
topping it off, with nothing at all;
tiny tight shirt, much too small.
Thick silver chains,
her jewelry no doubt,
Make it easy to keep track of her whereabouts
Thanks to the annoying sound they chime

They look ridiculous, as though enslaving her,
Forcing her to go out in public as she does
And yet, she seems confident,
Proud of her image
Security guard wonders when she'll grow up
He paces back and forth—impatiently
As if waiting for her to make the change
to "maturity"
Before even exiting the store

An adult—
Walks by with grace and class
Lengthy blond, businesswoman in designer clothing
Avoiding eye contact,
Dodging shoppers,
Heading directly towards the back of the aisle

The security guard suddenly remembers his objective
And searches for a young girl who seems to have
cleverly slipped away
He listens for the sounds of the chains
But everything is instantly drowned out
By the noise of the alarm system
JUSTICE.
With a smirk of satisfaction, he turns to face
the scene, to catch a glimpse
of the culprit

And as she lowers her blond head
in shame,
The red-headed teenager pays for her
blue nail polish.

Renée Gauvreau

Center Stage

Once upon a time, my life was as orderly as the inside of my locker. I took detailed notes, never talked out of turn, helped put away library books during my free periods, and went to track practice after school. But all that changed the day Mr. Soames made Sara McGee my partner in biology.

"If he thinks I'm touching this, he's dreaming," Sara whispered after Mr. Soames told us to make the first incision into the earthworms we were dissecting. She pushed her bangs—they were orange today as opposed to last week's green—out of her face and frowned.

I took the knife from her hand and split the earthworm neatly down its center.

"Thanks," she said. She rolled up her sleeves and her silver bangles clattered. "I know I'm a baby, but cutting open animals makes me sick."

I finished dissecting the worm, and when the period was over, Sara slipped her backpack over her shoulder and asked me to eat lunch with her.

"Okay," I said, surprised. I followed her to her locker,

where she opened a tube of tomato-red lipstick and thickly applied it.

"Want some?" she asked, but I shook my head "no."

"Just a tiny bit?" she asked again, and before I could stop her, she dabbed it on. Then she removed the tortoise-shell barrette I always wore and lifted my hair into a high ponytail, pulling two tendrils down on either side of my ears.

"Stunning!" she said, standing behind me so that I could see both of us in the little mirror that hung from a hook. Stunning? I wasn't so sure.

Soon, whenever Sara chewed Juicy Fruit gum in class, I did, too, even though I was careful not to get caught. I wore long skirts like Sara's, and dangle earrings. She hid in the stacks during study hall and read old magazines and, consequently, so did I. She took me to Papa Jimmy's and introduced me to double caffé lattes and biscotti dipped in chocolate. She liked to start arguments in world history class about personal freedom and even though I never could do that, I did find myself, miraculously, volunteering to read out loud in Mr. Bernard's English class.

It was Mr. Bernard, in fact, who pulled me aside and told me I had a flair for drama (we were reading *Romeo and Juliet*). He also said I should try out for the part of Laura in the junior class production of *The Glass Menagerie*.

"No way. I could never do that," I told Sara as soon as we left the room. Secretly, though, I was pleased he had asked.

"Of course you can. You'll be great," Sara said. "You have to try out!" She bugged me until I finally agreed.

At the audition, I read a scene with Joe Greenlaw, who I'd never said a word to before. I doubt he knew who I was, but I could recite his activities as if they were listed in alphabetical order under his picture in the yearbook: junior class vice-president; photo editor for the Park

Ridge *Banner*; captain, debate team; soccer goalie.

After we finished, Mrs. Layton, the director, just smiled and said, "Thank you *very* much," and the next day the casting list was posted on the bulletin board and there was my name, second from the top, with Joe Greenlaw's just above it.

I had play rehearsal almost every night, and so I had to use all my free time to catch up on my schoolwork and hardly ever had time to go to Papa Jimmy's with Sara. Slowly, though, a strange thing began to happen. Homework and chores, babysitting, and even Sara started to fade in importance, but the time I spent at rehearsals was as vivid as the glow-in-the-dark stars on my bedroom ceiling.

Joe talked to me, calling "Laura" from way down the hall. This made me so happy that I didn't even mind when I saw Rachel Thompson, who had waist-long hair that was shiny as glass, put her arm across his shoulder. One night, during dress rehearsal week, we were standing together on the fire escape outside the auditorium watching the snow flakes gather on the iron railing. Joe told me that deep down inside he was really shy and that he was glad he could be himself with me. "Maybe we should do things together," he said. "Go running, go to a dance, I don't know." And then we heard Mrs. Layton calling for us, so we ran back inside.

The next day, Sara stood by my locker just before homeroom. "Hi," she said.

"Hi."

"I never see you anymore. Except in classes, and that doesn't count." She tugged on one of the four stud earrings that lined her ear.

"I know," I said. "It's the play. I'm really busy. It'll be over soon." I looked closely at Sara, past her makeup, and her jewelry, and the long black cape that covered her shirt and her thick, black hiking boots. She always seemed so bold, the way she stated her opinions as if they were facts, and looked anybody in the eye. But now she was quiet, more like the old me than Sara. I gave her a hug.

"Let's do something," she suggested. She looked at the poster on the bulletin board just behind us. It was a drawing of a flapper girl twirling a strand of pearls. "Let's get a bunch of people together and crash the Winter Carnival dance. We'll go to the thrift shop and get some beaded dresses."

A dance. I thought of Joe and of our conversation the night before. And even though I knew, deep down, that it would be a white lie to say he'd invited me to that particular dance, I told her I was busy. "I can't," I said. She looked at me and waited. "Joe Greenlaw asked me."

"Yeah, right," she said.

"I'm sorry," I told her. "He did." Sara picked up her backpack from between her feet and started to walk away.

"Sara!" I called after her.

"Let me know when you can fit me into your busy schedule," she hissed.

* * * *

This is the part of my story that is really embarrassing—the part that I wish I could tell in third person, as if it really belonged to somebody else. A week after the play was over Joe found me during sixth-period study hall. "I'm sorry," he said.

I looked at him, not understanding.

"Sara McGee asked me if it was true we were going to the dance together. I'm sorry. I'm going with Rachel."

I looked down at my feet. The new me was going away, like a picture on a computer screen that fades out. I was sure my ears were bright red.

"I'm sorry," Joe continued. "It's nothing personal." He turned and looked like he was leaving, but then he came back. He put his hand on my arm. "Don't be embarrassed," he said. "You know, I should have asked you. I wish I had." And then he left.

Now Sara passed me in the hall without speaking. I spent most of my free time studying or practicing my sprints. I went back to wearing my plain, comfortable clothes and threw away my makeup. And I only talked when teachers called on me. As if nothing had changed.

But that wouldn't be true. To Sara, I might have looked the same. Still, deep inside, where she couldn't see, there was another me. I was brave, I was fun. I got a standing ovation in the middle of a stage, and a boy regretted not asking me to a dance. And it was Sara I had to thank for introducing that girl to me.

Jane Denitz Smith

Somehow, the Fegley High Drama Club's presentation of *Jaws* didn't quite measure up to the movie version.

Teenagers Are Amazing

Teenagers are amazing,
I wish the world would see,
just how beautiful we are,
how compassionate we can be.

I wish they could take back,
all the cynical things they've said,
and see how much we shine,
be positive instead.

Remark on our radiant smiles,
and the differences we make,
all of the people our lives touch,
all of the chances that we take.

Notice how we change,
each and every day,
wanting to leave childhood,
yet desperately wanting to stay.

I wish they could remember,
how tough our lives can be,
the promises that are broken,
the violence that we see.

Yet still we venture onward,
unsure of where the road may lead,
hoping they will take notice,
hoping they'll take heed,
of the changes that we've made,
of the power that we hold,
of the wisdom we have hidden,
of the stories yet untold.

I hope the world will notice,
what some have already seen,
teenagers are amazing people,
striving to follow their dreams.

Jamie Haskins

So I Am Told

I'm a fourteen-year-old girl with moss-colored hair,
    sparkles and funny clothes, who feels lonely
    sometimes.
I do not ask to be understood because *I* can't even
    understand myself.
I ask to be accepted,
I ask to be accepted as I am.
I do not want to be told what potential I have, or what
    my future holds.
I do not want to be told that I'm going nowhere in life
    because I skipped a math test.
I question my existence, my meaning.
I question what the "Real World" is, and why I'm not
    there.
I feel happy with no shoes on.
I feel lonesome in a crowded room.
Sometimes my heart bleeds and I cry,
Laughter echoes in my mind.
I am told to be different,
To be myself.
But then I am told what to wear and how to act.

I like to write and rumors hurt.
I don't know how to dance, but I try to anyway.
Please don't try to understand me, nor judge me too
   quickly.
My name doesn't matter,
My heart is open.

Alexei Perry

Automobile Ambivalence

Life consists not in holding good cards but in playing those you hold well.

Josh Billings

I know it sounds a little strange since I live in Detroit, the Motor City, but from the time I bought my first car as a new teenage driver I've been afflicted with an apparently unique condition. Automobile ambivalence.

When I got my driver's license I was excited beyond belief. I'd saved some money to buy a little unsightly, plodder of a vehicle, so appearance didn't matter to me. Of course, not having much money, appearance really couldn't matter. This was a classic clunker car.

It didn't matter what it looked like; I was no longer chaperoned. I could drive to school, and I could pick up my friends. (Okay, I admit some of my friends wouldn't be caught in my car for fear of picking up some strange germs or being convinced the whole thing was just going to fall apart, without warning, at any instant.)

On the other side of the carburetor, my not-that-much-older brother had a passion for cars. He subscribed to all the auto magazines, washed and waxed his car every Saturday morning and kept the inside of the vehicle pristine clean. Our two cars, sharing the driveway, were pretty much the Odd Couple of autos.

Fearing that some strange occurrence would happen to his car being parked too closely to mine, my brother put a blanket over his every night, kind of like one of those jackets the X-ray technician wears to avoid exposure to radiation. My brother was convinced my car was sending out some type of harmful emissions well beyond what came out of my broken muffler.

I admit that his car was clearly the Homecoming Queen, while mine was, well . . . mine was pretty much the end-of-the-bench junior varsity football player who got his uniform dirty because he fell in the mud on the way to the locker room after the game. Not much talent, not much speed, dirty as can be, but still able to move in the right direction. Most of the time.

When I first heard the term "all-purpose vehicle" I believed they were actually referring to my car. My vehicle was multifunctional: It served as a mobile closet, storage area for sports equipment, stockpile for nonperishable food items and a portable periodical section of newspapers and magazines. Every "purpose" was utilized when an impromptu basketball game was organized for the park after school and I needed my gym clothes, a pregame snack, a basketball and shoes.

My automobile ambivalence did create a few problems on the homefront. This was clear when my brother was required to borrow my car because his princess of a vehicle was in the shop for probably some type of face lift or tummy tuck.

I gave him the latest briefing as he sprayed a few layers of disinfectant throughout and laid a clean towel over the driver's seat. The info I provided included don't lock the door because the key won't open it, the driver's side window doesn't roll down, the trunk light remains permanently on and don't park in a position where you'll need to back up to leave. Getting the car to go in reverse is usually a fifty-fifty proposition. It's not worth playing the odds given the potential difficulties of having to enlist the services of a passerby to push your car into a position where you can actually drive away.

When my brother returned from his jaunt in my jalopy I knew that something was amiss when he threw down the keys and simply stared at me.

"Problem?" I meekly proposed.

"You didn't tell me it stalls at most stops!"

"I guess I forgot to mention that little peculiarity. However, if you pump the accelerator twice, pull the passenger-side seatbelt once, turn the radio to country music and roll down the rear passenger-side window, it should start right up."

He was as amused as the time I had to confess to him that I'd backed out of the garage into his car parked in the driveway. I had seen his pride-and-joy vehicle as I'd entered mine but, apparently, my short-term memory wasn't in full operation that morning. As I heard the sound of metal on metal, I knew it wasn't a good sign. I told him that maybe having Dad put up some traffic signals in our driveway would be a good idea. He wasn't amused.

One of the benefits of automobile ambivalence is there isn't an overwhelming disappointment when a little body damage occurs. Heck, with my car, I'd have been hard-pressed to notice anything. The dents and dings throughout made it resemble one of those antique-looking candelabras you hammered away at in seventh-grade shop class.

Before going to advise my brother of the two-car pileup in the driveway I surveyed the injuries. I remember actually being somewhat pleased that I'd accidentally achieved some symmetry given that the previous huge dent on the rear driver's side now matched the new dent on the opposite side. I thought, for whatever reason, that maybe I'd now get better gas mileage. Kind of some new aerodynamic action. More wind resistant.

After having had this first car for a couple years, I recall feeling a little sentimental as we approached an important milestone—one hundred thousand miles. Despite my general ambivalence, I did love my car, warts and all. I recall thinking for this big event I'd do something really special. I first thought a drive-thru car wash would be nice, but I was a little hesitant since I felt some of the dirt and rust may actually be holding the whole darn thing together.

I finally decided on a drive-in movie. Just a teenager and his car. In years since, I've had more cars and my auto ambivalence remains. But you only have one first car and although it's no longer intact, my memories are.

Bob Schwartz

Always a practical joker, the rubber leg that Diane kept
in her purse livened up many a first date.

$\overline{9}$

GROWING UP

*M*aturity begins to grow when you can sense
your concern for others outweighing your
concern for yourself.

John MacNaughton

Minimaxims for My Godson

The purpose of life is a life of purpose.

Robert Byrne

Dear Sandy,

Your nice thank-you note for the graduation present I sent you a few weeks ago just came in, and I've been chuckling over your postscript in which you say that such presents are great but you wish someone could give you "half a dozen foolproof ideas for bending the world into a pretzel."

Well, Sandy, I must admit, I don't have any very original thoughts of my own. But through the years I've encountered a few ideas of that kind—not platitudes but ideas sharp-pointed enough to stick in my mind permanently. Concepts that release energy, make problem-solving easier, provide shortcuts to worthwhile goals. No one handed them over in a neat package. They just came along from time to time, usually from people not in the wisdom-dispensing business at all. Compared to the great time-tested codes of conduct, they may seem like pretty small change. But each of them has helped to make my life a good deal easier and happier and more productive.

So here they are. I hope you find them useful, too.

1. *If you can't change facts, try bending your attitudes.* Without a doubt, the bleakest period of my life so far was the winter of 1942 to 1943. I was with the Eighth Air Force in England. Our bomber bases, hacked out of the sodden English countryside, were seas of mud. On the ground, people were cold, miserable and homesick. In the air, people were getting shot. Replacements were few; morale was low.

   But there was one sergeant—a crew chief—who was always cheerful, always good-humored, always smiling. I watched him one day, in a freezing rain, struggle to salvage a fortress that had skidded into an apparently bottomless mire. He was whistling like a lark. "Sergeant," I said to him sourly, "how can you whistle in a mess like this?"

   He gave me a mud-caked grin. "Lieutenant," he said, "when the facts won't budge you have to bend your attitudes to fit them, that's all."

   Check it for yourself, Sandy. You'll see that, faced with a given set of problems one man may tackle them with intelligence, grace and courage; another may react with resentment and bitterness; a third may run away altogether. In any life, facts tend to remain unyielding. But attitudes are a matter of choice—and that choice is largely up to you.

2. *Don't come up to the net behind nothing.* One night in a PTA meeting, a lawyer—a friend and frequent tennis partner of mine—made a proposal that I disagreed with, and I challenged it. But when I had concluded what I thought was quite a good spur-of-the-moment argument, my friend stood up and proceeded to

demolish it. Where I had opinions, he had facts; where I had theories, he had statistics. He obviously knew so much more about the subject than I did that his viewpoint easily prevailed. When we met in the hall afterward, he winked and said, "You should know better than to come up to the net behind nothing!"

It is true; the tennis player who follows his own weak or badly placed shot up to the net is hopelessly vulnerable. And this is true when you rush into *anything* without adequate preparation or planning. In any important endeavor, you've got to do your homework, get your facts straight and sharpen your skills. In other words, don't bluff—because if you do, nine times out of ten, life will drill a backhand right past you.

3. *When the ball is over, take off your dancing shoes.* As a child, I used to hear my aunt say this, and it puzzled me a good deal, until the day I heard her spell out the lesson more explicitly. My sister had come back from a glamorous weekend full of glitter, exciting parties and stimulating people. She was bemoaning the contrast with her routine job, her modest apartment and her day-to-day friends. "Young lady," our aunt said gently, "no one lives on the top of the mountain. It's fine to go there occasionally—for inspiration, for new perspectives. But you have to come down. Life is lived in the valley. That's where the farms and gardens and orchards are, and where the plowing and the work are done. That's where you apply the visions you may have glimpsed from the peaks."

It's a steadying thought when the time comes, as it always does, to exchange your dancing shoes for your working shoes.

4. *Shine up your neighbor's halo.* One Sunday morning, drowsing in a back pew of a little country church, I

dimly heard the old preacher urge his flock to "stop worrying about your own halo and shine up your neighbor's!" And it left me sitting up, wide-awake, because it struck me as just about the best eleven-word formula for getting along with people that I've ever heard.

I like it for its implication that everyone, in some area of life, has a halo that's worth watching for and acknowledging. I like it for the firm way it shifts the emphasis from self to interest and concern for others. Finally, I like it because it reflects a deep psychological truth: People have a tendency to become what you expect them to be.

5. *Keep one eye on the law of the echo.* I remember very well the occasion when I heard this sharp-edged bit of advice. Coming home from boarding school, some of us youngsters were in the dining car of a train. Somehow the talk got around to the subject of cheating on exams, and one boy readily admitted that he cheated all the time. He said that he found it both easy and profitable.

Suddenly, a mild-looking man sitting all alone at a table across the aisle—he might have been a banker, a bookkeeper, anything—leaned forward and spoke up. "Yes," he said directly to the apostle of cheating. "All the same—I'd keep one eye on the law of the echo, if I were you."

The law of the echo—is there really such a thing? Is the universe actually arranged so that whatever you send out—honesty or dishonesty, kindness or cruelty—ultimately comes back to you? It's hard to be sure. And yet, since the beginning of recorded history, mankind has had the conviction, based partly on intuition, partly on observation, that in the long run a man does indeed reap what he sows.

You know as well as I do, Sandy, that in this misty area there are no final answers. Still, as the man said, "I think I'd keep one eye on the law of the echo, if I were you!"

6. *Don't wear your raincoat in the shower.* In the distant days when I was a Boy Scout, I had a troop leader who was an ardent woodsman and naturalist. He would take us on hikes, not saying a word, and then challenge us to describe what we had observed: trees, plants, birds, wildlife, everything. Invariably, we hadn't seen a quarter as much as he had, nor half enough to satisfy him. "Creation is all around you," he would cry, waving his arms in vast inclusive circles, "but you're keeping it out. Don't be a buttoned-up person! Stop wearing your raincoat in the shower!"

I've never forgotten the ludicrous image of a person standing in the shower with a raincoat buttoned up to his chin. The best way to discard that raincoat, I've found, is to expose yourself to new experiences in your life *all your life.*

All these phrases that I have been recalling really urge one to the same goal: a stronger participation, a deep involvement in life. This doesn't come naturally, by any means. And yet, with marvelous impartiality, each of us is given exactly the same number of minutes and hours in every day. Time is the raw material. What we do with it is up to us.

A wise man once said that tragedy is not what we suffer, but what we miss. Keep that in mind, Sandy.

Your affectionate godfather,

Arthur Gordon

No Longer a Child

Jordana was a twelve-year-old girl like every other; she worried about her clothes, hair and boys. She always had a smile on her face and a warm hug to share. What most people did not know about her was that this little girl had some very grown-up problems. Her father caused these problems. He had sexually abused her when she was five and physically abused her for years after. The emotional scars left her in hidden shambles. Her mother and father divorced when Jordana was eight, leaving her mother with sole custody.

When we met in seventh grade, years after the abuse had stopped, she seemed like every other twelve-year-old girl. We became instant best friends, gossiping about movie stars, rock bands and boys. Jordana seemed happy living with her mother and stepfather, and when I asked about her father she only told me that she did not see him anymore.

One June day, I found out one of her biggest secrets. It was hot that day after school, and we went in Jordana's backyard to tan in tank tops and shorts. It was then that I noticed cuts on her arms, mirrored by scars of cuts that had already healed. When I asked her where she received the cuts, she turned to me and began to cry stories of the past, horrors flowing from her lips as fast as the tears fell from her eyes. Jordana told me that she had cut herself because she felt so much anger towards her father. She told me about the nights of terror, about beatings and the bruises. I didn't know what to do so I just listened, consoled and counseled to the best of my ability.

Not until I had gone home did I realize what had just happened. Jordana had trusted me with information that she had hidden deep inside for a dozen years. She had chosen my hand to reach out to and pleaded silently for me to reach back.

As the weeks went on the cuts became more frequent, as if she was using her body as a personal canvas. I became increasingly scared. I was too young to handle this myself. I realized soon that I did not have the means to help her, and my decision lay before me like a shallow grave. That day after school when Jordana was at basketball practice I went to her house and knocked on the door and reached out the only way I knew how, "Mrs. Brown, I have something I have to tell you." It was then that I realized I was no longer a child.

Hilary E. Kisch

Finding a Vision

Six years ago, I went blind. Due to a severe herpes simplex virus in my eyes, I lost one of my most precious possessions: my eyesight. Tiny cold sores covered the surface of my eyes, scarring my cornea. I wasn't allowed to stand in direct sunlight or even in a brightly lit room. The light would penetrate my eyelids and cause too much pain. At the age of seventeen, I was unprepared to find myself in a dark world. Who would I be without my ability to see?

All I wanted throughout the entire summer was to be able to see people. What new cute bathing suit styles was everyone wearing? Who had cut their hair or dyed it purple? I would have a conversation with someone and realize that I had no idea what facial expressions he was making. I no longer had the ability to make eye contact, a privilege I had taken for granted before. I longed to talk with my eyes. I just wasn't whole without my vision.

My parents became my sole support system. Hoping for a miracle, they took me to an eye specialist every day. No one was sure if I would ever completely recover, and if so, how long the healing process would take. Meanwhile, Mom and Dad adjusted their own lives in order to keep

my spirits up. They would take me to baseball games and
out to dinner—anything to get me out of the house.
However, going places was difficult. I had to wear eye
patches and dark sunglasses to ease the pain of bright
light. As a seventeen-year-old, this wasn't exactly the
fashion statement I was trying to make.

My parents had to take care of me everywhere. At
restaurants they ordered my food, arranged it on the
table, and then explained where everything was on my
plate so I could finally eat it. My fifteen-year-old brother
took this opportunity to rearrange the food on my plate.
My mom was amazing. Each day she would brush my
hair and lay out a decent looking outfit so I could walk out
of the house with a little bit of pride. She was determined
to keep my self-esteem as high as possible. I relied on my
mom to make me feel pretty. At an age when I should
have been gaining my independence, I found myself
becoming increasingly dependent on my parents.

I wasn't able to drive or visit my friends. Movies were
completely out of the question. Life seemed to just go on
without me, as if I was never there. Fortunately, I had a
wonderful friend who knew how to make me feel special.
Donny and I had dated a couple of times before I lost my
vision, but at that time we were just friends. He would
come to my house to sit and talk with me. If the TV were
on, he'd watch and I'd listen. One time, Donny took me to
a baseball barbecue and introduced me to all of his
friends. I had never been so happy in my entire life. He
didn't care that I couldn't see his friends. He held my
hand proudly and led me around. I may not have been
able to see all the people I met that day, but their voices
are clear in mind. I can still separate whose laughter
belonged to whom. When I close my eyes now and try to
remember that day, I mostly see darkness. But I can still
smell the sausage and brisket cooking on the grill. I can

hear the happiness around me and Donny's voice saying, "This is my girlfriend, Talina."

I slowly began to make progress toward the end of the summer. Little by little, I was able to open my eyes. My vision was still blurred but this achievement called for a celebration. My parents were still concerned and Donny continued to stay by my side. Then I began to worry, *Will I have to start my senior year wearing my thick glasses that everyone still refers to as Coke bottles?* I didn't want to think about it. August crept up on me, though, and I started school with limited vision and thick glasses. As I walked through the halls, I struggled to look confident. I had a harder time cheering at pep rallies and football games. My lack of clear vision and concern with my physical appearance took the fun out of everything that I used to love. My level of self-confidence had diminished to an unrecognizable point.

At a time in my life when I expected my only concern to be to have fun, I was learning a powerful lesson. I could no longer rely on appearance to make me feel better about myself. I had to go deeper. With the support of my family and friends, I realized that feeling good about who I am on the inside is far more important. Believing that I can overcome the obstacles that I face is crucial. My identity wasn't my thick glasses. My identity was my inner strength. This inner strength allowed me to love life even when I was unable to see it. Losing my eyesight could not take away my ability to hear the voices of the people who love me. It could not steal away the fresh smell of morning or the lingering aroma of my mom's cooking. Most important, my loss could never take from me the feel of my boyfriend's hand around my own.

Six years later, I continue to need steroid eyedrops to keep the virus from reoccurring. The scar tissue is slowly improving. Recently, I began to wear both contacts, which is a huge accomplishment. A day doesn't go by that I am not thankful for my progress and the lesson I learned. I am incredibly thankful for my special friend who visited me, introduced me as his girlfriend and is now my husband.

I am currently preparing for my first year of teaching. I think about which of my personal qualities I might be able to share with my students. I know how difficult it is to grow up and I want my students to believe that I understand them. If I can't teach them anything else, I hope I can get across the lesson that changed my teenage experience: True beauty is not about what you *see* on the outside but what you feel, sense and love from within.

Talina Sessler-Barker

No More What Ifs

It was August 2, 1999, a day I would never forget. Indeed, it was my dad's fifty-third birthday, but something else about that day was also very special. I called my dad up to see if he would like to have lunch together for his birthday. He agreed, and half-an-hour later I arrived at his school. (He's an elementary principal.) He ordered us BLTs at a nearby restaurant.

We walked together to the small fast-food restaurant. As we neared the door, two young girls walked in: two beautiful goddesses. They recognized my father, and approached us. "Hey Mr. Margheim," they happily chimed.

My dad had been their elementary-school principal, so he introduced us. "Chance, this is Stephanie."

"Uh, hi," I said. I didn't catch her friend's name. I was under the assumption that they were both college students. My dad must have read my mind because he asked them their ages. Embarrassed, I rubbed my hands over my face, paranoid. *Do they know that I'm interested, am I obvious?*

"Juniors," they said in unison. *Perfect,* I thought. I am a senior.

The conversation pretty much ended there, unfortunately. They were both working, so I figured that it would be best not to talk to them too much. My dad and I sat down. He ate, I couldn't. My stomach was doing flips; I was secretly waiting for Stephanie to approach me, hair blowing, eyes sparkling . . .

I guess we waited for some time before my dad gave me the old nudge. "Gotta get back to work," he whispered.

As we left, Stephanie gave me the usual, "Bye, nice to have met you."

"You, too," I crooned, lowering my voice.

The car ride back was silent. I am usually the conversation starter, but I was too deep in thought. I stared out the car window, thinking. I thought to myself as I got out of the car and walked into my father's office. After much contemplation, I decided, I was going to ask this girl out! I gave my father a hug, wished him a happy birthday and left.

My mind was asking a million questions. *No more what ifs*, I said to myself. *I am tired of what ifs.*

I pulled into the parking lot of the fast-food restaurant, and sat in my car for a good half-hour, contemplating my move. I was nervous, very nervous, heart-popping-out-of-my-chest nervous. I literally felt like I was having a heart attack! I took a deep breath, prayed and walked into the restaurant. She was talking to someone, so I waited by the counter. Her eyes met mine, and she walked over to me. After what seemed like an hour of staring at her, I opened my mouth and let the words fall out.

"Umm, I know this is gonna sound crazy, but would you like to go out sometime?"

What a relief! I finally asked someone out! I studied her face, reading her reaction.

"Awww, that's nice, but I am serious with someone right now."

"Oh, yeah, okay, don't worry about it," I said, "that's fine."

"It was a good try though, right?" We both laughed. Our chat ended with a friendly handshake, and a "see you later."

Surprisingly enough, I wasn't disappointed. True, I would have loved to come home that night telling everyone that I finally had a date; and yet, I felt great! I had finally faced my fear and bit the bullet. I was prouder of myself at that moment than I had ever been in my life.

For the first time in seventeen years, I had faced my fear. I went home that day, and for once, I didn't have to ask myself, *what if?*

Chance Margheim

All the More Beautiful

At seventeen, I wanted desperately to be an adult, and believed I was making progress. I shaved almost every other day, and had my own wheels. The only thing I needed was the girl.

I saw her from a block away. She was tall, with long brown hair. We went to the same public school, but she often wore this plaid skirt, like a private-school girl. I drove up from behind, in my car, the only place I didn't feel short, and something amazing happened. She looked back at me. It felt just like one of those cheesy movies, slow motion, hair flowing, a halo of light surrounding her. She followed me with her eyes as I passed. That day, I felt tall wherever I went.

My luck didn't stop there. It turned out that she and my cousin were friends. He gave me her name and number. That afternoon, my sweaty, shaking hand picked up the phone, and I spoke to Kristen for the first time. That weekend, I drove down the same street where our eyes first met, to pick her up for our first date, my first real date ever.

I pictured myself sitting next to this perfect girl, in her

perfect living room, being interrogated by her perfect parents. I arrived, and all my expectations began to be challenged. There was no playful dog in the front yard, and no white picket fence to keep him from running away. Before I could knock on the door, Kristen opened it just enough to slip out. Then she smiled and all was perfect again. We went miniature golfing and laughed together for the first time.

After that night, we were inseparable, sickening all our friends. She made me feel like a big man, even though she called me her little guy. I had never felt so close to anyone before. But some mornings, when I'd pick her up for school and she'd slip out her door, something was different. She wouldn't have that perfect smile. She'd stare out the window and she seemed lost. I'd ask her what was wrong, and she'd say, "Nothing."

No answer could have been worse. It drove me crazy. I wanted to help. I wanted her to smile. Most of all, I wanted to be let inside. If I was an adult, it was time to start acting like one.

I confronted her; told her I knew there was something wrong. I knew she had problems at home, and I knew I could help if she'd just let me. Then she started to cry. I felt utterly helpless.

She put her arms around me and pressed her face into my chest. I felt her hot tears seeping through my shirt.

I soon learned that Kristen suffered from anxiety and depression. At home, she couldn't escape her past. Outside, with me, she could pretend all was perfect. When she started crying, she stopped pretending, and let me inside. I also stopped pretending. There were times when I didn't feel strong, when I didn't feel wise. There were times when I didn't feel like an adult.

During these past six years, Kristen and I have shared many laughs and tears together. I have had time to study her smile. I realize it is not perfect and, therefore, all the more beautiful. She continues to challenge and surpass all my expectations, teaching me more about life than I ever imagined there was to know. We talk about marriage and a family of our own, but we're in no hurry to grow up.

Marc Gaudioso

Return to High School

Don't be afraid to take a big step. You can't cross a chasm in two small jumps.

David Lloyd George

On September 15, 1998, two landmark events occurred that I'd been anticipating my entire life: I turned eighteen, and I began college. When my parents, my sister, our dog, four boxes, three oddly shaped duffel bags and our gray station wagon drew near to the university where I would spend the next four years of my life, I was terrified.

I fidgeted, played with my clothing and my hair, then tried to distract myself by passing a lost ant from hand to hand for fifteen minutes, before releasing it safely by the side of the road as we pulled up to the dorm. My ant-gazing left me nearly cross-eyed and largely unconsoled. By the time we reached the front steps, my fear had left an "anxiety wrinkle" in my forehead, one that I swear I can still see today.

Meanwhile, orientation passed in a blur, like racing down a water slide, from which I plunged into the first day of classes. I went to the wrong building for three of

my classes and the wrong side of campus for another. As
I race-walked from class to class, I kept thinking I saw
high school classmates, and had to remind myself that
most of them were now living on the other side of the
country.

Only six months later, on the occasion of my sister's
debut in the school musical, I would return home for spring
break and revisit high school; again, I felt terrified. As a
freshman in high school, I had felt like a shadow-
person until I found my place on the stage, where the true
me found expression in drama. In one of the great ironies of
my high school years, I felt the freest when my words were
scripted and my gestures rehearsed. Offstage, and out of
the classroom, I had felt like an outcast before the unfor-
giving eyes of my peers. Now, as a visitor from college who
had not quite escaped the ghosts of high school past, I was
going to watch my sister act, dance and sing on stage.

I arrived at my old high school two minutes before the
musical was to begin, intending to sneak in and out, like a
shadow in the night. But I'd forgotten that the shows
always started late, that there was an intermission, and
that I'd have to wait for my sister at the end to congratu-
late her. I would see everyone, and in the garish light of
the lobby, everyone would see me. I escaped temporarily
into the ladies' bathroom and practiced relaxed smiles,
only to discover that as the corners of my mouth went up,
the anxiety wrinkle in my brow deepened. With a sigh, I
went out to watch the show.

Taking my seat as the lights and sound dimmed and the
overture began, I tried to sit serenely. But I fidgeted, just
as I had during the last few minutes of that two-hour
drive to college, only this time, I had no ants to save. As I
watched my sister perform, I couldn't help feeling as
though I should be up on that same stage. And in that
moment, I genuinely missed high school, the place where,

as a senior, I had finally nearly fit in. Now I was a freshman all over again.

When the musical ended, I wove through the crowd, hugging classmates who had never really known me, searching for my sister. As I passed several of my former classmates, I looked them over carefully. Like me, they looked pretty much the same, as uncomfortable as I. One of them, a girl who might have become a good friend if social status had not divided us, asked me if I felt out of place, no longer a high school student, no longer a member of the cast. "Of course," I wanted to say, but now this seemed trivial. In high school, I'd almost always felt out of place. Only now had the sensation become manageable, like holding your breath under water, knowing that any second, you can pop back up and take a deep breath of air.

So I laughed and said, "Tonight I'm just the sister." She laughed too, but it was an awkward laugh. Now, she also understood what it was like to feel out of place, and suddenly I understood something about her, about the rest of my classmates. That night, the last night of our past together, we were all the same. I squeezed her hand, and, then, I had no trouble smiling a real smile, with both forgiveness and regret, before saying good-bye.

As I left the theater, I saw a few figures in the distance. Thinking I recognized them, I raised my arm and prepared to call their names. Then one figure turned toward me; realizing my error, I laughed. I had mistaken my sister's classmates for two of my college friends. In that moment, I knew where I belonged. Taking a fond last look at my high school, and my past, I walked through the gates to my car. A streetlight rose from behind a hedge, and my shadow pulled back and let me by.

Sierra Millman

Inspirations

Courage is the discovery that you may not win.
    and trying when you know you can lose.

Honor is standing for what you believe—
    not for what you know.

Life isn't about living without problems.
Life is about solving problems.

If you plow the field every day—
    the only thing that grows is resentment.

Compassion is passion with a heart.

The only thing in the whole universe people need to
    control are their attitudes.

How a person wins and loses is much more important
than *how much* a person wins and loses.

If you only do what you know you can do—
you never do very much.

There are no failures—
just experiences and your reactions to them.

Getting what you want is not nearly as important
as giving what you have.

Going on a journey with a map requires following
directions—
going on a journey without one requires following
your heart.

Talent without humility is wasted.

If you don't want it bad enough to risk losing it—
you don't want it bad enough.

When life knocks you down you have two choices—
stay down or get up.

Tom Krause

Who Is Jack Canfield?

Jack Canfield is a best-selling author and one of America's leading experts in the development of human potential. He is both a dynamic and entertaining speaker and a highly sought-after trainer with a wonderful ability to inform and inspire audiences to open their hearts, love more openly and boldly pursue their dreams.

Jack spent his teenage years growing up in Martins Ferry, Ohio, and Wheeling, West Virginia, with his sister Kimberly (Kirberger) and his two brothers, Rick and Taylor. The whole family has spent most of their professional careers dedicated to educating, counseling and empowering teens. Jack admits to being shy and lacking self-confidence in high school, but through a lot of hard work he earned letters in three sports and graduated third in his class.

After graduating college, Jack taught high school in the inner city of Chicago and in Iowa. In recent years, Jack has expanded this to include adults in both educational and corporate settings.

He is the author and narrator of several bestselling audio- and videocassette programs. He is a regularly consulted expert for radio and television broadcasts and has published twenty-five books—all bestsellers within their categories—including nineteen *Chicken Soup for the Soul* books, *The Aladdin Factor, Heart at Work, 100 Ways to Build Self-Concept in the Classroom* and *Dare to Win*.

Jack addresses over one hundred groups each year. His clients include professional associations, school districts, government agencies, churches and corporations in all fifty states.

Jack conducts an annual eight-day Training of Trainers program in the areas of building self-esteem and achieving peak performance. It attracts educators, counselors, parenting trainers, corporate trainers, professional speakers, ministers and others interested in developing their speaking and seminar-leading skills in these areas.

For further information about Jack's books, tapes and trainings, or to schedule him for a presentation, please contact:

The Canfield Training Group
P.O. Box 30880 • Santa Barbara, CA 93130
phone: 800-237-8336 • fax: 805-563-2945
e-mail: *speaking@canfieldgroup.com*
Web site: *www.chickensoup.com*

Who Is Mark Victor Hansen?

Mark Victor Hansen is a professional speaker who, in the last twenty years, has made over four thousand presentations to more than two million people in thirty-three countries. His presentations cover sales excellence and strategies; personal empowerment and development; and how to triple your income and double your time off.

Mark has spent a lifetime dedicated to his mission of making a profound and positive difference in people's lives. Throughout his career, he has inspired hundreds of thousands of people to create a more powerful and purposeful future for themselves while stimulating the sale of billions of dollars worth of goods and services.

Mark is a prolific writer and has authored *Future Diary, How to Achieve Total Prosperity* and *The Miracle of Tithing*. He is the coauthor of the *Chicken Soup for the Soul* series, *Dare to Win* and *The Aladdin Factor* (all with Jack Canfield) and *The Master Motivator* (with Joe Batten).

Mark has also produced a complete library of personal empowerment audio- and videocassette programs that have enabled his listeners to recognize and better use their innate abilities in their business and personal lives. His message has made him a popular television and radio personality with appearances on ABC, NBC, CBS, HBO, PBS, QVC and CNN.

He has also appeared on the cover of numerous magazines including *Success, Entrepreneur* and *Changes*.

Mark is a big man with a heart and a spirit to match—an inspiration to all who seek to better themselves.

For further information about Mark, please contact:

Mark Victor Hansen & Associates
P.O. Box 7665
Newport Beach, CA 92658
phone: 949-759-9304 or 800-433-2314
fax: 949-722-6912
Web site: *www.chickensoup.com*

Who Is Kimberly Kirberger?

Kimberly is the president and founder of Inspiration and Motivation for Teens, Inc. (I.A.M. for Teens, Inc.) a corporation formed entirely to work with and for teens. It is her strong belief that teens deserve recognition, a more positive image and better treatment within our society.

When she is not writing, Kimberly spends her time working for the empowerment of teenagers and the improvement of teen education. She provides a Web site that is designed as a safe and comfortable environment for teens to discuss complex issues, and give each other support and encouragement.

She reads the thousands of e-mails, letters, and stories sent to her each month and travels around the country speaking to high-school students and parents, using humor and compassion to bridge the gap of miscommunication. She has appeared as a teen consultant on television and radio shows, including *Geraldo*, MSNBC, Fox Family Channel's *Parenting 101* and the *Terry Bradshaw Show*.

Kimberly created the *Teen Love* series in answer to the questions teens most often ask her, and to enable them to gain wisdom and choose more wisely when making decisions in love and relationships. The bestselling *Teen Love: On Relationships* and *Teen Love: A Journal on Relationships* are the first books in the series. She is co-author of the *New York Times* bestseller, *Chicken Soup for the Teenage Soul;* the *New York Times* number-one bestseller *Chicken Soup for the Teenage Soul II; Chicken Soup for the Teenage Soul Journal* and *Chicken Soup for the College Soul*. She is also coauthor of the forthcoming *Chicken Soup for the Parent's Soul*.

Kimberly is involved in several nonprofit organizations. St. Anne's (a residential home for unmarried mothers), Yellow Ribbon Project (for the prevention of teen suicide), Challenge Associates (teen leadership training), and Dyslexia Awareness and Resource Center have all been recipients of her time and proceeds from her books.

As cofounder of the Teen Letter Project (T.L.P.), Kimberly saw her utmost dream come to fruition. With donations from sales of the books, the T.L.P. was developed. Staffed by teens, under the guidance of Kim, the project is responsible for answering the thousands of heartfelt letters received from teenagers. Together, they reach out to teens in trouble and encourage them, letting them know people care, that they can seek outside help and support for their problems, and that they are not alone in these challenging years.

Contributors

Liz Alarie passed away since submitting her story at the age of fourteen. Her family, which includes her mom and dad, one sister and two brothers, reside in Petersburg, Ontario, Canada. They can be reached at RR#2, Petersburg, ON., Canada, N0B 2H0 or via e-mail at *ralarie@continuum.org*.

Dani Allred is a resident of North Ogden, Utah. She will be graduating from high school this spring. She enjoys music and writing, and is involved in her school and community. She believes you should be glad about life, for it gives you a chance to love, to work, to play and to look at the stars. She welcomes your e-mail at *elisemckenna@hotmail.com*.

Andrea Barkoukis wrote her story while in high school at Gilmour Academy in Cleveland, Ohio. She loves to read, be with friends and write. She has always wanted to be a writer and hopes to pursue writing as a career. She can be reached via e-mail at *Heaven675@aol.com*.

Libby Barnes is a freshman in high school in Minnesota. She enjoys writing poems, songs, music, stories and also loves to sing. Although she has never been published before, she hopes that it's not the last opportunity she gets to share her writing. Libby dedicates "China's Story" to her friends, whom she loves with all of her heart. She wants to thank them for sticking with her through thick and thin.

Sarah Barnett is a student and freelance writer in Ft. Worth, Texas. She has written many poems and other works for various publications including The National Library of Poetry and the Iliad Press. Her story was told to continually remind herself and others that such a simple thing, brought on by a simple person, can conquer so much. There are no limits. She can be reached via e-mail at *Duchess305@aol.com*.

Michele Bender is a freelance writer in New York City. She has written for many publications, including the *New York Times, Glamour, Jump, Cosmopolitan, Cosmo Girl, Ladies' Home Journal, Fitness* and *Marie Claire*. She can be reached via e-mail at *Mbender878@aol.com*.

Sarah Bercot is currently a freshman in high school in Indiana. She has had poems published in three different compilation volumes and a cartoon published in *All About You*. Her recent letter to the magazine's editor sparked a local television appearance. Her passions include drawing, painting, writing and reading.

Laura Bloor is a student in high school in Ohio. Her hobbies include playing tennis, piano, writing, listening to music and being an active participant in many school clubs. Her future aspirations include writing for *Rolling Stone* or aiding in communications for MTV Network. Her story is dedicated to Colleen, whom she hopes never gives up on such an emotionally and mentally challenging disease. She can be reached via e-mail at *LoBlo311@aol.com.*

Stacy Brakebush is eighteen years old and is starting college in the fall. She plans to major in psychology at Saddleback Community College and transfer wherever God leads her. She is a leader in AWANA's at her church to third and fourth grade girls. She dedicates her story to her grandfather, James Smith, who passed away. He was a true example of human compassion and kindness and a soldier for Christ.

Bonnie Brightman's stories and historical articles have appeared in magazines such as *Highlights, Cricket, Boys' Life,* and *Guideposts for Teens.* One of her stories will appear in Meadowbrook Press's adventure series, *Girls to the Rescue,* vol. 7 and her biography of Jimi Hendrix will be published in Spring 2000 by Lerner Publications. She lives in Idaho with her husband, son and dachshund, Minnie. She can be reached via e-mail at *rmarkel@micron.net.*

Michelle Wallace Campanelli is a national bestselling author. She was born on the Space Coast of Florida where she still resides with her husband, Louis. She is a graduate of Melbourne High School, Writers' Digest School and Keiser College. She is the author of *Hero of Her Heart,* by Blue Note Books and *Margarita,* by Hollis Books. She is also a short-story author in several nationally distributed anthologies published by Simon and Schuster's *Chocolate For a Woman's Heart* series. She has always enjoyed writing and painting as outlets for artistic expression. Currently, she is working on the sequel to *Margarita.* She can be reached via e-mail at *MCAMPANELLI@juno.com.*

Melissa Cantor is a senior at the American School of Tegucigalpa. She plans to study creative writing and has already won several prizes for her writing. Her story is dedicated to her parents, who gave her the opportunity to travel, and to the amazing people she has met during her travels. She can be reached via e-mail at *melissacantor@hotmail.com.*

Nathen Cantwell is a high-school student in Aberdeen, South Dakota. He lives with his parents and little brother, and he enjoys drawing, writing, hunting, fishing and golfing. He wrote the story "Angel" for his mother for a mother's day gift in 1998.

Dave Carpenter has been a full-time cartoonist since 1981. His cartoons have appeared in a variety of publications, including *Reader's Digest, Barron's, Harvard Business Review,* the *Wall Street Journal,* the *Saturday Evening Post, Better Homes and Gardens, Good Housekeeping, Forbes, Woman's World,* as well as numerous other publications. Dave can be reached at P.O. Box 520, Emmetsburg, IA 50536.

Vidhya Chandrasekaran is a freshman in high school in Rockford, Illinois. She hopes to pursue a career in medicine. She has been writing short stories and poetry most of her life, and her various works have been published in books and local newspapers. Vidhya has also enjoyed playing the violin and dancing for a number of years and plans to continue. She can be reached via e-mail at *Vidhya85@aol.com.*

Harlan Cohen is twenty-six years old and one of the country's most widely read and respected syndicated columnists among people in their teens and twenties. His nationally syndicated *Help Me, Harlan!* advice column can be read in over sixty local daily and college newspapers across the country. When not writing his column, Harlan can be found speaking at college campuses, offering advice online and completing his first book. His speaking topics include dating, relationships, sex and the college experience. You can reach Harlan via e-mail at *harlan@helpmeharlan.com* or visit him online at *www.helpmeharlan.com*. Please forward all other inquiries c/o Harlan Cohen, 2506 N. Clark Street, Suite 223, Chicago, IL 60614.

Kelly Cook is presently a secondary-school teacher in the areas of mathematics and science. She spent a year working as a substitute teacher, principally with young adolescents with special learning needs. In her spare time she likes to dabble in drawing and writing. This story is dedicated to her family and friends, particularly her parents, Bill and Brenda, brother Darrell and friends Scott, Jane and Tracy: "Thanks for always being there."

David Cooney's cartoons and illustrations are published in a variety of magazines including *USA Weekend, American Legion, Mutual Funds* and the *Chronicle of Higher Education*. Through the scientific journals that feature his work, his cartoons are seen in over fifty countries. David's cartoons are also published in *The New Breed*, a cartoon feature distributed by King Features Syndicate. His cartoons run in numerous newspapers under the title *Twisted View*. David lives with his wife Marcia and two children in the small Pennsylvania town of Mifflinburg. His Web site is *www.davidcooney.com* and he can be reached via e-mail at *david@davidcooney.com*.

Liz Correale is a New Jersey native who currently attends college in New England. She is a psychology major with high hopes of a career in governmental intelligence. Liz attributes much of her inspiration to her deep faith and her mother's lively sense of humor. She remains happy by writing, running and guessing what color her sister's hair will be this week— fuchsia or royal blue?

Cheryl Costello-Forshey is a freelance writer, poet and songwriter who resides in Ohio. Her poem, "Making Sarah Cry," appears in *Chicken Soup for the Teenage Soul II* and *Stories for a Teen's Heart*. Cheryl's poetry can also be found in other *Chicken Soup* books: *A 4th Course, A 5th Portion* and *College Soul*, as well as the upcoming book, *Stories for a Faithful Heart*.

Emily Crane is a student at Kansas State University. She is majoring in advertising and is a member of the Alpha Kappa Chapter of Alpha Xi Delta. Her poem is dedicated to her cherished sisters of the pink rose and written for Josh. She can be reached via e-mail at *crane_emily@hotmail.com*.

Leesa Dean is a recent graduate from Mount Baker High School in Cranbrook, British Columbia, Canada. She is planning to further her education in order to one day teach high-school English. Her hobbies include reading, writing, traveling, going on outdoor adventures and talking to people. Her life goals include having fun, saving the Earth and making a difference! She can be reached via e-mail at *leesadean@hotmail.com.*

Brad Dixon was born when his mother was twenty-two years old. She later divorced his father who then left him and his sister. Their mother remarried and they were raised by a man named "My Dad." He was his best friend growing up and laid down a foundation for him and his sister surrounded by love. Brad has had a nice life and is still learning.

Stacey Doerner is seventeen years old and will be a member of the high-school graduating class of 2000. She enjoys playing soccer, running, spending time with her friends and family as well as reading and writing. She has been elected class treasurer the past three years and is a member of the NHS. Currently, she is looking forward to graduating and attending college.

Danielle Eberschlag is an OAC graduate and will be entering the University of Toronto. She enjoys writing poetry, short nonfiction stories and formal essays during her spare time. She can be reached via e-mail at *tayskiss_scottslove@themoffatts.com* or *hansonlives@hotmail.com.*

Sydney Fox was born on November 1, 1982 in Tulsa, Oklahoma. Her parents' ministry to the homeless and the poor moved the family to the Washington, D.C. area. Helping the needy sparked her writing desires. It transformed daily journal entries into inspirational anecdotes about poverty's struggles. She works in a camera store and hopes to couple photography with her writings. She loves drama, plays the violin and cello and sings. She's planning her future and college major.

Derek Gamba is an aspiring actor/filmmaker in North Augusta, South Carolina. He is currently a sophomore honors student at Winthrop University, where he is a theater major. He has had poetry published in *Anthology for Young American Poets,* and is thrilled to be in this book. Aside from writing, acting, singing and looking for a break in the film industry, Derek enjoys hiking, tennis, karaoke, theme parks, movies (anything by his idols, Steven Spielberg, Kevin Williamson and Wes Craven), music and spending time with his family and friends. Derek can be reached via e-mail at *Dstargg@aol.com* or *Dstargg@yahoo.com.*

Joanna Gates is a senior at Columbine High School and will graduate in May 2000. She lives in Littleton, Colorado with her parents, brother and a variety of pets. Joanna is an aspiring artist and writer and plans to major in visual arts in college. She also enjoys spending time with friends, singing and basketball. She can be reached via e-mail at *jgates123@yahoo.com.*

Marc Gaudioso is an aspiring screenwriter in Hollywood, California. He has a B.A. in English with an emphasis in creative writing from the University of Southern California, where he wrote a number of short stories. He can be reached via e-mail at *slvrscrn76@aol.com.*

Zan Gaudioso is a freelance writer whose stories have appeared in newspapers across the country. Zan earned her degree in special education for the deaf and went on to teach sign language, as well as teaching deaf children and adults. She became part of a landmark program that was the first to utilize sign language in order to foster verbal language skills in autistic children. From there, with additional training, she went on to become a surgical nurse. With writing as an integral driving force in her life, she continued to write and be published in newspapers and in family medical journals. She currently lives with her fiancé and their dog, Delilah, in Pacific Palisades, California. She can be reached via e-mail at *justzan@usa.net.*

Renée Gauvreau is seventeen and a senior in high school in Sudbury, Ontario. She loves music and enjoys writing poetry in her free time. "Suspicion" is her first published work. Thank-you to her friends and family for their support and encouragement and to Kevin, Howie, Brian, A. J. and Nick for the inspiration to live life to its fullest. Renée can be reached at *ReNeH@thespark.com.*

Jennifer Gearhart is a student at Baylor University majoring in professional writing. She is a member of Alpha Chi Omega sorority, and plans to go to law school. Her story is dedicated to her amazing parents, the family she adores, her alter ego Leigh Ann, the precious Mayos, her friends and Pantego Christian Academy. Above all Jennifer thanks Jesus for giving her hope and unconditional love. Jennifer loves you all very much. She can be reached via e-mail at *jjjgea@hotmail.com.*

Celine Geday is fourteen years old and is an honor-roll student in Washington. She enjoys writing short stories, poems and essays, reading, acting, dancing, listening to music and skateboarding. She is working on fulfilling her dreams and furthering her talents in all of these areas. She can be reached via e-mail at *NJCCGEDAY@juno.com.*

Randy Glasbergen has had more than twenty-five thousand cartoons published in magazines, books and greeting cards around the world. He also creates *The Better Half,* which is syndicated to newspapers by King Features Syndicate. You can find more of Randy's cartoons online at *www.glasbergen.com.*

Danette Julene Gomez is currently pursuing a career in the fashion industry, however writing remains her true passion, one she indulges in whenever possible. This piece was inspired by the joy and unconditional love she has shared with the two people who mirror her soul: her sisters, Darlene and Desiree. She resides in Los Angeles, California and this will be the first time her work has been published. She can be reached via e-mail at *DGomez6457@aol.com.*

Andrea Gonsalves is a student in her final year of high school in Ontario, Canada. She plans to study English literature at a university and become a novelist. She enjoys writing daily, finding it to be an effective medium for making sense of a confusing world. She hopes to use her writing to help and inspire others. Andrea can be reached via e-mail at *gonsalvesa@usa.net.*

Arthur Gordon was born in Savannah, Georgia. He has been managing editor for *Good Housekeeping,* editor in chief for *Cosmopolitan* and editorial director for *Guideposts* and *Airforce Magazine.* He has written two books, *Reprisal* and *A Touch of Wonder.*

Jennie Gratton graduated from Central High School in Manchester, New Hampshire in 1999, where she was president of the drama club and played trumpet in the band. She is currently attending Northeastern University majoring in English and theater. She has been writing on her own for years, keeping a journal and writing poetry and short stories. Jennie hopes to pursue a career in writing or costume design, and can be reached via e-mail at *Butrcup123@aol.com.*

Alison Hamby is a senior in high school, where she plays on the varsity basketball team and is drum major in the band. She enjoys writing in her free time.

Kelly Harrington is studying psychology at the University of Southern California. She is a member of Psi Chi, a national honors society in psychology, and teaches elementary education at a local battered women's shelter. She has many passions, all of which are reflected in her writings. Her poetry is published in *Mystical Night* and *America at the Millennium.* From the psychology perspective, she will witness her dreams, as well as the dreams of many others, come to life. She can be reached via e-mail at *kellz94@aol.com.*

Jamie Haskins is a sophomore in high school. She is captain of the Visual Effects Color Guard. She enjoys spending time with her friends, shopping, writing and twirling in the guard. She lives with her father and mother and her adorable cat. Her poem is dedicated to the many people who made her feel amazing and have helped her throughout the recent difficult times—you know who you are! She can be reached via e-mail at *sunkissed_daze@hotmail.com.*

Amy Huffman is a seventeen-year-old student in high school in St. Louis, Missouri. Her favorite pastime is horseback riding, but she also enjoys writing, reading, listening to music, and spending time with her friends and her boyfriend. She gives many thanks to her family and friends for their continual support and belief in her and her dreams. And special thanks to "Buddy," who has made many of those dreams realities.

Laurie Kalb is a member of the Class of 2000 at the Annenberg School for Communication at the University of Pennsylvania. Writing has been a passion of hers since she was a little girl. She also enjoys running, sculpture and nature photography. Although the lifestyle of a bohemian poet will always be appealing, she ultimately hopes to utilize her interest in human behavior and interpersonal relationships to encourage others to believe in the power of their own voices. She can be reached via e-mail at *Laurie248@aol.com.*

Molly Karlin is currently a high-school senior in Connecticut. She is class valedictorian, drama club vice president, student council secretary, reporter for the school newspaper and an active member of chorus and the National Honor Society. She aspires to write and star in a successful film or play. She would like to dedicate her story to the friends who have stayed by her through hard times (you know who you are). She can be reached via e-mail at *Sky1414@aol.com*.

Kendal Kelly was born on October 2, 1982, the second of four children. She lives in Bristow, Oklahoma, near Tulsa. She is a high-school junior with a GPA of 3.97. She runs cross country and track, and plans to take state championship before she graduates. She loves little kids and babies, and writes in her spare time. She plans to attend college.

Hilary E. Kisch, a resident of Toronto, Canada, has finished her first year of university as an English major. "No Longer A Child" is her first piece of work submitted to a publisher. Aside from her passion for writing, she enjoys singing, playing guitar, and participating in a variety of sports including rugby and wakeboarding. She would like to dedicate this piece to her mother and thank her friends, Meghan and Greg, for their continued support. She can be reached via e-mail at *Hilary79@excite.com*.

Tom Krause is a motivational speaker, teacher and coach. He is the founder of Positive People Presentations and speaks to teenagers, teaching staffs, any organization dealing with teen issues and business organizations in the area of motivation and stress reduction. He is the author of *Touching Hearts— Teaching Greatness,* "Stories from a coach to touch your heart and inspire your soul," a motivational book for teenagers and adults. He can be reached via e-mail at *justmetrk@aol.com*.

Thad Langenberg is a student in Shawnee Mission, Kansas. His poetry has been published by *Indian Lore* and by the Kansas State Poetry Society's *Sunflower Petals.* His poem demonstrates how a single act of warmth and kindness can preserve life. It is dedicated to people who think they mean nothing to the world. He can be reached via e-mail at *langy999@earthlink.net*.

Melissa Lew is a seventeen-year-old high-school senior in Fountain Valley, California. She lives with her parents and her older brother, Chris. She looks forward to graduating this year, but until then she is kept busy as the FVHS Colorguard Captain. She can be reached via e-mail at *MissaStar@aol.com*.

Brian Leykum is a freshman at New York University. He grew up on Long Island, but his family recently moved to Massachusetts. "My Friend Mike" is Brian's first published piece. He can be reached via a-mail at *CurlyJ81@aol.com*.

Kathryn Litzenberger is a member of the Class of 2000 in Cromwell, Connecticut. This is her first published work, though she has always loved to write. In her spare time she sings, acts, writes and spends time with her friends. She dedicates this story to those who encouraged her to reach for her dreams: her friends, her family, her teachers and to the little girl who inspired her story—Rikki. She can be reached via e-mail at *Jewel0442@aol.com*.

Laura Loken is now a seventeen-year-old student in Crosby, North Dakota. Her story, "Don't Cry, Dad," was written on Christmas Eve in 1998 when she was sixteen years old. She enjoys singing, writing music, working in a nursing home and hanging out with friends. She is active in FCCLA, Youth Alive and her church youth group. She can be reached via e-mail at *fire_blue62@hotmail.com.*

Chance Margheim is a high-school student from Blacksburg, Virginia. He enjoys writing in his leisure time and takes much pride in his work. He plans to attend a college in the near future and major in the field of communications, where he will work in the area of public relations. He can be reached via e-mail at *chance@bburg.net.*

Selina E. Matis is a native of southwestern Pennsylvania, and was born in December 1984. She wrote the poem "Ability" for an English assignment when she was thirteen years old. Her inspiration for "Ability" came from her English teacher and classmates. Selina is currently a high-school freshman, planning to graduate with the class of 2003.

Dianna McGill was born and raised in a small town about an hour north of New York City. Her parents moved from the Bronx about two years before she was born. She is the youngest of eight born to strict Irish Catholic parents. Her family overcame many adversities together financially, as well as emotionally, and they remain close. She is thirty-two years old and works as a senior client service rep in a very large insurance agency. Reading and writing are two of her favorite hobbies and she hopes to write a novel someday.

Sierra Millman's teenage years form a collage of creative expression in academics and arts at the Branson School and Stanford University, where she pursues her passion for theater, dance and writing. An honor student, National Merit Finalist and member of the Cum Laude Society, Sierra's first play, *Eccentricities*, won grand prize at the Rocky Mountain Playwriting Festival; she has published essays and articles, with stories in development, a children's book out with an agent and new ideas percolating. She can be reached via e-mail at *smillman@leland.stanford.edu.*

Morgan Mullens-Landis was born Morgan Nicole Maylee Mullens on December 28, 1982 in Gainesville, Florida. Her dad died a few weeks before her fourth birthday in December 1986. She was put in foster care in October 1995. She became Morgan Amithyst Landis on July 20, 1998 when she was adopted by Brian and Jackie Landis. She can be reached via e-mail at *amirose46@hotmail.com.*

Jennifer Orendach is a sixteen-year-old high school student in Allentown, Pennsylvania. She is extremely happy to have been given the opportunity to display her work to such a large amount of people. Her life has always revolved around using her writing to help others better understand her feelings. She would like to dedicate this piece to her family, her many friends, and the kind people at *Chicken Soup for the Soul*. She can be reached at P.O. Box 4065, Bethlehem, PA 18018.

Alexei Perry is a fifteen-year-old girl with a passion for writing. She has delighted in playing with words since she was two years old. If you should chance to see a young girl scribbling on a piece of candy paper, table napkin, feather or birch bark it is likely to be Alexei. In her poetry, she documents the pain and promise of life. She can be reached at P.O. Box 51, Site 2, RR#1 Elora, Ontario, N0B 1S0, Canada.

Jessica Pinto is a freshman majoring in English at the University of California, Santa Barbara. She was invited to appear on National Public Radio to read her poetry and had two poems published by the 1999 Marin Poetry Contest. She was accepted to the California State Summer School for the Arts in 1998 for creative writing, where she composed "Ode to Shoes." She can be reached at P.O. Box 202, Mill Valley, CA 94942.

Shad Powers is a freelance writer in Battle Creek, Michigan. He has written for magazines such as *All About You, Jump* and *U. Magazine*. He is currently a sports writer for the *Battle Creek Enquirer* and can be reached via e-mail at *ShadP40@aol.com*.

Kate Reder is seventeen years old and lives in San Francisco with her parents and her older sister, Libby. She is a senior in high school, where she is the editor of the newspaper and of a literary magazine. She recently spent a fabulous summer in a Native Alaskan village writing, thinking and doing community service.

Rick Reed is a business owner, franchise developer and motivational speaker, as well as a youth travel hockey coach. His story is dedicated to his loving wife, Amy, and his two awesome sons, Patrick and Calvin, to whom he commits his story as proof of a life lesson learned—one he hopes they can learn without direct involvement. He can be reached via e-mail at *RReed12879@aol.com*.

Daphna Renan is a recent graduate of Yale University. This is her fourth story in the *Chicken Soup for the Soul* series. She can be reached via e-mail at *daphna.renan@yale.edu*. This story is dedicated to her mother.

Danielle Rosenblatt is a sixteen-year-old student who enjoys theater, dancing, running, writing and laughing with her friends. She plans to pursue writing as a career and hopes to publish her own book one day. Danielle would like to thank her family and friends who have filled her life with love and encouraged her to reach for her dreams.

Lisa Rothbard is a seventeen-year-old senior in high school. She has been involved with the *Chicken Soup for the Teenage Soul* series since she was thirteen. She can be reached via e-mail at *Rothie99@hotmail.com*.

Jamie Rowen is currently a student at Swarthmore College in Pennsylvania, studying International Relations. She loves to write, especially children's stories. This is her first published poem and she dedicates it to the victims of the Columbine tragedy.

Bob Schwartz is a freelance humor writer with a concentration in the area of family life. He has a weekly column in a Michigan newspaper and his humorous writings have appeared in many national magazines and regional parenting publications. He also provides a monthly humorous column on running for numerous regional running magazines. He lives in Huntington Woods, Michigan with his wife and three children and can be reached via e-mail at *rschwartz@s4online.com.*

Talina Sessler-Barker, age twenty-three, graduated in 1998 from the University of Texas where she was a member of the Longhorn Cheerleading Squad. She currently teaches language arts and coaches cheerleading at Leander Middle School, while seeking her masters of education degree from Southwest Texas University. Her goal is to help young people realize that true beauty lies within themselves. She resides in Leander, Texas with her husband Donny.

Kristin Sester is sixteen years old and a junior in high school in Saint Charles, Illinois. She enjoys writing for both her advanced creative writing class and for pleasure. Currently active with her church, Kristin is a volunteer peer leader to confirmation students. She is also involved in extracurricular activities within her school, including Spanish National Honor Society in which she holds an office. Her favorite hobby is photography.

JoLynn Shopteese is eighteen years old and lives in Savage, Minnesota. She wrote "Forever Changed," as a speech that she was asked to give after a missions trip to Mexico. She is hoping that she can be leader on the same trip next year. In the fall, she will be a freshman at Bethel College. She is planning to major in Spanish and go into social work and maybe writing. She would like to thank her family, especially her mom for "putting up with her." She can be reached via e-mail at *volleyball13jo@mailexcite.com.*

Jane Denitz Smith is the author of two young adult novels, *Mary by Myself* (1994), and *Charlie Is a Chicken* (1998), both published by HarperCollins Publishers, and both Harper Trophy paperbacks. She is also the author of a board book, *Baby and Kitty and Mommy and Daddy* (Workman Publishing, 1994) and has written several plays, as well as novels. She writes and teaches in Williamstown, Massachusetts, where she lives with her husband and three children.

Sara Strickland is an amateur writer. She enjoys writing short stories and writing poetry. She is a student and a model. This story is dedicated to Kyle, the most important lesson she ever learned. She can be reached via e-mail at *SJStrickland@webtv.net.*

Elizabeth Stumbo will graduate as a member of the class of 2000. She participates in sports, scenery for school and community theaters, and is editor of her high-school yearbook. She hopes to pursue a career in the arts and communications field. She can be reached at P.O. Box 338, Ogden, IA 50212.

Ruth Ann Supica is a fourteen-year-old student in high school in Overland Park, Kansas. She really enjoys writing and is thrilled to have her first published piece be in *Chicken Soup for the Teenage Soul III*. This story is dedicated to her best friend, Laura Halvorson, who has stood beside her for all fourteen years of her life; to Teresa Hogan, one of her biggest inspirations; and to her wonderful family. She can be reached via e-mail at *Rootie14@aol.com*.

Julia Travis is a high-school junior in Livonia, Michigan, where she is class president and a member of the soccer team. Her work has been published in *A Celebration of Michigan's Young Poets—1999*. She would like to thank the friends who have always been there for her. She can be reached via e-mail at *Julesorama@aol.com*.

Micah Twaddle lives in Maryville, Missouri, with her mother, father and three brothers. She is currently a freshman. "Voices" is her first published writing. The past two years she has struggled with anorexia and, although she still has her days, she is slowly getting a hold on it. Her experiences with anorexia are what initially inspired her writing. She can be reached via e-mail at *mtstars_@hotmail.com*.

Kathryn Vacca is a seventeen-year-old senior in high school in Boulder, Colorado. She is the opinion editor of her high-school newspaper, as well as the captain of the dance team and the debate team. Dance is her first passion, but she enjoys writing and is looking forward to a career in journalism.

Tal Vigderson was born in San Diego, California. Tal has an undergraduate degree in film from San Diego State University. He has had careers in photography, entertainment-marketing research and teaching in several grade levels, including special education in a junior high school in south central Los Angeles. Tal attended law school at Loyola of Los Angeles and passed the California Bar. He is currently working as an entertainment attorney in Los Angeles representing filmmakers, writers, directors, producers, Internet companies and major studios in various forms of transactional work. Tal likes to travel and enjoys tennis, hiking and photography. He can be reached via e-mail at *TOV3@aol.com*.

Danni Villemez loves riding her horse Cal-o-Kashif, also known as Marshmallow because he is so fat. She only likes to ride him bareback because he is so comfy. When she rides she has lots of thoughts come to her and she makes sure she writes them down afterward. It drives her trainer crazy seeing sheaves of paper all over the tack room. Riding helps her to relax and is a great opportunity for her to reflect and pray.

Christine Walsh is a comedian and actress in the greater Boston area. She is a freelance writer who loves all genres of literature, but favors writing for children and adolescents the most because it encourages boundless creativity. This story is dedicated to Brad, the person who taught her how to believe in herself.

Whitney Welch is thirteen years old and in the eighth grade in Prineville, Oregon. She loves writing, especially poems and reading. In addition to cross-country running and track, she is active in tap and jazz dance. She travels as much as possible with her family and to date has been to twenty-eight states and Washington D.C. She plans to have a career as a teacher.

Kristy White is a fifteen-year-old sophomore in high school in Grass Valley, California. She enjoys acting, writing and playing the piano. She can be reached via e-mail at *eleemosynary29@hotmail.com.*

Tom Witte was a writer and graphic arts designer in Denver, Colorado. He wrote this poem for his nephew, Ben, on the occasion of his bar mitzvah. His "Message for Ben" was written with great love, and Ben is proud and honored to have it published in memory of Tom, who died of AIDS at the age of forty-six. Ben can be reached via e-mail at *BMR@one.net.*

Cecile Wood is a British citizen, studying at the College of William and Mary in Virginia. She is currently doing a semester abroad in Buenos Aires, Argentina. She is grateful to *Chicken Soup for the Soul* for giving her a chance to share her stories.

Rebecca Woolf is an eighteen-year-old currently living in Los Angeles, California. She works for Kimberly Kirberger and I.A.M. for Teens, Inc. She has concocted her own book of poetry, *Through Broken Mirrors,* and is working on a screenplay, as well as other various projects. She has been published in *Chicken Soup for the Teenage Soul II* and *Teen Love: On Relationships,* among others. She has appeared as a guest on MSNBC, Fox Family Channel and CBS's *Woman to Woman.* Becca frequently attends booksignings with Kim and speaks to elementary and middle schools about the importance and influence of writing. She is currently working hard furthering her career as a writer and a poet. She wishes to thank all the wonderful people in her life, including Kim and her wonderful parents, for their support and love. She can be reached via e-mail at *rebeccawoolf@hotmail.com.*

Lynne Zielinski, mother of seven and "Nana" to thirteen grandkids, resides in Huntsville, Alabama. She believes that life is a gift from God and what we do with it is our gift to God. She tries to write accordingly. Lynne can be reached by calling 256-883-1592 or 256-880-9052.

Permissions

We would like to acknowledge the many publishers and individuals who granted us permission to reprint the cited material. (Note: The stories that were penned anonymously, that are in the public domain, or that were written by Jack Canfield, Mark Victor Hansen or Kimberly Kirberger are not included in this listing.)

Never Been Dissed—Until Now. Reprinted by permission of Shad Powers. ©2000 Shad Powers.

Loving Yourself First. Reprinted by permission of Harlan Cohen. ©2000 Harlan Cohen.

Dear Girl. Reprinted by permission of Derek Whittier. ©2000 Derek Whittier.

Experience Is a Teacher. Reprinted by permission of Julia Travis. ©2000 Julia Travis.

Dear Boy. Reprinted by permission of Sarah Bercot. ©2000 Sarah Bercot.

A Crush. Reprinted by permission of J. Leigh Turner. ©2000 J. Leigh Turner.

Sea Glass. Reprinted by permission of Stacey Doerner. ©2000 Stacey Doerner.

Kiss. Reprinted by permission of Emily Crane. ©2000 Emily Crane.

He Finally Said, "I Love You." Reprinted by permission of Jennifer Orendach. ©2000 Jennifer Orendach.

The Funeral of My Rose. Reprinted by permission of Derek Gamba. ©2000 Derek Gamba.

My Childhood Sweetheart. Reprinted by permission of Leesa Dean. ©2000 Leesa Dean.

I Had to Let Him Go. Reprinted by permission of Andrea Barkoukis. ©2000 Andrea Barkoukis.

I Never Thought It Would End This Way. Reprinted by permission of Jennifer Gearhart. ©2000 Jennifer Gearhart.

Please Sign My Yearbook. Reprinted by permission of Stacy Brakebush. ©2000 Stacy Brakebush.

My Knight on His White Horse. Reprinted by permission of Rebecca Woolf. ©2000 Rebecca Woolf.

Fading Fast. Reprinted by permission of Kendal Kelly. ©2000 Kendal Kelly.

Why Rion Should Live. Reprinted by permission of Sarah Barnett. ©2000 Sarah Barnett.

My Fairy Tale. Reprinted by permission of Kathryn Vacca. ©2000 Kathryn Vacca.

Purification in Tibetan Buddhism

The Practice of the Thirty-Five Confession Buddhas

Geshe Jampa Gyatso

Edited by Joan Nicell

Foreword by Lama Zopa Rinpoche

Wisdom

Wisdom Publications
199 Elm Street
Somerville, MA 02144 USA
wisdompubs.org

Library of Congress Cataloging in Publication data is available.
Names: Jampa Gyatso, Geshe, 1932– author. | Nicell, Joan, editor
Title: Purification in Tibetan Buddhism : the practice of the thirty-five
   confession Buddhas / Geshe Jampa Gyatso ; edited by Joan Nicell ; foreword
   by Lama Zopa Rinpoche.
Other titles: Everlasting rain of nectar
Description: Somerville, MA : Wisdom Publications, 2016. | Includes
   bibliographical references.
Identifiers: LCCN 2015045434 (print) | LCCN 2016000523 (ebook) | ISBN
   9781614293262 (paperback : alk. paper) | ISBN 1614293260 (paperback : alk.
   paper) | ISBN 9781614293385 (eISBN) | ISBN 9781614293385 () | ISBN
   1614293384 ()
Subjects: LCSH: Byang chub sems dpa'i ltung bshags. | Sangs-rgyas-ye-shes,
   Mkhas-grub, 1525-1591. Ltung ba bshags pa'i òtåikka. | Confession
   (Prayer)—Buddhism. | Atonement (Prayer)—Buddhism. | Spiritual
   life—Buddhism. | BISAC: RELIGION / Buddhism / Tibetan. | RELIGION /
   Buddhism / Rituals & Practice. | RELIGION / Prayer.
Classification: LCC BQ5594.C65 B93335 2016 (print) | LCC BQ5594.C65 (ebook) |
   DDC 294.3/4446—dc23
LC record available at http://lccn.loc.gov/201504543

ISBN 978-1-61429-326-2   ebook ISBN 978-1-61429-336-1
20 19 18 17 16
5   4   3   2   1

Cover design by LZD. Interior design by LJ Sawlit.. Set in Village Titling and the Adobe Garamond family, 11/13. Cover image courtesy of University Museum of Zurich: Thirty-Five Confessional Buddhas thangka. Line drawings by Peter Iseli, Bern, Switzerland.

Wisdom Publications' books are printed on acid-free paper and meet the guidelines for permanence and durability of the Production Guidelines for Book Longevity of the Council on Library Resources.

● This book was produced with environmental mindfulness
.For more information, please visit wisdompubs.org/wisdom-environment.

Printed in the United States of America.

Contents

Foreword

Students, all my brothers and sisters in the Dharma, this book contains *The Bodhisattva's Confession of Downfalls*, a practice for purifying negativities and downfalls, together with a commentary by Geshe Jampa Gyatso. Geshe-la is a highly qualified virtuous friend who possesses the three most important qualities of merit, warm heart, and pure morality. He has been teaching Dharma for many years in the West, particularly in Italy, and has been extremely kind to innumerable Westerners.

When we have enough merit, we will be able to understand the reasons why the practice of the Confession of Downfalls should be done by everyone who wants happiness and does not want suffering. Success in achieving happiness and avoiding problems, both now and in the future, depends upon two requisites. These requisites function whether we believe in them or not. For example, we might not believe that a particular tiny seed planted in the ground can grow into a tree with thousands of branches covered in leaves, so huge that it can provide shade for five hundred horse carriages; however, that does not mean that this tree does not exist. In fact, there is such a tree in India, the *nyagrodha* tree. Likewise, even though we may not believe in reincarnation and the law of action and result, nor believe that this practice purifies our negativities, frees us from obstacles to generating the realizations of the path to enlightenment, frees us from the problems of this life and future lives, such as obstacles, illnesses, disharmony, harm, bad treatment, and abuse by others, and brings happiness and peace, both worldly and ultimate, it does not signify that this practice does not function to do so. Similarly, if we were to explain to a primitive person about rockets going to the moon, or about television, although he may not believe in the existence of these things, the mere fact that he does not believe in them does not mean that they do not exist. Reality is not necessarily as we believe it to be.

One of the requisites for success in achieving happiness and avoiding problems is to purify the causes of suffering, negativities created in the past. However, although this is of benefit, merely to purify them alone is

not sufficient; we also need to stop committing negativities in the future, the second requisite for achieving happiness. We need to change our own mind and our own actions; otherwise, we would be like the elephant who goes into the water to wash only to emerge and once again lay down in the sand—there would never be an end to our purification practice. This is why the practice of the Confession of Downfalls (which is done in conjunction with the four opponent forces) includes the force of turning away from faults in the future, the determination to not commit a particular negative action again, i.e., henceforth, to live in morality. With these two requisites, the purification of negativities already committed and the abstention from committing them again, we can purify all obstacles to our happiness.

Why are we not able to perfectly work for the benefit of sentient beings, to free them from suffering and cause them to attain happiness, and, especially, to lead them to enlightenment? It is because we are sentient beings whose minds are obscured; if instead, we were enlightened beings, buddhas, we would not have any obscurations whatsoever in our mental continua and would be able to perfectly benefit others. Therefore, since the practice of purification enables us to purify negative actions, the obscurations that prevent us achieving the realizations of the path to enlightenment, it is extremely important. By engaging in it, we will be able to perfectly work to free sentient beings from the depthless ocean of suffering and lead them to happiness; the very purpose of our lives.

When we mindfully and correctly practice the Confession of Downfalls even once, it has the power to purify even very heavy negative actions, such as the five actions of immediate retribution. This is the reason why Lama Tsongkhapa performed many hundreds of thousands of prostrations in conjunction with the recitation of the names of the thirty-five buddhas. This practice is extremely powerful; in some texts it is said that just by reciting the first name, that of Guru Shākyamuni Buddha, eighty thousand eons of negativities are purified. In fact, the mere recitation of each of the names of the thirty-five buddhas has the power to purify many eons of different types of negative actions. When this practice is performed together with prostrations (even the mere folding of the hands together in front of a statue of Buddha), we accumulate inconceivable merit. Therefore, it would be a great loss if we were not to take advantage of this opportunity to do this practice. In short, *The Bodhisattva's Confession of Downfalls*, the recitation of the names of the thirty-five buddhas, particularly when done in conjunction

with prostrations, is an unbelievably powerful purification, and enables us to accumulate extensive merit.

May this book composed by Geshe Jampa Gyatso greatly benefit numberless sentient beings by enabling them to purify their minds and achieve full enlightenment as quickly as possible.

Lama Thubten Zopa Rinpoche

Publisher's Acknowledgments

The publisher thanks the Hershey Family Foundation, Chiu-Nan Lai, Fiorella Bonolis and Luigi Carpineti, Magda Cavalieri, Sante Cinti, Laura Coccitto, Istituto Lama Tzong Khapa, Joan Nicell, Tagden Shedrub Ling Monastery, and Thubten Tsognyi for their kindness in sponsoring the production of this book.

Editor's Preface

The practices of purifying negativities and accumulating merit are the heart of the many methods taught in the Buddhist sutra and tantra teachings for attaining enlightenment. To gain any mental, or spiritual, development whatsoever, it is absolutely necessary to purify the negativities of body, speech, and mind that we have accumulated throughout our beginningless lives. These negativities have left imprints on our mental continuum that at some future time will ripen in the experience of suffering. Therefore, to avoid rebirth in the lower realms and the experience of unhappiness in future lives, and to gain liberation and enlightenment, it is essential to purify our mental continuum.

In addition to purifying negativities, we need to accumulate merit, or positive energy, to achieve enlightenment. This is done by engaging in virtuous actions, such as the practice of the six perfections—generosity, morality, patience, joyous effort, concentration, and wisdom. By means of these practices a bodhisattva, a being who is striving to attain enlightenment, is able to accumulate the merit necessary to bring about the mental development that reaches its zenith in the state of complete omniscience.

The advantage of engaging in the practice of *The Bodhisattva's Confession of Downfalls* is that it enables us both to purify our negativities and to accumulate merit. By applying the four opponent forces, which counteract our negativities, we purify our mental continuum of negative energy; by rejoicing in all the virtues created by ourselves and others and dedicating them to unsurpassed enlightenment, we accumulate great stores of positive energy.

For these reasons, the practice of *The Bodhisattva's Confession of Downfalls* is an essential method enabling both beginners and advanced practitioners to achieve spiritual development. A well-known story illustrates the benefit of this practice: Lama Tsongkhapa himself engaged in extensive purification through reciting this sutra and performing one hundred thousand prostrations to each of the thirty-five tathāgatas—a total of three and a half million prostrations.

During the Easter weekend of 1993 Geshe Jampa Gyatso, the resident teacher at Istituto Lama Tzong Khapa, Pomaia, Italy, gave an oral commentary to *The Bodhisattva's Confession of Downfalls* based on the Tibetan commentary *A Significant Sight (Byang chub sems dpa'i ltung ba bshags pa'i ṭīkka don ldan)* by Sanggye Yeshe. Prior to the course, I hurriedly produced an extremely rough translation that was subsequently revised with much help from Geshe-la and George Churinoff. Since the practice of *The Bodhisattva's Confession of Downfalls* has enormous benefits, I hope that these two commentaries on the practice—one by a noted lineage guru of the stages of the path (lamrim) teachings and one by a contemporary teacher thoroughly familiar with the Western mind—will inspire many people to engage in this profound practice.

THE LIFE OF SANGGYE YESHE

This short biography of Sanggye Yeshe summarizes the main points of the extensive life story in Yeshe Gyeltsen's *Biographies of the Lineage Gurus of the Stages of the Path.*[1]

Sanggye Yeshe was born in 1525 in the small village of Druggya in the Tsang valley of Tibet. Auspicious signs occurred at his birth, and even at a very young age his behavior was uncommonly mature and subdued. He was often seen playing at teaching Dharma, meditating, and debating and, although very young, he often expressed the wish to become a monk. This behavior is attributed to his familiarity with the morality of renunciation gained in many previous lives when he had been born as a learned scholar and yogi in India. The renowned Gyelwa Ensapa, considered by Tibetans to be the first Panchen Lama, foreseeing that Sanggye Yeshe was to become his successor as a lineage holder, urged the parents to take special care of their son.

At the age of ten, the young boy received lay vows (*upāsaka, dge bsnyen*)[2] from his first teacher, Yönten Zangpo, and was given the name Chökyab Dorje. He studied reading and writing with this teacher, demonstrating remarkable ease in understanding whatever he was taught. Later, upon receiving the vows of a novice monk (*shrāmaṇera, dge tsul*) from this same master, he became known as Sanggye Yeshe.

At the age of fifteen Sanggye Yeshe entered Tashilünpo Monastery and began studying the philosophical subjects with Tsöndru Gyeltsen. The following year, when considering whether to go study at Sera Monastery with

Sanggye Yeshe (1525–1591)

Jetsün Chökyi Gyeltsen, a friend advised him to study instead under the tutelage of that master's disciple, Jamyang Gendün Lozang, who was considered a manifestation of Manjushri. Sanggye Yeshe studied Pramāṇa logic and epistemology with this master and then returned to Tashilünpo Monastery, where until the age of eighteen he studied Madhyamaka philosophy. At the age of nineteen he debated in front of a large gathering of abbots and monks at Tashilünpo and, undefeated, became renowned for his knowledge and understanding of the scriptures.

Sanggye Yeshe then studied the Perfection of Wisdom literature and the Vinaya, and once again his extraordinary depth of understanding was noted by his teachers. At the age of twenty-six, following the advice of Gendün Lozang, he became the disciplinarian at Tashilünpo. At the conclusion of these duties, Sanggye Yeshe traveled to Gangchen Chöpel Monastery, where

he received many teachings from Panchen Rinpoche Dönyö Gyeltsen on both sutra and tantra, including the transmission of many teachings on mind training (*lojong*). He then attended the Lower Tantric College, where he studied and mastered the tantras, rituals, ritual dance, mandala drawing, ritual music, chanting, and the rituals associated with burnt offerings. During this time a severe bout of leg pain made Sanggye Yeshe determine to return to Tsang following the completion of his studies at the Lower Tantric College. This pain is attributed to Palden Lhamo, a Dharma protector, who had been directed by Gyelwa Ensapa to bring Sanggye Yeshe back to him. Subsequently, Sanggye Yeshe went to study with Gyelwa Ensapa and received the transmission of the teachings on the stages of the path (*lamrim*) from this learned master, who became his root guru. Sanggye Yeshe spent many years in meditation based on these teachings, greatly pleasing his teacher. Having requested Gyelwa Ensapa for permission to receive the vows of a fully ordained monk, he received them from the abbot of Riwo Gepel Monastery, Chogle Nampar Gyelwa. After receiving teachings from this abbot, Sanggye Yeshe returned to Ensa Monastery, where he received the transmission of a great number of tantra initiations and commentaries from Gyelwa Ensapa. Upon the passing away of this precious master, Sanggye Yeshe made many offerings to the monastery and commissioned the making of many images.

Twice Sanggye Yeshe became the abbot of Riwo Gepel Monastery and in this position turned the wheel of Dharma for the benefit of his many disciples. Later, returning to Ensa, he gave extensive teachings on both the sutras and tantras. During this time, he took great care of Gyelwa Ensapa's incarnation, Lozang Chökyi Gyeltsen, bestowing upon him first the lay and later the novice vows as well as many teachings and the blessings of numerous initiations.

In short, Sanggye Yeshe's entire life was dedicated to Dharma practice—the suppressing of the mental afflictions and the practice of deity yoga. He passed away in 1591 at the age of sixty-seven, his death being accompanied by many marvelous signs. Various rites were conducted during the forty-nine days in which his body remained enclosed in a special structure built for the cremation. Following the cremation, uncommonly large relic pills, one the size of a pea, were found amassed together in the shape of eyes, brain, tongue, heart, and central channel. His main disciple, Panchen Lozang Chökyi Gyeltsen, had a stupa constructed on the cremation site to contain the relics and commissioned the making of a huge gold-covered

copper statue of Sanggye Yeshe. It was upon the passing away of his precious root guru, Sanggye Yeshe, that Panchen Lozang Chökyi Gyeltsen was inspired to write the *Guru Puja* (*Lama Chöpa*). Although Sanggye Yeshe had many well-known disciples, the best is said to have been Lozang Chökyi Gyeltsen, the reincarnation of Gyelwa Ensapa, who although considered by Westerners to be the first Panchen Lama, is considered by Tibetans to be the second.

TECHNICAL NOTE

The root text, *The Bodhisattva's Confession of Downfalls*, translated by George Churinoff and included here with his kind permission, is set in italic type to distinguish it from *A Significant Sight*, Sanggye Yeshe's explanation. Both the root text and Sanggye Yeshe's explanation have been indented to set them apart from Geshe Jampa Gyatso's commentary. I have abbreviated and modified some of the titles and subtitles in Sanggye Yeshe's explanation and have added extra subtitles at many points. A complete translation of the original outline can be found in the appendices.

For the sake of readability, phrases such as "This is taught (or shown) by saying…," or "The meaning of this is…," that occur in Sanggye Yeshe's commentary, respectively before and after each section of the root text, have been omitted. While these phrases are necessary in the Tibetan to show the demarcation between the root text and Sanggye Yeshe's explanation, I felt them to be unnecessary in the English, as this demarcation has been accomplished typographically. Also, while the commentary generally cites only the first and last few words of each of the relevant sections of the root text, here complete citations have been included for easier reference.

The chart indicating the colors and hand positions of the thirty-five tathāgatas is translated from Lama Tsongkhapa's *Practice of the Thirty-Five Buddhas and a Description of the Deities' Bodies*.

Most of the commentary by Geshe Jampa Gyatso included here is a transcription of his 1993 teachings on *A Significant Sight*. However, the detailed explanations of actions and their results—the four characteristics of actions (included in the introduction), the four types of results (included in the chapter "The Four Opponent Forces"), and the four branches of a complete path of action, as well as the ten non-virtues (included in the chapter "The Force of Total Repudiation" under the heading Negativities Included in the Ten

Non-Virtues)—have been incorporated from Geshe-la's teachings on Panchen Lozang Yeshe's *Quick Path* (*Lam rim myur lam*) given at Istituto Lama Tzong Khapa, August 2–8, 1984. The subsection The Mind of Enlightenment included in the chapter "The Force of the Basis" is a transcription of Geshe-la's commentary given at Istituto Lama Tzong Khapa February 23–24, 1985, on a text from *The Collected Works on Mind Training* by Kyabje Trijang Rinpoche. At Geshe-la's suggestion I myself wrote the very brief overview of the seven-point meditation for developing the mind of enlightenment. This is not included in a more detailed format since extensive explanations of this meditation are already available in other English commentaries on the stages of the path. The lists of the eight qualities of the Buddha, Dharma, and Sangha Jewels (included in the subsection Refuge in the chapter "The Force of the Basis") are an abbreviated translation from Jetsün Chökyi Gyeltsen's *Ocean Playground of the Lord of the Nāgas*. In addition, when I felt that a certain point needed further explanation, I personally questioned Geshe-la about it and then added his clarifications to this text.

Words already familiar to most Western Buddhist readers—such as dharani, Mahayana, nirvana, sangha, stupa, and sutra—have been treated as English words throughout the text and consequently the Sanskrit diacritical marks have been omitted.

The transliteration of Sanskrit words is according to the standard international system except that for ease of reading in English ś is written as sh, ṣ as ṣh, c as ch, and ch as chh. The transliteration of the Tibetan follows the system of Turrell Wylie, with the root letter rather than the initial letter capitalized in proper names and titles. Except for names of contemporary Tibetans, which are rendered according to precedent, I have written Tibetan proper names and the phonetics of *The Bodhisattva's Confession of Downfalls* in a simplified manner to facilitate their reading rather than striving for perfect pronunciation.

ACKNOWLEDGMENTS

The translation of the text *A Significant Sight* was made possible only due to Geshe Jampa Gyatso's infinite patience in answering my seemingly never-ending questions.

I am also extremely grateful to Venerable George Churinoff (Gelong

Thubten Tsultrim), who not only encouraged me to learn Tibetan and taught me how to read it but also went over the entire Tibetan text with me, thereby allowing me to improve the translation and to correct inaccuracies that would otherwise have gone unnoticed. I am also deeply indebted to Ven. George for his permission to include his translation of *The Bodhisattva's Confession of Downfalls* in this publication.

I would also like to extend my sincere thanks to Acharya Ngawang Lodoe for the help that he gave me in translating some of the more difficult grammatical points in the Tibetan text as well as for his help in writing the biography of Sanggye Yeshe.

I am indebted to Peter Iseli for taking time out from his busy schedule to provide the line drawing of Sanggye Yeshe above and the beautiful illustrations of how to do prostrations.

In addition, I would also like to express my appreciation to Venerable Massimo Stordi (Gelong Thubten Tsognyi), the director of Istituto Lama Tzong Khapa, for supporting me at the institute during the period of my work on this project.

Last, but definitely not least, a big thank you to the staff of Wisdom Publications, in particular Venerable Connie Miller, Editorial Projects Manager, for their advice, encouragement, and patience during all stages of this work.

Joan Nicell (Getsulma Tenzin Chöden)

A Significant Sight

*An Explanation of
the Bodhisattva's Confession
of Downfalls*

by Sanggye Yeshe

Commentary by Geshe Jampa Gyatso

Introduction

From a Buddhist point of view our experiences, pleasant and unpleasant, come about as a result of our own previous actions, virtuous and non-virtuous. These actions can be physical, verbal, or mental. However, in each of these cases the action originally stems from the mind since, prior to engaging in an action, a wish or intention to do that particular action always arises. Following upon the intention, we actually engage in the action. We experience its corresponding result later on, generally in a future life but possibly even in the same life. Since all our experiences are the result of our previous actions, the Buddha emphasized the law of cause and result in his teachings. For example, Buddha taught that actions have four general characteristics: (1) actions are definite, (2) actions increase, (3) actions not done will not be experienced, and (4) actions done will not go to waste.

1. Actions are definite

Virtuous actions definitely bring the result of happiness and never bring the result of suffering. Likewise, non-virtuous actions definitely bring the result of suffering and never bring the result of happiness. Internal causes and results function along much the same principles as external causes and results. An example of an external cause is planting an apple seed in the ground; in accordance with the cause—the apple seed—the result of an apple tree is produced. Were we to plant a pepper seed, a pepper plant would arise instead. An apple seed cannot give rise to a pepper plant, nor can a pepper seed give rise to an apple tree.

Internal causes and results function in the same manner; in accordance with the cause, virtuous actions, we definitely experience the result of happiness. Likewise, in accordance with the cause, non-virtuous actions, we definitely experience the result of suffering. Just as the small pleasure of a cool breeze on a hot day is the result of a past virtuous action, similarly, the

small suffering of a thorn pricking the sole of the foot is the result of a past non-virtuous action.

2. Actions increase

In the same way that a tiny seed can produce the result of a huge tree, a very small virtuous or non-virtuous action can bring a great result. This is because an action continues to increase as long as its antidote is not applied. If a non-virtuous act is purified using an appropriate method, we may not completely avoid experiencing its result, but we will at the very least be able to prevent it from increasing. Conversely, we destroy our virtuous actions through giving in to anger or holding wrong views.

3. Actions not done will not be experienced

Not having planted seeds in the ground, we will not reap a crop in the autumn. Likewise, if we have not done a particular virtuous or non-virtuous action, we will not experience its respective result of happiness or unhappiness.

4. Actions done will not go to waste

Having done a virtuous or non-virtuous action, if it is not destroyed by its antidote, its result will manifest when the necessary conditions come together. An action will never go to waste due to the passage of time. When we put our money in a bank, it remains there as long as we do not withdraw it, and in the meantime it continually produces interest; likewise, when we do an action, if it is not destroyed by its antidote, it will not disappear but will continually increase.

In addition to explaining the detailed functioning of actions and results, the Buddha also explained, by way of his clairvoyant powers, why a particular person was experiencing certain problems. He often told how at one time such-and-such a person had taken such-and-such a birth, did such-and-such an action, and was thereby experiencing such-and-such a result. Many examples of these stories can be found in *The Hundred on Karma Sutra* (*Karmashataka-sūtra*) and *The Sutra of the Wise and the Foolish* (*Damamūkosūtra*).

Through understanding that virtuous actions bring happiness and non-virtuous actions bring suffering, we see how important it is to continually strive to develop a good motivation and to engage in virtuous actions. At

the same time, we understand that we must completely abandon committing even seemingly insignificant non-virtuous actions so as to avoid experiencing further suffering and problems in the future. We may understand this intellectually, but because our mind is not subdued and is therefore influenced by many types of negative emotions or afflictions, we continue to commit non-virtuous actions. Our negative emotions are very strong while our positive thoughts are generally quite weak, and these two are always in competition. Most of the time the weaker positive side loses and the more powerful negative side wins, and our minds remain dominated by afflictions that in turn cause us to continue engaging in non-virtue.

Therefore, just as we clean our dirty clothes with soap and water, we need to purify our mental continuum of non-virtuous actions of body, speech, and mind. To avoid experiencing their unpleasant results, it is vital that we develop the habit of regularly purifying our inner dirt, the impure mind. For this purpose we engage in a practice of purification such as *The Bodhisattva's Confession of Downfalls*. When this practice is done in conjunction with the application of the four opponent forces, not only will we purify the non-virtuous actions committed in this life, we will also purify those committed during all our beginningless lives in cyclic existence. This practice is therefore essential in our quest for spiritual, or mental, development.

> I devoutly prostrate to the thirty-five tathāgatas, the gurus, the
> special deities, and all those worthy of prostration.

At the beginning of his commentary, Sanggye Yeshe pays homage, or prostrates, to the thirty-five tathāgatas, the gurus, the special deities, and all those worthy of prostration. Tathāgata, a Sanskrit epithet for a buddha, literally translated as One Gone Thus, indicates that a buddha simultaneously knows all phenomena as well as their thusness, or emptiness. "Guru" in Sanskrit, "lama" in Tibetan, "spiritual teacher" in English, refer to both the teachers from whom we directly receive teachings as well as to the lineage gurus from whom we indirectly receive teachings. The syllable *gu* of guru derives from the Sanskrit word *gun*, meaning "quality," while *ru* derives from *rup*, meaning "heavy" or "weighty." Therefore, the Sanskrit word *guru* signifies "one with weighty qualities."

In the context of Buddhism there are four classes of tantra: action, performance, yoga, and highest yoga tantra. The deities of these four classes are

called special deities. Four special, or main, deities are practiced in the Kadampa tradition: Shākyamuni Buddha, Avalokiteshvara (Chenrezig), Tārā (Drolma), and Achalā (Miyowa). Shākyamuni Buddha is the founder of the doctrine; Avalokiteshvara is the compassion of all the buddhas of the three times manifested as a deity; Tārā is the manifestation of all the buddhas' activities; and Achalā is the manifestation of all the buddhas' energy or power. By practicing these four deities, we are able to make rapid progress in our spiritual, or mental, development.

"All those worthy of prostration" refers to the objects of prostration: the buddhas, bodhisattvas, solitary realizers (*pratyekabuddha*), hearers (*shrāvaka*), dākas, dākinīs,[3] and Dharma protectors.[4] Prostrations are a way of showing respect for the objects we venerate. The Tibetan word for prostration is *chag-tsel* (*phyag 'tshal*) with the particle *lo* often added at the end of the phrase. Although *chag* in most contexts is the honorific word for "hand," here in relation to the objects of prostration it means, "You who possess the qualities of perfect compassion, wisdom, skill, and so on." *Tsel* means "to desire"—in this context, "I desire to attain your realizations." And *lo* here signifies, "Please bestow on me your realizations."

Prostrations are performed with the body, speech, and mind. We prostrate with our bodies by touching our legs, arms, and head to the ground, with our speech we recite verses of praise, and with our mind we generate faith through remembering and rejoicing in the qualities of the objects of prostration.

> I will express a mere portion of the meaning of the profound
> *Sutra of the Bodhisattva's Confession of Downfalls.*

The author of the commentary promises to give a short explanation of the *Sutra of the Bodhisattva's Confession of Downfalls* in a very simple way that is easy to understand.

> Our unsurpassed teacher, lord of the subduers, taught us, the
> disciples of the three realms, eighty-four thousand collections of
> doctrine as antidotes to be used against the eighty-four thousand
> afflictions—attachment and so forth.

The teachings of Shākyamuni Buddha are said to be able to subdue the dis-

ciples of the three realms—the beings of the desire, form, and formless realms. However, there is some debate as to whether the beings of the formless realm can actually be Shākyamuni Buddha's disciples since, lacking the aggregate of form, they do not have sense faculties and consequently can neither see Buddha nor listen to his teachings. The conclusion is that Buddha's disciples do in fact exist in the formless realm since a superior (*ārya*)[5] who was Buddha's disciple in a previous life can be reborn there.

There is a total of eighty-four thousand afflictions because there exist twenty-one thousand types of attachment, anger, and ignorance, respectively, as well as twenty-one thousand afflictions that are a combination of the three. Buddha gave his teachings, the eighty-four thousand collections of doctrine, as the antidotes to corresponding afflictions in accordance with the various dispositions, interests, and thoughts of the many sentient beings.

> In the profound *Sutra Indicating the Four Dharmas* (*Chatur-dharmanirdesha-sūtra*), which is like the foundation, or base, and root of the [eighty-four thousand collections of doctrine], it is taught, "Furthermore, when a non-virtuous action is performed, the function of total repudiation is to develop regret for it."

The four dharmas are the four opponent forces, the four essential aspects of every purification practice. The sutra that explains them is called the foundation, base, and root of the eighty-four thousand collections of doctrine, all Buddha's teachings, because these antidotes to the eighty-four thousand afflictions can be subsumed in the four opponent forces, which are the means to purify all negativities.

The meaning of this [quotation] is explained in the *Compendium of Instructions* (*Shikṣhāsamuchchaya*) through dividing [the explanation] into two: the confession of the heap of negativities in general, and the confession of the downfalls of a bodhisattva in particular.

A heap, or aggregate, implies many things brought together; in this case, our non-virtuous actions. Shāntideva in his *Compendium of Instructions* explains in general how to purify the many negative actions we have committed in both this and previous lives, as well as explaining in particular how to purify those committed by a bodhisattva. Although the term bodhisattva usually refers to a being who has generated the actual mind of enlightenment (*bodhichitta*), in this context it includes any person who

even aspires to develop the wish to attain enlightenment for the sake of all sentient beings.

> Furthermore, four confessions of downfalls are taught in *The Heap of Jewels Sutra* (*Ratnakūṭa-sūtra*), the delineation of the Vinaya requested by Upāli: (1) confession to a group of ten, (2) confession to a group of five, (3) confession in front of one or two—these being from the point of view of the gravity of the downfall—and (4) confession in the presence of the thirty-five buddhas. Among them, the topic on this occasion is the sutra taught to show how to confess negativities and downfalls before the thirty-five buddhas.

As taught in *The Heap of Jewels Sutra,* downfalls are confessed in front of larger or smaller groups of fully ordained monks in dependence on the gravity of the downfall. We should confess our heavier, or more serious, downfalls before a group of ten monks, our lesser downfalls before a group of five, and our least serious transgressions before one or two monks. Alternatively, we can confess our negativities in the presence of the thirty-five buddhas through reciting *The Sutra of the Bodhisattva's Confession of Downfalls* in conjunction with performing prostrations. The explanation of the latter method for confessing downfalls is the topic of this commentary.

Part One

Purifying Negativities and Downfalls

1. The Four Opponent Forces

As taught, "Especially due to the importance of purifying karmic obscurations, continually cherish reliance on all four forces," it is necessary to confess negativities and downfalls by means of all four opponent forces.

This quotation from Lama Tsongkhapa's *Lines of Experience* (*Nyams mgur*) emphasizes the importance of purifying our negativities and downfalls through applying all four opponent forces. The term "negativity" (*papa, sdig pa*) includes all non-virtuous actions of body, speech, and mind. The term "downfall" (*apatti, ltung ba*), also sometimes translated as transgression, literally means to fall down, signifying that the result of this type of action is to fall down into the lower realms, i.e., to be reborn there in the future. Although all non-virtuous actions are downfalls, the term particularly refers to actions that involve the transgression of a vow, which may or may not be non-virtuous. A transgression of a vow is non-virtuous if it involves committing a natural misdeed (*prakṛti-sāvadya, rang bzhin gyi kha na ma tho ba*) (e.g., transgressing the vow to abandon killing) or a formulated misdeed (*pratikṣhepaṇa-sāvadya, bcas pa'i kha na ma tho ba*) (e.g., transgressing the vow to abandon dancing) accompanied by an attitude of contempt for the vow. Examples of these non-virtues are, respectively, a person with individual liberation vows killing a sentient being and a fully ordained monk dancing with the thought that it does not matter that he has a vow to abandon dancing. However, if a monk dances with the motivation of benefiting others, although he would commit a downfall, it would not become a non-virtuous action.

The four opponent forces are (1) the force of the basis, (2) the force of applying all antidotes, (3) the force of total repudiation, and (4) the force of turning away from faults in the future. The force of the basis includes both

going for refuge to the Buddha, Dharma, and Sangha, and generating the mind of enlightenment in order to benefit sentient beings. Thus, the first opponent force is completed with the generation of these two minds.

The force of applying all antidotes means to apply one of the six types of antidotes as a countermeasure to purify our negativities and downfalls. The six antidotes are (1) recitation of sutras, (2) meditation on emptiness, (3) recitation of mantras[6] such as the hundred-syllable mantra of Vajrasattva, (4) making or commissioning statues or paintings of the buddhas, (5) making offerings to buddhas or stupas (*stūpa, mchod rten,* reliquary monument),[7] and (6) recitation of the names of buddhas such as the thirty-five tathāgatas. However, in addition to these, any positive action done with the purpose of purifying can become an antidote to the imprints left on our mental continuum by the negative actions we have committed.

The force of total repudiation is the generation of a deep sense of regret for the negative actions we have done. Accepting or acknowledging that a mistaken action was our own fault is one way of demonstrating this regret.

The force of turning away from faults in the future means to strongly determine, or resolve, not to do, or at least to try not to do, a negative action again. Through making such a firm determination we will eventually be able to completely stop engaging in that particular action.

When each of these four opponent forces is present in our confession we can totally purify our negative actions. However, if our purification lacks even one of them it will not be completely effective since each of the forces acts as a specific antidote to the four results that arise from a complete path of action. These are (1) the maturation result, (2) the result corresponding to the cause as an experience, (3) the result corresponding to the cause as an activity, and (4) the environmental result. Having committed a non-virtuous action such as killing, our maturation result is a future rebirth in one of the three lower realms as a hell being, hungry ghost, or animal—this is purified by the force of applying all antidotes. The result corresponding to the cause as an experience is the experience of suffering and difficulties when we are once again reborn as a human; for example, as a result of having killed, our life will be short and we will experience many illnesses—this is purified by the force of total repudiation. The result corresponding to the cause as an activity is that when once again reborn as a human we will spontaneously engage in that specific non-virtuous action due to our previous familiarity with it; for example, due to having killed in a past life we

will engage in killing or torturing insects and small animals even as a young child—this is purified by the force of turning away from faults in the future. The environmental result refers to the particular physical environment in which we take rebirth as a human; for example, the environmental result of killing is rebirth in a place where food and medicines are either of poor quality or difficult to obtain—this is purified by the force of the basis. Similarly, the other nine non-virtuous paths of action when complete produce the four types of result.[8] Therefore, to purify all four results of our negativities it is of utmost importance to include each of the four opponent forces in our purification practice.

Lama Tsongkhapa also stressed the need to continually purify our negativities and downfalls since we continually engage in committing them. It is not at all sufficient to confess them merely once a year, or even once a month.

2. The Force of the Basis

I go for refuge to the Buddha.
I go for refuge to the Dharma.
I go for refuge to the Sangha.

The force of the basis is going for refuge from the depths of our hearts
to the Three Jewels, the Buddha and so on, for the purpose of cleansing
and purifying our negativities and downfalls, by means of reflecting
that they know all our negativities and downfalls.

Even though I should explain the individual identification of the
refuges, how to go for refuge, and so forth, I will not write about this
here as it would be too long.

Although going for refuge to the guru is included in the refuge verse of
the root text it is not mentioned here in the commentary. Going for refuge
to the Three Jewels—the Buddha, Dharma, and Sangha—and generating
the wish to attain enlightenment to benefit all sentient beings comprises the
first opponent force, the force of the basis. It is called the force of the basis
because our collection of virtuous, non-virtuous, and unpredicted, or neutral, actions are committed with respect to either of two referent objects,
the Three Jewels or sentient beings. In turn we need to rely upon them to
purify our non-virtuous actions. By going for refuge to the Three Jewels we
purify negativities committed in relation to them, and by generating the
wish to attain enlightenment we purify negativities committed in relation
to sentient beings. Just as when we fall down on the ground, the ground
itself acts as our basis, or support, for being able to stand up again; likewise,
when we commit negative actions against the Three Jewels and sentient
beings, they themselves act as the basis of our purification. For this reason

we rely on the force of the basis—refuge and the mind of enlightenment—to purify our negativities.

I) REFUGE

Identifying the Three Jewels

Explained very simply the actual Buddha Jewel is any omniscient being such as Shākyamuni Buddha who has abandoned all faults and achieved all realizations. More precisely the actual Buddha Jewel is the final object of refuge that possesses the eight qualities of being uncompounded and so forth (see below). It includes the four bodies of a buddha: the nature body (*svabhāvikakāya, ngo bo nyid sku*), truth body (*dharmakāya, chos sku*), enjoyment body (*saṃbhogakāya, longs sku*), and emanation body (*nirmāṇakāya, sprul sku*).[9] The Buddha Jewel also encompasses the body, speech, and mind of a buddha—the results of a bodhisattva's collection of merit and wisdom over three countless great eons. The conventional Buddha Jewel is any representation of a buddha, such as a statue or painting.

The actual Dharma Jewel is any true path or true cessation; respectively, the method to abandon an object of abandonment and the abandonment itself. The conventional Dharma Jewel is any text or book of the Buddha's teachings.

The actual Sangha Jewel is any single person who has attained the path of seeing (i.e., has directly realized emptiness) and is thereby a superior. Thus, the Sangha Jewel is those beings who have acquired the realizations of true paths and true cessations, the real Dharma Jewel, in their mental continuum. The conventional Sangha Jewel is a group of four or more fully ordained monks or nuns.

The meaning of Buddha, Dharma, and Sangha can be more easily understood by making a simple illustration. We ourselves can be likened to university students, the Buddha to our professor, the Dharma to the subject matter, and the Sangha to our classmates. The professor, having already mastered a particular subject, teaches us according to his or her own knowledge and experience; similarly, the buddhas teach us the path to enlightenment based on their own knowledge and experience of it. When we study a particular subject well we gain some knowledge concerning it, this knowledge is comparable to the Dharma Jewel, the knowledge that actually protects us from

suffering and problems. While at university we rely upon our classmates and friends for help and support; likewise, the Sangha are the virtuous friends who help us to attain buddhahood. Through putting effort into learning the subject that the professor teaches us, we ourselves can become university teachers; correspondingly, through studying, meditating, and correctly practicing the Dharma that was taught by the Buddha, we ourselves can become buddhas. Reflection on this simple illustration can help us to understand the significance of the Three Jewels and thereby deepen our practice of taking refuge.

The Qualities of the Three Jewels

To develop stable faith, confidence, and appreciation that Buddha, Dharma, and Sangha are in fact valid objects of refuge we need to deepen our knowledge concerning their individual qualities. Having done this, when we recite the refuge verse and simultaneously remember and reflect on the particular qualities of each of the Three Jewels, the practice of taking refuge will be much more effective since it will come from our heart.

The qualities of the Buddha Jewel can be subdivided into the qualities of a buddha's body, speech, and mind. In brief, the inconceivable qualities of a buddha's body are manifested in the thirty-two major marks and eighty minor marks with which it is adorned, each of which is a result of having collected its respective cause.[10]

The melodious speech of a buddha has sixty-four qualities.[11] Due to its power even a single word is heard and understood in accordance with the dispositions, interests, and thoughts of the various listeners. For example, once when Shākyamuni Buddha said the I is impermanent, one disciple heard the I is suffering, another the I is empty, and another the I is selfless. Simultaneously, due to the power of Buddha's speech, these disciples each heard a different teaching appropriate to their own particular level of spiritual development.

A buddha's mind has many inconceivable qualities; for example, the twenty-one divisions of uncontaminated exalted wisdom that include the divisions of the ten strengths, the four fearlessnesses, the four individual knowledges, the eighteen unique qualities, and so forth.[12]

ભ ⚜ ભ

Eight qualities of each of the Three Jewels are further elaborated in Maitreya's *Sublime Continuum of the Great Vehicle* (*Mahāyāna-uttara-tantra-shāstra*).

The Buddha Jewel has the eight qualities of
1. uncompoundedness
2. spontaneously and effortlessly accomplishing all
3. inconceivability and inexpressibility
4. knowledge of ultimate and conventional truths
5. mercy
6. ability
7. [fulfillment of] the welfare of self
8. [fulfillment of] the welfare of others

The Dharma Jewel has the eight qualities of being
1. unimaginable
2. without the two, contaminated actions and afflictions
3. free from conceptualization
4. pure
5. clear
6. an antidote
7. true cessations
8. true paths

The Sangha Jewel has the eight qualities of
1. conventional knowledge
2. ultimate knowledge
3. inner knowledge (i.e., knowledge of the five sciences— medicine, literature, arts, dialectics, and philosophy)
4. being purified of obscurations of attachment (i.e., afflictive obscurations)
5. being purified of obstructive obscurations (i.e., obscurations to omniscience)
6. being purified of inferior obscurations (i.e., self-cherishing)
7. knowledge
8. freedom

The Two Causes of Going for Refuge

There are two main causes of going for refuge to the Three Jewels—these are fear and faith. In the context of refuge, fear refers to a fear of cyclic existence with all its sufferings and difficulties in general, as well as to a fear of the sufferings of the lower realms in particular. Having fear and wishing to be separated from the problems of cyclic existence, we seek someone or something that can provide us protection, just as a frightened person with problems looks for help and protection from someone more powerful. Through understanding the qualities of the Buddha, Dharma, and Sangha Jewels we develop faith and confidence that they can free us from the sufferings of cyclic existence. Thus, with fear and faith as a cause, we go for refuge to the Three Jewels.

Causal and Resultant Refuge

There are two ways of going for refuge—going for causal refuge and going for resultant refuge. Going for refuge to the beings who have already become enlightened is going for causal refuge to the Buddha Jewel; going for refuge to our own resultant buddha, the buddha we will become, is resultant refuge. Going for refuge to the realizations of true paths and true cessation in others' mental continua is causal refuge in the Dharma Jewel; going for refuge to our own future realizations is resultant refuge. Going for refuge to the superiors who have already become sangha is causal refuge in the Sangha Jewel; going for refuge to the sangha, the superiors we ourselves will become, is resultant refuge. Wishing to attain enlightenment, we should go for refuge to our own future resultant Buddha, Dharma, and Sangha as this will generate more interest in the practice of going for refuge and consequently we will put more energy into it.

Buddha Nature

When reciting the verse of refuge we should be completely convinced that we can definitely eliminate all our obscurations and thereby attain buddhahood. The reason for this certainty is that according to the sutra teachings every sentient being has buddha nature, or buddha lineage, and, in a similar context, the tantra teachings speak of tantra of basis. The explanation, common to

both sutra and tantra, is that these refer to the mind's emptiness of inherent, or true, existence. On a deeper level, tantra of basis is explained to be the subtle mind and subtle wind that transform into a buddha's body and mind. Due to the presence of buddha nature each and every sentient being has the potential to become buddha. Therefore, if we put effort into purifying our negativities and accumulating positive energy, or merit, we can be absolutely certain that we ourselves can become a buddha.

Refuge Advice

Upon deciding to take the Three Jewels as our main objects of refuge, we should abandon some actions and adopt others. In relation to the Buddha Jewel we should not take inferior mundane beings as our final refuge and we should respect all images of the Buddha equally, irrespective of the quality of the statue, painting, or drawing. To put our refuge in the Dharma Jewel into practice we should avoid harming sentient beings by abandoning the ten non-virtuous actions and engaging in the ten virtuous actions. Also we should respect all texts and books containing Dharma teachings. To uphold our refuge in the Sangha Jewel we should avoid people who influence us in a detrimental way and we should respect even the robes of the ordained. In addition to following the specific advice given in relation to each of the Three Jewels individually, we should also mentally recite one of the refuge prayers three times during the day and three times at night while remembering the qualities of the Buddha, Dharma, and Sangha. In this way we will continually develop and deepen our refuge in the Three Jewels.

II) THE MIND OF ENLIGHTENMENT

Although the force of the basis includes both going for refuge and generating the mind of enlightenment, the generation of the mind of enlightenment is not explained in the commentary. However, it is an essential part of the practice of confession since negative actions committed in relation to sentient beings are purified by generating the mind that wishes to lead them to the perfect happiness of complete enlightenment.

We know of two methods to develop the mind of enlightenment, (1) the meditation on the seven, the six causes and one effect, and (2) the medita-

tion on exchanging self and others. Since we will not be able to develop the mind of enlightenment as long as we continue to hold on to our biased attitudes toward sentient beings, each of these meditations is necessarily preceded by the preliminary practice of developing an attitude of equanimity toward all sentient beings.

1) The Seven: The Six Causes and One Effect

THE PRELIMINARY PRACTICE: MEDITATION ON EQUANIMITY

When developing the mind of enlightenment through meditating on the seven—six causes and one effect—the equanimity meditation is performed in relation to our friends, enemies, and strangers. The purpose of training in equanimity toward these three categories of people is to abandon the habit of generating hatred toward enemies, attachment toward friends, and indifference toward strangers. Through familiarizing ourselves with this meditation we will gradually stop making this distinction and learn to see all sentient beings as equal. This type of equanimity is common to both the Lesser Vehicle (*hīnayāna, theg dman*) and Great Vehicle (*mahāyāna, theg pa chen po*) traditions of Buddhism.

Begin the meditation by visualizing an enemy, a friend, and a stranger as if they were present in front of yourself. Having done so examine how you feel in regard to each of these people. You will probably find that toward the enemy you have a sense of aversion and repulsiveness; toward the friend warmth and attraction; and toward the stranger no emotion whatsoever. Then ask yourself, "What are the reasons I make these distinctions of enemy, friend, and stranger?" You will discover that you think of one person as your enemy because he or she has harmed you or your loved ones in the past, is presently harming you or your loved ones, or will harm you or your loved ones in the future. The reason you consider someone else a friend is that he or she has helped you or your loved ones in the past, is helping you or your loved ones in the present, or will help you or your loved ones in the future. You regard another person as a stranger because he or she has neither helped nor harmed you or your loved ones. As a result of these experiences you respectively feel hatred, attachment, and indifference toward these people. By analyzing this situation with wisdom we will come to the conclusion that we do not have valid reasons for making these distinctions since our perception of friends, enemies, and strangers is not at all stable. In fact, our relationships are constantly changing. Today's dearest friend can become tomorrow's enemy, today's worst enemy can become an intimate friend tomorrow, and someone now a stranger may eventually become a beloved friend or a hated enemy. From the level of our personal relationships up to the level of relationships between nations there is constant change.

Both in this life and throughout our beginningless succession of lives we have had many different relationships with each sentient being and in our future lives we will continue to have many different relationships with them. In addition to having had these three types of relationship with every sentient being, each one has also been our mother and has cared for us with infinite kindness and, even when they were not our mother, they helped and benefited us. Therefore, there is no reason to hate some sentient beings, to be attached to others, and to be indifferent toward still others.

These disturbing emotions bring us endless problems. For example, the pain of being abandoned by a friend is mainly due to our attachment. This attachment in turn can give rise to anger as a result of, for example, the jealousy we feel upon seeing our friend talking and laughing with another person. Since these and many other problems arise from attachment we should continually try to diminish and eventually eliminate it altogether. Reflecting on this we must make a firm decision that from now on we will not generate these harmful emotions toward other people.

THE ACTUAL MEDITATION ON THE SEVEN POINTS

Based on the development of equanimity we engage in the actual seven-point meditation composed of six causes and one effect. The first cause is the understanding that each and every sentient being has been our mother at some time during our beginningless lives in cyclic existence. Upon developing this understanding we go on to contemplate the second cause, remembering the kindness that we have received from our present mother (or another primary caretaker) that is then extrapolated to include all sentient beings. Thirdly, based on a deep sense of gratitude for the kindness we have received, we generate the wish to return this kindness. This in turn leads to the development of the fourth and fifth causes, love and compassion; respectively, the thought that wishes each sentient being happiness and the thought that wishes them to be free from suffering. As a consequence of developing love and compassion we develop the sixth cause, the special, or altruistic, attitude that is the decision to take upon ourselves the personal responsibility to bring all sentient beings happiness and freedom from suffering. Upon considering how to accomplish this we reach the conclusion that the only effective method is to achieve our own enlightenment. Thus, the effect, or outcome, of the previous six causes is the seventh point, the generation of the mind of enlightenment.[13]

2) EXCHANGING SELF AND OTHERS

The Preliminary Practice, Meditation on Equanimity

The second technique for developing the mind of enlightenment is the meditation on exchanging self and others, or more precisely, exchanging the attitude of cherishing ourselves for the attitude of cherishing others. The preliminary equanimity meditation associated with this practice is superior to, and more profound than, that of the equanimity meditation related to the seven causes and effect meditation. This is because the equanimity of the seven causes and effect meditation merely entails equalizing our attitude toward sentient beings while, in the context of exchanging self and others, equanimity is the strong intention to equally benefit and help all sentient beings without any partiality whatsoever. This type of equanimity eliminates the thought, "I will benefit this sentient being but not that sentient being." To develop this attitude it is necessary to depend on logical reasons, which are divided into (1) reasons based on the conventional truth and (2) reasons based on the ultimate truth.

(1) Reasons Based on the Conventional Truth

(a) Three reasons from the viewpoint of others
(i) We do not want to experience the slightest problem even in a dream and we are not satisfied even when we enjoy the greatest happiness. Likewise, even tiny sentient beings such as ants want only to experience happiness and do not want to experience even the smallest suffering. Since we are all equal in wanting happiness and not wanting suffering it is not right to be attached to our friends and to want to help them, and to hate our enemies and want to harm them. We should wish to benefit all sentient beings equally.

(ii) When we give food to a group of beggars, it would not be right to give food to some and not to others since all are equal in their hunger and need for food. Similarly, ourselves and all other ordinary sentient beings completely lack uncontaminated happiness and do not even experience perfect contaminated happiness. Since we are all equal in lacking happiness, although constantly wishing to obtain it, it would not be right to have the thought wishing to give happiness to some and not to others. We should wish to benefit all sentient beings equally.

(iii) In a hospital where there are many sick and suffering patients, it would not be right to treat some people while neglecting others. Likewise, ourselves and all sentient beings are completely the same in that each one of us is ill due to the three mental poisons of attachment, hatred, and ignorance. In consequence, we wander in cyclic existence experiencing the three types of suffering: the suffering of suffering, the suffering of change, and pervasive compounding suffering. The suffering of suffering includes both physical and mental suffering; the suffering of change refers to an experience that originally appears to be happiness but eventually changes into suffering; and pervasive compounding suffering is our contaminated aggregates, the bases of our present suffering and the creators of our future suffering. Since all sentient beings are equal in not wanting suffering yet continually experiencing it, we should have the strong wish to benefit all of them equally without the bias of thinking to help some and to neglect others.

Having meditated on these points and understanding that all sentient beings are equal, we may still wonder, "Why should I take the responsibility upon myself to help them?" To answer this question we contemplate the following three reasons.

(b) Three reasons from the viewpoint of self
(i) Each one of us has been taking rebirth in cyclic existence since beginningless time and in each of these many lives we have been dependent on sentient beings. Each sentient being has been our mother, relative, and friend and has helped and looked after us. In addition, sentient beings have provided us with, and are providing us with, the three essentials for our daily happiness—food, clothes, and a good reputation. For example, the food we eat comes from the hard work of farmers and the flesh of animals, the clothes we wear come from the textile makers and the skins of animals,

and the encouragement and support we need come from other people. Without depending on others we would not have even these basic happinesses. In addition, luxuries such as the ability to travel quickly and comfortably are also due to the kindness of others, the scientists, engineers, and so on. Even from the point of view of Dharma, the development of all our inner qualities is dependent on sentient beings who serve as the objects of our love, compassion, patience, and so forth. Consequently, even the highest happinesses, liberation and enlightenment, are dependent on sentient beings. Since all sentient beings are equal in having been kind to us and in having benefited us, we should firmly decide not to abandon any sentient being and to help each one without the slightest partiality.

(ii) We might think that while sentient beings have benefited us they have also harmed us. In response to this doubt we should think that sentient beings have definitely benefited us more than they have harmed us. In this life and in past lives the amount of benefit we have received from other sentient beings far outweighs the amount of harm. Therefore, it would not be right to abandon some sentient beings, we should have the intention to equally benefit all.

(iii) Although the moment of our death is uncertain, we will definitely die. It is the same for all other sentient beings. Since we are all caught in the web of impermanence, there is no sense in being attached to some sentient beings and to hate others. For example, a group of criminals who are scheduled for execution tomorrow do not hold feelings of attachment or hatred for each other, since all are going to die simultaneously. Likewise, since we and all other sentient beings are definitely going to die, there is no sense in discriminating. We should decide not to abandon even one sentient being and to help each one in whatever way we can.

This completes the six reasons in relation to the conventional truth from the viewpoint of both self and others. The next three reasons are in relation to the ultimate truth.

(2) Reasons Based on the Ultimate Truth

(i) Through mistaken conceptions we impute "friend" on the sentient beings who help us and "enemy" on those who harm us. If friend and enemy did in fact truly exist from their own side, rather than being mere imputations, Shākyamuni Buddha would have realized it. However, the Buddha made no distinction between a person who was applying oils and perfumes to one side of his body and another who was cutting the flesh of the other side. Therefore, since enemy and friend are just imputed by our own thought and do not exist from their own side we should decide to benefit all sentient beings equally.

(ii) In addition, if the enemy were truly existent he or she would always be an enemy and the truly existent friend would always be a friend. However, the reality is that our relationships, as well as our social status, wealth, and so on, are far from being stable. In fact they change frequently because there is no certainty at all in cyclic existence. Even this precious human rebirth is not stable—eventually we will die, take rebirth, and once again die. Therefore, we should abandon our concrete ideas concerning friends and enemies and resolve to benefit all sentient beings equally.

(iii) Self and others are dependent upon each other. For example, I refer to myself as "I" and to another person as "you," while that person would say "you" when referring to me and "I" when referring to himself or herself. I and you are established in dependence on each other and are not established independently from their own side. In the same way, tall and short, here and there, up and down, father and son, etc., only exist in relation to each other. A single person can be both father and son in dependence, respectively, on his relation to his son and his relation to his father. If these were not imputed by thought and established relatively, but instead existed inherently, then a father would always be a father and could never be a son. Likewise, enemy and friend are not truly existent but established in dependence. Therefore, there is no reason to be attached to the friend and to hate the enemy. Instead, we should wish to help all sentient beings equally.

THE ACTUAL MEDITATION ON EXCHANGING SELF AND OTHERS

Through relying on these nine reasons, we can equalize our attitude toward self and others and develop the wish to benefit all sentient beings equally. Having cultivated this equanimity we then strive to generate the mind of

enlightenment by contemplating the following five points, each of which leads to a particular decision related to a verse from *The Offering to the Guru* (*Guru Puja, Lama Chöpa*).

(1) The Decision to Benefit All Sentient Beings Equally

Having contemplated the nine reasons based on the conventional and ultimate truths, we can see that there is no reason to develop attachment for friends, feeling them to be close, and hatred for enemies, feeling them to be distant. The afflictions that are most harmful to us in this and future lives are attachment and hatred. They are the causes of hundreds of sufferings. They are like a prison guard preventing us from leaving the prison of cyclic existence. They lead us to rebirth in hell. Even the unhappiness and suffering we experience in a dream are caused by attachment and hatred. Like a tumor growing within our body they continually cause us pain and suffering. Therefore, just as we would attempt to free ourselves of a tumor by seeking medical treatment, we should strive to eliminate attachment and hatred from our mental continuum.

The thought to benefit all sentient beings and to separate them from suffering is the best tool to obtain the goal of temporal and ultimate happiness for ourselves and others. Since the profound practice of all bodhisattvas is to cultivate the attitude wishing to benefit sentient beings, all the buddhas of the past, present, and future have traveled this path. Therefore, we too should develop the thought, "Whatever sentient beings from their side do to me it does not matter. Whether they help me or harm me is of no importance. From my side I will try to generate good thoughts toward them. I will help and benefit them in any way I can." Thinking like this, decide to develop the thought to benefit all sentient beings equally and request your guru, who is inseparable from the deity, to bless you to develop this kind of attitude by reciting the following verse from *The Offering to the Guru:*

> Never desiring the slightest suffering,
> Never satisfied with the happiness we have,
> There is no difference between myself and others;
> Please bless me to generate joy in others' happiness.

While reciting this verse, contemplate its meaning and firmly decide to benefit and help all sentient beings without any partiality whatsoever

(2) The Decision to Abandon Self-Cherishing

Having equalized self and others, we should now begin the meditation on exchanging self and others (i.e., exchanging self-cherishing for cherishing others). To do this it is necessary to first contemplate the numerous disadvantages of cherishing ourselves. For example, self-cherishing is the cause of all suffering, from the problems of human beings up to rebirth in hell. Self-cherishing is the reason why the foe-destroyers of the Lesser Vehicle fall into the extreme of nirvana.[14] Although they are liberated from cyclic existence, they remain in equipoise in a state of peace due to thinking of themselves more than others. Also some bodhisattvas take an especially long time to reach enlightenment, in spite of having generated the mind of enlightenment, because they still have some remaining traces of self-cherishing.

In short, all the defects of cyclic existence and beyond cyclic existence (liberation) are caused by self-cherishing. In our present life and in all our future lives the suffering that we will experience is caused by our attitude of cherishing ourselves more than others. Self-cherishing is like a poisonous seed that, when not destroyed, prevents the attainment of happiness and enlightenment. Therefore, we need to make the firm decision, "I will not generate the self-cherishing thought even for an instant," and then request the guru and the deity for blessings to be able to carry out this practice with the following verse from *The Offering to the Guru:*

> Having seen this chronic disease of self-cherishing
> As the cause producing unwanted suffering,
> Please bless me to blame, begrudge, and
> Destroy the great demon of selfishness.

Contemplate this verse and firmly decide to abandon self-cherishing. Although we may be afraid of the external demons who sometimes cause us illness and disease, in actuality the inner demon of self-cherishing is much more dangerous because it is the source of all our problems and suffering. When we experience problems, instead of pointing out the cause as other peoples' faults and mistakes, we should point to our own self-cherishing as

the one to blame. Other sentient beings are, in fact, the source of all our happiness and good qualities.

If we were to fight with ordinary external enemies and then decide to give the victory to them, the problem would be solved and the conflict finished. However, we should never give the victory to our inner enemy, our self-cherishing. Instead, we should continually fight to conquer this enemy completely. Geshe Langri Tangpa in his *Eight Verses on Mind Training* said, "I will take the losses and defeats upon myself and I will give the victories and gains to others." By developing this attitude we will eventually achieve the stable, uncontaminated, everlasting happiness of the state of buddhahood and thereby possess the capacity to spontaneously and effortlessly fulfill the benefit of all sentient beings.

(3) The Decision to Cherish Others

Following upon the decision to abandon self-cherishing we need to contemplate the advantages of cherishing others. For example, whatever qualities, happiness, and good reputation we possess, all are the result of having cherished others. The happiness of humans and gods up to the bliss of buddhahood are the results of cherishing others.

Also, in terms of our Dharma practice, whether at the time of the base, path, or result, sentient beings are absolutely essential to us. At the time of the base (prior to entering the path of accumulation) we need sentient beings as referent objects toward whom we can develop compassion. At the time of the path, when practicing the six perfections, we need sentient beings as objects of our practice; for example, to practice generosity we need someone to accept our offerings. At the time of the result, the attainment of enlightenment, we also need sentient beings since a buddha turns the wheel of Dharma (i.e., teaches) only for their benefit. Therefore, sentient beings are absolutely essential to us at the beginning, middle, and end of our practice.

Having contemplated the advantages of cherishing others the third decision is, "From the side of sentient beings whether they harm me or benefit me it does not matter. I will hold them all as equal. I will cherish all sentient beings as I cherish my guru and my deity. I will not abandon any sentient being but will always cherish each of them. I will not abandon the attitude of cherishing others even for an instant." Then request the guru and the deity to bless you to be able to do this by reciting this verse from *The Offering to the Guru:*

Having seen the mind that cherishes my mothers and
Would set them in bliss as the gateway to the arising of infinite
    qualities,
Even should these migrators arise as my enemies,
Please bless me to cherish them more than my life.

(4) The Decision to Exchange Self and Others

Having examined the disadvantages of self-cherishing and the advantages of cherishing others we should actually practice exchanging the thought that cherishes self for the thought that cherishes others. However, at this point we might experience some doubts concerning the difficulty of making this exchange and perhaps think that it is not actually possible to accomplish it. To eliminate this doubt we need to consider that in the past even Shākyamuni Buddha was an ordinary person just like ourselves. In fact, at times we were born together with him in cyclic existence. However, unlike ourselves, the Buddha put effort into the practice of exchanging self and others and thereby succeeded in attaining enlightenment. Instead, we, who have continued to cherish ourselves since beginningless time and have been concerned only with fulfilling our own aims, are still wandering in cyclic existence. Reflecting upon this we will realize that we too are indeed capable of exchanging ourselves with others, we just need to make the necessary effort. Through familiarity with the attitude of cherishing others, we can even arrive at the point of thinking of others' bodies as our own, just as now, due to familiarity, we cherish our body, although at one time it was merely the combination of our mother's egg and father's sperm and therefore belonged to them.

Understanding that it is possible to cherish others as we now cherish ourselves, we should make the decision, "Since I can exchange myself and others, I will do so right now," and then request the guru and the deity for blessings to be able to do so by reciting this verse from *The Offering to the Guru:*

In brief, the childish work only for their own welfare,
While the buddhas work solely for the welfare of others;
With a mind realizing the contrast between their respective faults and
    qualities,
Please bless me to be able to equalize and exchange myself and others.

(5) The Decision to Make Our Heart Practice the Exchanging of Self
and Others

To reinforce the decision to exchange ourselves and others, we should alter-
nately contemplate the disadvantages of self-cherishing and the advantages
of cherishing others. Think, for example, that due to cherishing ourselves
we engage in killing other sentient beings and thereby will experience the
consequences of rebirth in hell and, later on when reborn again as a human
being, a short life. Then think that through cherishing others and thereby
refraining from killing, we will experience the happy results of rebirth in
the higher realms and a long life as a human being. In this manner, alter-
nately consider the suffering results of each of the ten non-virtuous actions
and the benefits of engaging in the corresponding virtuous action. Having
done so the conclusion reached is that all faults, misery, and unpleasantness
are generated by self-cherishing while all qualities, benefits, and fortune
come about through cherishing others. At this point we should make the
decision to definitely exchange ourselves with others thinking, "No matter
whom I encounter I will not abandon the practice of cherishing others. I
will make my heart practice the exchanging of self with others." To be able
to do so request the guru and the deity for blessings by reciting the following verse from *The Offering to the Guru:*

> Self-cherishing is the gateway to all misfortune,
> While cherishing my mothers is the foundation of every quality;
> Therefore, please bless me to make my heart practice
> The yoga of exchanging self and others.

Then, on the basis of having made the decision to cherish others, we
engage in the actual practice of exchanging self and others by way of a
meditation known as "taking and giving." Begin by visualizing your self-
cherishing in the form of a heap of black dust at your heart. In front of
yourself visualize all sentient beings who, due to having committed negative
actions, are experiencing suffering and difficulties. Motivated by compassion, imagine taking their suffering from them in the form of thick black
smoke that leaves their bodies through their right nostrils. This smoke
enters into your own left nostril and, descending, strikes the self-cherishing

at your heart exploding it into tiny pieces. Your self-cherishing completely disappears. Imagine that all sentient beings are freed from their suffering. Then, motivated by love, breathe out all your roots of virtue, possessions, and happiness of the past, present, and future through your right nostril in the form of white light. This light enters the sentient beings through their left nostrils giving them every desired happiness, from the mundane up to the supreme happiness of unsurpassed enlightenment.

Although by doing this meditation on "taking and giving" we cannot actually take away the suffering of sentient beings nor can we give them our happiness, we can increase our good heart while decreasing our self-cherishing and self-grasping. If we are able to do this practice daily, even for just a few minutes, it will definitely bring beneficial results. In addition, we can continue to develop our good heart throughout the day, whether walking, eating, sitting, or resting, by constantly thinking to benefit others and to avoid causing them harm. This good heart is the essence of cherishing others.

3. The Force of Applying All Antidotes

*I prostrate to [Teacher] Bhagavan Tathāgata Foe-Destroyer Perfectly
   Complete Buddha Glorious Conqueror Shākyamuni.*
I prostrate to Tathāgata Thoroughly Destroying With Vajra Essence.
I prostrate to Tathāgata Radiant Jewel.
I prostrate to Tathāgata Nāga-Lord King.
I prostrate to Tathāgata Army of Heroes.
I prostrate to Tathāgata Delighted Hero.[15]
I prostrate to Tathāgata Jewel Fire.
I prostrate to Tathāgata Jewel Moonlight.
I prostrate to Tathāgata Meaningful to Behold.
I prostrate to Tathāgata Jewel Moon.
I prostrate to Tathāgata Immaculate.
I prostrate to Tathāgata Bestowed With Courage.[16]
I prostrate to Tathāgata Purity.
I prostrate to Tathāgata Bestowed With Purity.
I prostrate to Tathāgata Water-God.
I prostrate to Tathāgata Water-God Deity.
I prostrate to Tathāgata Glorious Excellence.
I prostrate to Tathāgata Glorious Sandalwood.
I prostrate to Tathāgata Infinite Splendor.
I prostrate to Tathāgata Glorious Light.
I prostrate to Tathāgata Glorious Sorrowless.
I prostrate to Tathāgata Son of Cravingless.
I prostrate to Tathāgata Glorious Flower.
I prostrate to Tathāgata Pure Light Rays Clearly Knowing by Sporting.

I prostrate to Tathāgata Lotus Light Rays Clearly Knowing by Sporting.
I prostrate to Tathāgata Glorious Wealth.
I prostrate to Tathāgata Glorious Mindfulness.
I prostrate to Tathāgata Glorious Name Widely Renowned.
I prostrate to Tathāgata Most Powerful Victory Banner King.
I prostrate to Tathāgata Glorious Utterly Suppressing.
I prostrate to Tathāgata Totally Victorious in Battle.
I prostrate to Tathāgata Glorious Suppressing Advancement.
I prostrate to Tathāgata Glorious All-Illuminating Manifestations.
I prostrate to Tathāgata Jewel Lotus Suppresser.
I prostrate to Tathāgata Foe-Destroyer Perfectly Complete Buddha
*   Mountain-Lord King Firmly Seated on Jewels and a Lotus.*

When the benefits of prostrating to the thirty-five tathāgatas and reciting their names are explained from the outset, a strong interest will arise in the confession of negativities; therefore, I will mention them.

Reciting, "I prostrate to Tathāgata Shākyamuni," purifies the negativities of ten thousand eons. Similarly, Vajra Essence purifies the negativities of ten thousand eons; Radiant Jewel purifies the negativities of twenty thousand eons; Nāga-Lord King purifies the negativities of one thousand eons; Army of Heroes purifies the negativities of one thousand eons; Delighted Hero purifies the negativities of two thousand eons; Jewel Fire purifies the negativities of two thousand eons; Jewel Moonlight purifies the negativities of eight thousand eons; Meaningful to Behold purifies the negativities of one eon; Jewel Moon purifies the negativities of the five actions of immediate [retribution]; Immaculate purifies the negativities of the five secondary [actions]; Bestowed With Courage purifies the negativities motivated by hatred; Purity purifies the negativities motivated by attachment; Bestowed With Purity purifies the negativities of ten thousand eons; Water-God purifies the negativities of one thousand eons; Water-God Deity purifies the negativities of five thousand eons; Glorious Excellence purifies the negativities of five thousand eons; Glorious Sandalwood purifies the negativities of seven eons; Infinite Splendor purifies the negativities of seven eons; Glorious Light is said to be of immeasurable benefit; Glorious Sorrowless purifies the negativities motivated by ignorance; Son of Cravingless purifies the negativities instigated by imprints; Glorious

Flower purifies all obscurations of body; Pure Light Rays purifies all obscurations of speech; Lotus Light Rays purifies all obscurations of mind; Glorious Wealth purifies all obscurations of misusing the possessions of the sangha; Glorious Mindfulness purifies all obscurations of disparaging people; Glorious Name purifies all obscurations motivated by jealousy; Most Powerful Victory Banner purifies all obscurations motivated by pride; Utterly Suppressing eliminates all types of divisive speech; Totally Victorious in Battle eliminates all types of afflictions; Suppressing Advancement eliminates the negativities of having caused others to commit [negativities]; Glorious All-Illuminating Manifestations eliminates the obscurations of rejoicing in [negativities] committed by others; Jewel Lotus eliminates the obscurations of having abandoned the Dharma; and Mountain-Lord King eliminates the obscurations of having degenerated our commitments to the guru.

It is said in the sutra that reciting or remembering the names of these tathāgatas one time purifies the negativities of countless eons. Keeping these benefits in mind you should put effort into confession.

Merely reciting the names of the thirty-five tathāgatas purifies the many negativities, even very heavy ones, that have been accumulated over a period of eons. Indeed, saying the mantra of Shākyamuni Buddha, "Tayathā Om Muni Muni Mahāmunaye Shākyamunaye Svāhā," is equivalent to saying, "I prostrate to Teacher Bhagavan Tathāgata Foe-Destroyer Perfectly Complete Buddha Glorious Conqueror Shākyamuni." As it says in the commentary, merely reciting Shākyamuni Buddha's name purifies the negativities accumulated over a period of ten thousand eons. Therefore, when we are either too tired or too busy to recite the names of each of the thirty-five buddhas to purify whatever negativities we may have committed during the day, it is enough to merely recite Shākyamuni Buddha's name.

A BRIEF EXPLANATION OF THE NEGATIVITIES

The five actions of immediate retribution (*ānantarya, mtshams med*),[17] discussed in more detail below (see pp. 51–52), are, in brief, (1) killing your mother, (2) killing your father, (3) killing a foe-destroyer, (4) causing blood to flow from the body of a tathāgata with evil intent, and (5) creating a

schism in the sangha. According to Vasubandhu's *Explanation of the "Treasury of Knowledge"* (*Abhidharmakoshabhāṣhya*) the result of any of the first four actions is rebirth in the immediately subsequent life in one of the hell realms, while the result of creating a schism in the sangha is to definitely be reborn in the hell of greatest suffering, Unrelenting Torment (*avīchi, mnar med*).

The five secondary, or close, actions of immediate retribution (*upā-nantarīya, nye pa'i mtshams med*) are similar to the five actions of immediate retribution although they are somewhat less grave. The five are (1) killing a bodhisattva abiding in certainty (i.e., one who is certain to achieve buddhahood within one hundred eons); (2) killing a superior; (3) destroying a stupa, monastery, temple, etc. with hatred; (4) raping a fully ordained nun who is a foe-destroyer; and (5) appropriating the provisions of the sangha (i.e., stealing statues or the sangha's belongings). Like the five actions of immediate retribution the five secondary also bring rebirth in hell in the immediately subsequent life.

The negativities committed due to the motivating force of the three poisonous minds, attachment, hatred, and ignorance, include the ten non-virtuous paths of actions, which consist of the three of body (killing, stealing, and sexual misconduct), the four of speech (lying, divisive speech, harsh words, and idle talk), and the three of mind (covetousness, malice, and wrong view).

There are two explanations of the meaning of obscurations of body (*lus kyi sgrib pa*). In some contexts, obscurations of body are explained to mean that the bodies of some sentient beings, such as those of animals, are obscured in the sense that when a being is born with that type of body the mind is obscured. Several stories from the vinaya teachings illustrate this. One tells of a fully ordained monk who, having achieved the power of magical emanation, transformed himself into a tiger. As a result his mind became completely obscured and he was no longer able to remember that he was actually a human being and a monk. This particular type of obscuration of body is also known as a maturation obscuration (*vipāka-āvaraṇa, rnam smin gyi sgrib pa*). Although at the moment we have clear minds and are intelligent, if we were to take rebirth as, for example, a sheep, our minds would become completely obscured by ignorance; consequently, we would become extremely foolish. While the mind of that sheep would be the continuity of our present mind, the change in body causes the mind to become obscured.

Obscurations of body can also refer to the obscurations, or negativities, accumulated by the three non-virtuous paths of action of the body. Therefore, purifying the obscurations of body includes purification of the causes for being reborn with an obscured mind due to an inferior body, as well as purification of the negativities created through actions of the body.

Obscurations of speech (*ngag gi sgrib pa*) are the negativities accumulated by the four non-virtuous paths of action of speech.

Obscurations of mind (*yid kyi sgrib pa*) are the negativities accumulated by the three non-virtuous paths of action of the mind as well as the afflictions that obscure, or cover, the mind.

Obscurations of misusing the possessions of the sangha refer to negativities accumulated through using the belongings of the sangha without permission, damaging them, or even throwing them away. Since these objects should be taken care of and treated with respect, misusing them is very negative and causes our minds to become obscured.

Obscurations of disparaging people, whether individuals or the sangha as a group, are the negativities of verbally belittling others by saying that they do not have qualities that they do in fact possess.

Obscurations motivated by jealousy refer to negativities committed out of jealousy, a mental factor that cannot bear the happiness of others. It derives from the root affliction, anger, and is the cause of many negative actions.

Obscurations motivated by pride refer to negativites committed due to pride. Pride is a huge obstacle to gaining new knowledge as it either causes us to think we know something that we do not know, or else it prevents us from admitting that we do not know something that we do not. In different contexts pride is divided into three, seven, or nine types, the worst type being the pride that is similar to the view of the transitory collection, that of a very strong sense of I. This sense of I, and its consequent sense of mine, are the causes of many obscurations.

Divisive speech means to purposely speak in such a way as to create a division between people, whether bringing about a rift between those who were harmonious or bringing about a greater rift between those who were already in discord.

All types of afflictions include the six root afflictions (attachment, anger, pride, ignorance, doubt, and afflicted view) and twenty secondary afflictions (belligerence, resentment, concealment, spite, jealousy, miserliness, deceit, dissimulation, haughtiness, harmfulness, non-shame, non-embarrassment,

lethargy, excitement, non-faith, laziness, non-conscientiousness, forgetfulness, non-introspection, distraction),[18] the causes of all our negativities.

The negativities of making others commit negativities are created by ordering, asking, or paying someone else to engage in a negative action, such as murder. Even though we did not do the action directly ourselves, if it is carried out successfully, it is a complete action of killing and therefore brings the same results as if we had in fact actually committed it.

Obscurations of rejoicing in negativities done by others refer to the negativities we create through rejoicing that someone else has committed a negative action; for example, being happy and thinking that a hunter has done something good by successfully shooting and killing an animal.

Abandoning the Dharma, said to be the heaviest of all negative actions, causes the mind to become very obscured. *The Guhyasamāja Tantra* mentions that although the five actions of immediate retribution can be purified by the practice and recitation of that tantra, it cannot purify the negative action of having abandoned the holy Dharma. We commit the action of abandoning the Dharma by, for example, putting Dharma texts under inferior objects or by sitting on them. We also abandon the Dharma through criticizing our own or other religions. Practicing a religion for some time and later coming to feel uncomfortable with it and, as a result, deciding to stop practicing it for a while, is not the negative action of abandoning the Dharma. However, if we were to think that the religion is mistaken, has no result, and consequently completely reject it, the action would be that of abandoning the Dharma.

Obscurations of having degenerated our commitments to the guru occur by, for example, verbally criticizing or physically striking him or her.

In conclusion, reciting or remembering the names of the thirty-five tathāgatas purifies the many types of negativities that we have committed in this and previous lives. By understanding and reflecting on these benefits, even if we recite the names of the tathāgatas just once, we will purify the negativities accumulated over many eons.

THE VISUALIZATION

When doing the confession, visualize in the space in front of yourself the conqueror Shākyamuni in the middle, with the other tathāgatas in

the four directions, above, and below, [each of whom is] seated on a moon cushion, a lotus, and a throne ornamented with jewels. Then, with your body prostrate; with your speech recite the names of the tathāgatas; and with your mind devoutly pay homage by remembering the benefits of prostrations and the qualities of the tathāgatas.

When doing the confession in the presence of the thirty-five tathāgatas visualize Shākyamuni Buddha seated on a large throne in front of yourself at the level of your eyebrows. He is surrounded in space by the other thirty-four buddhas, each of whom also has one face, two arms, wears the three robes of a fully ordained monk, and is seated on a moon cushion, lotus, and throne. Imagine that they are all actually present and, if possible, clearly visualize the specific colors and hand positions of each buddha. If you are unable to do this extensive visualization, merely visualize Shākyamuni Buddha seated on a moon cushion, lotus, and large throne and feel that the other tathāgatas are also present.

Then, with a clear visualization, whether detailed or simple, begin the confession by reciting the verse of going for refuge to the Three Jewels while simultaneously generating the wish to attain enlightenment for the benefit of all sentient beings. Develop a deep sense of regret for the many negative actions you have committed since beginningless time up to now. Then make a firm resolution to at least try to refrain from engaging in them in the future. With these states of minds—refuge, the mind of enlightenment, regret, and resolve—perform the actual antidote, the recitation of the names of the tathāgatas together with prostrations. By performing the confession in this manner, all four opponent forces are present and, with faith in the efficacy of this practice, we will definitely purify our negativities.

಍ ‡ ಍

COLORS AND HAND POSITIONS OF THE THIRTY-FIVE TATHĀGATAS

TATHĀGATA	COLOR	HAND POSITION
Shākyamuni	yellow	right pressing down the earth left meditative equipoise
Thoroughly Destroying With Vajra Essence	yellow	two hands expounding Dharma
Radiant Jewel	red	two hands meditative equipoise
Nāga-Lord King	blue below neck white above neck	two hands at the heart, thumbs aligned in the middle, two [index] fingers straight, the tips slightly apart, [other fingers intertwined and] curled inward
Army of Heroes	yellow	right granting refuge left slightly drawn aside from the heart, the thumb and palm facing outward
Delighted Hero	yellow	two hands expounding Dharma
Jewel Fire	red	right pressing down the earth left meditative equipoise
Jewel Moonlight	white	right pressing down the earth left meditative equipoise
Meaningful to Behold	green	right granting refuge left slightly drawn aside from the heart, the thumb and palm facing outward
Jewel Moon	white	[two hands] expounding Dharma
Immaculate	blue	[two hands] meditative equipoise
Bestowed With Courage	yellow	[two hands] expounding Dharma
Purity	yellow	right pressing down the earth left meditative equipoise
Bestowed With Purity	red	[two hands] expounding Dharma
Water-God	white	[two hands] meditative equipoise
Water-God Deity	white	[two hands] expounding Dharma
Glorious Excellence	yellow	right granting refuge left slightly drawn aside from the heart, the thumb and palm facing outward

TATHĀGATA	COLOR	HAND POSITION
Glorious Sandalwood	white	right pressing down the earth left meditative equipoise
Infinite Splendor	red	[two hands] expounding Dharma
Glorious Light	blue	[two hands] expounding Dharma
Glorious Sorrowless	pink	[two hands] meditative equipoise
Son of Cravingless	yellow	[two hands] expounding Dharma
Glorious Flower	yellow	right granting refuge left slightly drawn aside from the heart, the thumb and palm facing outward
Pure Light Rays	yellow	right pressing down the earth left meditative equipoise
Lotus Light Rays	red	right pressing down the earth left meditative equipoise
Glorious Wealth	blue	[two hands] meditative equipoise
Glorious Mindfulness	yellow	[two hands] meditative equipoise
Glorious Name Widely Renowned	white	right expounding Dharma left meditative equipoise
Most Powerful Victory Banner	blue	right hoists a victory banner in direction of left shoulder left meditative equipoise
Utterly Suppressing	blue	right holds a sword at the heart left meditative equipoise
Totally Victorious in Battle	blue	two hands hold a yellow coat of mail
Suppressing Advancement	blue	two hands pressing down the earth
All-Illuminating Manifestations	red	right granting refuge, left meditative equipoise
Jewel Lotus Suppresser	orange	right granting refuge left meditative equipoise
Mountain-Lord King	yellow	two hands meditative equipoise holding a mountain

OBJECTS OF PROSTRATION

If it is asked, "Well then, to which objects should we prostrate and how should we prostrate?" Among the prostrations to the thirty-five tathāgatas—the objects—how to prostrate to the conqueror Shākyamuni, who is situated in the middle, is shown at the beginning saying, "I prostrate to Bhagavan Tathāgata Foe-Destroyer Perfectly Complete Buddha Glorious Conqueror Shākyamuni."

If the meaning of these [epithets] are explained a little:

Since he has destroyed (*bcom*) the four demons (*māra, bdud*), is endowed with (*ldan*) the four bodies and five exalted wisdoms, and has transcended (*'das*) cyclic existence and nirvana, he is called Bhagavan (*bcom ldan 'das*, Transcendent Endowed Destroyer).

Since he knows that he has gone (*gshegs pa*) to the direct perception of all phenomena and the thusness (*de bzhin nyid*) of all phenomena, he is called Tathāgata (*de bzhin gshegs pa*, One Gone Thus).

Since he has destroyed (*bcom*) the foes (*dgra*), which are the afflictions, he is called Foe-Destroyer (*arhat, dgra bcom pa*).

Since he has completed (*rdzogs pa*) all qualities perfectly (*yang dag pa*), precisely as they should be, he is called Perfectly Complete (*samyaksaṁ, yang dag par rdzogs pa*).

Since he has awakened (*sangs*) from the sleep of the afflictions and has expanded (*rgyas*) his awareness to all objects of knowledge, he is called Buddha (*sangs rgyas*, Awakened-Expanded). It is said, "Due to having awakened from the sleep of the afflictions and having expanded his awareness to objects of knowledge, the Buddha, like a lotus, is awakened and expanded."

Since he is endowed with the perfection of high status (*abhyudaya, mngon mtho*) and definite goodness (*niḥshreyasa, nges legs*), he is called Glorious (*shrī, dpal*).

Since he has conquered (*rgyal*) all objects of abandonment, the discordant class, he is called Conqueror (*jina, rgyal ba*).

Since he was born in the Shākya lineage, he is called Shākya.

Since he has subdued (*thub*) the foes that are the afflictions, he is called Muni (*thub pa*, Subduer).

ॐ ✿ ॐ

"Bhagavan" is an epithet given to a fully enlightened buddha, such as Shākyamuni Buddha. The etymology explained here accords with the Tibetan translation as *Chom-den-de* (Transcendent Endowed Destroyer). *Chom*, destroyer, indicates that the Buddha has destroyed all four demons, or māras: (1) the demon of the aggregates, (2) the demon of the afflictions, (3) the demon of death, and (4) the demon of the sons-of-the-gods. The demon of the aggregates in this particular context specifically refers to our contaminated body. Our body is called a demon because it is the base of all our suffering and problems. The demon of the afflictions refers to the mental afflictions of attachment, anger, ignorance, and so forth. They are called demons because they destroy our present happiness and create our future suffering. Death is called a demon because it causes harm to our body and mind through ending their relationship. The demon of the sons-of-the-gods refers to actual beings of the highest level of the desire realm, that of Controlling Others' Emanations, who harm us by sending five arrows, or negative energies, that disturb our peace of mind. When we feel angry right from the moment of waking it is because we have been struck by the arrow of anger, a type of negative energy, sent by the sons-of-the-gods. On the other hand, if from the time of waking we feel very slow and stupid it is a result of having been struck by the arrow of ignorance. When we are overcome with strong attachment it is due to having been struck by the arrow of attachment; being filled with excessive pride is due to the arrow of pride; and being tormented by jealousy is due to the arrow of jealousy. Each of us has, at some time, definitely experienced the results of the negative, harmful energy sent by the sons-of-the-gods.

Shākyamuni Buddha and all other buddhas are called Destroyer because they have completely destroyed their own demons of the aggregates, afflictions, and death, as well as having destroyed the demon of the sons-of-the-gods in the sense that a buddha can no longer be harmed by them.

The *den* of *Chom-den-de* means "to be endowed with" or "to possess." Since the Buddha possesses the four bodies and five exalted wisdoms he is called Endowed. The four bodies are the nature body, wisdom body, enjoyment body, and emanation body of an enlightened being. The five exalted wisdoms are the mirror-like wisdom, the wisdom of equality, the wisdom of individual realization, the wisdom of accomplishing activities, and the wisdom of the sphere of phenomena.[19]

De means "transcended" or "gone beyond." The Buddha is called

Transcendent because he has transcended both cyclic existence and the nirvana of the hearer and solitary realizer foe-destroyers. Cyclic existence is the joining with contaminated aggregates again and again (i.e., the uncontrolled taking of rebirth) by the power of contaminated actions and afflictions. Nirvana, explained simply, is the attainment of a personal peaceful state of continuous meditative equipoise. Unlike ordinary sentient beings who are trapped in cyclic existence and the Lesser Vehicle foe-destroyers who have merely achieved their own peace, a buddha has attained a state of enlightenment that is free from both the faults of cyclic existence and those of nirvana and has thus fulfilled both his own and others' welfare.

In summary, the title of Bhagavan signifies that a buddha such as Shākyamuni Buddha, has abandoned all faults and has attained all qualities and is therefore worthy of our prostrations.

The Buddha is also called Tathāgata, One Gone Thus, because he has gone to, or reached, the simultaneous direct perception of all phenomena together with their thusness (i.e., emptiness). A tathāgata is also known as a *sugata* (*bde bar gshegs pa*, One Gone to Bliss) of which there are two types, the actual sugata being the realization of uncontaminated exalted wisdom. In addition, the complete abandonment of all objects of abandonment, the afflictions and so on, is also called sugata. Since a buddha has developed these qualities of realization and abandonment in his mental continuum he is called a sugata.

Although in many contexts the title of foe-destroyer refers specifically to the hearers and solitary realizers who have achieved their own personal liberation, it is also an epithet of the Buddha, since a foe-destroyer (*dgra bcom pa*) is a being who has completely destroyed (*bcom*) the inner foes, or enemies (*dgra*), the afflictions. The afflictions are called enemies because they harm us, just as do our external enemies. Recognizing that all our past, present, and future suffering is caused by our real enemies, the afflictions, we should continually strive to weaken them and finally destroy them altogether. In this way, we too will become foe-destroyers.

The Buddha is said to be Perfectly Complete since he has achieved the perfect completion of all qualities of body, speech, and mind. These qualities can be summarized, respectively, as the one hundred and twelve major and minor marks that adorn a buddha's body, the sixty-four qualities of a buddha's melodious speech, and the twenty-one divisions of uncontaminated exalted wisdom of a buddha's mind.

The Buddha is Glorious in that he possesses the perfection of high status, rebirth in the upper realms as a human, and the perfection of definite goodness, the state of omniscience that is endowed with qualities common to the hearers and solitary realizer foe-destroyers, and with qualities unique only to a buddha.

The Buddha is called Conqueror since he has conquered, or destroyed, the objects of abandonment, the afflictive obscurations that prevent liberation, and the obscurations to omniscience, or the obscurations to objects of knowledge, that prevent enlightenment. In other contexts, the epithet of Conqueror is explained to mean that a buddha has conquered the four demons.

The Buddha is known as Shākya since Shākya is the name of his family lineage or clan. The title of Muni, Subduer, demonstrates that the Buddha has subdued, or defeated, all the afflictions.

Although each one of us was born together with Shākyamuni Buddha many times in the past and we wandered with him in cyclic existence, the difference between the Buddha and ourselves is that in his previous lives he made an effort to complete the two collections of merit and wisdom and was thereby able to attain the state of enlightenment. We too, through making an effort, can attain high status, rebirth as a human or god in our future lives, or achieve the state of definite goodness, liberation and enlightenment. However, as long as we do not make the necessary effort, we will continue wandering in cyclic existence. Therefore, in this very life we need to make effort—not to make money, money, money—but to purify our minds so that we ourselves can become holy beings.

How to Prostrate

How to prostrate to him, the Subduer, who was described so, is as taught in *The Sutra of the Prayer of Good Conduct* (*Ārya bhadracharyā-praṇidhānarāja, 'Phags pa bzang po spyod pa'i smon lam gyi rgyal po*):

Emanate bodies equaling the number of atoms in the world systems, then prostrate touching your five body parts to the ground while visualizing that the emanated bodies also prostrate touching their five body parts to the ground. Emanate countless heads on your own body and on each of the emanated bodies and countless tongues in each head, then with your speech recite the ocean-like

qualities of the objects of prostration, whichever of the thirty-five tathāgatas and so on. With your mind visualize the buddhas together with their children, who, equaling the number of grains of sand of the Ganges River, are seated on top of a single atom. Then, in brief, visualizing the entire earth and space filled with the buddhas together with their retinues of bodhisattvas, pay homage to them out of respect.

Likewise, the remaining root text (*grantha, gzhung*),[20] "I prostrate to Tathāgata Thoroughly Destroying With Vajra Essence" and so on, should also be understood in terms of this method of explaining by means of the two [divisions]: (1) to which objects to prostrate and (2) how to prostrate.

To perform actual physical prostrations (see appendix 7) begin by joining the palms of your hands with the thumbs folded inward. This represents offering a wish-fulfilling jewel to all the buddhas and surrounding bodhisattvas who are visualized in the space in front of yourself. Imagine emanating countless bodies each of which has many heads with many tongues and then touch your folded hands to four points in succession (crown, forehead, throat, and heart) or, if you prefer, to just three (crown, throat, and heart). As you prostrate, touch your five body parts (legs, arms, and head) to the ground and imagine that all the emanated bodies do the same. Simultaneously recite the name of the corresponding tathāgata while imagining that each of the emanated tongues also does the same. Since even doing a single prostration brings the result of taking rebirth as a universal monarch, we collect innumerable virtues by conjoining prostrations and recitation of the names of the tathāgatas with this visualization because, by doing so, it is equivalent to performing countless prostrations and recitations simultaneously.

OFFERINGS

The root text, [I prostrate to Tathāgata...], shows both the limb of prostration and the limb of offering since, having explicitly shown prostrations to the thirty-five buddhas, it also implicitly shows the necessity of making offerings.

In addition to prostrating to the thirty-five buddhas, we should also present various types of offerings to them. Outer offerings are either actual material substances such as the seven usually placed on an altar (drinking water, washing water, flowers, incense, light, perfume, and food) or mentally emanated offerings such as beautiful gardens, flowers, mountains, trees, lakes, and so on. In brief, all the enjoyable things that exist in this world can be mentally offered to the buddhas. In addition, we can offer our Dharma practice, our virtuous actions, just as the Tibetan saint Milarepa, who had no material offerings, offered his teacher, Marpa, his Dharma practice and realizations to repay the kindness he had received from him. In the context of tantra we offer even the objects of our attachment, hatred, and ignorance by including them in the *maṇḍala* offering, a representation of the universe that is purified and offered. By doing so we train ourselves to mentally offer the various objects that we, for example, presently hold so dear, just as Shākyamuni Buddha in his previous lives gave away everything he possessed, even his wife and child. Through making this type of offering the strength of our afflictions will gradually diminish.

4. The Force of Total Repudiation

These and others, as many tathāgata foe-destroyer perfectly complete buddha-bhagavans as are abiding, living, and residing in all the world systems of the ten directions, all buddha-bhagavans, please pay attention to me.

"These and others" indicates the thirty-five buddhas who were explained above. "As many buddha-bhagavans as are abiding...in all the world systems of the ten directions" indicates that they have attained the truth body. "Living and residing" indicates that they have attained the complete enjoyment body. "All buddha-bhagavans, [please pay attention] to me" indicates that they have attained the emanation body.

Saying, "Please pay attention to me," we request the thirty-five tathāgatas and all the other buddhas of the ten directions to listen to, or to witness, our confession. Since the buddhas who have attained the three bodies—the truth body, enjoyment body, and emanation body—completely know all that there is to know, they are therefore appropriate persons to whom to make our confession.

The truth body encompasses the special mental qualities of a buddha, such as the five exalted wisdoms. The enjoyment body, according to sutra, possesses the five qualities of (1) giving only Great Vehicle teachings, (2) being surrounded solely by bodhisattva superiors, (3) being adorned with the thirty-two major marks and eighty minor marks, (4) remaining until the end of cyclic existence, and (5) always dwelling in the Not Low pure land (*akaniṣṭa, 'og min*), so-called because it is the highest of the seventeen

levels of the form realm. For the purpose of benefiting ordinary sentient beings who are unable to perceive it directly the enjoyment body emanates many bodies, the emanation bodies, to different realms and places in accordance with their needs.

> Having requested such buddha-bhagavans, those who have achieved the three bodies, to pay close attention to us with great mercy saying, "Please witness my confession of negativities and downfalls," it is necessary to put effort, day and night, into the confession of negativities and downfalls because it is taught in *The Heap of Jewels*, "Bodhisattvas, downfalls that are together with the five [actions of] immediate [retribution], downfalls that occur through women, downfalls that occur through the hands, downfalls that occur through children, downfalls that occur through stupas, downfalls that occur through the sangha, and heavy downfalls other than those should be confessed day and night by yourself alone in the presence of the thirty-five buddhas."

The five actions of immediate retribution, as mentioned previously, are killing one's mother, one's father, or a foe-destroyer, causing blood to flow from the body of a tathāgata with evil intent, and creating a schism in the sangha. A downfall that occurs through women transpires when, for example, a man with the lay vow of refraining from sexual misconduct has sexual intercourse with another man's wife. Downfalls that occur through the hands are, for example, killing and stealing, both of which are generally accomplished with our hands. Downfalls that occur through children include such actions as abusing a child, abandoning a newborn baby, and fighting over a child. Downfalls that occur through stupas encompass such actions as destroying stupas, taking the offerings made to them, taking their decorations, and so forth. Downfalls that occur through the sangha can be committed in relation to either the conventional sangha, a group of four fully ordained monks or nuns, or the ultimate sangha, a single superior. Examples of this type of downfall are stealing the belongings of the conventional or ultimate sangha or creating a schism in the conventional sangha.

These and other heavy downfalls need to be confessed day and night in front of the tathāgatas by applying the four opponent forces. In brief, as

explained above, go for refuge from the depths of your heart to the Three Jewels while generating the wish to attain enlightenment to benefit all sentient beings, thereby completing the force of the basis. Then develop deep regret for the negative actions you have done and resolve to try not to do them again, thereby completing, respectively, the opponent force of total repudiation and that of turning away from faults in the future. With these three opponent forces as the foundation, prostrate while reciting the names of the tathāgatas, thereby completing the force of applying all antidotes. By confessing in this manner you will definitely be able to purify the negativities committed in this and previous lives.

Identifying Negativities and Obscurations

In this life and in all the states of rebirth in which I have circled in cyclic existence throughout beginningless lives, whatever negative actions I have done, caused to be done, or rejoiced in the doing of...

Negative actions [include] those directly committed in this life, those indirectly committed through having made others do them, and those of having rejoiced in others' doing of them, as well as those not committed in this life but committed throughout beginningless lives up to this life while continuously circling in cyclic existence by the power of actions and afflictions. In brief, the negativities to be confessed are shown to be (1) the negative actions that we have directly committed, (2) those that we have indirectly committed through having caused them to be done, and (3) those of having rejoiced in others' doing of them, in all the states of rebirth in which we have circled.

Here the root text clearly shows that it is necessary to confess and purify both the negativities committed in this life as well as those committed in previous lives. Although we have probably done many negative actions in this life, most likely we have not engaged in every single type. However, since our previous rebirths are without beginning we have certainly committed them at some time in the past. Therefore, it is extremely important to include all the negativities of this life and all those of our previous lives in the confession, whether they were committed directly, indirectly, or by rejoicing.

The Negativities of Misusing the Possessions of the Jewels

Whatever possessions of stupas, possessions of the sangha, or possessions of the sangha of the ten directions I have appropriated, made to be appropriated, or rejoiced in the appropriation of…

In this context a stupa is the Buddha Jewel and the Dharma Jewel; their possessions are their offering substances. Using them without permission is considered to be appropriating the possessions of a stupa. Thus, we have directly appropriated the possessions of the Buddha and Dharma Jewels. In addition, if, without permission, we directly use the possessions of the sangha—the belongings of superior beings, the actual Sangha Jewel—it is appropriating the possessions of the Sangha Jewel. Thereby, [the root text] indicates that the negativities of misusing the possessions of all three Jewels are negativities to be confessed.

"The possessions of the sangha of the ten directions" are the belongings of the sangha, a group of four or more, who live in the infinite places, the communities of sangha of the ten directions. Directly using [their possessions] without permission is appropriating the possessions of the sangha of the ten directions. This is also called appropriating the provisions of the sangha.

Since these objects are very delicate and these situations easily happen to us, I implore you to be careful concerning this point.

All our negativities of having appropriated the possessions of the Three Jewels as was explained—whether directly, indirectly (having made others appropriate them), or of having rejoiced in others' appropriating of them—are negativities to be confessed.

In this context the Buddha and Dharma Jewels are referred to by the term "stupa." The Buddha Jewel includes all enlightened beings as well as representations of them such as statues, paintings, and pictures. If, without asking permission, we were to use the offerings that have been made to them, we would commit the action of appropriating the possessions of the Buddha Jewel. The Dharma Jewel is represented by texts containing the Buddha's teachings. If, without asking permission, we were to take and use offerings placed before them, our action would be that of appropriating the possessions of the Dharma Jewel.

Taking the belongings of superiors without asking permission is appropriating the possessions of the Sangha Jewel. Taking the belongings of, or offerings made to, the conventional sangha, including a monastery or nunnery, without asking permission, is appropriating the possessions of the sangha of the ten directions.

In summary, the negativities, or objects to be confessed, comprise any of the above-mentioned actions that we ourselves have directly committed, indirectly committed, or accumulated through having rejoiced in others' doing of them.

The Negativities of the Five Actions of Immediate Retribution

> *Whatever of the five actions of immediate [retribution] I have done,*
> *caused to be done, or rejoiced in the doing of...*

The five actions of immediate [retribution] are causing blood to flow from the body of a tathāgata with evil intent, creating a schism in the sangha, killing a foe-destroyer, killing one's father, and killing one's mother. The negativities of having directly committed these actions ourselves, of having indirectly committed them through having made others do them, and of having rejoiced in others' doing of them are also negativities that are objects to be confessed.

There is a reason for calling these five "actions of immediate [retribution]": because if we commit any one of them, if it is not confessed, it will cause us to be thrown into hell after we die without another rebirth in between.

There is some difference of opinion between the Lesser and Greater Vehicles concerning whether or not we can actually commit the action of immediate retribution of causing blood to flow from the body of a tathāgata. According to the vinaya teachings this action can only be committed in relation to the body of Shākyamuni Buddha; consequently, it would be impossible for us to commit it. However, the Great Vehicle asserts that this action can be committed in relation to any tathāgata and, therefore, it would indeed be possible for us to commit it. Regardless of this difference of opinion, it is unlikely that we have committed this action in this life; nor is it likely that we have killed our father, our mother, or a foe-destroyer. On the other hand, it is impossible for us to have committed the action of

immediate retribution of creating a schism in the sangha. This is because this particular action of immediate retribution is specifically related to an event that occurred during the lifetime of Shākyamuni Buddha when Devadatta imposed five mandatory practices that resulted in controversy within the monastery. The five practices were (1) to not eat meat because it involves the killing of sentient beings, (2) to not eat salty food because it causes attachment, (3) to not drink milk because it harms the suckling calf, (4) to not wear cut and sewn clothes because it harms the weavers, and (5) to not stay in solitary places because it does not benefit other people. Fortunately, harmony was quickly restored by two of Buddha's disciples, Shāriputra and Maudgalyāyana. In consequence, their presence, as well as that of Shākyamuni Buddha himself, is necessary to commit the action of immediate retribution of creating a schism in the sangha. In this lifetime, if we were to cause a division among the sangha, while it would be a great negativity, it would not be an action of immediate retribution.

Furthermore, according to the root tantra of Guhyasamāja, abandoning the Dharma is equivalent to the action of immediate retribution of creating a schism in the sangha, and breaking or destroying a statue of the Buddha is equivalent to the action of immediate retribution of causing blood to flow from a tathāgata. Therefore, according to tantra, it is possible that we have committed all five actions of immediate retribution at some time in this or past lives. Although we may not have committed any of them in this life, since we do not know with certainty that we did not do them in other lives, we need to purify them. For this reason, the actions of immediate retribution that we have directly and indirectly committed and the negativities accumulated by having rejoiced in others' doing of them are indicated as negativities to be confessed.

The Negativities Included in the Ten Non-virtues

> *Whatever of the ten non-virtuous paths of action I have engaged in the adoption of, caused to be engaged in, or rejoiced in the engagement in...*

The negativities of adopting the ten non-virtuous paths of action taught as, "actions of body, three types," and so forth, are also negativities to be confessed, or negativities that are objects to be confessed, whether we have directly engaged in them, have caused others to

engage in them (i.e., have made others do them), or have rejoiced in others engaging in (i.e., doing) them.

The ten non-virtuous paths of action are the three accumulated by the body (killing, stealing, and sexual misconduct), the four accumulated by speech (lying, divisive speech, harsh words, and idle talk), and the three accumulated by mind (covetousness, malice, and wrong view). Each of these paths of action must consist of four branches, or parts, to be complete. These are (1) the basis (*gzhi*), (2) thought (*bsam pa*), (3) execution (*sbyor ba*), and (4) completion (*mthar thug*). The branch of basis refers to the particular object at which an action is directed. The branch of thought is further divided into three: recognition, affliction, and motivation. Recognition, or discrimination, is the clear and unmistaken identification of the object. The affliction is any of the three mental poisons: attachment, hatred, or ignorance. The motivation is the wish to engage in the action. The execution, or preparation, includes all the actions engaged in prior to the completion of the path of action. The completion is when the actual path of action is accomplished. By carefully analyzing the ten non-virtuous paths of action in terms of their four branches we will come to understand exactly what each one of them entails.

Killing. Taking the life of a sentient being, even that of the tiniest insect, is the most serious of the negative actions of body. The *basis* is the continuum of another sentient being. The *recognition* is the correct identification of the sentient being we wish to kill. The *affliction* involved can be any of the three poisons; for example, killing for food is done out of attachment, killing out of aversion is due to hatred, and killing for enjoyment is caused by ignorance. The *motivation* is the wish to kill. The *execution* of the action can be done directly—using a weapon, poison, mantra power, and so forth—or indirectly by causing someone else to kill. The *completion* of the action is that the other sentient being dies first. Consequently, if two people were to mortally wound each other simultaneously, the person who dies first would not create the complete action of killing. Likewise, although suicide is a very heavy negative action, it is not the complete path of action of killing.

Stealing. Stealing is taking the wealth or possessions of others without them having been given. The *basis* is an object possessed by another being. The *recognition* is the clear unmistaken identification of the object we intend to

take. The *affliction* can be any one of the three—attachment, hatred, or ignorance. The *motivation* is the wish to take an object that has not been given (i.e., to separate that object from the person to whom it belongs). The *execution* can be carried out directly—using either force, stealth, or deceit— or indirectly by causing someone else to steal. The *completion* is, after taking the object, to feel a sense of satisfaction thinking, "Now it is mine."

Sexual misconduct. Sexual misconduct occurs in relation to four types of *basis*: an unsuitable person, an unsuitable bodily part, an unsuitable time, and an unsuitable place. An unsuitable person is someone else's partner, a close relation, a minor, or someone with a vow of chastity. An unsuitable bodily part is, for example, the mouth or anus. An unsuitable time is day-time, during pregnancy, or when one of the partners has taken the eight Mahāyāna precepts, since these include refraining from all sexual activity for twenty-four hours. An unsuitable place is in front of our guru, parents, or images of the buddhas, near a stupa, or in a temple. The correct *recognition* of our partner is not necessary to complete the path of action of sexual misconduct. The *affliction* accompanying sexual misconduct is generally attachment but can be hatred (e.g., rape) or ignorance (e.g., thinking that sexual intercourse is a way to gain spiritual realizations). The *motivation* is the wish to engage in sexual activity. The *execution* is sexual activity with an unsuitable person, with an unsuitable bodily part, at an unsuitable time, or in an unsuitable place. The *completion* is experiencing the pleasure of orgasm.

Lying. The *basis* is a person who is capable of understanding our words. The *recognition* is knowing that we are altering our discrimination; for example, saying that we have seen someone whom we have not seen or saying that we have not seen someone whom we have seen. The *affliction* can be either attachment, hatred, or ignorance. The *motivation* is the wish to alter the truth. The *execution* can be done by speaking, by making a physical gesture, or by remaining silent. The *completion* is that the other person understands what we have communicated.

Divisive speech. The *basis* is two or more people who have either a harmo-nious or a disharmonious relationship. The *recognition* of these people should be unmistaken. The *affliction* can be any of the mental poisons. The *motivation* must be to cause discord between harmonious people or to cause

further discord between those who are already in disharmony. The *execution* involves speaking true or false words with an end to causing discord; for example, speaking in such a way as to cause a complete breakup of an already strained relationship between two friends. The *completion* is that the other people understand what we have said.

Harsh words. The *basis* is another sentient being. The *recognition* of the person we wish to hurt with our words should be unmistaken. The *affliction* can be any of the three mental poisons. The *motivation* is the wish to cause harm with our words. The *execution* involves saying something true or untrue, in either a rude or polite way. The *completion* is that the other person understands our words.

Idle talk. The *basis* is something trivial or insignificant. The *recognition* of what we are saying should not be mistaken. The *affliction* can be any of the three mental poisons. The *motivation* is the wish to say the insignificant words. The *execution* is to speak without a good purpose; for example, teaching Dharma for the purpose of gaining money or fame, reading books that decrease our interest in Dharma, singing worldly songs, telling jokes, and habitually complaining. The *completion* is to finish speaking the insignificant words. Although this non-virtuous action is by nature light, it can become heavy by way of committing it frequently.

Covetousness. The *basis* is the possessions or qualities of another person. The *recognition* is the correct identification of the object we desire to possess. The main *affliction* is attachment. The *motivation* is the wish to possess the object. The *execution* is the thought process considering how to obtain the object. The *completion* is the decision to obtain the object.

Malice. The *basis* is another sentient being. The *recognition* of the sentient being we desire to harm must be unmistaken. The main *affliction* is hatred. The *motivation* is the wish to harm by striking, beating, and so on. The *execution* is the thought process planning to harm that sentient being. The *completion* is the decision to harm that sentient being.

Wrong view. The *basis* is a phenomenon that exists, such as past and future lives, the law of action and result, the Three Jewels, the four noble truths,

and the two truths. The *recognition* is thinking that what we believe is completely correct when in fact it is incorrect. The main *affliction* is ignorance. The *motivation* is the wish to deny the existence of the object. The *execution* is undertaking the denial, of which there are four types: (1) denying that causes, virtue and non-virtue, exist; (2) denying that the four types of result exist; (3) denying that functions exist (including, [i] denying that parents are needed to produce a child, [ii] denying that a seed is needed to produce a plant, [iii] denying the existence of coming and going—i.e., past and future lives, and [iv] denying the existence of miraculous rebirth); and finally (4) denying the existence of foe-destroyers. The *completion* is deciding to actively deny the object; for example, deciding to tell other people that past and future lives do not exist.

According to the vinaya teachings, eight of the ten non-virtuous paths of action—sexual misconduct, the four of speech, and the three of mind—must be committed directly to become a complete action, while killing and stealing can be complete actions even when we cause someone else to do them. However, according to the abhidharma teachings, the four non-virtuous paths of action of speech can also be completed by causing someone else to do them.

In summary, whether we have directly done these ten non-virtuous actions, caused others to do them, or rejoiced that others have done them, these negativities are objects to be confessed.

How to Confess Negativities and Downfalls

Whatever karmic obscurations due to which I and sentient beings, having become obscured, will go to hell, an animal mode of rebirth, or the land of the hungry ghosts; will be reborn in border areas, reborn as barbarians or as long-life gods; will have imperfect faculties, hold wrong views, or will not be delighted with the arising of a buddha—in the presence of the buddha-bhagavans who are exalted wisdom, who are eyes, who are witnesses, who are valid, and who see with knowledge, I admit and confess all these karmic obscurations. I do not conceal or hide them.

Confess Negativities with Intense Regret

Among the negative actions that were explained above, if we remember having committed any of them whatsoever in this life, it is necessary to confess it with intense regret. Not only that, even if we have not committed those negativities and downfalls in this life, since we cannot certify whether we have or have not done them throughout beginningless cyclic existence up to this life, and since we have [indeed] committed those very negativities, although we do not actually remember it now, we therefore need to confess them with intense regret. Furthermore, this regret should be similar to that of, for example, having ingested poison. However, while ingesting poison does not produce anything other than the suffering of death or the suffering of merely coming close to death, having committed negativities, if they are not confessed and purified, not only will they produce the suffering of death and the suffering of coming close to death in this life but also, by the power of these karmic obscurations, we will definitely be thrown into the leisureless states (*akṣhaṇa, mi khom pa'i gnas*) in future lives.

The Result of Not Confessing Negativities—The Eight Leisureless States

If it is asked, "Well then, how many leisureless migrations projected by [these karmic obscurations] are there?" In regard to that, the root text indicates that there are the [following] eight: the three leisureless [states] with respect to the bad migrations, hell and so forth, since "will go to hell" means "will migrate to hell"; and the five leisureless [states] with respect to the happy migrations, barbarians and so forth. Moreover, being born as a long-life god is the leisureless [state] with respect to the gods. The four leisureless [states] of birth in a border area or as a barbarian, of being dumb with imperfect faculties, of being like the Cast-Afar (*ayata, rbyang phan pa*)[21] who hold wrong views, and of not being delighted with the arising of a buddha in the world—not enjoying and hating it like the malicious demons—are the leisureless [states] with respect to humans.

The meaning of this, in brief, is that having committed a negative action, such as one of the ten non-virtuous actions, if it is not confessed and purified, it will eventually cause us to be reborn in one of the eight leisureless states. Leisureless, in this context, refers specifically to a lack of time and opportunity to engage in Dharma practice.

The second link of the twelve links of dependent arising, actions or karmic formations, includes both virtuous and non-virtuous actions. These actions are called projecting causes because they function to project us into a future rebirth. For example, non-virtuous actions project us into the leisureless rebirths of the lower realms as hell beings, hungry ghosts, and animals.

The leisureless state of a long-life god refers to a particular god rebirth in a part of the fourth concentration of the form realm called Without Discrimination. Rebirth there is due to having cultivated its specific cause—meditation on the Absorption Without Discrimination on the basis of calm abiding—in the immediately preceding life. At the very moment of taking life as a long-life god, the thought occurs, "Now I am born," and when dying, the thought occurs, "Now I am dying." Besides these two thoughts no other mental activity occurs and these gods remain as unconscious as statues for eons of time. This state is said to be without leisure since the beings born there cannot even listen to Dharma teachings let alone actually practice Dharma.

Four leisureless states are specified regarding rebirth as a human being. A border area is a barbaric place in which there is no culture, written language, or religion. Birth in such a place is a leisureless state due to the total absence of Dharma teachings. Being born with imperfect or impaired mental or sense faculties is a leisureless state because, for example, with a dull mental faculty it would be almost impossible to practice Dharma. Our main activities would be eating and sleeping and our life would not be much different from that of an animal. Being born as a human but holding wrong views like the Cast-Afar, the Hedonists, who do not accept the law of action and result, past and future lives, etc., is said to be a leisureless state since wrong views result in a lack of interest in Dharma practice. The fourth leisureless state of human beings is usually said to be birth as a human being during a dark eon, a time when no buddha arises in the world. It is a leisureless state since without a buddha the Dharma teachings would not exist in the world and, in consequence, we would not be able to

practice Dharma. Although here the root text says that the fourth leisureless state is to be unhappy like the demons with the arising of a buddha in the world, this actually means to be born in a dark eon when no buddha arises in the world.

To avoid taking rebirth in these leisureless states without the opportunity to practice the holy Dharma, we need to take care to purify each and every negativity and downfall that we have committed in this and past lives.

The Appropriateness of Confessing to the Buddha-bhagavans

> Since the buddha-bhagavans precisely realize all phenomena in general and how all our white and black actions were done in particular, they are called exalted wisdom. Moreover, since they directly and clearly see, just as eyes see forms, they are called eyes. Due to distinguishing the excellent and the faulty, the virtuous and non-virtuous actions that we have done, they are called witnesses. Having witnessed like that, since they are unmistaken and infallible in distinguishing the excellent and the faulty, they are valid persons.
>
> All the karmic obscurations mentioned above that eventually bring rebirth in the eight leisureless [states] are to be admitted and confessed in the presence of the tathāgatas who directly know and precisely see the mode in which phenomena abide, emptiness.

The buddha-bhagavans are called "exalted wisdom" because they directly realize all phenomena, everything that exists, including all our actions. They are called "eyes" because they possess the wisdom eyes that directly see, or know, whatever actions we do, both the black, negative ones as well as the white, virtuous ones. Just as we directly see the colors and shapes of visible forms with our eyes, the buddhas directly perceive all phenomena. Since they see, or witness, our non-virtuous and virtuous actions, the buddhas are also called "witnesses." They are "valid" persons due to their ability to unmistakenly and infallibly distinguish between what is right and what is wrong. Since the buddhas possess such exalted qualities, it is appropriate to confess our negativities in their presence.

Confess Negativities Openly and Honestly

The difference between admitting and confessing is that saying "admit" is telling someone, "I did this and that negativity and downfall," while, in addition to the former, saying "confess" is making a confession, by regretting what we did in the past, and a vow, by making a strong determination to restrain ourselves hereafter.

Saying "I do not conceal them"; although we have committed some kind of negativity or downfall, to not conceal it is to not entertain the wish to keep it secret from the very moment it is committed. Otherwise, it would become a negativity or downfall that is together with concealment.

Saying "I do not hide them"; like hiding stolen property in a worldly sense, to hide is to say that we have not committed a negativity or downfall that we have in fact done. Not doing so, but saying "done" with respect to the done and "not done" with respect to the not done is, when stated truthfully, to not hide it. Having committed a negativity or downfall it would be unwise to hide it because, although when hidden from someone such as a deaf mute it would not be known by him, when hidden from the perfectly complete buddhas who directly see all phenomena, since they pay attention to everything we do, any negativities and downfalls whatsoever, they would be displeased with us once more. Even if we were to commit such minor faults as digging earth, cutting grass, or drawing designs in the earth without a purpose, since the tathāgatas pay attention to it we should rely on conscientiousness by imagining ourselves as though situated in front of the tathāgatas and reflect on the inappropriateness of transgressing the advice of the sugatas. This is mentioned here because it says in *Engaging in the Bodhisattva Deeds* (*Bodhisattva-charyāvatāra, Byang chub sems dpa'i spyod pa la 'jug pa*), "I always abide in the presence of all the buddhas and bodhisattvas who are endowed with unobstructed sight regarding all," and, "If you dig earth, cut grass, draw designs in the earth, and so forth without a purpose, upon remembering the advice of the sugatas, out of terror immediately give it up."

To admit our negative actions is to say, "I did such and such a negative action" in accordance with what we have actually done. If instead we commit a negative action and then, on top of that, say that we did not do it, this would make the buddhas, who directly see each of our actions, even more ashamed of and displeased with us. Since the buddhas know even the very minor faults we commit, such as the faults fully ordained monks and nuns create through engaging in such activities as digging earth, picking or cutting grass, or tracing designs in the earth without a specific purpose, we should truthfully admit and purify whatever negative actions we have done. Whether we remember them specifically or not does not matter since, although we may not have done a specific action in this life, it is quite likely that we have done it in a previous life. Through reflecting on this we will develop the wish to purify each and every negative action and will therefore put effort into the practice of confessing our negativities with the four opponent forces.

5. The Force of Turning Away from Faults in the Future

From now on, I will stop and refrain from them.

Not only should we confess the negativities and downfalls that we committed in the past, we should also make a firm determination to restrain ourselves from now on (i.e., hereafter), thinking, "I will desist from doing those negativities and downfalls that I have been doing and I will not do those that have not been done."

In addition to purifying the negativities already done, it is extremely important to stop committing them in the future. Saying, "From now on, I will stop and refrain from them," signifies that, although we have committed negative actions in the past, from now on we will not do them again. This firm determination, or resolution, to stop engaging in negativities is the opponent force of turning away from faults in the future. Although the text says, "I will stop and refrain from them," some teachers say that it is better to say, "I will try not to do them again," because this is likely to be more truthful. They say that if we were to promise definitely not to do a particular action again but then, some time later on, were to engage in it, our confession would become similar to a lie. However, even if, due to the strength of our afflictions, this were to happen, we should immediately apply the four opponent forces to purify the negative action.

Closing the Four Doors

To prevent ourselves from committing negativities in the future, we also need to close our four doors, the four means by which we continue to commit negativities. Just as, for example, if the four doors of a house are left

open many unwanted things such as thieves, animals, dust, and wind can easily come inside; if we leave our four doors open we will continually engage in creating more negativities and downfalls. The four doors are (1) a lack of conscientiousness, (2) a lack of respect for others, (3) our many afflictions, and (4) a lack of knowledge. We can close these doors through applying their respective antidotes: (1) the development of mindfulness, introspection, and conscientiousness; (2) the cultivation of respect; (3) the application of a specific antidote; and (4) meditation on dependent arising and emptiness. Each of the afflictions has its own specific antidote, for example, the antidote to anger is meditation on love and compassion, the antidote to pride is analytical meditation on the eighteen constituents, and the antidote to too many thoughts is concentration on the breath. As a general antidote to all our negativities we need to cultivate the mental factors of mindfulness and introspection as this will enable us to avoid engaging in negativities and, if we find that we have engaged in them, it will enable us to purify them immediately.

The Efficacy of Purification

> In summary, the meaning of the preceding explanations is that we should put effort into confessing negativities and downfalls with intense regret by relying on all four opponent forces. If we make such an effort, no matter how many negativities and downfalls we have done in the past, through purifying them afterwards with the confession of the four forces, we will become an appropriate vessel for accomplishing the higher paths, even though our mental continuum was previously polluted by negativities and downfalls. This is like, for example, the moon that becomes beautiful due to its light in the middle of a clear sky once the cover of clouds has been cleared away. As taught in [Nāgārjuna's] *Friendly Letter* (*Suhṛllekha*), "Beautiful as the cloudless moon is one who, though once reckless, later becomes conscientious, like Nanda, Aṅgulimālā, Ajātashatru, and Shaṅkara."

To illustrate the efficacy of purification the text compares our mental continuum to the beauty of the cloud-free moon in that just as the moon in its

purity is revealed when the clouds are blown way, so too the natural beauty, or purity, of our mental continuum is revealed when we purify our negative actions. Nanda, Aṅgulimālā, Ajātashatru, and Shaṅkara, each of whom was overcome by a particularly strong affliction, are mentioned to emphasize that even the strongest afflictions can be eliminated from our minds, like clouds from the sky. Nanda, a cousin of Shākyamuni Buddha, had such strong attachment for his wife that he could not bear to be separated from her for even a minute. However, through the knowledge and skill of Shākyamuni Buddha who, by his clairvoyance, perceived when the moment was ripe to subdue his cousin's mind, Nanda was able to overcome his attachment, purify his mind, and attain the state of foe-destroyer. To subdue Nanda, one day Buddha went to Nanda's house begging for alms. He gave Nanda his bowl to be filled with food but instead of accepting the filled bowl turned around and began to walk back toward his monastery. Nanda, fearing to offend the Buddha, followed with the bowl until they reached the monastery. When they entered inside, the Buddha told Nanda to have his hair cut and to take ordination as a monk. Nanda did so but, continually reminded of his beautiful wife, planned to escape from the monastery at the very first opportunity. One day his chance came but before he had gone very far he saw Buddha coming toward him and feeling ashamed he returned to the monastery. Some time later, one of Buddha's chief disciples, Maudgalyāyana, known for his magical powers, suggested to Nanda that they go for a walk together. During the walk Maudgalyāyana emanated a beautiful park in which there were many extremely attractive goddesses, each of whom was much more beautiful than Nanda's wife. Maudgalyāyana told Nanda that if he kept his vows well he would be able to enjoy the company of the goddesses in his next life. This motivated Nanda to remain in the monastery and to make more effort to keep his vows. On another occasion Maudgalyāyana, again though his psychic powers, showed Nanda a horrible place with a huge pot filled with bubbling melted iron. When Nanda questioned him about this pot, Maudgalyāyana replied that it was for a person named Nanda who would be reborn in it if he did not keep his vows purely. Nanda, very frightened by hearing this, developed strong renunciation, abandoned all attachment, completely purified his mental continuum, and eventually became a foe-destroyer.

Aṅgulimālā, a very angry person, had killed nine hundred and ninety-nine people when he met Shākyamuni Buddha. However, he too, through

the skillful actions of the Buddha, was able to purify his mental continuum and become a foe-destroyer. King Ajātashatru killed his father, a highly realized being, to usurp the throne, but later he too was able to become a realized being through deeply regretting his action and engaging in purification practices. Although Shankara killed his mother, he too was able to attain high realizations in that same life due to purifying his negativities. Each of these examples confirms that we too can attain the state of a holy being through striving in the practice of purification.

CONFESSION PREVENTS NEGATIVITIES FROM INCREASING

> When we confess well, the essential point of the quote, "Even the heavy negativities of the wise are light; even the light negativities of the foolish are heavy," is as though present in [the confession].

Even very heavy negativities become light when we use our wisdom and immediately apply the four opponent forces. This is because by purifying a negativity as soon as it is done, even if the action cannot be completely purified, a wise person prevents it from increasing and thereby daily becoming more and more heavy. However, the negativities of a foolish person, who thinking that it does not matter does not purify his or her negative actions, become heavy, even though initially they may have been very light. For example, if today we were to kill a single ant and did not purify this negativity, tomorrow the action would increase to equal that of having killed two ants, the next day to that of having killed four, and so on, continuing to multiply each day as long as the action is not purified. Like this, the enormity of the action continues to increase and an initially minor action becomes very serious. Consequently, it is extremely important to purify our negative actions every day since by doing so, even though we may not be able to completely purify our negative actions, at least we will be able to stop them from increasing.

THE ESSENCE OF CONFESSION

> Therefore, from the very beginning do not be stained by faults and downfalls. However, if, due to the power of the great strength of the

afflictions, you do become stained by faults and downfalls, minor and so on, it is necessary to confess them with the four forces explained previously by reciting *The Sutra of the Three Heaps*. Likewise, it is also taught in *Engaging in the Bodhisattva Deeds,* "I, with a mind fearing sorrow, having kneeled with folded hands directly in front of the Protector, confess all negativities," and, "Again and again during the day and night recite *The [Sutra of the] Three Heaps."*

This concludes the explanation of how to confess negativities.

In conclusion, the essence of the practice of confession is, whenever you realize that you have done a negative action, to visualize the thirty-five buddhas, kneel down in front of them with your hands folded, and remembering the qualities of the Buddha, Dharma, and Sangha, go for refuge to them. Reflecting that you did such and such a negative action, and understanding that it was wrong, develop sincere regret. Then, making a firm decision to try not to do this action again, prostrate while reciting the names of the thirty-five tathāgatas. Faith and belief that this purification practice will bring beneficial results in the long run is an important factor in determining its efficacy. Do not think that you will experience the result very quickly, perhaps tomorrow or the day after tomorrow. However, by continually doing this practice you will actually purify your negative actions and eventually you will be able to achieve the realizations that lead to enlightenment.

The Bodhisattva's Confession of Downfalls is also known as *The Sutra of the Three Heaps* because it contains three heaps, or aggregates: the heap of confession, the heap of dedication, and the heap of rejoicing. The explanation of the first heap, confession, which entails the purification of negativities through the application of the four opponent forces, is concluded.

Part Two

Accumulating Merit

6. Dedicating Virtues

Request the Buddha-bhagavans to Witness the Dedication

All buddha-bhagavans, please pay attention to me.

We appeal to the conquerors together with their sons, who are the thirty-five buddhas and so forth, saying, "Earlier, you very kindly witnessed my confession of negativities. Now, paying attention with great mercy, please witness my dedication."

Visualizing the buddhas and bodhisattvas in the space in front of ourselves, as is explained above, and feeling confident that they are really present even though we cannot actually see them, we appeal to them to witness our dedication. Although they are in fact present, we are unable to see them at the moment because our mind is obscured by afflictions. Upon attaining the great level of the path of accumulation we will be able to directly see, and even to communicate with, the buddhas and bodhisattvas. At that time we will also see images of the buddhas as actual emanation bodies and will be able to receive teachings directly from them. When we attain the path of seeing and become a bodhisattva superior we will see images of the buddhas as their actual enjoyment bodies. However, until then, we should feel confident that all the buddhas and bodhisattvas, in particular the thirty-five tathāgatas, are actually present in front of us. Then, with this awareness, we should respectfully request them to witness the dedication of the merit accumulated through engaging in virtuous actions in this and other lives. Through dedicating that we ourselves and all sentient beings may attain enlightenment, our merit will never be lost or exhausted until enlightenment is attained. Like putting a single drop of water into the ocean, until the ocean dries up, the drop will not dry up.

To illustrate the importance of dedicating merit, there is a traditional story of two Tibetans who met on their way to Lhasa. One man was carrying a large sack of roasted barley flour while the other had only a small sack of dark roasted pea flour. The person with the pea flour suggested to the other that they mix the two flours together, to which he kindly agreed. After some days of eating the resulting mixture the person who owned the bigger sack told the other man that the latter's portion of the flour had been consumed. However, the owner of the smaller sack disagreed and told him to take a look inside the bag of flour. Sure enough, it was possible to distinguish the darker particles of pea flour from those of the light colored barley flour. Therefore, the owner of the larger sack could not rightly claim that the other's flour had been finished. Just as the smaller sack of roasted flour is not completely consumed until the larger one is finished, likewise, when we dedicate our merit for the purpose of attaining enlightenment, due to the power of the dedication, the potential of even our smallest virtuous actions will not be consumed until every sentient being has attained enlightenment.

Identifying the Virtues to Be Dedicated

In this life and in the other states of rebirth in which I have circled in cyclic existence throughout beginningless lives, whatever roots of virtue there are from my generosity, be it as little as having given one morsel of food to a being born in the animal realm; whatever roots of virtue there are from my having guarded morality; whatever roots of virtue there are from my pure conduct; whatever roots of virtue there are from my having fully ripened sentient beings; whatever roots of virtue there are from my having generated bodhichitta; and whatever roots of virtue there are from my unsurpassed exalted wisdom: all these, assembled and gathered, then combined together…

Thus, the virtues to be dedicated are shown to be all the roots of virtue of generosity and so forth that we have created—however many roots of virtue we have created having been illustrated with the six perfections—in this life and in the other states of rebirth in which we have circled in cyclic existence throughout beginningless lives up to this life by the power of actions and afflictions. Having said above, "all

the states of rebirth in which I have circled," there is a reason for saying here, "in the other states of rebirth," because it is said like that through considering that the lives in which we created virtues are almost non-existent in comparison to the lives in which we created negativities.

If it is asked, "Well then, how are the virtues illustrated by the six perfections created?" Whatever our, the dedicators', generosity in this life and in all lifetimes, having been illustrated by the roots of virtue of the generosity of giving a small thing, a mere morsel of food, to ordinary recipients, beings in the animal realm and upwards, it also [includes] the virtues of offering all great things, our bodies, possessions, and roots of virtue, to special recipients, superiors such as the perfectly complete buddhas, as well as the generosity of Dharma of appropriately explaining the profound Dharma to the ocean-like surrounding [beings]. By showing these as virtues that are objects to be dedicated, the root text also shows the limb of offering.

Similarly, whatever roots of virtue (i.e., all whatsoever) of our having guarded morality, such as the morality of abandoning the ten non-virtues, are virtues that are objects to be dedicated.

Purity is liberation, nirvana; and pure conduct is meditating on the four immeasurables, love and so forth, for the sake of obtaining it. Moreover, [pure conduct] is the root of virtue of cultivating patience since the four immeasurables, love and so forth, destroy anger.

The [roots of] virtue of undertaking the effort that especially delights in creating virtue, indicated by saying "having fully ripened sentient beings," are the virtues of undertaking the effort that especially delights in ripening sentient beings who are not yet fully ripe and liberating those who are ripe.

The roots of virtue of cultivating concentration are generating the mind of supreme unsurpassed enlightenment and then abiding single-pointedly on it.

Unsurpassed exalted wisdom is the wisdom truth body (*jñāna-dharmakāya, ye shes chos sku*), while the roots of virtue of investigating the meaning of selflessness with analytical wisdom are for the sake of obtaining it.

Any of these whatsoever, that we have directly created, are virtues that are objects to be dedicated.

The objects to be dedicated are the roots of virtue created through the practice of the six perfections in this life as well as in previous lives. The commentary mentions two types of generosity in regard to the roots of virtue created through the practice of the perfection of generosity: the generosity of giving material objects and the generosity of giving the Dharma. Merely giving one mouthful of food to a being who is experiencing a bad rebirth, such as an animal, constitutes the practice of generosity and is therefore worthy of dedication. Since the practice of generosity can involve something as simple as giving a handful of grain to some birds or ants, it would seem quite easy to practice it. However, the real practice of generosity is not so much the actual action of giving as it is the development of the wish to give. It is the attitude that is completely opposite to miserliness—a tight mind and a tight fist. As such the practice of generosity also includes making mental offerings of such valuable things as our own body, possessions, and roots of virtue to special objects such as the buddhas, as well as teaching the Dharma of the vast and profound lineages to sentient beings, who are like an ocean in number and extent. By giving other people the Dharma teachings we help them to develop their knowledge, wisdom, and good qualities and to ultimately achieve every happiness. While the commentary only explicitly mentions the generosity of giving material objects and the Dharma, also the roots of virtue of having practiced the generosity of giving protection from harm and the generosity of giving love are objects to be dedicated.

The perfection of morality, like that of generosity, involves developing a particular mental attitude; in this case, the wish to completely abandon all non-virtuous actions. Three types of morality are taught: (1) the morality of abandoning, or refraining from, the ten non-virtuous actions; (2) the morality of practicing, or guarding, the ten virtuous actions; and (3) the morality of benefiting sentient beings. All the roots of virtue that we have accumulated through practicing these three types of morality, in this life and in previous lives, are objects to dedicated.

The perfection of patience is illustrated in the root text saying, "Whatever roots of virtue there are from my pure conduct." Purity is liberation or nirvana, literally the state of having gone beyond the sorrow, or suffering, of cyclic existence. To achieve this we need to create its cause, meditation on the four immeasurables: immeasurable love, compassion, joy, and equanimity. The four immeasurables are the antidotes to anger and hatred—the

wish to harm sentient beings—since they are based on the wish to benefit sentient beings. For this reason, meditation on the four immeasurables is included in the perfection of patience. Whatever roots of virtue we have created by our practice of the four immeasurables in this and previous lives are therefore objects to be dedicated. When we recite the verses of the four immeasurables during our daily practices we should try to mentally generate thoughts of immeasurable love, compassion, joy, and equanimity, since by doing so we will accumulate many roots of virtue. These should be immediately dedicated for the purpose of achieving enlightenment so as to prevent anger from destroying them. Dedicating, like putting money in the bank to prevent thieves from stealing it, prevents anger from stealing away our virtues.

The roots of virtue accumulated through performing particular actions to ripen sentient beings who are not ripe and to liberate those who are ripe, are included in the perfection of joyous effort. In addition to those actions, any effort whatsoever that we put into creating virtue is included in the practice of the perfection of joyous effort. As such it is also an object to be dedicated.

The roots of virtue of generating the mind of enlightenment and then focusing on it single-pointedly are included in the perfection of concentration and are objects to be dedicated. The mind of enlightenment is composed of two aspirations, a causal aspiration and an accompanying aspiration. The causal aspiration is the great compassion that taking all sentient beings as its referent object wishes them to be free from suffering. This aspiration is the main cause for generating the mind of enlightenment. The second aspiration, the wish to attain enlightenment, accompanies the primary mind, the mind of enlightenment.

Through the practice of these five perfections—generosity, morality, patience, joyous effort, and concentration—we complete the collection of merit needed to attain the form body (*rūpakāya, gzugs sku*) of a buddha.

"Whatever roots of virtue there are from my unsurpassed exalted wisdom" refers to analytical meditation on emptiness, or selflessness, which is included in the perfection of wisdom. To attain the truth body of a buddha, we need to complete the collection of wisdom; for this purpose we meditate on emptiness. The roots of virtue thereby created are also objects to be dedicated.

In summary, all the roots of virtue accumulated through our practice of the six perfections are objects to be dedicated.

Dedicating Our Own and Others' Virtues

Then, if it is asked, "What is the difference between the three, 'assembled,' 'gathered,' and 'combined together'?" The difference between the three is like this. Saying "assembled" indicates, "All the virtues I have created in the three times are assembled into a group." "Gathered" is an old term, which in new terminology means assembled. It indicates that the virtues accumulated in the three times by other beings are also assembled into a group. "Combined together" indicates that both the virtues created by ourselves and the virtues created by others, combined together, are the virtues to be dedicated to complete enlightenment.

"Assembled" indicates that the virtues that we ourselves have created in the three times—past, present, and future—are collected into a group. "Gathered" indicates that the virtues created in the three times by all other beings are also collected into a group. "Combined together" indicates that our own collection of virtues as well as the collections of virtues of all other sentient beings are brought together and then dedicated to enlightenment. Consequently, the objects to be dedicated include both our own collection of virtues as well as that of every other sentient being. By dedicating in this way the practice of dedication becomes very effective.

I offer this king of wish-fulfilling jewels, a highly cherished system of explanation from the treasury of excellent explanations, to my guru in order to repay his kindness.

How to Dedicate

I totally dedicate to the unsurpassed, the unexcelled, that higher than the high, that superior to the superior; thereby, do I totally dedicate to unsurpassed, perfectly complete enlightenment.

Just as the buddha-bhagavans of the past totally dedicated, just as the buddha-bhagavans of the future will totally dedicate, and just as the buddha-bhagavans presently abiding totally dedicate, I too similarly totally dedicate.

A fervent aspiration will arise at the beginning of making a dedication when we excellently connect [the objects to be dedicated with the aim of the dedication]. Although in general there are many ways of dedicating, the supreme and perfect ways of connecting them are (1) dedication as a cause of the flourishing of the doctrine, the source of benefit and happiness; (2) dedication as a cause of being cared for by a guru, the source of attainments; and (3) dedication to unsurpassed complete enlightenment.

Furthermore, dedicating as a cause of the flourishing of the doctrine is considered an unsurpassed dedication, since in dependence on the survival of the doctrine we become manifestly completely enlightened and then solely enact the welfare of others, such as accomplishing the benefit and happiness of all sentient beings. Also, dedicating as a cause of being cared for by holy gurus is considered an unsurpassed dedication since all temporal and ultimate qualities depend on the holy guru and by dedicating virtues in this way we will be gladly cared for by holy gurus in all our lives, in dependence upon which all qualities will arise. Also, as taught in *The Stages of the Path*, dedicating to unsurpassed complete enlightenment is considered an unsurpassed dedication because, just as, for example, when for the purpose of growing barley or rice, we plant their seeds and, even though unwanted, the stalks arise, likewise, when we dedicate virtues for the purpose of attaining unsurpassed complete enlightenment, incidentally, all other qualities will arise. Therefore, my holy guru, the lord of wisdom, glorious Tsongkhapa, having seen this powerful fact, also dedicated every virtue to all these dedications, any of the three. Among the ways of dedicating, in this context the dedication is to complete enlightenment.

Furthermore, [the root text] states "the unsurpassed" and "the unexcelled." Although unsurpassed and unexcelled are, in general, synonymous, here it is not considered to be an error to state both because "the unsurpassed" indicates the form body while "the unexcelled" indicates the truth body. The difference between saying "that higher than the high" and "that superior to the superior" is also similar because "that higher than the high" indicates the enjoyment body and "that superior to the superior" indicates the emanation body. There is a reason for calling the enjoyment body "that higher than the high," because "the high" is said in regard to the bodhisattvas on the tenth

ground, while the enjoyment body is higher than the bodhisattvas on the tenth ground. There is a reason for calling the emanation body "that superior to the superior," because "the superior" is said in regard to the hearer and solitary realizer foe-destroyers and the bodhisattvas abiding on the pure grounds, while the emanation body is superior even to them.

Who has formerly seen or heard an explanation like this? It has excellently come forth thus from the compassion of the deity and the guru.

Therefore, since the virtues explained previously are dedicated for the purpose of attaining the form body and the truth body, this is the meaning of saying, "I totally dedicate to unsurpassed, perfectly complete enlightenment." Moreover, just as, for example, the previous buddha-bhagavans of the past dedicated virtues to complete enlightenment, just as the buddha-bhagavans of the future will also dedicate, and just as the buddha-bhagavans presently abiding are totally dedicating virtues to complete enlightenment, we too similarly totally dedicate virtues to complete enlightenment.

The best type of dedication is the dedication to complete enlightenment, praying that our virtuous actions become the cause for ourselves and all sentient beings to achieve enlightenment—the truth and form bodies, or the holy mind and holy body, of a buddha. However, we can also dedicate to the flourishing and abiding of the doctrine, to always being cared for in all our lives by holy gurus, or in fact to any virtuous purpose whatsoever. In short, we should dedicate our virtues in the same way as the buddhas of the past dedicated, as the future buddhas will dedicate, and as the present buddhas are dedicating.

Take Care to Dedicate

We should take great care to dedicate our virtues to complete enlightenment because the lord of yogis, Milarepa, taught, "The two, a great meditator meditating in a cave and the benefactor who supplies him with the necessities of life, have the auspiciousness of equally serving to awaken," and, "How is there auspiciousness? The heart of auspiciousness is dedication. Afterwards, take care to dedicate." By dedicat-

ing virtues—illustrated by the virtues of supplying the necessities of life—as the cause of attaining buddhahood, we will attain buddhahood through the auspiciousness of having dedicated to it. [Milarepa] also said to disciples who came later, "After you have created virtue, take care in the dedication."

To emphasize the importance of making a dedication after every virtuous action, Milarepa gave the example of a meditator in a cave and the person providing his needs, both of whom dedicate their actions for the purpose of attaining enlightenment. Due to the power of the dedication—the cause—both the meditator and the benefactor create the auspiciousness (*pratītyasamutpāda, rten 'brel*), or the dependent relation, to simultaneously attain buddhahood, the result.

In fact, the teachings on mind training (*blo sbyong*) state that two things are important in regard to creating virtuous actions. At the beginning of the action it is important to generate a good motivation and at its conclusion it is important to dedicate the virtue created. If we do both of these we can collect many virtues, since even our daily actions of eating, drinking, sleeping, walking, dressing, and washing can be transformed into virtuous actions when done with a good motivation. If we practice like this, whatever we do will be done with the good intention of benefiting others. Just as, for example, the bodhisattvas who follow the sutra teachings eat and drink with the intention of nourishing the many thousands of tiny organisms that live within their bodies, we too should likewise try to practice generosity. Alternatively, if we are mainly practicing tantra we can practice generosity through offering our food and drink to our guru visualized at our heart as inseparable from the deity.

എ ⚡ എ

In brief, at the moment we have a human body with eighteen special qualities that is better than a wish-fulfilling jewel; however, it is extremely difficult to obtain again. Therefore, rejoicing in how fortunate we are, we should use this body to the best of our ability to benefit other sentient beings as well as ourselves. Rather than using it as if it were a vessel containing negativities, we should use it to become a pure vessel of the perfections of generosity, morality, patience, joyous effort, concentration, and wisdom.

7. The Seven Limbs

The Manner in Which There Are the Seven Limbs

I confess all negativities individually.
I rejoice in all merit.
I urge and request all buddhas.
May I attain the supreme excellence of unsurpassed exalted wisdom.

The meaning of "I confess all negativities individually," is [the follow-ing]: since negativities accumulated by way of the body need to be con-fessed by prostrations and so forth; since negativities accumulated by way of the speech need to be confessed by saying the names of the tath-āgatas, reciting profound mantra-dharanis (*dhāraṇī, gzungs sngags*),[22] and since negativities accumulated by way of the mind [need to be] confessed by way of meditating on the path; this is eluci-[dated by] "I confess them individually."

["I confess] all negativities individually" shows the limb of confessing [negativi]ties, that were indicated above, and the limb of offering [by] combining them together. In addition to these two, [the root verse shows]: the limb of rejoicing in all merit, the virtues created by our-[selves and] others; the limb of urging all the buddhas of the ten directions to turn the wheel of Dharma; the limb of requesting them to not show the aspect of passing beyond sorrow but to remain as long as the eons are not emptied; and, having summarized the ways of dedicating explained above by saying, "May I attain the supreme excellence of unsurpassed exalted wisdom," it shows the limb of dedication. We should thereby understand that the seven limbs are shown in their entirety.

The Sutra of the Bodhisattva's Confession of Downfalls includes the entire seven-limb prayer, an essential method for purifying negativities and accumulating merit. The first limb, the limb of prostration was explained earlier in regard to the lines of the root text, "I prostrate to Tathāgata...." Since physical prostrations purify the negativities created by the body; recitation of the names of the thirty-five tathāgatas purifies the negativities created by the speech; and meditation on, or related to, the path—love, compassion, emptiness, the four immeasurables, and so forth—purifies the negativities created by the mind; it is important to do all three together.

The second limb, the limb of offering, was explained as being implicitly included in the root text in both the lines of prostration, "I prostrate to Tathāgata...," as well as in the dedication of the roots of virtue of generosity. We can make various types of offerings, such as the four types of offerings taught in tantra, the outer, inner, secret, and suchness offerings. As explained previously the outer offerings are both actual material substances and mentally imagined ones. The inner offering, according to highest yoga tantra, is composed of ten impure substances transformed into nectar. The secret offering is the offering of bliss to our guru who is visualized as inseparable from the deity. The suchness offering is the offering of our realization of emptiness.

The third limb, confession, involves the application of the four opponent forces to purify our negativities. The fourth limb, rejoicing, specifically refers to the practice of rejoicing in our own and others' virtuous actions. The fifth limb is the limb of urging that urges, or exhorts, the buddhas to turn the wheel of Dharma—in other words to teach the Dharma. The sixth, the limb of requesting, requests all the buddhas to not pass away. These six limbs serve to accumulate virtues that are then dedicated, together with other virtuous actions created by ourselves and others, in order that we and all other sentient beings may attain enlightenment. This is the seventh limb, that of dedication.

Each of the seven limbs also functions to reduce a particular mental affliction. The limb of prostration is the antidote to pride; presenting offerings is the antidote to miserliness; confession is the antidote to the three mental poisons, attachment, hatred, and ignorance; rejoicing is the antidote to jealousy; urging the buddhas to turn the wheel of Dharma is the antidote to having abandoned the Dharma in the past; and requesting them to not pass away is the antidote to negative actions committed in relation to our

guru. Therefore, with this one simple practice we can purify eons of negativities and accumulate a huge amount of merit.

> The light rays of the compassion of the deity and guru have caused the lotus of intelligence to excellently blossom, producing this new system of explanation, the essence of honey, that I have now revealed. How wonderful!

This sutra is also called *The Sutra of the Three Heaps* because it was explained as such since it expresses the three: the heap of confessing negativities, the heap of dedicating virtues, and the heap of rejoicing.

GOING FOR REFUGE TO THE THREE JEWELS AGAIN

> *To the best of humans, the conquerors who are presently abiding, those of the past, and likewise those of the future, to all those whose exalted qualities are like an infinite ocean, folding my hands, I approach for refuge.*

Having explicitly shown, "Folding my hands (i.e., venerating them), I approach (i.e., go) for refuge to the conquerors who are the best of humans—the buddhas who are presently abiding; the buddhas of the past (i.e., those who already came before); and, likewise, the buddhas of the future—with their infinite qualities of body, speech, and mind, the infinitely praised, all the buddhas of the three times who are like a great ocean," it implicitly shows going for refuge to the Dharma Jewel and the Sangha Jewel.

At the end of the prayer we go for refuge once again to the Three Jewels saying, "Folding my hands, I approach for refuge." This implies placing our complete trust in the Buddha, Dharma, and Sangha.

SIGNS OF PURIFICATION

When confessing negativities and downfalls by means of the seven limbs, there is a manner in which signs [of purification] occur in dreams. It is taught in *The Dharani That Exhorts* (*Chundādhāranī*) that

signs in dreams of purifying negativities are vomiting bad food; drinking yogurt, milk, and so on; seeing the sun or the moon; traveling in the sky; [seeing] a blazing fire; defeating a buffalo or a person [wearing] black; seeing a sangha of fully ordained monks or nuns; climbing a tree spouting milk; mounting an elephant or a bull; climbing a mountain, a lion throne, or a mansion; listening to the Dharma; and so forth.

If we recite the names of the thirty-five buddhas while doing prostrations and at the same time generate the four opponent forces in our mind, we will experience great benefit. Signs in dreams of, for example, vomiting bad food, drinking white liquids such as milk or yogurt, wearing white clothes, and so on, confirm that we are successfully purifying our negativities.

Part Three

Conclusion

8. Overcoming the Afflictions

In addition to confessing negativities it is also extremely important to analyze how the various afflictions arise in your mind. This analysis enables us to apply their respective antidotes before they lead us to engage in negative actions. For example, examine how attachment, one of the strongest mental afflictions, arises in your mind. You will find that whenever you come into contact with an attractive object, immediately and automatically attachment arises. For example, when you smell the pleasant odor of food cooking, the attachment of wishing to eat it arises. When you hear good music, immediately something in your mind awakens and attachment arises. When you see attractively designed clothes, immediately attachment follows and you think "I like that. I want it."

Anger, or hatred, is another of our strongest afflictions. It arises when we come into contact with people or objects that we consider unpleasant. Although anger is not always present, when certain conditions come together it easily arises. If we examine our mind well, we will probably find that, like most ordinary people, we get angry as often as once a day, if not more often.

Another of our root, or principal, afflictions is ignorance. Ignorance is the main cause of all our problems because a lack of knowledge and understanding leads us to easily make many mistakes. The result of these mistakes is problems, difficulties, and a lot of suffering.

Another affliction is pride; for example, the pride that thinks, "I am beautiful," "I am very good," or "I am very skillful." Pride causes us to become swollen up with ourselves.

Doubt, the inability to make a decision, is also present in our mental continuum. Doubt causes us to think, "Maybe yes. Maybe no. Maybe this. Maybe that." It becomes a cause of problems when it continually interferes

with our ability to come to a decision and thereby prevents us from achieving success in any of our undertakings.

Jealousy is another very harmful affliction. If we examine how it arises we will find that when something nice happens to another person, jealousy automatically arises in our mind. For example, if we see our boyfriend or girlfriend talking with someone else, immediately we want to know why he or she is talking to that person. We begin to suspect that he or she is planning to leave us and start a relationship with that other person. Consequently, jealousy is the cause of disharmony in our relationships and brings us many problems in our day-to-day life.

You should check to see whether or not you have these afflictions in your mental continuum. You will probably find that almost all of the root and secondary afflictions are present, except perhaps, some of the wrong views such as holding an inferior view as supreme or holding bad conduct and bad morality as supreme. However, even though we may not have those particular afflictions, we have many other afflictions in our mind and consequently we need to purify them.

Apply the Specific Antidotes to the Afflictions

The afflictions are our enemies because they harm us, not only by disturbing our present peace of mind, but also by causing us to engage in negative actions that eventually result in suffering. However, although our main enemies are within our own mind, generally we do not recognize this fact and, instead, point to our enemy as being someone external to ourselves. We consider someone to be our enemy if he or she has harmed us, our friends, or our relatives. Considering our afflictions using the same line of reasoning, we will see that our negative emotions are our real enemies, since they can bring us much more harm than any external enemy. To destroy the inner enemies of the afflictions, we have no need of physical weapons, only the development of our own inner qualities serves to accomplish their destruction.

We need to apply specific antidotes to each of the various afflictions. By doing so, the strength of our afflictions gradually diminishes and we will become much more relaxed and happy. This is the tangible result of our Dharma practice, the employing of methods to improve and develop our mind. We have two types of mind—quality mind and faulty mind. We

need to purify the faulty mind and develop the quality mind. In this way, we will gain the realizations of a bodhisattva. *Sattva* means "person" or "being," while *bodhi* means "big mind" or "big heart"; therefore, a bodhisattva is a being with a big heart who wishes to attain complete enlightenment for the benefit of all sentient beings.

Anger. The method to diminish our afflictions is meditation. For example, if anger is our main problem, we need to engage in doing specific meditations that develop compassion and love. When we are angry we have the wish to harm, to beat, to hit, to insult. As a remedy we need to develop compassion and love, the main causes of our mental peace and relaxation.

Compassion is the attitude wishing that all sentient beings could be free from suffering. We meditate in order to make this attitude manifest, to transform our mind into the nature of compassion. Having accomplished this, we try to hold this attitude in our mind and focus upon it. However, it will probably quickly disappear and we will find that we need to make an effort to develop it once again. At first the compassion we generate will last only a minute, or maybe just a second, but by developing it again and again it will come to last for five minutes, ten minutes, fifteen minutes, and so on, gradually becoming more and more stable. By making a constant effort day after day, some result will definitely come—the hatred and anger will lessen and we will gradually find ourselves becoming more patient and relaxed.

We can also meditate on love to overcome anger. In this context, love does not refer to the kind of love we mean when we say, "I love you." Generally, when we say "I love you," we mean "I am attached to you." Real love is the mental attitude wishing that all sentient beings have happiness. Through meditation we make this kind of mind manifest, we transform our mind into the nature of love and then hold and focus on this attitude. This is what is known as meditation on love.

Attachment. Attachment arises through exaggerating the good qualities of a particular object. At first we may think that the object is beautiful, then that it is the most beautiful. Thinking this way, our attachment for the object grows. If we examine how we react to attractive objects we will see that we have had this experience many times. Then, when we are unable to acquire the desired object, we become unhappy and suffer. To diminish our

attachment to an object, we can meditate to diminish its beautiful appearance and to see it in its reality. If we are unable to do this, as Vasubandhu says in the *Abhidharmakosha*, the best way for ordinary people to reduce attachment is to put a distance between themselves and the object. This distance can be physical, mental, or both. Physical distance implies staying away from the object. Mental distance means to stop thinking about the object of attachment. If we are able do this the manifest attachment for that object will gradually diminish.

Ignorance. There are various antidotes to ignorance, one of which is the meditation analyzing how phenomena exist as dependent relations. An example of a dependent relation is the appearance of a particular person as our enemy that arises in dependence upon our considering him or her an enemy. Since this appearance arose in dependence upon our own point of view, we can work to change our way of thinking. From our own side we can make an effort to become friends with that person and thereby bring about a transformation in the relationship. In fact, whether we have a good or bad relationship with a specific person depends entirely upon ourselves.

It is essential to understand how everything exists as a dependent relation, or dependent arising. By way of this realization, we come to understand the final, or ultimate, nature of all phenomena—emptiness (*shūnyatā, stong pa nyid*). The realization of emptiness is called wisdom (*prajñā, shes rab*) or mother. The mind of enlightenment, great compassion, is called method (*upaya, thabs*) or father. The union of mother and father, wisdom and method, the realization of emptiness and bodhichitta, gives birth to the child of a buddha, a bodhisattva.

There are many different types of ignorance. The ignorance that is the root of cyclic existence is the ignorance that grasps at a truly, or inherently, existing self. The main antidote to this ignorance is the wisdom realizing emptiness. Emptiness means that a self of persons and a self of phenomena lack inherent existence, they are empty of true existence. This realization destroys self-grasping, the grasping at an inherently existing self, the source of all our other afflictions. Therefore, it is extremely important to meditate on emptiness.

During meditation on emptiness we first develop an image of emptiness in our mind and then focus on it. Consequently, at first it is only a mental

image, a mere reflection of actual emptiness. By continuing to meditate on emptiness using a specific process of analysis, the image gradually becomes more and more clear until eventually we realize emptiness by way of a direct perceiver (*pratyakṣha, mngon sum*). At this point emptiness is understood directly without any further need to use reasoning, just as we directly see an object held in our hand.

Pride. Through understanding dependent relation we are able to understand that all phenomena do not inherently exist. Why do they not inherently exist? Only because they exist as dependent relations. We should use this reasoning to analyze the mode of existence of the self or I. For example, when we think, "I know everything," pride arises. To reduce this pride we should examine where, and what, is this I. We begin by checking whether the form aggregate, our body, is I. If the body is I then which part of it is I? The head, the arms, the legs…? Nowhere in the body do we find an I. Our body is a collection of eight types of atoms: those of the four root elements (earth, water, fire, and wind) and those of the four secondary elements (visible form, odor, taste, and tangible object). Which of these is I? Again we find that none of them is I. Why? If this body were I, then the I would continue to exist in our corpse when we die. However, it is not so.

Next check whether or not the feeling aggregate is I. If it seems to be I, is the I pleasant, unpleasant, or neutral feeling? Then check whether the discrimination aggregate is the I. Examine whether it is the wrong discrimination that discriminates the impermanent as permanent, the suffering as happiness, the impure as pure, and the selfless as having a self. Or is it the right discrimination that discriminates these four correctly? Check the compositional factors aggregate for the I. Forty-nine mental factors and fourteen non-associated compositional factors are included in this aggregate. Is it one of them? We will find that none of the feelings, discriminations, or compositional factors are I.

Finally, check the consciousness aggregate to determine whether or not it is I. Is the eye, ear, nose, tongue, body, or mental consciousness I? Is virtuous mind, non-virtuous mind, or neutral mind I? In this way, we should examine the five aggregates and the eighteen constituents for the I, the self. However, even though we may check, we will not find an I. There is no concrete "beautiful I" or "knowledgeable I." We can look for

it but it cannot be found. Reflect on this. Doing this type of analytical meditation reduces pride.

Doubt. Doubt often arises in our minds. In order to counteract it we can do one of many different kinds of breathing meditations. For example, focus your mind on the breath as you inhale and exhale and, with a part of the mind, count each cycle from one up to twenty-one. This meditation functions to diminish the thoughts, or conceptions, arising in our minds. Another type of breathing meditation is to imagine that as you exhale you breathe out black smoke which is in the nature of all your doubts, worries, afflictions, sicknesses, and unhappiness. When you inhale imagine that your breath has the aspect of white light which is in the nature of all the qualities of the holy beings, their love, compassion, energy, and wisdom, as well as all the good energy in the universe from the mountains, lakes, oceans, and trees. Imagine that you receive the blessings of all the holy beings and let your mind become completely relaxed. If you find that your mind is very disturbed by many thoughts, put the emphasis on the visualization of exhaling black smoke, your negative energy. When your mind is more relaxed put the emphasis on receiving the positive energy of all the holy beings.

Although there are many different breathing meditations, all of them involve applying a particular antidote to our negative emotions. There is real benefit from doing this type of meditation. Just as your stomach discomfort is finished when you succeed in vomiting up the food that caused the problem, imagine that by expelling all your negative energy your mental disturbance finishes and your mind becomes quiet and relaxed. This type of meditation provides one of the conditions for our positive energy to develop and increase.

However, although meditation on the breath is one way to reduce doubt, the main antidote to doubt is the development of wisdom. The more wisdom we develop, the less doubt will arise.

Jealousy. As mentioned previously, rejoicing in the good qualities, actions, and fortune of others is the main antidote to jealousy. Rejoicing is a mind that delights in others' happiness and as such is completely opposite to the mind of jealousy. Through rejoicing we create the cause to experience that happiness ourselves in the future.

In conclusion, put effort into purifying your negative actions using a method such as *The Bodhisattva's Confession of Downfalls* and strive to overcome your mental afflictions by meditating on their specific antidotes. By doing so, gradually all your faults will diminish and all your qualities will increase.

9. Final Dedications

Sanggye Yeshe's Dedication

This is mentioned here from the compassion of all the gurus along with the deities. I, Buddhajñāna (*Sangs rgyas ye shes*), a saffron-robed individual liberation being, wrote down in script this excellent account explaining a mere portion of the meaning of the profound *Sutra of the Three Heaps* for the purpose of delighting the fortunate ones of new awareness. Due to whatever collection of pristine virtues has arisen from it, may the negativities and downfalls, together with their imprints, accumulated continuously in life after life from beginningless time by myself and the kind ones, be cleansed and purified and then, may we quickly attain the ultimate—buddhahood that is free from obscurations and complete in all qualities. Also, temporally, may the day and night be filled with the light of benefit and happiness from the rising of a pair, the sun and the moon of study and practice, the means of spreading and developing the precious doctrine of the Subduer in all directions and times.

I, faithfully and devoutly, request the gurus together with the deities, as well as the hosts of scholars, to forgive whatever faults I have made in composing this method. Please mercifully let me be without obscurations.

The Sutra of the Three Heaps is like a door blocking negative ones like myself from falling into an abyss. Having abandoned stains of errors in the words and meaning, close the door to the lower realms. Fortunate ones, abide joyfully. Be faithful by having seen the heroes that destroy doubt. Prostrate to the treasures of compassion, the

assembly of thirty-five tathāgatas. Upon hearing their names the unbearable sufferings of cyclic existence, without an exception, are destroyed in a single instant.

The Sutra of The Confession of Downfalls with the four forces in their entirety is the best of antidotes to the eighty-four thousand afflictions.

THE SPONSOR'S DEDICATION

This source of attainments clarifying the words and meanings was printed due to me, Samdrub Tsering (*bsam grub tshe ring*). Due to these virtues may the precious doctrine spread and flourish. May the lotus feet of the holy doctrine holders without exception be firm. May my parents and relatives be victorious in the battle with the two obscurations and may they each accomplish every aim of this and future [lives]. For the sake of eliminating the torment of migrators, I devoutly offer this excellent explanation, medicine for migrators, to Tse [Chog] Ling with a mind of benefiting migrators, for the purpose of augmenting the welfare of migrators.

Appendices

The above diagram corresponds to the placement of the figures in the cover thangka of the thirty-five confession buddhas. The numbers correspond to the order in which the buddhas are enumerated in the prayer, *The Bodhisattva's Confession of Downfalls.*

1. *The Bodhisattva's Confession of Downfalls*

I, (*say your name*), for all time, go for refuge to the guru;
I go for refuge to the Buddha;
I go for refuge to the Dharma;
I go for refuge to the Sangha.

I prostrate to [Teacher] Bhagavan Tathāgata Foe-Destroyer Perfectly
   Complete Buddha Glorious Conqueror Shākyamuni.
I prostrate to Tathāgata Thoroughly Destroying With Vajra Essence.
I prostrate to Tathāgata Radiant Jewel.
I prostrate to Tathāgata Nāga-Lord King.
I prostrate to Tathāgata Army of Heroes.
I prostrate to Tathāgata Delighted Hero.
I prostrate to Tathāgata Jewel Fire.
I prostrate to Tathāgata Jewel Moonlight.
I prostrate to Tathāgata Meaningful to Behold.
I prostrate to Tathāgata Jewel Moon.
I prostrate to Tathāgata Immaculate.
I prostrate to Tathāgata Bestowed With Courage.
I prostrate to Tathāgata Purity.
I prostrate to Tathāgata Bestowed With Purity.
I prostrate to Tathāgata Water-God.
I prostrate to Tathāgata Water-God Deity.
I prostrate to Tathāgata Glorious Excellence.
I prostrate to Tathāgata Glorious Sandalwood.
I prostrate to Tathāgata Infinite Splendor.
I prostrate to Tathāgata Glorious Light.
I prostrate to Tathāgata Glorious Sorrowless.
I prostrate to Tathāgata Son of Cravingless.

I prostrate to Tathāgata Glorious Flower.
I prostrate to Tathāgata Pure Light Rays Clearly Knowing by Sporting.
I prostrate to Tathāgata Lotus Light Rays Clearly Knowing by Sporting.
I prostrate to Tathāgata Glorious Wealth.
I prostrate to Tathāgata Glorious Mindfulness.
I prostrate to Tathāgata Glorious Name Widely Renowned.
I prostrate to Tathāgata Most Powerful Victory Banner King.
I prostrate to Tathāgata Glorious Utterly Suppressing.
I prostrate to Tathāgata Totally Victorious in Battle.
I prostrate to Tathāgata Glorious Suppressing Advancement.
I prostrate to Tathāgata Glorious All-Illuminating Manifestations.
I prostrate to Tathāgata Jewel Lotus Suppresser.
I prostrate to Tathāgata Foe-Destroyer Perfectly Complete Buddha
  Mountain Lord King Firmly Seated on Jewels and a Lotus.

These and others, as many tathāgata foe-destroyer perfectly complete buddha-bhagavans as are abiding, living, and residing in all the world systems of the ten directions, all buddha-bhagavans, please pay attention to me.

In this life and in all the states of rebirth in which I have circled in cyclic existence throughout beginningless lives, whatever negative actions I have done, caused to be done, or rejoiced in the doing of; whatever possessions of stupas, possessions of the sangha, or possessions of the sangha of the ten directions I have appropriated, made to be appropriated, or rejoiced in the appropriation of; whatever of the five actions of immediate [retribution] I have done, caused to be done, or rejoiced in the doing of; whatever of the ten non-virtuous paths of action I have engaged in the adoption of, caused to be engaged in, or rejoiced in the engagement in; whatever karmic obscurations due to which I and sentient beings, having become obscured, will go to hell, an animal mode of rebirth, or the land of the hungry ghosts, will be reborn in border areas, reborn as barbarians or as long-life gods, will have imperfect faculties, hold wrong views, or will not be delighted with the arising of a buddha—in the presence of the buddha-bhagavans who are exalted wisdom, who are eyes, who are witnesses, who are valid, and who see with knowledge, I admit and confess all these karmic obscurations. I do not conceal or hide them. From now on, I will stop and refrain from them.

All buddha-bhagavans please pay attention to me. In this life and in the other states of rebirth in which I have circled in cyclic existence throughout beginningless lives, whatever roots of virtue there are from my generosity, be it as little as having given one morsel of food to a being born in the animal realm; whatever roots of virtue there are from my having guarded morality; whatever roots of virtue there are from my pure conduct; whatever roots of virtue there are from my having fully ripened sentient beings; whatever roots of virtue there are from my having generated bodhichitta; and whatever roots of virtue there are from my unsurpassed exalted wisdom: all these, assembled and gathered, then combined together, I totally dedicate to the unsurpassed, the unexcelled, that higher than the high, that superior to the superior; thereby, do I totally dedicate to unsurpassed, perfectly complete enlightenment.

Just as the buddha-bhagavans of the past totally dedicated, just as the buddha-bhagavans of the future will totally dedicate, and just as the buddha-bhagavans presently abiding totally dedicate, I too similarly totally dedicate.

I confess all negativities individually.
I rejoice in all merit.
I urge and request all buddhas.
May I attain the supreme excellence of unsurpassed exalted wisdom.

To the best of humans, the conquerors who are presently abiding, those of the past, and likewise those of the future, to all those whose exalted qualities are like an infinite ocean, folding my hands, I approach for refuge.

2. Woodblock Prints of the Thirty-Five Tathāgatas

The following woodblock prints are believed to have originally come from a Nyingma text titled *Dharma Treasure of the Confession of All Negativities: A Golden Razor for Confessing Negativities* (*sDigs bShags gSer gyi sPu gri*), and accord quite closely with the cover thangka of the thirty-five tathāgatas.

The images of the woodblock prints do not correspond directly with the descriptions of the thirty-five buddhas from Lama Tsongkhapa's vision, as explained in his text *Practice of the Thirty-Five Buddhas and a Description of the Deities' Bodies* (see chart on pp. 38–39). Although the mudras depicted in these prints may differ, according to advice from Geshe Jampa Gyatso one can still visualize the individual buddhas according to their colors as described in Lama Tsongkhapa's text.

These woodblock prints have been included in the hope that readers will derive benefit from them in their personal visualization practice.

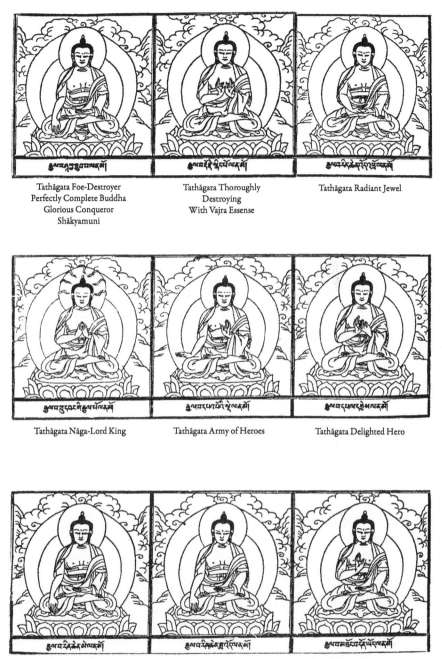

Tathāgata Foe-Destroyer Perfectly Complete Buddha Glorious Conqueror Shākyamuni

Tathāgata Thoroughly Destroying With Vajra Essense

Tathāgata Radiant Jewel

Tathāgata Nāga-Lord King

Tathāgata Army of Heroes

Tathāgata Delighted Hero

Tathāgata Jewel Fire

Tathāgata Jewel Moonlight

Tathāgata Meaningful to Behold

Tathāgata Jewel Moon   Tathāgata Immaculate   Tathāgata Bestowed
                                                            With Courage

Tathāgata Purity   Tathāgata Bestowed   Tathāgata Water-God
                          With Purity

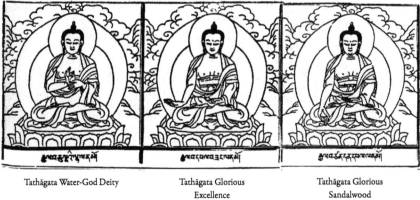

Tathāgata Water-God Deity   Tathāgata Glorious   Tathāgata Glorious
                                   Excellence   Sandalwood

Tathāgata Infinite Splendor

Tathāgata Glorious Light
Victorious in Battle

Tathāgata Glorious
Sorrowless

Tathāgata Son
of Cravingless

Tathāgata Glorious Flower

Tathāgata Pure Light
Rays Clearly Knowing
by Sporting

Tathāgata Lotus Light Rays
Clearing Knowing
by Sporting

Tathāgata Glorious Wealth

Tathāgata Glorious
Mindfulness

Tathāgata Glorious Name
Widely Renowned

Tathāgata Most Powerful
Victory Banner King

Tathāgata Glorious
Utterly Suppressing

Tathāgata Totally
Victorious in Battle

Tathāgata Glorious
Suppressing Advancement

Tathāgata Glorious
All-Illuminating
Manifestations

Tathāgata Jewel
Lotus Suppresser

Tathāgata Foe-Destroyer
Perfectly Complete Buddha
Mountain Lord King
Firmly Seated on
Jewels and a Lotus

3. Phonetics of *The Bodhisattva's Confession of Downfalls*

Dag (*say your name*) zhe gyi wa
Dü tag tu la ma la kyab su chi o
Sang gye la kyab su chi o
Chö la kyab su chi o
Gen dun la kyab su chi o

Tön pa chom den de de zhin sheg pa dra chom pa yang dag par dzog pe sang gye pel gyel wa sha kya tub pa la chag tsel lo
De zhin sheg pa *dor je nying pö rab tu jom pa* la chag tsel lo
De zhin sheg pa *rin chen ö tro* la chag tsel lo
De zhin sheg pa *lu wang gi gyel po* la chag tsel lo
De zhin sheg pa *pa wö de* la chag tsel lo
De zhin sheg pa *pel gye* la chag tsel lo
De zhin sheg pa *rin chen me* la chag tsel lo
De zhin sheg pa *rin chen da ö* la chag tsel lo
De zhin sheg pa *tong wa dön yö* la chag tsel lo
De zhin sheg pa *rin chen da wa* la chag tsel lo
De zhin sheg pa *dri ma me pa* la chag tsel lo
De zhin sheg pa *pel jin* la chag tsel lo
De zhin sheg pa *tsang pa* la chag tsel lo
De zhin sheg pa *tsang pe jin* la chag tsel lo
De zhin sheg pa *chu hla* la chag tsel lo
De zhin sheg pa *chu hle hla* la chag tsel lo
De zhin sheg pa *pel zang* la chag tsel lo
De zhin sheg pa *tzen den pel* la chag tsel lo
De zhin sheg pa *zi ji ta ye* la chag tsel lo
De zhin sheg pa *ö pel* la chag tsel lo

De zhin sheg pa *nya ngen me pe pel* la chag tsel lo
De zhin sheg pa *se me kyi bu* la chag tsel lo
De zhin sheg pa *me tog pel* la chag tsel lo
De zhin sheg pa *tsang pe ö zer nam par röl pe ngön par kyen pa* la chag tsel lo
De zhin sheg pa *pe me ö zer nam par röl pe ngön par kyen pa* la chag tsel lo
De zhin sheg pa *nor pel* la chag tsel lo
De zhin sheg pa *dren pe pel* la chag tsel lo
De zhin sheg pa *tsen pel shin tu yong drag* la chag tsel lo
De zhin sheg pa *wang pö tog gi gyel tsen gyi gyel po* la chag tsel lo
De zhin sheg pa *shin tu nam par nön pe pel* la chag tsel lo
De zhin sheg pa *yül le shin tu nam par gyel wa* la chag tsel lo
De zhin sheg pa *nam par nön pe sheg pe pel* la chag tsel lo
De zhin sheg pa *kün ne nang wa kö pe pel* la chag tsel lo
De zhin sheg pa *rin chen pe me nam par nön pa* la chag tsel lo
De zhin sheg pa *dra chom pa yang dag par dzog pe sang gye rin po che dang pe
ma la rab tu zhug pa ri wang gi gyel po* la chag tsel lo

De dag la sog pa – chog chü jig ten gyi kam tam che na – de zhin sheg pa
dra chom pa yang dag par dzog pe sang gye chom den de gang ji nye chig
zhug te – tso zhing zhe pe sang gye chom den de de dag tam che – dag la
gong su söl

Dag gi kye wa di dang – kye wa tog me ta ma ma chi pa ne – kor wa na kor
we kye ne tam che du – dig pe le gyi pa dang – gyi du tzel wa dang – gyi pa
la je su yi rang wam – chö ten gyi kor ram – gen dün gyi kor ram – chog
chü gen dün gyi kor trog pa dang – trog tu chug pa dang – trog pa la je su
yi rang wam – tsam ma chi pa nge le gyi pa dang – gyi du tzel wa dang –
gyi pa la je su yi rang wam – mi ge wa chü le kyi lam yang dag par lang wa
la zhug pa dang – jug tu tzel wa dang – jug pa la je su yi rang wam – le kyi
drib pa gang gi drib ne dag sem chen nyel war chi wam – dü drö kye ne su
chi wam – yi dag kyi yül du chi wam – yül ta kob tu kye wam – la lor kye
wam – hla tse ring po nam su kye wam – wang po ma tsang war gyur wam
– ta wa log par dzin par gyur wam – sang gye jung wa la nye par mi gyi par
gyur we le kyi drib pa gang lag pa de dag tam che – sang gye chom den de
ye she su gyur pa – chen du gyur pa – pang du gyur pa – tse mar gyur pa –
kyen pe zig pa – de dag gi chen ngar töl lo – chag so – mi chab bo – mi be
do – len che kyang chö ching dom par gyi lag so

Sang gye chom den de de dag tam che dag la gong su söl – dag gi kye wa di
dang – kye wa tog me ta ma ma chi pa ne – kor wa na kor we kye ne zhen
dag tu – jin pa ta na dü drö kye ne su kye pa la ze kam chig tzam tzel we ge
we tza wa gang lag pa dang – dag gi tsül trim sung pe ge we tza wa gang lag
pa dang – dag gi tsang par chö pe ge we tza wa gang lag pa dang – dag gi
sem chen yong su min par gyi pe ge we tza wa gang lag pa dang – dag gi jang
chub chog tu sem kye pe ge we tza wa gang lag pa dang – dag gi la na me pe
ye she kyi ge we tza wa gang lag pa – de dag tam che chig tu dü shing dum
te dom ne – la na ma chi pa dang – gong na ma chi pa dang – gong me yang
gong ma – la me yang la mar yong su ngo we – la na me pa yang dag par
dzog pe jang chub tu yong su ngo war gyi o

Ji tar de pe sang gye chom den de nam kyi yong su ngö pa dang – ji tar ma
jön pe sang gye chom den de nam kyi yong su ngo war gyur wa dang – ji
tar da tar zhug pe sang gye chom den de nam kyi yong su ngo war dze pa –
de zhin du dag gi kyang yong su ngo war gyi o

Dig pa tam che ni so sor shag so – sö nam tam che la ni je su yi rang ngo –
sang gye tam che la ni kül zhing söl wa deb so – dag gi la na me pe ye she
kyi chog dam pa tob par gyur chig

Mi chog gyel wa gang dag da tar zhug pa dang – gang dag de pa dag dang
de zhin gang ma jön – yön ten ngag pa ta ye gya tso dra kun la – tel mo jar
war gyi te – kyab su nye war chi o

4. Sanskrit Names of the Thirty-Five Tathāgatas

The English translation of the tathāgatas' names can be replaced with the names in their original Sanskrit.

1. Shākyamuni Tathāgata Arhat Samyaksaṁ-buddha
2. Vajra-garbha-pramardin
3. Ratnārcis
4. Nāgeshvara-rāja
5. Vīrasena
6. Vīra-nandin
7. Ratnāgni
8. Ratna-chandra-prabha
9. Amogha-darshin
10. Ratna-chandra
11. Nirmala (or Vimala)
12. Shūradatta
13. Brahmā
14. Brahma-datta
15. Varuṇa
16. Varuṇa-deva
17. Bhadra-shrī
18. Chandana-shrī
19. Anantaujas
20. Prabhāsa-shrī
21. Ashoka-shrī
22. Nārāyaṇa
23. Kusuma-shrī
24. Brahma-jyotir-vikrīḍitābhijña
25. Padma-jyotir-vikrīḍitābhijña

26. Dhana-shrī
27. Smṛti-shrī
28. Suparikīrtita-nāmadheya-shrī
29. Indra-ketu-dhvaja-rāja
30. Suvikrānta-shrī
31. Yuddhajaya (or Vijita-saṃgrāma)
32. Vikrānta-gāmin-shrī
33. Samantāvabhāsa-vyūha-shrī
34. Ratna-padma-vikrāmin
35. Ratna-padma-supratiṣṭhita-shailendra-rāja Tathāgata Arhat Samyaksaṃ-buddha.

5. The Tibetan Text:
The Bodhisattva's Confession of Downfalls

འཕགས་པ་ཕུང་པོ་གསུམ་པའི་མདོ། །

༄༅། །ན་མོ། བྱང་ཆུབ་སེམས་དཔའི་ལྟུང་བ་བཤགས་པ། བདག་མིང་འདི་
ཞེས་བགྱི་བ། དུས་རྟག་ཏུ་བླ་མ་ལ་སྐྱབས་སུ་མཆིའོ། སངས་རྒྱས་ལ་སྐྱབས་སུ་
མཆིའོ། ཆོས་ལ་སྐྱབས་སུ་མཆིའོ། དགེ་འདུན་ལ་སྐྱབས་སུ་མཆིའོ།།

སྟོན་པ་བཅོམ་ལྡན་འདས་དེ་བཞིན་གཤེགས་པ་དགྲ་བཅོམ་པ་ཡང་དག་པར་
རྫོགས་པའི་སངས་རྒྱས་དཔལ་རྒྱལ་བ་ཤཱཀྱ་ཐུབ་པ་ལ་ཕྱག་འཚལ་ལོ།
དེ་བཞིན་གཤེགས་པ་རྡོ་རྗེ་སྙིང་པོ་རབ་ཏུ་འཇོམས་པ་ལ་ཕྱག་འཚལ་ལོ། །
དེ་བཞིན་གཤེགས་པ་རིན་ཆེན་འོད་འཕྲོ་ལ་ཕྱག་འཚལ་ལོ། །
དེ་བཞིན་གཤེགས་པ་ཀླུ་དབང་གི་རྒྱལ་པོ་ལ་ཕྱག་འཚལ་ལོ། །
དེ་བཞིན་གཤེགས་པ་དཔའ་བོའི་སྡེ་ལ་ཕྱག་འཚལ་ལོ། །
དེ་བཞིན་གཤེགས་པ་དཔལ་དགྱེས་ལ་ཕྱག་འཚལ་ལོ། །
དེ་བཞིན་གཤེགས་པ་རིན་ཆེན་མེ་ལ་ཕྱག་འཚལ་ལོ། །
དེ་བཞིན་གཤེགས་པ་རིན་ཆེན་ཟླ་འོད་ལ་ཕྱག་འཚལ་ལོ། །
དེ་བཞིན་གཤེགས་པ་མཐོང་བ་དོན་ཡོད་ལ་ཕྱག་འཚལ་ལོ། །
དེ་བཞིན་གཤེགས་པ་རིན་ཆེན་ཟླ་བ་ལ་ཕྱག་འཚལ་ལོ། །
དེ་བཞིན་གཤེགས་པ་དྲི་མ་མེད་པ་ལ་ཕྱག་འཚལ་ལོ། །
དེ་བཞིན་གཤེགས་པ་དཔལ་བྱིན་ལ་ཕྱག་འཚལ་ལོ། །
དེ་བཞིན་གཤེགས་པ་ཚངས་པ་ལ་ཕྱག་འཚལ་ལོ། །
དེ་བཞིན་གཤེགས་པ་ཚངས་པས་བྱིན་ལ་ཕྱག་འཚལ་ལོ། །
དེ་བཞིན་གཤེགས་པ་ཆུ་ལྷ་ལ་ཕྱག་འཚལ་ལོ། །

དེ་བཞིན་གཤེགས་པ་ཆུ་ཀླུང་གི་ལྷ་ལ་ཕྱག་འཚལ་ལོ། །

དེ་བཞིན་གཤེགས་པ་དཔལ་བཟང་ལ་ཕྱག་འཚལ་ལོ། །

དེ་བཞིན་གཤེགས་པ་ཚན་དན་དཔལ་ལ་ཕྱག་འཚལ་ལོ། །

དེ་བཞིན་གཤེགས་པ་གཟི་བརྗིད་མཐའ་ཡས་ལ་ཕྱག་འཚལ་ལོ། །

དེ་བཞིན་གཤེགས་པ་འོད་དཔལ་ལ་ཕྱག་འཚལ་ལོ། །

དེ་བཞིན་གཤེགས་པ་མྱ་ངན་མེད་པའི་དཔལ་ལ་ཕྱག་འཚལ་ལོ། །

དེ་བཞིན་གཤེགས་པ་སྲེད་མེད་ཀྱི་བུ་ལ་ཕྱག་འཚལ་ལོ། །

དེ་བཞིན་གཤེགས་པ་མེ་ཏོག་དཔལ་ལ་ཕྱག་འཚལ་ལོ། །

དེ་བཞིན་གཤེགས་པ་ཚངས་པའི་འོད་ཟེར་རྣམ་པར་རོལ་པས་མངོན་པར་མཁྱེན་པ་ལ་ཕྱག་འཚལ་ལོ། །

དེ་བཞིན་གཤེགས་པ་པདྨའི་འོད་ཟེར་རྣམ་པར་རོལ་པས་མངོན་པར་མཁྱེན་པ་ལ་ཕྱག་འཚལ་ལོ། །

དེ་བཞིན་གཤེགས་པ་ནོར་དཔལ་ལ་ཕྱག་འཚལ་ལོ། །

དེ་བཞིན་གཤེགས་པ་དྲན་པའི་དཔལ་ལ་ཕྱག་འཚལ་ལོ། །

དེ་བཞིན་གཤེགས་པ་མཚན་དཔལ་ཤིན་ཏུ་ཡོངས་གྲགས་ལ་ཕྱག་འཚལ་ལོ། །

དེ་བཞིན་གཤེགས་པ་དབང་པོའི་ཏོག་གི་རྒྱལ་མཚན་གྱི་རྒྱལ་པོ་ལ་ཕྱག་འཚལ་ལོ། །

དེ་བཞིན་གཤེགས་པ་ཤིན་ཏུ་རྣམ་པར་གནོན་པའི་དཔལ་ལ་ཕྱག་འཚལ་ལོ། །

དེ་བཞིན་གཤེགས་པ་གཡུལ་ལས་ཤིན་ཏུ་རྣམ་པར་རྒྱལ་བ་ལ་ཕྱག་འཚལ་ལོ། །

དེ་བཞིན་གཤེགས་པ་རྣམ་པར་གནོན་པས་གཤེགས་པའི་དཔལ་ལ་ཕྱག་འཚལ་ལོ། །

དེ་བཞིན་གཤེགས་པ་ཀུན་ནས་སྣང་བ་བཀོད་པའི་དཔལ་ལ་ཕྱག་འཚལ་ལོ། །

དེ་བཞིན་གཤེགས་པ་རིན་ཆེན་པད་ྨ་རྣམ་པར་གནོན་པ་ལ་ཕྱག་འཚལ་ལོ། །

དེ་བཞིན་གཤེགས་པ་དྲ་བཙོམ་པ་ཡང་དག་པར་རྫོགས་པའི་སངས་རྒྱས་རིན་པོ་ཆེ་
དང་པད་ྨ་ལ་རབ་ཏུ་བཤུགས་པ་རི་དབང་གི་རྒྱལ་པོ་ལ་ཕྱག་འཚལ་ལོ། །

དེ་དག་ལ་སོགས་པ་ཕྱོགས་བཅུའི་འཇིག་རྟེན་གྱི་ཁམས་ཐམས་ཅད་ན་དེ་བཞིན་
གཤེགས་པ་དྲ་བཙོམ་པ་ཡང་དག་པར་རྫོགས་པའི་སངས་རྒྱས་བཅོམ་ལྡན་
འདས་གང་རྗེ་སྟེད་ཅིག་བཞུགས་ཏེ་འཚོ་ཞིང་གཞེས་པའི་སངས་རྒྱས་བཅོམ་ལྡན་
འདས་དེ་དག་ཐམས་ཅད་བདག་ལ་དགོངས་སུ་གསོལ།

བདག་གི་སྐྱེ་བ་འདི་དང་། སྐྱེ་བ་ཐོག་མའི་ཐ་མ་མ་མཆིས་པ་ནས་འཁོར་བ་ན་
འཁོར་བའི་སྐྱེ་གནས་ཐམས་ཅད་དུ་སྱིག་པའི་ལས་བགྱིས་པ་དང་། བགྱིད་དུ་
བསྩལ་བ་དང་། བགྱིད་པ་ལ་རྗེས་སུ་ཡི་རང་བའམ། མཆོད་རྟེན་གྱི་དཀོར་
རམ། དགེ་འདུན་གྱི་དཀོར་རམ། ཕྱོགས་བཅུའི་དགེ་འདུན་གྱི་དཀོར་ཕྲོགས་པ་
དང་། འཕྲོག་ཏུ་བཅུག་པ་དང་། འཕྲོག་པ་ལ་རྗེས་སུ་ཡི་རང་བའམ། མཆམས་
མ་མཆིས་པ་ལྔའི་ལས་བགྱིས་པ་དང་། བགྱིད་དུ་བསྩལ་བ་དང་། བགྱིད་པ་ལ་
རྗེས་སུ་ཡི་རང་བའམ། ལས་ཀྱི་སྒྲིབ་པ་གང་གིས་བསྒྲིབས་ནས་བདག་སེམས་ཅན་
དམྱལ་བར་མཆི་བའམ། དུད་འགྲོའི་སྐྱེ་གནས་སུ་མཆི་བའམ། ཡི་དགས་ཀྱི་ཡུལ་
དུ་མཆི་བའམ། ཡུལ་མཐའ་འཁོབ་ཏུ་སྐྱེ་བའམ། ཀླ་ཀློར་སྐྱེ་བའམ། ལྷ་ཚེ་རིང་
པོ་རྣམས་སུ་སྐྱེ་བའམ། དབང་པོ་མ་ཚང་བར་འགྱུར་བའམ། ལྟ་བ་ལོག་པ་འཛིན་
པར་འགྱུར་བའམ། སངས་རྒྱས་འབྱུང་བ་ལ་མཉེས་པར་མི་བགྱིད་པར་འགྱུར་
བའི་ལས་ཀྱི་སྒྲིབ་པ་གང་ལགས་པ་དེ་དག་ཐམས་ཅད་སངས་རྒྱས་བཅོམ་ལྡན་

འདས་ཡེ་ཤེས་སུ་གྱུར་པ། སྤྱན་དུ་གྱུར་པ། དཔལ་དུ་གྱུར་པ། ཆད་མར་གྱུར་པ། མཐྱེན་པས་གཟིགས་པ་དེ་དག་གི་སྤྱན་སྔར་མཐོལ་ལོ། ཆགས་སོ། མི་འཆབ་པོ། མི་སྲེད་དོ། སྤན་ཆད་ཀྱང་བཅོད་ཅིང་སྡོམ་པར་བགྱིད་ལགས་སོ།

སངས་རྒྱས་བཅོམ་ལྡན་འདས་དེ་དག་ཐམས་ཅད་བདག་ལ་དགོངས་སུ་གསོལ།

བདག་གི་སྐྱེ་བ་འདི་དང་། སྐྱེ་བ་ཐོག་མའི་ཐ་མ་མ་མཆིས་པ་ནས་འཁོར་བ་ན་འཁོར་བའི་སྐྱེ་གནས་གཞན་དག དུ་སྐྱིན་པ་ཐ་ན་དུད་འགྲོའི་སྐྱེ་གནས་སུ་སྐྱེ་པ་ལ་ཟས་ཁམ་གཅིག་ཙམ་སྩལ་བའི་དགེ་བའི་རྩ་བ་གང་ལགས་པ་དང་། བདག་གིས་ཚུལ་ཁྲིམས་བསྲུངས་པའི་དགེ་བའི་རྩ་བ་གང་ལགས་པ་དང་། བདག་གིས་ཚངས་པར་སྤྱོད་པའི་དགེ་བའི་རྩ་བ་གང་ལགས་པ་དང་། བདག་གིས་སེམས་ཅན་ཡོངས་སུ་སྨིན་པར་བགྱིས་པའི་དགེ་བའི་རྩ་བ་གང་ལགས་པ་དང་། བདག་གིས་བྱང་ཆུབ་མཆོག་ཏུ་སེམས་བསྐྱེད་པའི་དགེ་བའི་རྩ་བ་གང་ལགས་པ་དང་། བདག་གིས་བླ་ན་མེད་པའི་ཡེ་ཤེས་ཀྱི་དགེ་བའི་རྩ་བ་གང་ལགས་པ་དེ་དག་ཐམས་ཅད་གཅིག་ཏུ་བསྡུས་ཤིང་བསྡོམས་ཏེ་བསྒོམས་ན་བླ་ན་མ་མཆིས་པ་དང་། གོང་ན་མ་མཆིས་པ་དང་། གོང་མའི་ཡང་གོང་མ། བླ་མའི་ཡང་བླ་མར་ཡོངས་སུ་བསྔོས་ནས་བླ་ན་མེད་པ་ཡང་དག་པར་རྫོགས་པའི་བྱང་ཆུབ་ཏུ་ཡོངས་སུ་བསྔོ་བར་བགྱིའོ།

ཇི་ལྟར་འདས་པའི་སངས་རྒྱས་བཅོམ་ལྡན་འདས་རྣམས་ཀྱིས་ཡོངས་སུ་བསྔོས་པ་དང་། ཇི་ལྟར་མ་བྱོན་པའི་སངས་རྒྱས་བཅོམ་ལྡན་འདས་རྣམས་ཀྱིས་ཡོངས་སུ་བསྔོ་བར་འགྱུར་བ་དང་། ཇི་ལྟར་ད་ལྟར་བཞུགས་པའི་སངས་རྒྱས་བཅོམ་ལྡན་འདས་རྣམས་ཀྱིས་ཡོངས་སུ་བསྔོ་བར་མཛད་པ་དེ་བཞིན་དུ་བདག་གིས་ཀྱང་ཡོངས་སུ་

བསྒོ་བར་བགྱིའོ། །ཕྱག་པ་ཐམས་ཅད་ནི་སོ་སོར་བཤགས་སོ། །བསོད་ནམས་ཐམས་
ཅད་ལ་ནི་རྗེས་སུ་ཡི་རང་ངོ་། །སངས་རྒྱས་ཐམས་ཅད་ལ་ནི་བསྐུལ་ཞིང་གསོལ་བ་
འདེབས་སོ། །

བདག་གིས་བླ་ན་མེད་པའི་ཡེ་ཤེས་ཀྱི་མཆོག་དམ་པ་ཐོབ་པར་གྱུར་ཅིག །མི་མཆོག་
རྒྱལ་བ་གང་དག་ད་ལྟར་བཞུགས་པ་དང་། །གང་དག་འདས་པ་དག་དང་དེ་བཞིན་
མ་བྱོན། །ཡོན་ཏན་མངགས་པ་མཐའ་ཡས་རྒྱ་མཚོ་འདྲ་ཀུན་ལ། །ཐལ་མོ་སྦྱར་བར་
བགྱིས་ཏེ་སྐྱབས་སུ་ཉེ་བར་མཆིའོ།

འཕགས་པ་ཕུང་པོ་གསུམ་པ་ཞེས་བ་ཐེག་པ་ཆེན་པོའི་མདོ་རྫོགས་སོ།། །།

6. Outline of *A Significant Sight*: A Commentary to *The Bodhisattva's Confession of Downfalls*

(*Many of the outline headings found here have been abbreviated in the translation, several have been modified, and IC2a and IC2b have been omitted altogether.*)

I. How to confess negativities and downfalls
IA. How to confess negativities and downfalls by means of showing the force of the basis
IB. How to confess negativities and downfalls by means of showing the force of applying all antidotes
IC. How to confess negativities and downfalls by means of showing the force of total repudiation
  IC1. Request to witness the confession of negativities and downfalls
  IC2. Identifying the negativities and obscurations to be confessed
    IC2a. Shown in brief
    IC2b. Explained extensively
      IC2b-1. Explaining the negativities of misusing the possessions of the Jewels
      IC2b-2. Explaining the negativities of the five [actions of] immediate [retribution]
      IC2b-3. Explaining the negativities included in the ten non-virtues
  IC3. How to confess those negativities and downfalls
ID. How to confess negativities and downfalls by means of showing the force of turning away from faults in the future

II. How to dedicate virtues
IIA. Request to witness the dedication
IIB. Identifying the virtues to be dedicated
IIC. How to dedicate

III. Summarizing the meaning, showing the seven limbs in their entirety

IIIA. Explaining the manner in which there are seven limbs

IIIB. For the purpose of showing the seven limbs, again showing how to go for refuge to the Three Jewels

7. How to Perform Full-Length Prostrations

(1) Put the palms of your hands together with the thumbs aligned and tucked into the center of your palms. Your folded thumbs represent offering a wish-fulfilling jewel to the buddhas.

Note: Having visualized the thirty-five buddhas in the space before you, imagine that you emanate countless bodies, each of which has many heads with many tongues. As you prostrate, imagine that all the emanated bodies, visualized surrounding you, do the same.

(2) Place your folded hands upon the crown of your head. This creates the cause to obtain the crown protuberance (*ushnisha*) of a buddha.

Note: Simultaneously recite the phrase of prostration to the corresponding tathāgata while imagining that each of the emanated tongues also does the same. Continue to repeat that same phrase of prostration until the prostration is complete.

(3) Touch your folded hands to your forehead (optional). This purifies negative actions committed by the body and creates the cause to obtain the treasure hair of a buddha.

Note: If you prefer to do prostrations without touching your hands to your forehead, visualize that touching your crown purifies negative actions committed by the body.

(4) Touch your folded hands to your neck. This purifies negative actions committed by speech and creates the cause to obtain the melodious speech of a buddha with its sixty-four qualities.

(5) Touch your folded hands to your heart. This purifies negative actions committed by mind and creates the cause to obtain the qualities of a buddha's mind, such as the twenty-one divisions of uncontaminated exalted wisdom.

Note: While touching your hands to the forehead (or crown), neck, and heart visualize that white light and nectar radiate from the corresponding place of the body of the buddha to whom you are prostrating and enter, respectively, into your own forehead, neck, and heart, completely purifying all your negativities of body, speech, and mind. If you find this visualization difficult, merely visualize that white light and nectar radiate from the heart of the buddha to whom you are prostrating, enter into your body through your forehead, and purify all your negativities of body, speech, and mind. Visualize that all your negativities leave your body through your lower orifices in the form of filthy dirt, snakes, scorpions, and so forth. These fall into the gaping mouth of the Lord of Death, who is visualized seven levels under the ground below your feet. The Lord of Death becomes extremely blissful and satisfied.

(6) Bend forward and place your hands flat on the ground with your fingers very slightly apart.

(7) Lower your knees and stretch your body out full-length on the ground with your arms extended forward.

Note: It is said that the amount of negative actions purified by a single prostration is in proportion to the number of atoms of earth covered by the extended body; therefore, also visualize that your body is extremely huge and covers an enormous amount of earth.

(8) Either (a) lift merely your palms up off the ground or (b) bend your elbows and bring your folded hands over the back of your head; then lower your palms once again to the ground.

Note: While doing this, visualize that a replica of the buddha to whom you are prostrating absorbs into you, thereby, blessing you.

(9) To stand up bring your hands back to shoulder level, raise up on your knees, place your hands on the ground close to the level of your knees, raise your knees off the ground, then raise your hands, and stand up straight.

(10) Begin the next prostration by immediately placing your folded hands on the crown of your head.

Note: At the end of the final prostration once again touch your folded hands to the crown, forehead (optional), neck, and heart. Visualize that your body is completely pure and transparent, like clear crystal, and feel convinced that all your negative actions of body, speech, and mind have been completely purified.

How to Perform Short Prostrations

(1) Touch your folded hands, with thumbs tucked inside the palms, to your crown, forehead (optional), neck, and heart as above.

(2) Bend forward, place your hands flat upon the ground, lower your knees to the ground, and touch your forehead to the ground.

Note: Five points of the body should always touch the ground—the hands, knees, and head.

(3) When standing up, first the head leaves the ground, then the knees, and finally the hands.

Note: You should come to a straight standing position before beginning the next prostration.

(4) Begin the next prostration by immediately placing your folded hands on the crown of your head.

Note: At the end of the final prostration once again touch your folded hands to the crown, forehead (optional), neck, and heart. Short prostrations are generally performed at the beginning and end of Dharma teachings, during the Restoring and Purifying Ceremony of monks and nuns, etc.

How to Perform Very Simple Prostrations

(1) Hold your folded hands, with thumbs tucked inside your palms, at your heart.

Note: The practice of confession to the thirty-five buddhas is usually accompanied by full-length prostrations but can be done with either the short or very simple prostrations when space or health do not permit full-length prostrations.

Notes

1. For a complete version see Janice D. Willis's *Enlightened Beings.*
2. The five lay vows are the vows taken by lay Dharma practitioners to abandon killing, stealing, sexual misconduct, lying, and taking intoxicants.
3. Dakas and dakinis are, respectively, male and female Dharma practitioners who have the appearance of gods. There are three types: (1) the mantra born (*sngags skyes*), who are practitioners of the generation stage of tantra; (2) the simultaneously born (*lhan skyes*), who are practitioners of the completion stage of tantra; and (3) the field born (*zhing skyes*), who are born in a special place, such as one of the twenty-four holy places of Heruka.
4. Supermundane Dharma protectors are wrathful emanations of buddhas who eliminate hindrances to our Dharma practice. Mundane Dharma protectors are worldly beings who have pledged to protect the Dharma and the beings who practice it.
5. A superior is a being who has directly realized emptiness, the ultimate mode of existence of all phenomena. The exalted wisdom realizing emptiness cuts through the ignorance grasping at an inherently existent self of persons and self of phenomena, the source of all other mental afflictions.
6. The syllable *man* of *mantra* means "mind," while *tra* means "to protect." Therefore, a mantra is that which protects the mind. According to the sutra teachings, mantras protect the mind from the afflictions, while according to the tantra teachings, mantras protect the mind from ordinary appearances and grasping at ordinary appearances.
7. A stupa is a Buddhist reliquary monument representing the omniscient mind of a buddha. It contains relics—whether of a highly realized being or an ordinary person—that have been purified and consecrated by particular rituals and thereby transformed into objects worthy of veneration.

8. For an explanation of the four results in relation to each of the ten non-virtuous paths of actions see *An Anthology of Well-Spoken Advice*, pp. 339–342; *Liberation in Our Hands*, part 2, pp. 256–257; and *Liberation in the Palm of Your Hand*, pp. 452–453.

9. For an extensive explanation of the qualities of a buddha's four bodies see Haribhadra's *Clear Meaning Commentary and Liberation in Our Hands*, part 2, appendix E.

10. For an extensive explanation of the thirty-two major marks see *An Anthology of Well-Spoken Advice*, pp. 243–249, and for an explanation of both the major and minor marks see *Liberation in Our Hands*, part 2, appendix E, pp. 308–314.

11. For an extensive explanation of the qualities of a buddha's speech see *The Sixty Branches of Melodious Speech* included in Chandrakīrti's *Supplement to (Nāgārjuna's) "Treatise on the Middle Way,"* translated by T. Jampa and G. Churinoff; and lam-rim texts such as *An Anthology of Well-Spoken Advice*, pp. 251–257, and *Liberation in Our Hands*, part 2, appendix E, pp. 315–320.

12. For an extensive explanation of the qualities of a buddha's mind see *An Anthology of Well-Spoken Advice*, pp. 258–262; and *Liberation in Our Hands*, part 2, appendix E, pp. 294–307.

13. For a detailed discussion of the meditation on the seven, the six causes and one effect, see lam-rim texts such as *Liberation in the Palm of Your Hand*, pp. 566–587.

14. Nirvana, or liberation, is the state achieved when the afflictions and their seeds are completely eliminated from the mental continuum. The foe-destroyers who have achieved nirvana have reached a state of personal peace but, unlike the buddhas, they do not work to free all sentient beings from suffering.

15. It seems likely that a change in the Tibetan text has occurred since the original Sanskrit word *vīra* (meaning hero, brave, courageous, etc.), which would have been correctly translated into Tibetan as *dpa'* (also meaning hero, brave, courageous, etc.), here, however, appears as *dpal* (glorious). Probably over time the Tibetan *a* was changed to *la*. It has been translated here in accordance with the original Sanskrit.

16. Here again the Tibetan *dpa'* (hero, brave, courageous, etc.) seems to have been changed to *dpal* (glorious), since the Sanskrit *shūra* (as does

vīra) means hero, brave, courageous, etc. Again here it has been translated in accordance with the original Sanskrit.

17. The five actions of immediate retribution are also called the five heinous
crimes, the five extreme negative actions, and the five immediate karmas.

18. For a detailed discussion of the root and secondary afflictions see
Meditation on Emptiness, pp. 255–266.

19. For an explanation of the first four wisdoms see *Liberation in Our
Hands,* part 2, appendix E, pp. 291–293. The fifth, the wisdom of the
completely pure sphere of phenomena, although called a wisdom, actually refers to the nature body of a buddha. However, generally speaking
it can be said to mean the wisdom realizing emptiness.

20. Root text (*gzhung*) refers to the actual *Sutra of the Bodhisattva's
Confession of Downfalls.*

21. Cast-Afar is a synonym of Hedonist (*charvaka, tshu rol mdzes pa*).
The followers of this particular philosophical school, which existed in
India at the time of Buddha, are so-called because they are considered
by the Buddhist schools to have cast afar, or to have rejected, the correct view concerning the law of actions and results, past and future
lives, and so on.

22. The actual meaning of dharani (retention) is recollection and wisdom.
A mantra-dharani, or dharani of mantra, is a mantra that brings about
the development of recollection and wisdom by enabling us to retain,
or to hold, words and their meanings in our mind. Therefore, this is a
case of giving the name of the result to its cause.

Glossary

English	Sanskrit	Tibetan
action	karma	las
action tantra	kriyātantra	bya rgyud
affliction	klesha	nyon mongs
afflictive obscuration	kleshāvaraṇa	nyon mong pa'i sgrib pa
aggregate/heap	skandha	phung po
anger	pratigha	khong khro
animal	tiryagyoni	dud 'gro
antidote/opponent	pratipakṣha	gnyen po
attachment	rāga	'dod chags
attainment	siddhi	dngos grub
auspiciousness	pratītyasamutpāda	rten 'brel
barbarian	turuṣhka	kla klo
basis	ādhāra/vastu	gzhi
benefit	anushamṣha	phan yon
bodhisattva	bodhisattva	byang chub sems dpa'
border area	prānta	yul mtha' khob
branch	aṅga	yan lag
buddha	buddha	sangs rgyas
Cast-Afar	ayata	rbyang phan pa
cause	hetu	rgyu
collections of doctrine	dharmaskandha	chos kyi phung po
commitment	samāya	dam tshigs
compassion	karuṇā	snying rje
completion	—	mthar thug
compositional factor	saṃskāra	'du byed
concealment	mrakṣha	'chab pa

concentration	dhyāna	bsam gtan
confession	deshana	bshags pa
conqueror	jina	rgyal ba
consciousness	vijñāna	rnam par shes pa
constituent	dhātu	khams
conventional truth	saṃvṛtisatya	kun rdzob bden pa
covetousness	abhidhyā	brnab sems
cyclic existence	saṃsāra	'khor ba
daka/dakini	ḍāka/ḍākiṇī	mkha' 'gro (ma)
dedication	pariṇāma	bsngo ba
definite goodness	niḥshreyasa	nges legs
demon	māra	bdud
dependent relation	pratītyasamutpāda	rten 'brel
desire realm	kāmadhātu	'dod khams
Dharma	dharma	chos
Dharma protector	dharmapāla	chos skyong
direct perception/perceiver	pratyakṣha	mngon sum
disciple	vineya	gdul bya
discipline	vinaya	'dul ba
discordant class	vipakṣha	mi mthun pa'i phyogs
discrimination	saṃjñā	'du shes
divisive speech	paishunya	phra mar smra ba
doctrine	dharma	chos
doubt	vichikitsā	the tshom
downfall	āpatti	ltung ba
emanation body	nirmāṇakāya	sprul sku
emptiness	shūnyatā	stong pa nyid
enemy/foe	ari	dgra
enjoyment body	sambhogakāya	longs sku
enlightenment	bodhi	byang chub
environmental result	ādhipatiphala	bdag po'i 'bras bu
eon	kalpa	bskal pa
equanimity	upekṣhā	btang snyoms
exalted wisdom	jñāna	ye shes
execution/preparation	prayoga	sbyor ba

faith	shraddhā	dad pa
feeling	vedanā	tshor ba
foe-destroyer	arhat/arhan	dgra bcom pa
force of applying all antidotes	—	gnyen po kun tu spyod pa'i stobs
force of the basis	—	rten gyi stobs
force of total repudiation	—	rnam par sun 'byin pa'i stobs
force of turning away from faults in the future	—	nye pa las slar ldog pa'i stobs
form	rūpa	gzugs
form body	rūpakāya	gzugs sku
form realm	rūpadhātu	gzugs khams
formless realm	ārūpyadhātu	gzugs med khams
formulated misdeed	pratikṣhepaṇa-sāvadya	bcas pa'i kha na ma tho ba
fully ordained monk	bhikṣhu	dge slong
fully ordained nun	bhikṣhunī	dge slong ma
generosity	dāna	sbyin pa
god	deva	hla
Great Vehicle	mahāyāna	theg pa chen po
ground	bhūmi	sa
happiness	sukha	bde ba
harsh words	pārushya	tshig rtsub smra ba
hatred	dveṣha	zhe sdang
heap/aggregate	skandha	phung po
hearer	shrāvaka	nyan thos
Hedonist	chārvāka	tshu rol mdzes pa
hell	naraka	dmyal ba
high status	abhyudaya	mngon mtho
highest yoga tantra	anuttarayogatantra	rnal 'byor bla med rgyud
homage	nāmo	'dud pa
human	manuṣhya	mi
hungry ghost	preta	yi dvags

idle talk	pralapa	ngag 'khyal
ignorance	avidyā/moha	ma rig pa/gti mug
immeasurable	apramāṇa	tshad med
immediate [retribution]	ānantarya	mtshams med pa
imprint	vāsanā	bags chags
introspection	samprajanya	shes bzhin
jealousy	īrṣhyā	phrag dog
Jewel	ratna	dkon mchog
joyous effort	vīrya	brtson 'grus
karmic obscuration	karmāvaraṇa	las kyi sgrib pa
killing	prāṇātighāta	srog gcod
lay vows	upāsaka/upāsikā	dge bsnyen
leisureless	akṣhaṇa	mi khom pa
Lesser Vehicle	hīnayāna	theg dman
liberation	mokṣha	thar pa
limb	aṅga	yan lag
love	maitri	byams pa
lying	mṛṣhāvāda	rdzun du smra ba
major mark	nimitta	mtshan bzang
malice	vyāpāda	gnod sems
maturation result	vipākaphala	rnam smin gyi 'bras bu
meaning	artha	don
meditation	bhāvanā	sgoms pa
meditative stabilization	samādhi	ting nge 'dzin
mental factor	chaitta	sems byung
mercy	anukampā/dayā	brtse ba
merit	puṇya	bsod nams
method	upāya	thabs
migrator/migration	gati	'gro ba
mind	chitta	sems
mind of enlightenment	bodhichitta	byang chub kyi sems
mindfulness	smṛti	dran pa
minor mark	anuvyañjana	dpe byad

morality	shīla	tshul khrims
motivation	samutthāna	kun nas slong ba
natural misdeed	prakṛti-sāvadya	rang bzhin gyi kha na ma tho ba
nature body	svabhāvikakāya	ngo bo nyid sku
negative action	pāpakarma	sdig pa'i las
negativity	pāpa	sdig pa
nirvana	nirvāṇa	mya ngan las 'das pa
non-associated compositional factor	viprayukta-saṃskāra	ldan min 'du byed
non-virtue	akushala	mi dge ba
Not Low	akaniṣhṭa	'og min
novice monk	shrāmaṇera	dge tsul
object	viṣhaya	yul
object of abandonment	prahātvya (?)	spang bya
object of knowledge	jñeya	shes bya
obscuration	āvaraṇa	sgrib pa
obscuration of maturation	vipāka-āvaraṇa	rnam smin gyi sgrib pa
obscurations to omniscience/objects of knowledge	jñeyāvaraṇa	shes sbya'i grib pa
offering	pūjā	mchod pa
One Gone Thus	tathāgata	de bzhin gshegs pa
One Gone to Bliss	sugata	bde bar gshegs pa
opponent force	pratipakṣhabala	gnyen po stobs
path	mārga	lam
patience	kṣhānti	bzod pa
perfection	pāramitā	pha rol tu phyin pa
perfectly complete	samyaksaṃ	yang dag par rdzogs pa
performance tantra	charyātantra	spyod rgyud
person/being	pudgala/puruṣha	gang zag/skyes bu
phenomenon	dharma	chos
poison	viṣha	dug
pride	māna	nga rgyal

prostration	abhivandana	phyag 'tshal
pure conduct	brahmacharyā	tshangs spyod
quality	guṇa	yon tan
realm	dhātu	khams
recognition	saṃjñā	'du shes
refuge	sharaṇa	skyabs
regret	kaukṛtya	'gyod pa
rejoice	anumodana	rjes su yid rang ba
respect/devout	ādara/bhakti	gus pa
result	phala	'bras bu
result corresponding to the cause	niṣhyandaphala	rgyu mthun gyi 'bras bu
(1) as an activity	—	byed pa rgyu mthun gyi 'bras bu
(2) as an experience	—	myong ba rgyu mthun gyi 'bras bu
retention	dhāraṇī	gzungs
root of virtue	kushala-mūla	dge ba'i rtsa ba
root text	grantha	gzhung
sangha	saṅgha	dge 'dun
secondary action of immediate retribution	upānantarīya	nye ba mtshams med pa
sentient being	sattva	sems can
sexual misconduct	kāmamithyācāra	'dod pas log par g.yem pa
solitary realizer	pratyekabuddha	rang sangs rgyas
son-of-the-gods	devaputra	hla'i bu
spiritual teacher	guru	bla ma
stealing	adattādāna	ma byin len
stupa	stūpa	mchod rten
Subduer	muni	thub pa
suffering	duḥkha	sdug bsngal
superior	ārya	'phags pa
sutra	sūtra	mdo
thought	chintā	bsam pa

Three Jewels	triratna	dkon mchog gsum
three poisons	triviṣha	dug gsum
thusness/suchness	tathatā	de bzhin nyid
Transcendent	bhagavan	bcom ldan 'das
true cessations	nirodhasatya	'gog pa'i bden pa
true origins	samudayasatya	kun 'byung bden pa
true paths	mārgasatya	lam gyi bden pa
true sufferings	duḥkhasatya	sdug bsngal bden pa
truth	satya	bden pa
truth body	dharmakāya	chos sku
ultimate truth	paramārthasatya	don dam bden pa
unpredicted/neutral	avyākṛta	lung ma bstan
Unrelenting Torment	avīchi	mnar med
unsurpassed/highest	anuttara	bla na med pa
view	dṛṣhṭi	lta ba
virtue	kushala	dge ba
wisdom	prajñā	shes rab
wisdom truth body	jñānadharmakāya	ye shes chos sku
Without Discrimination	asaṃjña	'du shes med pa
world system	lokadhātu	'jig rten gyi khams
wrong view	mithyādṛṣhṭi	log par lta ba
yoga tantra	pratidesaniya	rnal 'byor rgyud

Bibliography

Abbreviations:

P   *The Tibetan Tripiṭaka.* Peking edition, edited by Dr. Daisetz T. Suzuki. Tokyo, Japan: Suzuki Research Foundation, 1962.

D   *A Complete Catalogue of the Tibetan Buddhist Canons.* Derge edition, edited by Hakuju Ui, Munetada Suzuki, Yensho Kanakura, Tokan Tada. Sendai, Japan: Tohoku Imperial University, 1934.

1. SUTRAS AND TANTRAS

Dharani That Exhorts. Chuṇḍādhāraṇī. bsKul byed kyi gzungs. Not listed in P or D.

Guhyasamāja Tantra. gSang ba 'dus pa. P81, D442. Partial translation in Alex Wayman's *The Yoga of the Guhyasamājatantra* (Delhi: Motilal, 1977).

Heap of Jewels Sutra. Ratnakūṭasūtra. dKon mchog brtsegs pa'i mdo. Not technically a sutra but a collection of sutras, including the *Questions of Upāli.* P760 vols. 22–24.

Hundred on Karma Sutra. Karmashatakasūtra. mDo sde las brgya pa. P1007, D340.

King of Prayers of Good Conduct. Bhadracharyāpraṇidhānarāja. bZang po spyod pa'i smon lam gyi rgyal po. P716, D1095. Translation by Martin Willson, "The Noble King of Vows of the Conduct of Samantabhadra," in *Shakyamuni Puja* (Boston: Wisdom Publications, 1988).

Sutra Indicating the Four Dharmas. Chaturdharmanirdeshasūtra. Chos bzhi bstan pa'i mdo. D249.

Sutra of the Bodhisattva's Confession of Downfalls. Byang chub sems dpa'i ltung ba bshags pa. See *Sutra of the Three Heaps.*

Sutra of the Three Heaps. Triskandhakasūtra. Phung po gsum pa'i mdo. P950, D284. Translations in Kathleen McDonald, *How to Meditate* (Boston: Wisdom Publications, 1984, 1995) and in Pabongka Rinpoche, *Liberation in the Palm of Your Hand* (Boston: Wisdom Publications, 1991).

Sutra of the Wise and the Foolish. Damamūkosūtra. mDzangs blun mdo. P1008, D341. Translation from the Mongolian by Stanley Frye, *The Sutra of the Wise and the Foolish,* or *The Ocean of Narratives (üliger-ün dalai)* (Dharamsala: Library of Tibetan Works and Archives, 1981).

2. SANSKRIT AND TIBETAN TREATISES

Chandrakīrti (Zla-ba-grags-pa). *Supplement to [Nāgārjuna's] "Treatise on the Middle Way." Madhyamakāvatāra. dBu ma la 'jug pa.* P5262, D3861. Unpublished translation by Thubten Jampa and George Churinoff (Pomaia, Italy: Istituto Lama Tzong Khapa, 1990).

Gendün Drub (dGe-'dun grub), First Dalai Lama (1391–1474). *Clarifying the Path to Liberation: A Complete Explanation of the Treasury of Abhidharma. mDzod tig tar lam gsal byed.* Sarnath, India: The Pleasure of Elegant Sayings Printing Press, 1973. Partial translation by David Patt (1993 Ph.D thesis) and the introduction and chapters 1 and 2 by George Churinoff (Pomaia, Italy: Istituto Lama Tzong Khapa, 1992).

Gyeltsab (rGyal-tshab, 1364–1432). *The Benefits of the Names of the Thirty-Five Buddhas. Sangs rgyas sum cu so lnga'i mtshan gyi phan yon bzhugs.* Included in *The Collected Works of Gyeltsab Dharma Rinchen (rGyal tshab dar ma rin chen gyi gsung 'bum),* vol. 1. New Delhi: Guru Deva, 1982.

Haribhadra (Seng-ge bzang-po). *Clear Meaning Commentary. Sphūṭārtha. 'Grel ba don gsal.* D3793.

Jaitāri (dGra las rgyal ba). *Stages of Training of a Bodhisattva: A Commentary to the Bodhisattva's Confession of Downfalls. Bodhyāpattideshānavṛtti-bodhisattvashikṣhākrama. Byang chub kyi ltung ba bshags pa'i 'grel pa byang chub sems dpa'i bslab pa'i rim pa.* D4006.

Jetsün Chökyi Gyeltsen (rJe-btsun chos-kyi rgyal-mtshan). *The Ocean Playground of the Lord of the Nāgas. Klu dbang gi rol mtsho (Shes rab kyi pha rol tu phyin pa'i man ngag gi bstan bcos mngon par rtogs pa'i rgyan 'grel pa dang bcas pa'i rnam bshad rnam pa gnyis kyi dka' ba'i gnas gsal bar byed pa legs bshad skal bzang klu dbang gi rol mtsho zhes bya ba).* Xining, China: mTso sngon mi rigs par khang, 1991.

Lang-ri Tangpa Dorje Seng-ge (gLang-ri thang-pa rdo-rje seng-ges, 1054–1123). *Eight Verses on Mind Training. bLo sbyong tsig rkang brgyad ma lo rgyus dang bcad pa.* Included in *Sems dpa' chen po dkon mchog rgyal mtshan gyis phyogs bsgrigs mdzad pa'i blo sbyong brgya rtsa dang dkar chag gdung sel zla ba bcas.* Compiled by dKon mchog rgyal mtsan. Dharamsala: Shes rig par khang, 1973. Translation by Brian Beresford, "Thought Transformation in Eight Stanzas," in Geshe Rabten and Geshe Dhargyey's *Advice from a Spiritual Friend* (Boston: Wisdom Publications, 1984, 1996).

Maitreya (Byams-pa). *Sublime Continuum of the Great Vehicle. Mahāyāna-uttara-tantra-shāstra* (also known as *Ratna-gotra-vibhāga*). *Theg pa chen po rgyud bla ma'i bstan bcos.* P5525, T4024. Translated by E. Obermiller, *Sublime Science of the Great Vehicle to Salvation* (Acta Orientalia, XI, ii, iii, and iv); and by J. Takasaki, *A Study on the Ratnagotravibhāga* (Rome: Is.M.E.O, 1966).

Nāgārjuna (Klu-sgrub). *Commentary to the Bodhisattva's Confession of Downfalls. Bodhyāpattideshanāvṛtti. Byang chub kyi ltung ba bshags pa'i 'grel pa.* D4005. Translation by Brian Beresford, *The Commentary to the "Declaration of Downfalls of an Awakening (Warrior)" in Mahāyāna Purification* (Dharamsala: Library of Tibetan Works and Archives, 1980).

———. *Friendly Letter. Suhṛllekha. bShes pa'i spring yig.* P5682, D4182 and 4496. Translation by Geshe Lobsang Tharchin and Artemus Engle, *Nāgārjuna's Letter* (Dharamsala: Library of Tibetan Works and Archives, 1979).

Panchen Lozang Chökyi Gyeltsen (Pan-chen blo-bzang chos-kyi rgyal-mtshan, 1569–1662). *Guru Puja.* a.k.a *Indivisibility of Bliss and Emptiness: A Ritual of the Profound Path of Offering to the Guru. Zab lam bla ma mchod pa'i cho ga bde stong dbyer med ma.* Reprinted in *bLa ma'i rnal 'byor dang yi dam khag gi bdag bskyed sogs zhal 'don gces btus.* Dharamsala: Shes rig par khang, 1979. Translations by Alexander Berzin, *The Guru Puja* (Dharamsala: Library of Tibetan Works and Archives, 1979); and by Thubten Jinpa in Tenzin Gyatso, *The Union of Bliss and Emptiness* (Ithaca, N.Y.: Snow Lion Publications, 1988).

Panchen Lozang Yeshe (Pan-chen blo-bzang ye-shes, 1663–1737). *Quick Path Stages of the Path. Lam rim myur lam.* Included in *The Collected Works of Panchen Lozang Yeshe. Pan chen blo bzang ye shes kyi gsung 'bum.* New Delhi: bKra shis hlun po Monastery, 1981.

Sanggye Yeshe (Sangs-rgyas ye-shes, 1525–91). A Significant Sight: An Explanation of the Bodhisattva's Confession of Downfalls. Byang chub sems dpa'i ltung ba bshags pa'i ṭīkka don ldan ces bya ba bzhugs. Listed among The Collected Works of Sanggye Yeshe but mistakenly included in The Collected Works of Tsechogling Yongdzin Yeshe Gyeltsen (Tshe mchog gling yongs 'dzin ye shes rgyal mtshan gyi gsung 'bum), vol. 14. New Delhi: Tibet House Library, 1974.

Shāntideva (Zhi-ba-hla). *Compendium of Instructions. Shikṣhāsamucchaya. bsLab pa kun las btus pa.* P5336, D3939. Translation by Bendall and Rouse, *Śikṣā Samuccaya* (repr. Delhi: Motilal Banarsidass, 1971).

———. *Engaging in the Bodhisattva Deeds. Bodhisattvacharyāvatāra. Byang chub sems dpa'i spyod pa la 'jug pa.* P5272, D3871. Translation by Stephen Batchelor, *A Guide to the Bodhisattva's Way of Life* (Dharamsala: Library of Tibetan Works and Archives, 1979).

Trijang Dorje Chang (Khri byang rdo rje 'chang, 1901–81). *Collected Works About Mind Training. bLo sbyong gi skor sogs gsung thor bu'i rigs rnams phyogs gcig tu bsdebs pa.* Included in *The Collected Works of Trijang Dorje Chang (Yongs rdzogs bstan pa'i mnga' bdag skyabs rje yongs 'dzin khri byang rdo rje 'chang chen po'i gsung 'bum)*, vol. ga. New Delhi: Guru Deva, undated.

Tsongkhapa (Tsong-kha-pa, 1357–1419). *Practice of the Thirty-Five Buddhas and a Description of the Deities' Bodies. Sangs rgyas so lnga'i mngon rtogs dang hla skua'i phyag tshad.* Included in *The Collected Works of Tsongkhapa (Kham gsum chos kyi rgyal po shar rgyal ba tsong kha pa chen po po'i gsung 'bum)*, vol. 11. New Delhi: Guru Deva, 1978.

———. *Lines of Experience,* or *The Abbreviated Meaning of the Stages of the Path. Nyams mgur, or Lam rim bsdus don.* In *Collected Works*, vol. 2. Translation by Robert A. F. Thurman, "Lines of Experience," in *The Life and Teachings of Tsong Khapa* (Dharamsala: Library of Tibetan Works and Archives, 1982).

Vasubandhu (dbYig-gnyen). *Explanation of the "Treasury of Knowledge." Abhidharmakoshabhāṣhya. Chos mngon pa'i mdzod kyi bshad pa.* P5591, D4090. Translation of La Vallée Poussin's French translation by Leo Pruden, *Abhidharmakośabhāṣyam*, 4 vols. (Berkeley: Asian Humanities Press, 1988).

Yeshe Gyeltsen, Tsechogling Yongdzin (Tse mchog gling yongs 'dzin ye shes rgyal mtsan, 1713–93). *Biographies of the Lineage Gurus of the Stages of the Path. Lam rim bla ma brgyud pa'i rnam thar.* Xining, China: mTso sngon mi rigs par 'debs bzo grva khang, 1990.

3. OTHER WORKS

Dhargyey, Ngawang. *An Anthology of Well-Spoken Advice.* Dharamsala: Library of Tibetan Works and Archives, 1982.

Hopkins, Jeffrey. *Meditation on Emptiness*. Boston: Wisdom Publications, 1983, 1996.

Pabongka Rinpoche (Pha-bong-kha). *Liberation in Our Hands, Parts One and Two*. Translated by Geshe Lobsang Tharchin with Artemus B. Engle. Howell, New Jersey: Mahayana Sutra and Tantra Press, 1990 and 1994.

———. *Liberation in the Palm of Your Hand*. Translated by Michael Richards. Boston: Wisdom Publications, 1991.

Willis, Janice D. *Enlightened Beings*. Boston: Wisdom Publications, 1995.

About the Author

Geshe Jampa Gyatso was born in Dham near Lhasa, Tibet, in early 1932, the eldest of seven children of a Tibetan nomad family. His parents named him Pelgye, and as an infant he suffered from frequent, sometimes life-threatening, illnesses. But at age four, his health dramatically improved, and that same year a visiting Nyingma lama predicted he would leave home at thirteen to become a monk and would never want for physical nourishment. At the age of seven he received the intermediate renunciate vows from the famed Purchog Jamgon Rinpoche of Sera Je Monastery. Purchog Rinpoche, recognized as the manifestation of the future Buddha Maitreya, gave the boy the name Jampa Gyatso, "ocean of love."

Jampa Gyatso did indeed leave home at age thirteen to live and study at Sera Je Monastery outside Lhasa. His routine for the next three years was strict: rising at four AM, he would clean the room and make offerings on the altar before making a fire for tea. At first his time was spent memorizing texts and helping with chores, though he would sometimes "escape" for a walk to Lhasa or to a nearby lake. At sixteen, Jampa Gyatso began his formal study of Buddhist philosophy with the textbook on Collected Topics, memorizing pages while he did his chores. He attended the various daily assemblies of monks in the main hall and began to learn and practice the art of philosophical debate.

It was at Sera that Jampa Gyatso met Lama Thubten Yeshe, who would become one of his dearest friends. Jampa Gyatso and Lama Yeshe were ardent debaters, forming debating groups among their friends to practice. When they weren't in class or debating, Jampa Gyatso, Lama Yeshe, and another friend would sneak off to Lama Yeshe's room, and behind the locked door they would read the songs and biographies of great meditators.

During this time Jampa Gyatso took ordination as a novice monk with the

great master Tagrig Dorje Chang, studied the vows, and received *lamrim* teachings from the tutor of the Dalai Lama. For six years he studied the Perfection of Wisdom (*prajñāpāramitā*) sutras while receiving additional teachings on the *lamrim*. Encouraged by his guru Geshe Tashi Bum, Jampa Gyatso took full ordination at age twenty-two.

Jampa Gyatso's life changed dramatically in March 1959, when the Chinese occupation of Tibet forced him, like thousands of other Tibetans, to flee his native land. Leaving his precious texts, sādhanas, and possessions behind, he followed his guru's advice and joined a party of thirty-five with Lama Yeshe to escape toward Bhutan and eventually on to India. The route was rigorous, and when Jampa Gyatso arrived in India, he fell gravely ill. He was immediately admitted to a regional hospital, where he remained for five months, then to a larger hospital in Rajasthan, where he stayed for almost a year and a half.

After nearly two years of hospitalization, Jampa Gyatso returned to his studies in 1961 at the monastic settlement in Buxa, near the border with Bhutan. There he continued with six years of study and debate. Then, in 1967, along with fifty other monks, Jampa Gyatso entered the newly instituted Buddhist studies program at the Sanskrit University in Varanasi to pursue the Acharya degree, which he received in 1970. At the request of the Religious Affairs Department of the Tibetan government in exile, Jampa Gyatso continued his studies at the tantric college of Gyume, which had been reestablished in exile. One year later, after completing the extensive examinations at a congregation of the three monasteries of Sera, Ganden, and Drepung, and having debated in Dharamsala at the annual prayer festival in 1972, he became a lharampa geshe, the highest level awarded.

Geshe Jampa Gyatso spent the next several years helping prepare the land that was donated by the Indian government to Gyume College until a request from the Religious Affairs Department petitioned him to take part in a new research program at the Central Institute of Higher Tibetan Studies in Varanasi. With the help of other scholars, Geshe Jampa Gyatso chose to investigate and compare the various interpretations of the aspects of the three knowers (a topic from the Prajñāpāramitā sutras) from the perspectives of the various philosophical schools. His research at Varanasi culminated in 1976 with a final thesis of 480 pages.

He returned immediately to Gyume College, but shortly thereafter he received a letter from his old friend Lama Thubten Yeshe, who had just founded of the Foundation for the Preservation of the Mahayana Tradition

(FPMT). For several years, Lama Yeshe had been teaching Buddhism to an ever-increasing number of Westerners, and he recruited Geshe Jampa Gyatso to travel to the West to teach. In 1980, after a brief stint teaching Westerners at Kopan Monastery in Nepal, Geshe Jampa Gyatso arrived at Istituto Lama Tzong Khapa in Pomaia, Italy, which had been founded in 1977, and he remained there for the next twenty-seven years. During this time he taught an enormous number of courses of varying lengths at Istituto Lama Tzong Khapa as well as at many other FPMT centers in Italy, Spain, France, and England. In addition, from 1983 to 1997 he completed extensive commentaries on three of the great treatises (Maitreya's *Abhisamayālaṃkāra*, Chandrakīrti's *Madhyamakāvatāra*, and Vasubandhu's *Abhidharmakosha*) as part of the newly created Geshe Studies Program. From 1998 to 2004 he taught the FPMT's first residential Masters Program, and from 2005–2007, together with Geshe Tenphel, he taught Istituto Lama Tzong Khapa's first residential Basic Program. He also acted as abbot of Nalanda Monastery in France and in Italy Takden Shedrup Dhargye Ling Monastery and Shenphen Samten Ling Nunnery.

Geshe Jampa Gyatso passed away November 27, 2007, remaining in the state of *tukdam* for one week during which there were no signs of physical decomposition. His body was cremated with a traditional ceremony at Istituto Lama Tzong Khapa.

Also from Wisdom Publications

BECOMING VAJRASATTVA
The Tantric Path of Purification
Lama Thubten Yeshe
Foreword by Lama Zopa Rinpoche

VAJRASATTVA MEDITATION
An Illustrated Guide
Khenpo Yeshe Phuntsok

THE WAY OF AWAKENING
A Commentary on Shantideva's Bodhicharyavatara
Geshe Yeshe Tobden
Foreword by His Holiness the Dalai Lama

WISDOM OF THE KADAM MASTERS
Tibetan Classics Series, Volume 2
Thupten Jinpa

ESSENCE OF THE HEART SUTRA
The Dalai Lama's Heart of Wisdom Teachings
His Holiness the Dalai Lama
Translated and Edited by Thupten Jinpa

CREATION AND COMPLETION
Essential Points of Tantric Meditation
Jamgön Kongtrul Lodrö Thaye

About Wisdom Publications

Wisdom Publications is the leading publisher of classic and contemporary Buddhist books and practical works on mindfulness. To learn more about us or to explore our other books, please visit our website at wisdompubs.org or contact us at the address below.

Wisdom Publications
199 Elm Street
Somerville, MA 02144 USA

We are a 501(c)(3) organization, and donations in support of our mission are tax deductible.

Wisdom Publications is affiliated with the Foundation for the Preservation of the Mahayana Tradition (FPMT).

Chicken Soup for the Soul

www.chickensoup.com

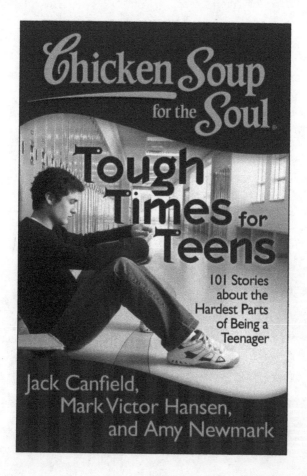

The teenage years are tough, and when bad things happen, the challenges can be overwhelming. Faced with illness, car accidents, loss of loved ones, divorces, or other upheavals, the obstacles to happiness can seem insurmountable. The 101 stories in this book describe the toughest teenage challenges and how other teens, with the same struggles, overcame them. This collection will be a support and companion for teenagers and will encourage, comfort, and inspire them, showing them that, as tough as things can get, they are not alone.

978-1-935096-80-1

Teenage years are tough, but this book will help teens as they journey through the ups and downs of adolescence. Teens will find support and inspiration in the 101 new stories from teens just like them. Stories in this book serve as a guide on topics about daily pressures of life, school, love, friendships, parents, and much more. This collection will show readers that as tough as things can get, they are not alone!

978-1-935096-72-6

Teens in high school have mainly moved past worrying about puberty and cliques, so this book covers topics of interest to older teens—sports and clubs, driving, curfews, self-image and self-acceptance, dating and sex, family, friends, divorce, illness, death, pregnancy, drinking, failure, and preparing for life after graduation. High school students will find comfort and inspiration in this book, referring to it through all four years of high school, like a portable support group.

978-1-935096-25-2

Being a teenager is difficult even under idyllic circumstances. But when bad things happen, the challenges of being a teenager can be overwhelming, leading to self-destructive behavior, eating disorders, substance abuse, and other challenges. In addition, many teens are faced with illness, car accidents, loss of loved ones, divorces, or other upheavals. These 101 stories from Chicken Soup for the Soul's library describe the toughest teenage challenges and how to overcome them.

978-1-935096-03-0

Chicken Soup for the Soul
for the Soul®

Our 101 BEST STORIES

Teens Talk Relationships

Stories about Family, Friends and Love

Jack Canfield
& Mark Victor Hansen
edited by Amy Newmark

The teenage years are difficult. Old friends drift away, new friends come with new issues, teens fall in and out of love, and relationships with family members change. This book reminds teenagers that they are not alone, as they read the 101 best stories from Chicken Soup for the Soul's library written by other teens just like themselves, about the problems and issues they face every day—stories about friends, family, love, loss, and many lessons learned.

978-1-935096-06-1

Chicken Soup for the Soul.

Teens Talk Growing Up

Our 101 BEST STORIES

Stories about Growing Up, Meeting Challenges, and Learning from Life

Jack Canfield
& Mark Victor Hansen
edited by Amy Newmark

Being a teenager is hard—school is challenging, college and career are looming on the horizon, family issues arise, friends and love come and go, bodies and emotions go through major changes, and many teens experience the loss of a loved one for the first time. This book reminds teenagers that they are not alone, as they read stories written by other teens about the problems and issues they all face every day.

978-1-935096-01-6

Share with Us

We all have had Chicken Soup for the Soul moments in our lives. If you would like to share your story or poem with millions of people around the world, go to chickensoup.com and click on "Submit Your Story." You may be able to help another reader, and become a published author at the same time. Some of our past contributors have launched writing and speaking careers from the publication of their stories in our books!

Our submission volume has been increasing steadily — the quality and quantity of your submissions has been fabulous. We only accept story submissions via our website. They are no longer accepted via mail or fax.

To contact us regarding other matters, please send us an e-mail through webmaster@chickensoupforthesoul.com, or fax or write us at:

Chicken Soup for the Soul
P.O. Box 700
Cos Cob, CT 06807-0700
Fax: 203-861-7194

One more note from your friends at Chicken Soup for the Soul: Occasionally, we receive an unsolicited book manuscript from one of our readers, and we would like to respectfully inform you that we do not accept unsolicited manuscripts and we must discard the ones that appear.

Improving Your Life Every Day

Real people sharing real stories — for nineteen years. Now, Chicken Soup for the Soul has gone beyond the bookstore to become a world leader in life improvement. Through books, movies, DVDs, online resources and other partnerships, we bring hope, courage, inspiration and love to hundreds of millions of people around the world. Chicken Soup for the Soul's writers and readers belong to a one-of-a-kind global community, sharing advice, support, guidance, comfort, and knowledge.

Chicken Soup for the Soul stories have been translated into more than 40 languages and can be found in more than one hundred countries. Every day, millions of people experience a Chicken Soup for the Soul story in a book, magazine, newspaper or online. As we share our life experiences through these stories, we offer hope, comfort and inspiration to one another. The stories travel from person to person, and from country to country, helping to improve lives everywhere.